THE SHELL GUIDE TO BRITISH
ARCHAEOLOGY

THE SHELL GUIDE TO BRITISH
ARCHAEOLOGY
Jacquetta Hawkes
with Paul Bahn

Photographs by Jorge Lewinski

MICHAEL JOSEPH
LONDON

To my grand-daughters
Camilla and Corinna

Frontispiece: *Pentre Ifan Chambered Long Barrow, Dyfed, Wales*

First published in Great Britain by Michael Joseph Ltd 1986
44 Bedford Square, London WC1B 3DP

Photographs © 1986 by Jorge Lewinski

Designed by Bob Vickers
Site plans by Martin Lubikowski

Designed and produced by
Bellew Publishing Company Ltd, 7 Southampton Place, London WC1A 2DR

British Library Cataloguing in Publication data
Hawkes, Jacquetta
    The Shell guide to British archaeology
    1. Great Britain–Antiquities–Guide-books
    2. Great Britain–Description and travel–1971
    –Guide-books
    I. Title   II. Bahn, Paul G.
    914.1   DA90

    ISBN 0 7181 2448 0

Printed and bound in Great Britain by W. S. Cowells

Although sponsoring this book, Shell UK Ltd would point out that the
authors are expressing their own views.

CONTENTS

The Gazetteer

FOREWORD

I am glad that this book is finished: it has taken a long time to write and assemble – so my first thanks should go to the producers and publishers for their patience. If I owe them thanks rather than apologies, it is because this is, after all, an unusually ambitious work. No other guide in this field covers England, Wales, Scotland and its Isles for Roman as well as prehistoric times, and gives details of the best way to reach every site. The Introduction, too, is an exceptionally full survey of the archaeological background – which moreover has been most kindly vetted for me by Professor Stuart Piggott. Add to all this Jorge Lewinski's photographs, ranging the whole territory even to the Hebrides and Shetlands, and it will be seen that this *Shell Guide to British Archaeology* is the product of much effort.

I want to thank Dr Paul Bahn, who wrote almost the whole text of the Gazetteer (though I am to be praised or blamed for the selection of sites). I am also indebted to him for keeping me in order over the changed county names and boundaries, which to anyone of my generation still seem strange and deplorable. If occasionally, when referring to monuments in Wales and Scotland, I have used the old county names, this is because they give a more precise location.

It was agreed that as the guide should have a long life ahead of it the metric system must be preferred for distances and dimensions – with some regret, because for most British and American readers miles, feet and acres are far more readily visualized.

The dating system adopted for prehistoric times is largely based on the now familiar radiocarbon (carbon 14) analysis. I have made some references in the text to uncertainties over such dates. These arise from the recent unhappy discovery that radiocarbon dates appear to become progressively 'younger' than the true calendar years the further back we extend them in prehistoric time. By the 4th millennium BC it is thought that the calendar dates may be as much as 700 years earlier than the radiocarbon readings. Since, however, these adjustments are not yet sure or stable, it has seemed wisest to keep to the unadjusted radiocarbon system.

There remains one other doubt-sown field where I must take the reader into my confidence. There is a school of thought, led by the distinguished engineer Professor Alexander Thom, which detects in our megalithic circles, stone rows and menhirs evidence that their builders were applying advanced astronomical and mathematical knowledge. I am among those who cannot find this evidence by any means sufficiently reliable to overcome the extreme historical improbability that our illiterate and innumerate Stone and Bronze Age farmers possessed mathematical and astronomical genius unique for their time – that they could, for example, foretell eclipses of the sun. Undoubtedly they were deeply interested in the solstice and movements of the moon and stars, probably for both practical farming and religious purposes. But this depended on simple observation and does not imply a scientific approach that emerged only among the later Babylonians and the Greeks. One must follow one's own judgement and so I have not included Dr Thom's findings in our accounts of the megalithic monuments concerned. Those who wish to study them should turn to his *Megalithic Sites in Britain*: I warn them that it will make heavy demands of their mathematical understanding.

It remains only to send this guide on its way with the hope that it will bring satisfaction to those who use it for their walks and excursions. If, just occasionally, they are inclined to curse Dr Bahn and myself for leading them towards mud, bogs, barbed wire or monuments hidden in summer bracken, I hope they will feel such bad moments to be greatly outweighed by hours of added interest and enjoyment.

No country in northern Europe has a richer inheritance of prehistoric and Roman antiquities than Great Britain. Just as within our small islands there is a wonderfully great variety of geological formations – from the relatively young soils of lowland England, through the geologically middle-aged uplands of chalk and limestone, to the most venerable rocks of the highlands – so the earthworks and stoneworks built by our early ancestors are exceptionally varied and yet tell a continuous story.

I want to guide interested travellers both to track down and understand the significance of all these antiquities – from tombs and sacred circles to dwellings and fortifications, and from the caves of the Old Stone Age to roads, villas, cities and military works left by the Romans. My hope is that their enjoyment of the countryside will be increased by visiting its antiquities armed with enough information to be able to judge roughly when and by what manner of people they were raised.

Exceptional sites will be starred in the Gazetteer, and for the rest I shall include only remains that are attractive enough in themselves, or in their natural setting, to repay, if need be, a stiff climb or a walk round a ploughed field. Perhaps a few of those who start making such visits in the most carefree spirit may become so badly infected by the archaeological virus that they will want to study the subject in more detail – even, if they are sociable, enrol as excavators.

Obviously, visitors will be attracted to monuments that are both striking and in fine country, such as Avebury or Maiden Castle, or full of historic interest and with notable things to look at, such as *Verulamium* (St Albans) and Bath. But so great is the lure of the past that many will be ready to seek out obscure earthworks or flock to dismal-looking excavations, wildernesses of holes and trenches, as soon as they hear that remains of the distant past are being dug up there.

I believe that the appeal of ancient monuments has much in common with the emotion most of us feel for the place where we spent our early childhood. We go to them to make contact with our origins, to be reminded for how long our forebears have been baking bread, ornamenting themselves and their possessions, worshipping and caring for their dead. In that mood, an old shoe preserved by chance in slime will seem a wonderful object empowered to move us. The more we are uprooted, forced into the position of modern nomads, obliged to adapt to bewildering changes, the greater, it seems, is our longing for continuity and the sense of 'belonging' that it brings.

Whatever the cause, there is no doubt that a lively interest in our origins has become a part of modern life. It can be seen not only in the crowds of visitors at our more famous monuments, but also in the popularity of books and television programmes on archaeology, and most of all, perhaps, in the hundreds, if not thousands, of men and women who now devote their lives to the advancement of archaeology in universities, museums and under the auspices of local authorities.

A HISTORY OF ARCHAEOLOGY IN BRITAIN

Antiquaries

Long before the dawn of modern archaeology, there were antiquaries who took an active interest in the material remains of the ancient peoples of Britain. Most of them were collectors eager to fill cabinets with 'curious' objects, but some were prepared to suffer hardship travelling the country to find and record the more conspicuous monuments and speculate with boldness as to who could have built them. Because the English gentry, and professional men in their retirement, were so fond of rural life, this country can be said to have surpassed all others in such open-air antiquarianism.

True historical antiquarianism was first born in Tudor England among scholars who formed a brilliant intellectual society in London and the old universities. Notable among them was John Leland who, under the patronage of Henry VIII, toured England and Wales and recorded what he saw of antiquity, principally medieval buildings, but also such prehistoric monuments as caught his interest. The Elizabethan age produced William Camden who, in 1586, published the first edition of his *Britannia*. It was an immediate success, running into several editions during the author's lifetime and translated into English

from the original Latin. This book remained every antiquary's indispensable companion through the seventeenth and eighteenth centuries, the final greatly expanded version of 1806 being issued in four fat volumes.

The outstanding figure of the seventeenth century was John Aubrey, offspring of an old family of landed gentry. Like Leland, he was an itinerant, but unlike his predecessor he made careful notes and sketches of prehistoric monuments. He recorded barrows and hillforts, and was the first to introduce the Avebury Sanctuary to the learned world, having come upon it in 1648 when out hunting. He was commissioned by Charles II to survey both Stonehenge and Avebury, and this work has been commemorated at Stonehenge in

the naming of the Aubrey Holes that he discovered. Less happily, he led the way in tentatively attributing the erection of these sanctuaries to the Druids, an error that has been a persistent nuisance to archaeology ever since.

The saddest aspect of John Aubrey's troubled life was that he failed to publish his invaluable field records. His major work, the *Monumenta Britannica*, lay in the Bodleian Library at Oxford until recently, when it was published in two magnificent gilt-edged volumes admirably edited by the novelist John Fowles.

Aubrey's successor (who made free use of the former's unpublished notes) was William Stukeley (1687–1765), by far the most remarkable field antiquary of his day. For some time he practised as a doctor and had wide scientific interests, but he was to become increasingly absorbed by his passion for antiquity, and from 1710 to 1725 he visited and made excellent drawings of many of the monuments included in this guide. On reaching Hadrian's Wall, he was overcome by 'this amazing scene of Roman grandeur in Britain' and deeply shocked by the heedless manner in which it was being destroyed.

His best work is to be found in his thorough surveys of Avebury and Stonehenge: at Stonehenge, he detected the inconspicuous Avenue (as he named it), and at Avebury, while recording the whole of this complex monument, he chanced to witness the destruction by a farmer of 'the Sanctuary', the stone circles at the end of the West Kennet Avenue. Hitherto, Stukeley had been an objective fieldworker whose careful plans and drawings were to be of immense value to archaeology, but after 1725 his nature seemed to change with the times as the scientific temperament of the seventeenth century began to be affected by the new Romanticism. He became obsessed with the Druids (taking holy orders in the belief that he had a mission to reconcile their supposedly 'patriarchal religion' with Christianity, and, above all, with the concept of the Trinity), and he began to weave absurd fantasies round the monuments he had studied. At Avebury, for example, he saw the rings and the sinuous course of the Avenue as 'a snake proceeding from a circle! ... the eternal procession of the son from the first cause'. Such notions ruined the text of his books on both Avebury and Stonehenge, but fortunately he

Stonehenge Sanctuary, Wiltshire

reproduced his original plans and drawings almost untouched.

In order not to leave William Stukeley, to whom we owe so much, as a deluded old man, it should be added that, in his rational younger days, he had been chosen as the first secretary of a distinguished group of 'gentlemen, well-wishers to Antiquities' who were founding a society. With meetings first held in the year 1707, this Society of Antiquaries of London is the oldest of its kind in the world.

With the advance of the Romantic movement, antiquarianism became fashionable: young gentlemen rode about the country in search of the Gothic and other even more ancient remains, while landowners took a new interest in the ancient monuments on their estates. Ideas about the Druids penetrated Romantic literature, as can be seen in Blake's mystical poetry and in Keats' visit to the Keswick stone circle, surely referred to in his 'dismal cirque of Druid stones upon a forlorn moor ...'

Archaeologists

Round the turn of the century, however, more sober work was done, which was now truly archaeological in that its devotees tried to use antiquities to reconstruct the prehistory of Britain. Among the first and best of these men was Sir Richard Colt-Hoare (1758-1838), who studied and excavated the abundant prehistoric remains in his own county of Wiltshire. His fine *Ancient History of North and South Wiltshire* (in two volumes) includes accounts of the position and contents of hundreds of barrows. However, Colt-Hoare died largely frustrated in his hope that so much digging would yield 'something that might supersede conjecture'.

A year before Colt-Hoare's death, C. J. Thomsen, a pioneer Danish archaeologist, devised the 'three-age system' (Stone, Bronze and Iron), which, despite its weaknesses, is still in use. It was the beginning of a classification that was to bring order and understanding to the reconstruction of the prehistoric past.

As the nineteenth century advanced, the social background of field archaeology changed with the changing structure of British society. The patronage of the gentry and wealthy landowners declined, and the direction of much research passed into the hands of professional men and was largely supported by the rising middle class. New national societies were founded, while all over the country, local antiquarian societies sprang up with an enthusiastic membership of squires, doctors, parsons and their interested ladies. They held meetings, went on excursions and set up museums in provincial cities to house all the antiquities that were brought to light by the upheavals of the Industrial Revolution and by their own excavations.

Among the leaders of all this activity, three were mainly concerned with barrow-digging in the hitherto rather neglected north of England. The earliest was Thomas Bateman of Derbyshire whose best-known book, *Ten Years' Diggings in Celtic and Saxon Gravehills*, published just before his death in 1861, already shows improving standards of excavation. In this he was to be far surpassed by William Greenwell, a canon of Durham, who was active in several regions during his immensely long life, but first and foremost among the legion of barrows on the Yorkshire Wolds. He was a careful and thoughtful excavator whose *British Barrows* (1877) marked a big step forward in British field archaeology. The canon was among the first to recognize the importance of pottery in dating sites. He classified the vessels he unearthed in his Bronze Age barrows under the now-familiar names of drinking cups (beakers), food vessels, incense cups and urns. His medical collaborator, Professor George Rolleston, made an exact study of human skulls, distinguishing between the long heads usual in the Stone Age burials and the rounded heads often found in those of the Bronze Age. This led to the popular notion of 'long barrow, long head and round barrow, round head,' which, while overly simple, still has racial significance.

In *British Barrows*, Canon Greenwell praised J. R. Mortimer, the third of these northern excavators, for having 'most carefully and exhaustively examined' barrows within his own territory of the Yorkshire Wolds. (In private, the canon had called Mortimer 'that scoundrel'.) However careful, Mortimer was also slow moving, and he failed to publish his results until 1905, when, as an old man, he produced *Forty Years' Researches in Brit-*

Beaker, overhanging-rim urn and other Bronze Age pottery (David Cripps)

Bronze Age urns (David Cripps)

ish and Saxon Burial Mounds of Yorkshire. Illustrated by his teenage daughter, it is a particularly handsome volume.

While these men were revealing the archaeological riches of the north of England, work was also, of course, continuing in the south. There was, for example, the Revd W. C. Lukis making surveys of the monuments of Devon and Cornwall. But surpassing them all was one of the most remarkable men in the history of field archaeology: General Lane-Fox Pitt-Rivers (1827–1900). Handsome, intelligent, well-born and energetic, he had combined a successful army career with a serious interest in the cultures of ancient and primitive peoples, which led him on to excavation, at first under the guidance of Canon Greenwell. He was digging at Cissbury as early as 1867, but it was only after 1880, when he inherited vast estates in Wiltshire and Dorset centred on his house in Cranborne Chase, that he flung himself into the exploration of the prehistoric and Roman remains on his land.

The general far outstripped the canon as a meticulous excavator. He saw the importance of excavating monuments in their entirety, of recording everything, however insignificant it might appear, by means of exact plans and sectional drawings. He also believed in prompt and thorough publication, achieving this in the shape of four large volumes bound in royal blue and gold, his now-famous *Excavations in Cranborne Chase*, which appeared, as the work was done, between 1887 and 1898. His finds and records, including exactly contoured models carved from mahogany, are now in the Salisbury and South Wiltshire Museum.

The name and fame of General Pitt-Rivers add a special distinction to the archaeology of Cranborne Chase, but many of the sites he dug are unspectacular. Among those most worth a visit today are the totally excavated Wor Barrow, Winkelbury hillfort and the late Roman Bokerley Dyke.

General Pitt-Rivers had no immediate successors to carry on his work; perhaps no ordinary individual dared attempt it. A generation was to pass before another exceptional man arrived to don the general's cloak: Dr R.E.M. (later Sir Mortimer) Wheeler (1890–1976). As a young man he had already been fired by *Excavations in Cranborne Chase*, and he developed an ambition to lead British archaeology towards a greatly improved standard of excavation.

Studies of such antiquities as pottery, tools and weapons had greatly expanded and refined the 'three-age system' before World War I. Immediately after, the use of aerial photography by the military was adapted to archaeology and gave fieldworkers a powerful new eye, but there had been no comparable improvement in digging methods. During the interwar years, however, excavations by Dr Wheeler and his wife, Tessa, were to revolutionize British field archaeology and give it a leading place in the scientific study of the past. Starting with carefully selected Roman sites in Wales, they launched their first ambitious excavation at *Verulamium* (St Albans, Herts), exploring both the Roman city and the historically associated Iron Age earthworks.

Next they transferred their now large and well-trained team of diggers to Maiden Castle in Dorset, where they worked through four strenuous seasons to 1937. By a skilful placing of trenches among the mountainous ramparts, the history of this huge tribal stronghold was largely disentangled and the famous 'war cemetery' laid bare in all its grimness. It was here, at the East Gate, that Dr Wheeler devised the invaluable grid method of excavation.

The British public flocked to the Dorset countryside to see these discoveries and watch the diggers at work. A deliberate part of Wheeler's policy for British archaeology had always been to popularize it; he wanted the public to understand and enjoy the subject and so be prepared to pay for its pursuit.

Already in Wales he had launched this policy, selling exclusive rights to the *Daily Mail* to publish news of the Caerleon excavations. At *Verulamium* and Maiden Castle, coverage by the media was much increased, while the Wheelers saw to it that the resulting hosts of visitors were conducted round the sites by intelligent guides. The money the public put into the collecting boxes made a worthwhile contribution to excavation expenses, while the ground was being prepared for the ample state-funding of archaeology that was to be accepted in post-war times. By then, of course, the publicity given by the press had been vastly increased by the immediate success of the subject on television – a success in which Dr Wheeler again played a leading part.

So the pursuit of antiquity, which had begun with the patronage of kings, now depends very largely on that of the people. Sir Mortimer Wheeler can be seen as a dominating figure in British archaeology in the line of Leland, Camden, Aubrey, Stukeley and Pitt-Rivers. He may well prove to be the last, since the role of giants is giving way to teamwork, increasing specialization and the co-operation of archaeologists with scientists of many disciplines. Although he dominated the inter-war period and the Fifties and Sixties, there was a vast amount of work being done by other men and women of high repute, some of them Wheeler's pupils, nearly all owing much to his standards and methods in excavation.

Because of this increased specialization and teamwork, it is difficult to single out contemporary archaeologists and their contributions. There are a few, however, whose important excavations have gradually built up the knowledge on which this guide is based.

Professor Vere Gordon Childe, a near contemporary of Wheeler's, was an eminent philosopher and theorist of world prehistory who worked primarily from literature and in museums. Nevertheless, he ventured into the field to uncover Skara Brae, Rinyo and Jarlshof in the bleak Orkneys and Shetlands, and a number of Iron Age hillforts and other sites in Scotland.

Christopher Hawkes's early dig at St Catherine's Hill, Winchester, laid the foundation for dating and understanding the history of the Celtic Iron Age. He followed this up by excavations at a number of southern hillforts (Buckland Rings, Bury Hill, Quarley Hill) and by several seasons' exploration of Cunobelin's capital at Colchester.

Avebury and nearby Windmill Hill were tackled by the marmalade prince, Alexander Keiller, ably assisted by the young Stuart Piggott, from 1925 to 1939. It was a herculean task: not only were their age and history established, but a great restoration was made, with buried stones discovered and replaced, fallen ones set upright and many, many empty sockets found and set with concrete markers. So an overgrown, squalid and ruined monument was restored to its present dignity and clarity of plan.

The corresponding effort to solve the historical problems of Stonehenge was carried out during the first half of the 1950s under the direction of Professor Richard Atkinson and, again, Stuart Piggott. As can be seen from the lengthy entry in the Gazetteer, they were successful in establishing a long and intricate history, though some dating difficulties remain.

Later, Professor Atkinson's research illuminated the wider problems of our henge monuments and he took on another major excavation – that of the gigantic Silbury Hill near

Roman statue from Verulamium
(David Cripps)

Avebury, until then assumed to be an outsized round barrow of the Bronze Age. The dig, in collaboration with the BBC, proved an awkward exercise in public relations, for the long-hoped-for discovery of a rich burial did not happen and the cameras were frustrated. (Silbury proved to date from the late New Stone Age.)

Stuart Piggott was later to exacavate two well-known megalithic tombs: the chambered long barrow of West Kennet, just to the south-east of Silbury Hill, and Wayland's Smithy, an eastern outlier of this type of tomb. These digs have added to the attraction of the monuments for visitors and also to the general study of megalithic architecture.

In the north of England, Star Carr (now reburied) was dug by Professor Grahame Clark, a pioneer in the study of prehistoric economics. The site told a great deal about the everyday and ritual life of Middle Stone Age hunters and fishers.

For Roman Britain, a subject particularly benefited by aerial photography, Professor Ian Richmond was outstanding. An elegant writer and a slow, meticulous excavator, he

Skara Brae Village Settlement, Orkneys. Houses of the late New Stone Age uncovered by Professor Vere Gordon Childe

dug the Roman camp at Hod Hill and led much of the work on Hadrian's Wall. After World War II, much else was accomplished in Roman field studies. In the City of London, particularly, excavation was undertaken ahead of rebuilding on bomb sites, while later building development revealed the Temple of Mithras. Then in the late 1960s, Barry Cunliffe, a leading figure of the younger generation of archaeologists, uncovered the unique Roman palace of Fishbourne and greatly added to the riches of Roman Bath.

—Present-day techniques— in archaeology

During the last 20 years, the main progress in archaeology has been in new ideas and techniques, using a bewildering variety of scientific aids. There has been the development of experimental archaeology–from the making and trying out of flint and bronze implements to the building of ramparts and ditches to observe their gradual erosion and silting. Also fascinating have been experimental reconstructions, such as the Roman fortifications at The Lunt, the Iron Age settlement at Butser Hill and the gallant experiment in prehistoric living endured for a year by a group of enthusiasts (with the support of the BBC) in Cranborne Chase. 'Rescue archaeology', where excavation has to keep ahead of destructive building, may demand new methods–for instance, to cope with hundreds of minor sites exposed during the construction of a motorway. Then there is the scrutiny of soils and pollen grains for information about climate, vegetation and local ecology.

Most significant are the scientific analyses that seek the sources of raw materials or the age of ancient remains. For example, the testing of stone axes has revealed how widely they were traded away from their quarries of origin. Dating analysis has become so varied and ingenious that it is a science in itself. Of all the methods, carbon 14, or 'radiocarbon', analysis is at present by far the most important, having sharpened and to some extent changed our ordering of prehistoric events.

PREHISTORIC AND ROMAN BRITAIN

In telling the story of our Roman and prehistoric past as it has been gradually built up by centuries of hard work there is one theme which gives it unity. This is man's gradual transformation of the face of Britain as he first changed the populations of wild animals by hunting, then century by century cleared the forests for arable and pasture while marking it forever with his dwellings, graves, temples and fortifications – and, after the Roman conquest, with his towns and highways.

The Old Stone Age

The first phase of British prehistory, the Old Stone Age (the Palaeolithic), dawned during the Great Ice Age – or the Pleistocene of geology. This period, extending up to two million years, was divided by four glaciations when vast ice sheets spread over much of northern and western Britain. During most of this time Britain was a western promontory of Europe.

Men were hunting in what was to become southern England during the warm interval between the second and third glaciations – if not before. We know of their presence from the flint implements found in the gravels of our river terraces, most abundantly in the Thames Valley. At that time there were lions, elephants and rhinoceroses living in a valley lined with verdant woodland. Small groups of human beings, still physically more primitive than ourselves, seem to have camped on the open ground beside the river where they could hunt the herds of deer, oxen and horses which came down to drink.

These hunters have left few sites worth visiting, although there are enthusiasts who devote themselves to watching gravel digging in the hope of finding flint implements. Most sought after are the well-proportioned pear-shaped tools, known as hand-axes, designed for butchering, chopping or digging for roots.

One such encampment site, however, is of exceptional interest. This is the Barnsfield gravel pit on the south bank of the Thames at Swanscombe. It has been called 'one of the most famous archaeological sites in the world', its fame being due to the discovery there of skull fragments that are the earliest human fossils from our country and among the earliest in Europe.

The people of Swanscombe seem to have hunted the Thames valley some 200,000 years ago when the climate was already deteriorating towards the third glaciation. The pitiful remains of one of them, nowadays held to represent a very early, thick-skulled breed of *Homo sapiens*, can be seen in the Natural History Museum in London, together with the elegant hand-axes that he or she flaked with so much skill and purposefulness.

As the glacial conditions intensified, with ice sheets spreading southward once more, these people gradually retreated towards warmer climes in southern Europe. When the climatic pendulum had swung once more and warmer conditions again prevailed in Britain, the same number did not return. It is possible that the rise in sea level, which always accompanied the melting of the ice, now breached the chalk of the Dover Straits, temporarily rendering Britain an island. This could explain why the human population was so low at a time when the British climate was little worse than the present one.

The last glacial period, which began about 70,000 years ago, was also the least severe: at the height of the freeze, the ice sheets never extended beyond a line running irregularly from south Wales to York. Something like 40,000 years ago, there was a pause in the advance of the glaciation, and much of Britain (now undoubtedly again part of the Continent) became open grassland supporting large herds of bison, reindeer and mammoth. To judge from their smaller, more specialized flint implements, the hunters attracted to the region by this abundant game were of the breed known as Neanderthal man, whose skeletal remains have often been found in Europe and Asia.

The cold and the nature of the hunting grounds encouraged these hunters to seek the shelter of caves. Among those where their implements have come to light, the most interesting are, in the south-west, Kent's Cavern and the Hyena Den by Wookey Hole, and in the north Midlands, Creswell Crags. The most significant thing about the Neanderthal folk is that they already had spiritual fears and longings that prompted them to bury their dead with care and simple rituals.

The Neanderthalers remained dominant, though probably never numerous, until about 30,000 years ago, when western Europe, including Britain on its outermost fringes, was occupied by races essentially

Creswell Crags, Derbyshire. Cave dwelling of the Old Stone Age

indistinguishable from ourselves – Neanderthal man has been labelled *Homo sapiens (neanderthalensis)*, while his successors are *Homo sapiens sapiens*. The relationship between the two stocks is much disputed, but there seems no doubt that in western Europe the Neanderthals were dispossessed and died out in the face of the superior intelligence, social organization and culture of the newcomers.

For their tools and weapons, the *Homo sapiens sapiens* had perfected a new method of producing long, narrow blades of flint that could be trimmed into various specialized forms. They built spear-throwers that added leverage to human muscle and must have greatly increased their success as hunters. This invention was soon followed by that of the bow and arrow. Their ritual and magical practices were elaborate and they liked to decorate themselves with beads and pendants, and probably with face-paint and feathers. In more favoured Continental regions, these late Old Stone Age peoples were developing the art of sculpture, often in the service of their religious practices.

In Britain, although game was plentiful, living conditions seem to have been too harsh to attract many hunters. A few open-air camp sites are known, but usually (as before) the hunters preferred the shelter of caves. Some reoccupied old Neanderthalers' cave-dwellings; elsewhere, as at the famous Goat's (Paviland) Cave on the Gower peninsula, they were the first human occupants.

When the last glaciation reached its greatest intensity about 25,000 years ago, even that large part of Britain remaining free of ice sheets is thought to have become uninhabitable. Such dire conditions lasted some ten millennia before, once again, temperatures began to rise, allowing people and animal herds, mostly horse and reindeer, to move back into the promontory that was to be Britain. In time, tundra gave way to birch and

pine and then to deciduous trees, while elk and the giant Irish deer roamed the country. The returning hunters, the last of the Old Stone Age, seem to have been more numerous than before: their remains have been found in many caves, but are best known from the group in the Cheddar Gorge and from several in the Creswell ravine where numbers of families may have been able to enjoy something of a community life. Their flint implements were in the old blade tradition, but tended to be smaller and they had by now devised stoutly barbed bone harpoon heads. Sadly for us, however, they appear still to have been too hard-pressed to practise the cave painting and sculpture then at their height in France and Spain.

As the climate continued to grow warmer, the way of life that depended on hunting game herds in open country was ended by the spread of forests and the dawn of the post-glacial age in which we are still living.

The Middle Stone Age

Once again, the small human communities had to adapt their way of life drastically to the changing conditions–though they remained dependent on hunting and food-gathering for several millennia. This was the Mesolithic period, the Middle Stone Age. Although there were deer, wild ox and boar in the forests, they were fewer, more widely scattered and generally harder to come by than the game herds of old. This put a premium on long-distance weapons, a need that was met most admirably by powerful bows (over two metres long) and a variety of arrows. The flint work during this period is distinguished by the very small and angular shapes devised to be set in wooden, bone or antler hafts as barbs, points and blades.

A further fundamental adaptation was brought about when the melting ice gave rise to streams, lakes and swamps where these Middle Stone Age people could fish and fowl. For this, they developed light canoes propelled by wooden paddles and a wide range of harpoons, fish spears, fish hooks and nets. Some groups also lived along the seashore, with shellfish and sea birds as their staple diet. Their huge shell wastepiles called *middens* can best be seen near Oban in Strathclyde and in the Hebrides, but most have been covered by the sea.

In their way of life and manufactures, the Middle Stone Age peoples of lowland England had much in common with those of north-west Europe, particularly of Denmark. This is not surprising, since during the earlier part of the period their territories were united by a land surface that was low and swampy but habitable and presumably rich in fish and wildfowl. However, around 6000 BC the steadily rising sea invaded these flat-lands and formed the North Sea, making Britain an island.

Like the Old Stone Age before it, this last phase of the hunting economy in Britain has left us little to look at in the field. The limited stock of cave-dwellings might still have been used for part of each year, but it was more common for small groups of hunters to live in flimsy huts on heaths or at the waterside, sometimes with sunken floors for greater warmth. One such hut can be seen at Abinger Common in Surrey.

Unfortunately, by far the most remarkable living place has now been reburied–although it is marked on Ordnance Survey maps. This is at Star Carr, a few miles south of Scarborough, where as early as 7500 BC there was a lakeside settlement of some 20 souls–prosperous hunters and fishermen. A platform of earth and brushwood, probably used as a landing stage for their canoes, rested on birch trees that had been felled with stone axes – the earliest known example of trees cut by man. Star Carr shows vividly that the Middle Stone Age peoples, though constructing nothing of any size, must have been a more conspicuous presence in the landscape than their predecessors.

The New Stone Age

During the succeeding New Stone Age (the Neolithic), the land clearance begun in the Middle Stone Age was vastly accelerated. The reason for this was the arrival, from about 4000 BC, of newcomers from across the Channel and the North Sea. They are generally supposed (though there is no direct evidence for it) to have come in sizeable skin-covered boats comparable with the old Irish *curraghs*. What is certain is that they brought with them grain seed, mainly wheat and barley, and livestock – cattle, sheep, pigs and pet dogs. The domestication of these plants and animals had begun in south-west Asia and Anatolia where their wild ancestors were native. The cereals were selected for their heavier grains, and the livestock for their smaller sizes and, presumably, docility. From the Orient, farming had spread westward, mainly, it seems, by way of the Mediterranean and the Danube valley. With their revolutionary agricultural economy, these colonists also brought new knowledge and skills, most significantly the making of pottery and of polished stone axes. Though primarily designed for tree-felling and woodworking, some of these axes or adze-like implements must have been used as hoes, while a more specialized agricultural tool was the straight sickle for lopping off the ears of corn. Their arrows had beautifully flaked, leaf-shaped heads – quite different from those made by the hunters (and a happy find for flint collectors!). Rather surprisingly, these enterprising immigrants do not seem to have practised spinning and weaving, but must have dressed in skins prepared with the scrapers that were a standard part of their flintwork.

Some of these settlers must have landed far up our Atlantic coasts for several of the earliest known sites (according to carbon 14 dating) are in the north-east of Ireland. From their landing places, they spread rapidly, clearing woodland on the lighter soils for grain plots and pasture, favouring for this task the uplands' chalk and limestone hills, river gravels and coastal strips, and avoiding such heavy, densely forested regions as the Midlands. For a time, some natives maintained their hunting life, but generally they appear to have been absorbed by the farming people or to have adopted some part of the new economy.

This period of land clearance and the building of farmsteads and small settlements, perhaps reinforced by further immigration, is thought to have occupied several generations. It was only after about 3500 BC that the pioneer farming communities commanded the numbers and resources to undertake projects on an ambitious scale. And, for the non-specialist, this is the welcome contrast between the Middle and New Stone Ages: for, while the Middle Stone Age left no spectacular remains, the New Stone Age saw the erection of many of our finest prehistoric monuments. From approximately 3500 BC through the third millennium (when advanced civilizations were being developed in Mesopotamia and Egypt), the farmers laboured to produce many of the remarkable monuments described in this book.

Flint mines and causewayed camps

While these early farmers put their greatest efforts into building for religious ritual and ceremony, they did develop an industry around the manufacture of the stone axes, adzes and hoes that were of such importance for land clearance and cultivation and for the advanced carpentry of which they were capable. There were excellent raw materials in the flint and tough volcanic rocks available in Britain, and trade in these tools began early.

Volcanic rocks were worked at many sites throughout the highland zone, from Cornwall to the Hebrides and Orkney. Usually the raw material was obtained from boulders or scree, but occasionally shallow mining was undertaken. The trade in axes made from hard stone was of great importance, covering hundreds of miles. The sites where these rocks were worked, however, are far from spectacular now: only the very prolific factory at Pike of Stickle, on the Langdale slopes

Pike of Stickle, Langdale, Cumbria. The site of a New Stone Age axe factory can be seen on the right

in Cumbria, is well worth the effort of finding.

For flint, although surface blocks could be used, by far the best material came from nodules embedded deep in the chalk. From as early as 3500 BC in Sussex, and later in Wessex and East Anglia, miners sank pits to reach these hidden beds, working with antler picks, with shovels made from the shoulder-blades of their cattle, and with no better light than a moss wick floating in animal fat. Once prised out, the nodules were hoisted to the surface in baskets and there split and worked into rough shapes for implements. It is thought that the miners themselves travelled and bartered this stock-in-trade, the final shaping of the tools being undertaken by or on behalf of the purchasers. Flint axes might be shaped by careful flaking alone, but were often smoothed by laborious grinding.

The most advanced mining was at Grimes Graves in Norfolk where many of the shafts were sunk through two beds of inferior flint to reach the best nodules at a depth of as much as 12 metres. Radial galleries were then driven along this lowest flint bed, some-

times breaking into old workings to form a bewildering underground network.

At most flint-mining areas, there is no more to be seen than grass-grown waste heaps and shallow pits where the backfill of the shafts has subsided, but at Grimes Graves at least one excavated mine has been kept open. A visit there is an experience as rewarding as any that prehistory can offer. The unique fertility shrine (when on view) serves to remind us that religious ideas were interwoven with industrial enterprise even as they were with farming, giving an essential unity to prehistoric people's understanding of life.

A comparable blending of ritualistic with practical activities inspired the construction of another type of monument distinctive of the New Stone Age in Britain. This is an odd kind of earthwork that has been endowed by archaeology with the clumsy and misleading name of 'causewayed camp'. These puzzling compounds, which began to be constructed after 3500 BC, consist of one to four rings of banks and ditches in which the ditches are invariably interrupted by causeways, and the banks are sometimes broken by corresponding gaps. Up to a score are known or suspected, nearly all of them in southern

England and most of them on hilltops or spurs of the chalk downlands. As they have been sadly denuded by time, and several are buried beneath Iron Age hillforts, they have no strong visual appeal, but they do have a considerable historical interest as the earliest large-scale constructions in Britain intended for social use.

The specific functions of these camps are still uncertain. The hilltop sites and the very large amount of chalk dug for embankments suggest some defensive intention, yet the flat bottoms of the ditches, the many causeways and, above all, the distance often found between the ringworks, disqualify causewayed camps as fortifications.

Excavation has proved that they were not permanently occupied, for only the westernmost, Hembury in Devon, has produced evidence of huts, one of them substantial, and other occupation litter. The rest often contain small storage pits and cooking places, while domestic rubbish, including potsherds, flints and animal bones, have been found in the ditches, sometimes in such a way as to suggest that they were the remains of communal feasts. Occasionally human bones have also been found in the fill of the ditches, seemingly deliberately put in place and covered.

Since the causewayed camps were certainly neither villages nor forts, the best-informed guess is that they were tribal rallying places where scattered farming communities came together at appointed times for such purposes as barter, initiation, seasonal dances or other tribal rites and ceremonies. Considering the large areas enclosed (up to nine hectares) and the supreme importance of cattle and sheep to these New Stone Age farmers, it seems likely that the handling of herds and flocks was in some way involved.

The site where the nature of causewayed camps and the way of life of their builders can best be appreciated is on Windmill Hill, near Avebury. There, ditches from large sectors of the three ringworks have been left open, while most of the finds are very well displayed in the Avebury museum. These include quantities of round-bottomed domestic pots and stone axes which came from as far afield as Cornwall and Cumbria.

Long barrows and chambered tombs

While the great economic and social significance of the flint mines and causewayed camps are enough to attract serious-minded visitors today, it is the long barrows and chambered tombs, already being built by 3000 BC, that comprise all the most alluring monuments of the New Stone Age. The earlier of the two classes of funerary monument is the long barrow, i.e. a mound very much longer than it is wide. Later came the chambered tomb - some, but not all, in long barrows. Both were designed for communal burial, but were also centres of the religious life of their communities - sacred places concerned with the primal mysteries of birth, death and rebirth, in the sense of renewed fertility.

Soon after 3500 BC, tribal groups were collaborating to build the earthen type of long barrow (a barrow without a stone chamber), probably as the last resting places for their leading families. Usually the bodies were exposed in enclosures or mortuary houses until they had decomposed, then on some appointed occasion, possibly the death of a particularly important personage, the bones were brought together and the heavy task of barrow building undertaken. Sometimes the mound appears to have been built over the existing mortuary house, and sometimes nearby, covering a new house or platform. Although the interment of disarticulated bones prevailed, fleshed bodies were also buried, usually in a crouched position. The number of individuals all or part of whose bones went into a single barrow varied enormously, from one to over 50 men, women and children. Although the earthen long barrows were communal tombs, rarely if ever were these mortuary houses reopened to admit further burials.

Grave goods - items buried with the dead to accompany them to and help in their afterlives - are rare in earthen long barrows. Only a few pots (perhaps ritually broken), stone axes and arrowheads have been found. It may have been thought that, by the time the flesh had decomposed, the spirits had departed, though honour still had to be paid to the ancestral bones. There are also few signs of elaborate rituals, although in some barrows, notably in Yorkshire, the mortuary houses had been either intentionally or accidentally burned.

The barrows range from about 30 to 80 metres in length and today, especially in chalk downland country, the turf-covered long barrows have a simple appearance: almost always wider and higher at the end pointing in a roughly easterly direction. When new, many must have looked like buildings, for the soil (usually dug from side ditches) of which they were constructed was contained within wooden walls, tapering from a broad façade at the east end, behind which the burials lay, to a lower and much narrower west end. There is good reason to think that they were derived from the long-houses typical of New Stone Age dwellings in north-west Europe, where wedge-shaped, though commonly stone-built, long barrows are also found.

In Britain, the overwhelming majority of earthen long barrows are on the chalk lands of England: throughout Wessex, on the South Downs of Sussex, and on the Chilterns and the Lincolnshire and Yorkshire Wolds. There are also long barrows on the Yorkshire moors and in Scotland, but there they inevitably merge into long cairns, where piled stones had to take the place of softer subsoils.

The chambered tombs – barrows with chambers built of massive stones or mega-liths – first appeared towards the end of the fourth millennium, when earthen long barrows were already widespread. Both forms were built and used for at least 1000 years – to the end of the New Stone Age – and, being contemporary, they and the uses to which they were put certainly had some traditions in common.

The most fundamental of these shared traditions was that of the collective burial of men, women and children – a custom sufficiently unusual among humankind to be truly significant. The most fundamental difference between them is that the chambered tombs, normally with free access to the chambers, could be used for successive burials over generations – in this resembling the family vaults still used among our highborn and royal. It seems that the most usual practice was inhumation (burying the whole body), with the bodies almost invariably being placed in the chamber with knees near chins, sometimes lying on their sides, sometimes in sitting or crouching postures near the walls. However, sometimes just the bones were buried, as in the earthen long barrows, and cremation was practised in south-west Scotland and occasionally elsewhere.

The number of interments tended to be larger in chambered tombs than in earthen long barrows – over 20 being quite common and many more not infrequent. The use of ancestral bones for religious and magical purposes appears to have been employed by the megalith builders. Careful excavation of

Belas Knap, Winchcombe, Gloucestershire. The false entrance of this New Stone Age chambered long barrow

burials in undisturbed side-chambers at West Kennet revealed that several skulls and long bones were missing. The skull is universally venerated, and it may be that thigh bones were chosen as symbols of generation and fertility.

The provision of grave goods for the dead was only slightly more generous in chambered tombs than in long barrows. It seems as if pottery vessels were left with food and drink for the dead, while beads and other ornaments have fairly often been found, though seldom in place on the corpses. Otherwise, as with the barrows, arrowheads and small flint implements are not uncommon, while stone axes are rarities; one elderly woman appears to have been buried with her pet dog. Although grave goods must often have been removed by antiquaries and earlier intruders, the paucity of finds when intact burials have been scientifically excavated suggests that individuals were not normally interred with their best possessions. This is in sharp contrast with what was to follow in the Bronze Age.

Although grave goods are few and poor, the bones of domestic animals and deer are plentiful in or near the tombs and sometimes may be the remains of funerary feasts. As with earthen long barrows, there was a ritual use of fires, and offerings for the dead might be left outside the entrances, the focal points of forecourts surely designed for ritual use. The entrances to the chambers were probably closed with a slab or other blocking stone after the interment ceremonies and were often carefully sealed when they were to be used no more.

The variety of detail in plan and construction of the British chambered tombs is almost infinite. There are, however, two principal forms that can be distinguished here: the gallery graves that are usually covered by long barrows, and the passage graves that are more often under round barrows.

The gallery graves were first being built before the end of the fourth millennium. They are commonly composed of megalithic uprights and roofing stones combined with drystone walling; occasionally the roofing stones may be partly supported by corbels. The entrance, which opens directly on to the easterly end of the long barrow, is often emphasized by even larger blocks forming the central feature of a forecourt recessed into this wider end of the barrow. The simplest, though not necessarily the oldest, type of gallery grave has one long, narrow, paral-

lel-sided chamber, but the more impressive and perhaps characteristic form – known as the transepted gallery grave – has one or more opposing pairs of side-chambers opening on to the central gallery.

The best-known gallery graves are the chambered long barrows of the Gloucestershire Cotswolds, all in lovely country. They include a number of the more elaborate transepted kind and, in Hetty Pegler's Tump at Uley, a tomb still wholly enclosed in its mound. In several examples, however, of which Belas Knap at Winchcombe is the best, a most curious feature is found: the imposing portal at the centre of the forecourt is a sham, there being no large gallery grave beyond it. Instead, relatively small

burial chambers are entered inconspicuously from the side of the mound. A possible device against tomb-robbers? Whatever the explanation, it proves the ritual importance of the portal to those for whom the sepulchre was sacred.

The Cotswold monuments are seen as belonging to a widespread group of gallery graves. To the east, there are a number on the Wiltshire downs, including the now-restored West Kennet, and others on the Berkshire downs where Wayland's Smithy (now in Oxfordshire) is familiar to users of the Ridgeway. The fine Stoney Littleton transepted gallery is among a few southerly outliers beyond the Bristol Avon. Then there are more across the Bristol Channel in what was

Wayland's Smithy Chambered Long Barrow, Oxfordshire

formerly Monmouthshire and south-west Wales to as far west as the Gower peninsula, and another compact and enjoyable group in the Black Mountains.

Another distinct and very numerous group of tombs that qualify as gallery graves can be found in south-west Scotland, most of them in Argyll and Arran, but a few scattered as far east as the area around Dumbarton. A large proportion of these Scottish galleries are distinguished by being divided into segments by low slabs set on edge across the floor; some, however, have only a single short chamber. Very similar gallery graves occur across the

sea on the Isle of Man and in the north of Ireland.

The second principal type of chambered tomb, the passage grave, was perhaps introduced a few centuries after the gallery grave. There is some perversity in the choice of its name since the important feature of this form is its single large chamber, often at the centre of its circular mound. It is, however, approached by a relatively narrow passage, the roof of which is sometimes much lower than that of the chamber. Both features are usually constructed of megalithic uprights combined with drystone work and may be roofed with large capstones – though in the finest examples, the chamber is corbelled and lofty.

There are a few passage graves in north-west Wales, by far the most interesting being Bryncelli Ddu in Anglesey with its single carved slab that links it with the symbolic passage-grave art of Ireland and Brittany. But the vast majority are in Scotland, most of which date from the third millennium. There is a group in the south-west in Dumfries & Galloway and a large (300 sites) and varied grouping covering Skye, the Hebrides, the northern Highlands, the Orkneys and Shetlands. In many of these, the chamber is partially divided by pairs of upright slabs projecting from the walls, a device reaching an extraordinary extreme in the stalled cairns of the Orkneys, such as Mid Howe on Rousay island, where the mound is lengthened to cover a long narrow chamber divided into as many as a dozen compartments. Here, in the far north, passage graves are occasionally found in a very odd kind of long barrow, with a recessed forecourt between projecting horns at the easterly end repeated at the much narrower and chamberless tail end. Notable examples are those of Camster and Yarrows in the Caithness district of Highland.

The finest megalithic tomb in Britain, rivalled only by the Irish New Grange, is the passage grave of Maes Howe on Mainland in the Orkneys. Not only is it large, but it was constructed with unparalleled precision: there is nothing rugged or romantic about Maes Howe architecture. What is so interesting is that, when a building material such as easily shaped flagstone was available, the New Stone Age builders of about 2500 BC were able and willing to achieve formality and symmetry.

Bryncelli Ddu, Anglesey. An important New Stone Age passage grave

The St Lythan's Chambered Long Barrow, Glamorgan

The entrance to the Maes Howe chamber points not towards sunrise, but south-west, and this is a peculiarity shared by the last group of Scottish chamber tombs to be described. There are eleven of these Clava tombs, remarkably uniform, and concentrated in a small area south of the Spey valley round Inverness. All are marked by a large round barrow enclosed by stone kerbing. They are true passage graves with a narrow passage leading to a perfectly circular chamber built entirely of dry walling, though with a more massive foundation course. The roofs are partially corbelled, then closed with a single capstone. As a final distinctive, indeed unique, feature, each of these mounds is surrounded by a circle of standing stones mounting in size towards the south-west sector. It would be wonderful to know what it was about the history and ideas of these people, perhaps a tribe, that led them to build these sepulchres to a design so neatly standardized and so much their own. It is thought that they were active rather late in the Scottish passage grave period, probably extending into the beginning of the second millennium.

Far away from the principal megalithic country of the west and north, there remains one other small local group of tombs by the river Medway in Kent, the best known of these being Kit's Coty. Typically, a rectangular chamber stands at the eastern end of a long barrow that is also rectangular (*not* wedge-shaped or oval) and enclosed by a stone kerb or upright stones.

In addition to the main groups of chambered tombs that have been described, in western Britain there are many much simpler megalithic chambers to be seen. The most striking are rounded or squarish in plan with stone uprights supporting a massive capstone, and look like tables for a gargantuan feast. These are still often known by the old antiquarian name of 'dolmen', and the best are in Cornwall and Wales.

The megalithic tombs of Britain are our most ancient true buildings, the megalithic our first architectural style, primitive and solemn. The sense of the immense labour that simple people gave to the expression of other-worldly ideas seems still to cling to these stones weathered by the passage of four or five thousand years.

Henges

Archaeologists like to divide the New Stone Age into an early and a late phase at about 2750 BC when, although much went on as before, a new type of sacred monument began to be built. This is known as the 'henge' after its most splendid example, Stonehenge.

Henges are an entirely British achievement without parallel elsewhere. In their simplest and earliest form, they were circular enclosures with a bank usually outside a ditch – the reverse of earthworks intended for defence. The oldest examples often have a single entrance, while later two were common; the huge bank and ditch of Avebury are broken by four entrances.

Henges range from a modest size to about 12 hectares for Avebury and Durrington Walls. They also show a great variety of internal features of which circles of standing stones are the most striking. These may often have been part of the original construction, but we know from the history of Stonehenge that they could be later additions. Durrington Walls had large circular constructions of wooden posts, while at Arminghall, in Norfolk, there was a horseshoe setting of massive tree trunks. Many contain pits – either scattered or arranged in rings inside the earthwork – that may have been intended for the pouring of libations or for other ritual acts, and which quite often were used for cremations. Stonehenge's single ring of pits, known as the Aubrey Holes, contained cremations.

As with the earlier barrows and tombs, the henges were centres of magico-religious activity. They were sacred enclosures where local groups or tribes met together, probably seasonally, for rites serving their most urgent needs: for the fertility of their flocks and herds, their fields and themselves, for death to be followed by regeneration. In all this, the presence of cremation burials must have played some part. Unhappily, material remains of cult practices are few.

At henges that had standing stones and rings of stone or wood, sky divinities were probably beginning to be in the ascendancy. There is little doubt that our Stone Age farmers observed the movements of the sun and moon with religious awe and that they used these movements as calendrical pointers. The summer and winter solstices were probably among the occasions for ritual gatherings, as suggested by the most famous instance of the marking of the midsummer sunrise approximately over the Heel Stone at Stonehenge. There are also features at Stonehenge that can be read as marking extreme rising and setting points of the moon.

The best of these sanctuaries are rewarding to visit, and therefore figure well in the Gazetteer. From the Stripple Stones of Cornwall, by way of Arbor Low in Derbyshire and the fully excavated Cairnpapple near Edinburgh, to the noble Ring of Brodgar in the Orkneys, they are among the most satisfying of our ancient monuments, while Avebury and Stonehenge, far surpassing the rest, are unquestionably the most extraordinary of all the monumental creations of the prehistoric peoples of Britain.

The Beaker Folk

When the oldest henges had been in existence for some 500 years, an event took place of great importance for the prehistory of Britain. This was the invasion and settlement of the Beaker Folk. The name comes, of course, from the shapely and well-made drinking vessels from which it can be assumed they quaffed their beer (they increased barley crops at the expense of wheat) and which they buried beside their dead.

Beaker people were widespread on the Continent, but those who determined to seek lands in Britain are thought to have crossed the North Sea from the Rhineland. So far as we know, the native farming communities did not put up much resistance: certainly the invaders spread quite rapidly throughout much of the country. Physically they would initially have stood out among the old population, since in addition to the roundheadedness of at least some of the groups among them, they tended to be taller and more strongly built, with well-marked features and, one may guess, somewhat fairer colouring.

That the Beaker Folk would have dominated the indigenous population, forming a ruling élite, is made more certain by the evidence that they were a more martial people. They were archers, using a new form of barbed arrowhead and wearing stone wristguards for protection against the strings of powerful bows, and some among them were armed with heavy battle-axes of polished stone. They also had knives and short daggers of copper and bronze, and decked themselves with earrings and other trinkets of gold. Thus they were the first to introduce knowledge of metal-working to Britain, but because stone remained the principal material for tools and weapons while the native traditions persisted in many ways, archaeology has decreed that the Beaker invasions are to be assigned to the late New Stone Age.

A martial, perhaps male-dominated, type of society can also be inferred from the abandonment of communal tomb building in favour of individual burial below round barrows. In contrast with the old communal rite, the chieftain would be laid in a single grave fully clothed and with his weapons and ornaments as well as a beaker and perhaps other vessels. Burials of women were sometimes as impressive as those of the warriors, with large mounds and rich grave furnishings. Although the prime burial was usually single, subsidiary interments are occasionally found (including cremations) and may have been those of the chieftain's followers and servants.

The type of barrow commonly raised by the Beaker Folk was a simple pudding-shaped mound, often directly surrounded by a ditch and covering a central grave cut into the subsoil, where the body was laid, commonly in a crouched position. In chalk country, what are now grassy mounds were once conspicuously white, for the usual practice was to pile the topsoil over the grave and then pack the chalk from the ditch over it to form a gleaming dome.

This simple form, known as the bowl barrow, was to remain a standard type of Bronze Age grave monument, found all over Britain even while, as we shall see, more elaborate variations were being developed in Wessex during the centuries following the Beaker settlement.

Round barrows were to become far and away the commonest of our conspicuous prehistoric monuments: some 6000 have been identified in Wessex alone, while the grand total is probably three times that number. They are seen at their best in the chalklands of southern England, East Anglia, and the Lincolnshire and Yorkshire wolds, where they could be most exactly built and have been least eroded. Yet they are abundant, too, on rocky subsoils as in Cornwall, Wales, the Peak district and the Yorkshire moors, where they may take the form of cairns with a stone cist for the grave and a stone kerb to retain the stony mound.

Almost all round barrows, then, that one comes across will probably have been raised between the end of the New Stone Age through the early and middle phases of our Bronze Age - that is to say, from about 2000 to 1200 BC. There are, however, some rare exceptions: about 100 round barrows built by the Romans are known in southern and south-eastern England, and (rarer still) there are the mounds built by our Anglo-Saxon ancestors, as can be seen in the little group beside the famous Sutton Hoo ship burial in Suffolk.

In spite of the wealth of Beaker burials that has been found in Britain, there are no considerable earthworks or buildings. Although some of their settlements have been excavated, remains of dwellings were either absent or were of the flimsiest oval or circular huts. It looks as though they led a partially nomadic or pastoral life. Although forming something of a warrior élite, they appear to have worked with those inhabitants whom they found in Britain, often continuing and, in time, vigorously developing, the native culture. The most significant mark that the Beaker Folk made on it was undoubtedly in the development of the religious and ceremonial activities centred on the henges.

Although henges were already being built before the invasions, the Beaker Folk played a great part in elaborating them, as is plain at Durrington Walls and, above all, at Avebury and Stonehenge. At Avebury, while the huge earthwork and its monumental circles had been raised before 2000 BC, the newcomers were responsible for adding the West Kennet Avenue and the double stone circle at the end of it (those that Stukeley saw destroyed). There were Beaker burials at the foot of three of the Avenue standing stones. At Stonehenge, the Beaker influence was felt in the second building period when the original simple henge was enhanced by the Avenue earthwork and the double 'bluestone' circles. Indeed, since the Beaker Folk were established in south Wales, some prehistorians believe that it was they who carried out

Grave goods from the Bush Barrow, Wiltshire, p. 32
(David Cripps)

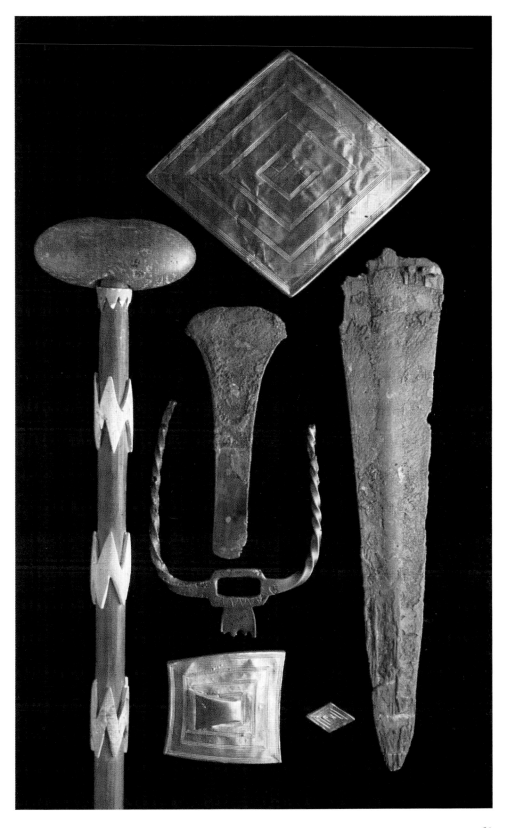

the amazing feat of transporting these huge blocks all the way from the Preseli mountains of Dyfed.

That the invaders and their immediate descendants recognized and identified themselves with the sanctity of our two greatest henges, as indeed with other lesser ones, is perhaps even more surely and tellingly revealed by the choice of their rulers to be buried nearby. Among the barrows that cluster round the temples, a number covered Beaker graves – such as, for example, one at the west end of the wonderful Normanton group that Colt-Hoare described as 'the most beautiful bowl barrow on the plains of Stonehenge'.

The coming of the Beaker Folk had an important impact on the more material aspect of life of the late New Stone Age. Their knowledge of metallurgy, however rudimentary, led them to prospect for copper, gold and tin and to find the ores in Ireland, south-west England and the west Midlands. They were, in fact, pioneers of the British bronze industry, preparing the way for the full early Bronze Age in Britain.

The Bronze Age

Barrows

In about 1700 BC, there appeared in Wessex, most conspicuously in Wiltshire and Dorset, a range of new barrow types raised over individual graves that were evidently those of wealthy, non-Beaker chieftains and their wives. These round barrows are standardized in form and laid out with great precision, and therefore provide an ideal pursuit for monument hunters.

All are strictly circular and can be said, in the typological sense, to be developments from the simple bowl barrow of the Beaker Folk. The bell type, which can be massively imposing, is like the bowl except that a level berm (narrow ledge) is left between mound and encircling ditch. It assumes a bell-like outline only because material from the mound has slid down over the berm before being stabilized by the covering turf. Occasionally (like the bowl) the bell barrow has a little bank round the outside lip of the ditch, and this is a relatively important feature in the three following varieties. In the *disc* form, the central mound is very slight, perhaps no higher than the outer bank; rarely there may be two or even three of these tumps within the disc. The mound of the *saucer* barrow is very low, only half a metre or so in height, but extends right to the ditch – for this reason it can be difficult to distinguish from a much eroded bowl. The last, the *pond*, is not really a barrow at all, for it consists of a shallow, carefully cut, circular hollow that occupies all the space within the outer bank.

One of the most interesting things about these Wessex barrows (there are about 500 in all) is that the forms are sex-related. The bowl, as the universal form, may cover either a man or woman, but the bell was usually raised for a man, and the disc type and, to a lesser extent, the saucer, for a woman. Of pond barrows little is known: their primary purpose may not have been for burials. Cremation was sometimes practised, most often for women, but the common rite for the chieftains' graves was inhumation, and once again, the body was usually laid on its side in a crouched position. However, in one of the most splendidly furnished of them all – the Bush Barrow, part of the Normanton group near Stonehenge – the corpse, that of a tall, stalwart man, seems to have been at full length on its back. He was buried with a round shield, a bronze axe, two bronze daggers, one enriched with intricate goldwork, a gold plaque on his breast, a knife in his right hand and a ritual mace or sceptre with a polished stone head and a slender, inlaid shaft.

The Bush Barrow is perhaps the richest, but many Wessex barrows yielded handsome grave goods in gold and bronze, and at Clandon in Dorset another sceptre came to light, its jet head embossed with gold. This chieftain had also been provided with a handled cup carved from a lump of amber. The women were usually buried with a variety of beads and elaborate necklaces of amber, faïence and gold, with small knives and with bronze awls, probably used for leather working.

It appears very likely that these rich warrior rulers represent infiltration from Brittany, on a far smaller scale than that of the Beaker Folk, but with force enough to dominate and, when necessary, organize the already large and prosperous population of Wessex. Together they were able to develop long distance trade: they supplied gold, copper and tin from Ireland to the Continent and in exchange acquired luxuries such as amber and faïence beads from Europe and Mediterranean lands.

The greatest interest centres on the part played by the Wessex chieftains in the colossal enterprise of developing Stonehenge from the first modest henge to the unique temple we now know from its ruins. Although carbon 14 dates have been interpreted to prove that Stonehenge was completed centuries before the time of the Wessex chieftains, archaeological opinion is shifting once more and it is now possible to believe that they were indeed the architects of its last and greatest development. Indeed it would seem that only the chieftains would have had the power, knowledge and ambition to transport and erect the great sarsens of this third period at Stonehenge. Certainly they were seeking to lie within the sacred aura of the place when they chose, as the Beaker Folk had done before them, to be buried on the neighbouring downs.

Through the early Bronze Age, while Wessex prospered and traded with Europe, the rest of Britain remained relatively poor and insular. The building of round barrows continued through the early and much of the middle Bronze Age. As time went by cremation returned to fashion until, during the last centuries of barrow-building, it had become an almost universal custom. The burnt bones were put in large urns and these were often buried, either upright or inverted in a single grave at the centre of the barrow. Like the construction of the barrows themselves, the variety of the interments was, in detail, almost infinite.

Stone circles

Perhaps the class of monument of the early and middle Bronze Age that can prove most stirring to visit is the stone circle. There are approximately 900 of these rings of standing stones in Great Britain, most of them, naturally enough, in the highland country where stone was readily available. They range in diameter from under 10 to over 100 metres and the stones themselves vary in shape and size. The stone circles may have been derived from henges or from circles set round chambered tombs as in the Clava passage graves, near Inverness. Circles of such kinds were set up by the late New Stone Age, but the typical, free-standing stone circles, though very difficult to date, are assigned to the Bronze Age, the latest known carbon 14 date being

about 1200 BC for a small circle in Tayside.

The main concentrations of these free-standing stone circles are in north-east Scotland and Orkney, Cumbria, Wiltshire and Cornwall, but they are well scattered over the high ground with large numbers of modest examples in Wales and on Dartmoor. There are also a few isolated examples, such as those in the Outer Hebrides and the famous Rollright Stones, curiously on their own in Oxfordshire. Some of them are connected with stone rows and avenues or have a single standing stone outside the ring. Among localized forms, a group of over 70 circles clustered among the Grampian foothills in north-east Scotland are distinctive enough to have been given a name of their own: recumbent stone circles. In these, the stones are graded in height, rising towards the tallest pair, usually facing south-westerly, that flanks a long and massive recumbent stone. First sight of this makes most people think of a sacrificial altar. It definitely was not that, but what purpose it did serve is never likely to be known.

The circles must have been raised to enclose sacred ground that served as a meeting place for tribes or smaller communities, probably on the occasion of seasonal festivals. In some, there may well have been sight lines on the rising or setting of the sun and moon. The stones of a few circles have been carved with symbols of religious meaning. In the south, axes or other weapons are simply depicted, while in the north, cup-and-ring symbols or the rarer spirals may be found. Some stone circles contain cremation burials, but this was not their primary purpose. It is noteworthy that the largest and finest of the free-standing circles seldom have any association with burials.

Free-standing stone circles are most often to be found in remote places, among rugged hills or on wild moorland. This is in part due to the necessity for suitable stone, but also to the sad fact that, in more populous regions, hundreds if not thousands of circles have been destroyed. However this may be, these sacred places of our forebears often have a romantic appeal greatly enhanced by their natural setting. This is most true of Castlerigg, or The Carles, just south-east of Keswick, where the stones stand in a pasture with a superb background of Lakeland fells.

Overleaf: Castlerigg Stone Circle, Cumbria. Possibly one of the earliest stone circles in Britain, Castlerigg contains an enigmatic rectangle of stones inside the circle

The erection of stone circles appears to have tailed away at about the same time as that of barrow building: during the century following 1300 BC. With them there came to an end the long period (probably over 2000 years) during which the peoples of Britain put their greatest creative efforts into building religious monuments. During the following five centuries of the later middle and late Bronze Age, virtually no monuments were constructed that were large or striking enough to survive and excite general interest today.

Settlements

Such a break in building is surprising, since the population of Britain was growing during that period and great advances were being made in metallurgical skills and in the design, quantity and variety of bronze tools and weapons. Improvements in the design of spears and the production first of rapiers, then of heavy slashing swords and bronze shields must prove that warfare was on the increase during this latter part of the Bronze Age. Indeed we shall see that the building of hillforts was already beginning, on a relatively small scale, before the dawn of the Iron Age in the seventh century BC.

Although there are no spectacular field monuments dating from this period, new types of settlement have left visible remains. Perhaps because the climate, warmer than our present one, was beginning to deteriorate, the communities practising mixed farming who had always been the basis of the social economy took to living in more substantial settlements: small groups of circular houses, presumably family dwellings, often enclosed together with a paddock within a fence or stone walling. Their settlements stood among small squarish fields, known to us as 'Celtic fields', which were cultivated by cross-ploughing with oxen and in which barley and lesser crops of emmer wheat were grown.

Remains of settlements of this kind are a familiar sight on Dartmoor: groups of 'hut-circles', some with a substantial surrounding wall. The hut-circles actually mark the location of the low stone walls that, together with central posts, supported roofs of turf or thatch. The nature of the adjoining fields and pens suggests that it was only on the drier east side of the moor that corn growing was important, the folk of the west and south depending very largely on their cattle and sheep.

In chalk country, the settlements are less conspicuous, although the banks and ditches of the enclosures may remain, together with traces of houses that, on excavation, reveal a ring of holes for stout roof posts. Here greater interest attaches to the 'Celtic fields' that in some areas still cover the downs in a vast net, most striking in the light of a rising or setting sun. This part of our heritage from the prehistoric past is, however, being rapidly destroyed by modern farming.

On the Yorkshire moors and elsewhere in the north, the same patterns of circular stone houses, enclosures and fields can be traced and are often associated with cemeteries of small cairns, as at Danby Rigg in North Yorkshire. Settlements of this kind were widespread and flourishing by the middle Bronze Age (after 1400 BC) and were maintained with little change by a conservative peasantry until the end of Roman times.

The Iron Age

This conservative tradition of small farmers provided the firm foundation of life in Iron Age Britain. The round houses remained much the same, though larger and better equipped against bad weather. In north-west Scotland, fortified dwellings – brochs, duns and wheelhouses – were developed just before and after the arrival of the Romans. The one important advance of these farming communities was the building of deep silos for the storage of food grains and raised granaries for seed corn: the capacity to store cereals in bulk made possible the accelerated increase in population during Iron Age times.

Continental influence

The social structure and culture of Britain was greatly affected by the arrival of groups of Celtic peoples from France and the Low Countries, giving rise to another warrior aristocracy.

There is disagreement among prehistorians as to how much the Continental influences were attributable to invasions and how much to trade and intercourse between tribal rulers. But that invaders did arrive at least in small numbers at various times and in different regions during the British Iron Age is certain. Although dates, too, are hotly disputed, the outline history of the British Iron Age can be roughly drawn.

Iron began to be used from about 700 BC, but it was not in plentiful supply for another two centuries, by which time a full iron-using culture of Continental Celtic origin was slowly spreading northwards and westwards across Britain. It was during this period that the building of hillforts first became a major activity. A second phase opened in about 300 BC with further invaders and cross-Channel contacts. It is probable that these movements introduced the use of the sling in warfare, a new armament that, as will be seen, brought about a great strengthening of hillfort defences. The third century saw a flowering of Celtic art that was to last until Roman civilization largely crushed it. This masterly decorative art reinforces the evidence of the hillforts – that is, that the Celtic rulers were devoted to martial values – for much of what survives is found on weapons, helmets and shields, horse-trappings and such adjuncts to the heroic life as war trumpets, gold neckrings and bronze tankards. Finely ornamented bronze hand mirrors for women have also been found.

The third period of the Iron Age, when Celtic Britain emerged into the first faint light of history, began about 120 BC with the invasion and settlement of south-eastern England by peoples of mixed German and Celtic stock coming from what is now Belgium – those whom Julius Caesar called the Belgae. Among the leading Belgic tribes were the powerful Catuvellauni, who spread widely north of the Thames with central strongholds near St Albans in Hertfordshire. A second wave of Belgic settlement, beginning before Caesar's expeditions of 55–54 BC, established the tribe of the Atrebates in a large southern area from Sussex to Hampshire and Berkshire, with principal towns near Chichester and at Silchester. These two tribes, with their allies, became deadly rivals, and their non-Belgic neighbours strove to check their expansion.

Belgic influence

The Belgae introduced progressive changes both before and after Caesar: they intro-

duced the potter's wheel and a much greater use of wheeled vehicles, and they replaced the primitive stone rubbers for grinding flour with the rotary handmill. Celtic coinage gradually came into use until the leading Belgic kings were issuing coins inscribed with their names and sometimes with the title of *Rex*. So for the closing phase of British independence, the names of many princes are known and their tribal struggles and intrigues can sometimes be followed. Of these, the most significant was the seizure of the Trinovantian kingdom by the ever-expanding Catuvellauni and their adoption of its capital at Colchester as their own. There followed the long and prosperous reign of the famous Catuvellaunian king Cunobelin (Shakespeare's Cymbeline), whose death in about AD 40 helped to precipitate the Roman invasion of AD 43. Meanwhile, Cunobelin and other Belgic kings of his time romanized their domestic life, importing wine, oil and good tableware, glass and other refinements, and exporting corn, cattle, iron and precious metals, pearls, slaves, hides and hunting dogs.

Normally the Belgic peoples did not fortify hilltops but defended far larger areas with long dykes. They made use of natural lowland obstacles such as rivers and marshes, and sometimes cut off the area between two confluent rivers. Within the space so defended, the actual settlement could be scattered, with room for cultivation and pasture. Earthworks of this kind at Belgic capitals (which they called *oppida*) can best be seen at Wheathampstead (Herts) and adjoining the later Roman towns at Colchester and Chichester.

Outside the settled tribal kingdoms in the south-east, however, the Belgae sometimes extended their rule by taking over and strengthening their neighbours' hillforts, as they did at Maiden Castle in Dorset, but in the greater part of Britain, beyond Belgic territory, the hillforts, our principal legacy from the Iron Age, remained in occupation as before.

Hillforts and fortified homesteads

Although defended hilltop settlements were already being established in the late Bronze Age, there may not have been many of them. It was not until after 500 BC that the building of hillforts became a major activity.

There are over 2000 in Britain, strikingly uneven in both distribution and size. Of over 1400 below Hadrian's Wall, nearly all are south-west of a line from the Dee to Dungeness; in Kent, East Anglia, Yorkshire and Lancashire there are few. The many hillforts in west and south Wales and in Cornwall tend to be small in contrast with those of England and north-east Wales. North of Hadrian's Wall there is a dense concentration in the Border Country, a scatter round the Firths of Forth, Tay and Moray and a very few near the north and west coasts. In Scotland generally, with rare exceptions, hillforts are not large.

The purpose for which they were built must have varied from region to region and, in some areas, from century to century. Many hillforts protected a single household, presumably from raiders or feuding enemies. The larger works, protecting villages and towns, may have been strongholds of powerful individuals ruling wide lands, the product of intertribal warfare, or raised against or by invaders. A few, especially coastal sites such as Hengistbury Head on the Dorset coast, may even have been trading centres. It may be that, in times of crisis, farmers from outlying homesteads would have fled with their cattle to hillforts for protection, and some hillforts may have been built solely as refuges with no permanent settlement.

In plan, most forts crown hilltops, often following the contours but taking care not to leave dead ground where a foe could approach unseen. Promontory forts in which ramparts protect the neck of a steep-sided headland are not uncommon, and have a variant in the picturesque cliff castles of the south-west, where the defences run from cliff to cliff of a promontory jutting out to sea.

The design of the ramparts ranged very widely, depending on tradition, the materials available and changing means of attack and defence. The most obvious division is, of course, between earthworks built from chalk or other yielding subsoils and the stone walls of the highland zone of the west and north.

The simplest form of earthwork was to dig a deep and usually v-shaped ditch and pile the soil along the inner lip, making as steep a slope as possible from ditch bottom to rampart top. This method could be used to great effect even on a large scale – as in the second period at Maiden Castle. Frequently, however, the earthwork was reinforced by a timber framework or lacing, usually to secure a vertical revetment (retaining wall) for the front, and sometimes the back, of the rampart.

In stony country, the walls were usually of rubble faced with drystone masonry, sometimes doubled on the front and stepped at the back for easy access to the rampart walk.

This stepping is well illustrated at Tre'r Ceiri in Gwynedd. There was always a danger that stresses might push the drystone outwards to the point of collapse, and to prevent this, timbers were often laid across the line of the wall as ties. The builders might conceal the timber ends behind the walling, or again they might be exposed along the face. This latter construction was commonly used in Scotland, where it showed a great weakness because it readily caught fire. This accounts for the Scottish vitrified forts, so-called when it was thought that the rock had been deliberately melted for greater toughness. It is now recognized that vitrification was caused

Maiden Castle, Dorset. A section of the mountainous Iron Age ramparts of this famous hillfort, which was excavated by Sir Mortimer Wheeler

by accidental burning or by enemy action, the slots for the timber forming flues that intensified the heat.

Since they were the weakest point in the defences, hillfort entrances were few and, in stony country, often narrow. The gates seem always to have been wooden, and usually in pairs, turning on hinge or pivot to meet at the centre. Sometimes, and characteristically in early, single-ramparted strongholds, the entrance was through a simple break in the ramparts, but this invited direct assault and various devices were employed to allow the defenders to use their missiles before the attackers reached the gates. The favourite

was to bend the rampart ends inwards to make a funnel-shaped or parallel-sided approach to the portal where the enemy could be attacked from the flanks. An alternative was to mask the entry with external outworks – a form that reached a fantastic extreme at Maiden Castle. Sometimes one or a pair of guard-chambers were built beside the gates, and there might be a bridge to carry the rampart walk across the opening.

It is impossible, except within localities, to proclaim one type of rampart construction invariably earlier or later than another. However, it does appear that the single rampart (well seen at Cissbury in West Sussex) was reinforced in response to the introduction of sling warfare after 300 BC. Widely separated ramparts were presumably designed for cattle marshalling (for example, in the Clovelly Dykes in Devon), and cliff castles are a feature of the south-western peninsula. The latter have close parallels in Brittany and must reflect the constant cross-Channel trafficking between the tribes of the two peninsulas long fostered by the trade in Cornish tin.

All along the Atlantic coasts of Scotland and on into the Orkneys and Shetlands, there developed towards the end of the Iron Age a fascinating variety of fortified homesteads: duns, brochs and wheelhouses. Duns consist of a thick, roughly circular drystone wall some three metres high and entered through a single narrow entrance. Often there are cells or small galleries within the thickness of the wall, but the main living space for the household was in the open central enclosure. They are found in numbers from southwest Scotland, along the west coast, and on the isles to the west, and some of the largest merge in form with small hillforts.

The main distribution of brochs is from the north-west of the Scottish mainland to the northern isles, with a concentration in Caithness and Orkney. They provide one of the outstanding attractions of Scottish archaeology and have been recognized as uniquely Scottish. Several appear in the Gazetteer, including the finest and best preserved, the Mousa Broch in the Shetlands. Here alone one can see what must have been one of the most striking aspects of these extraordinary round towers: the perfect drystone masonry gently incurving and unbroken by any opening except one diminutive doorway at the foot. Mousa Broch still stands to a height of 13 metres.

This external appearance of immense solidity is, in a way, belied by the fact that broch walls are double, like a thermos, the two skins about a metre apart and bonded by lintel slabs and accommodating a stairway curving up to the summit. The bonding slabs produce the effect of galleries, but these seem to have had no practical use (save that

Dun Carloway, Lewis. The walls of this well-preserved Iron Age broch still stand to 9m in height

Dun Carloway Broch, Lewis

one was found to have served as a privy), the accommodation being in the central court together with adjacent wall chambers. It is usually said that a lean-to was built on a raised floor round the courtyard, but another view is that the whole central space had a high-pitched roof.

A wheelhouse is a circular stone dwelling with stone piers projecting inwards radially from the walls, but stopping short of the centre to leave an open space. These presumably supported roofs of turf or heather. Such dwellings cover much the same territory as the broch: in north-west Scotland and in Orkney and Shetland, and are often found together with them, most notably at Jarlshof and Clickhimin in Shetland.

Duns and the simpler brochs may already have appeared as early as the late second century BC, but were certainly at their height during the next two centuries, some continuing to be occupied through Roman times. Though there may be earlier examples, wheelhouses were most popular during the second and third centuries AD.

The settlements the hillforts were built to protect seem usually to have consisted of irregular scatters of the traditional round houses with innumerable storage and rubbish pits and connecting pathways. Occasionally, as at Danebury Hill in Hampshire, orderly rows of rectangular buildings have been uncovered, but it is not certain that these were dwellings. No royal or chieftains' houses have as yet come to light (except possibly at Hod Hill); in fact, they were probably surprisingly rough and simple for rulers who were finely dressed and armed. It is likely that the hill settlements included at least one building that served for religious observances.

Many hillforts have neither natural water supplies nor tanks or wells within the defences, a lack that suggests that they were not generally expected to sustain prolonged attack or siege. It is probable, however, that hillfort defences could usually be held against the unsustained onslaughts of tribal wars. The adoption of the sling gave defenders the ability to hurl down missiles from a height on to men attempting to scale the outer ramparts. Attackers would have stormed the ramparts with showers of stones and would have undermined the walls, and fire, too, must often have been used against gates and wall timbers.

The defences of British hillforts were no match for Roman siege weapons and military discipline. This is made evident by the events of Caesar's expeditions and the early stages of the Roman conquest. Caesar's account of his second foray of 54 BC includes the earliest mention of a British hillfort and its storming. This almost certainly took place at Bigbury, near Canterbury, where the Britons, led by

King Cassivellaunus, had blocked the entrances with felled trees. The legionaries made a causeway of earth and faggots across the ditches and, with shields interlocked over their heads, had no difficulty in capturing the fort.

Again with the opening campaign of the conquest of AD 43 we shall see that Vespasian, commanding the 2nd Legion, easily stormed no fewer than 20 hillforts in southern England, including the massively fortified Maiden Castle.

Roman Britain

Roman conquest

The Roman conquest and the inclusion of most of Britain within a highly organized and literate empire means that the anonymous millennia of prehistory are abruptly succeeded by some four centuries when a vast amount is known of this northern province. Whereas hitherto it has been necessary to use the monuments to reconstruct history, now it is more a matter of relating history to the monuments although, of course, archaeology has done much to fill in and correct the written record.

Because our greatest Roman monument, Hadrian's Wall, is most intimately tied up with the military and political history of the province as a whole and of north Britain in particular, it is treated in a special account on pages 212–25. This makes it unnecessary to do more here than outline the early phases of the conquest in England and Wales and the romanization of the province, ending with a survey of our 'Roman remains'.

Although Caesar's expeditions proved to be no more than exploratory forays, contact between British princes and Rome continued and, as we have seen, was supported by a trade in luxuries that was highly profitable to Roman merchants. The idea of bringing Britain into the empire had not been abandoned in Rome and the Emperor Caligula got as far as building a grand lighthouse at Boulogne in preparation for an invasion. With Caligula's assassination in AD 41, his uncle Claudius assumed the purple with a deep personal ambition to win himself some military glory.

The Catuvellaunian king, Cunobelin, died at about this time, having extended his realm to cover most of south-east England. On succeeding him, his warlike son Caratacus determined to expand his kingdom yet further and drove the Atrebatic ruler, Verica, to flee to Rome and appeal for help against him. As the Atrebates were among the British tribes friendly to Rome, this appeal from a legitimate ruler and ally presented Claudius with the perfect opportunity to invade. In the spring of AD 43, an army of some 40,000 men (four legions and the usual auxiliaries of foot and cavalry) disembarked, unopposed, at what was almost certainly the natural harbour of Richborough on the east coast of Kent.

After skirmishes, the first battle with Caratacus and his massed tribesmen was at the crossing of the Medway, probably at Rochester; it was hard fought, but the Britons had to fall back to the Thames in the London area. Again they failed to prevent the Romans from crossing the river, though they harried them with some success in the marshy and forested country to the north. Caratacus was soon to make for Wales to rouse the resistance of the tough, anti-Roman mountain tribes. Claudius himself was now, by arrangement, summoned to lead his army in the capture of the Catuvellaunian *oppidum* of *Camulodunum* (Colchester). He arrived at the head of detachments of his Pretorian Guard, most of a fifth legion, and a contingent of elephants.

All went according to plan, *Camulodunum* was occupied, victory acclaimed – and after only 16 days in his new province-to-be, the emperor returned to Rome to celebrate. Within a few years a splendid temple dedicated to the 'divine' Claudius was raised in the Roman town now established close above the site of *Camulodunum*. The vaulted foundations of this temple can be visited below the Norman castle there.

The rapid conquest of lowland England followed immediately, aided by the support of old and new allies among the British tribes. Verica, an old man, was probably briefly reinstalled as a client-king in the Atrebatic *oppidum* at Chichester, to be succeeded by Cogidubnus, the prince who is thought to have owned the palace at Fishbourne in West Sussex. A ruler of the East Anglian Iceni was also granted a client-kingdom.

Meanwhile, the army made a three-pronged advance across England, building military roads with forts at strategic points.

The southern force, the 2nd Legion, led by Vespasian, having passed the friendly Atrebatic territory of Sussex and Hampshire, met with some resistance, most strongly it seems from the Durotriges of Dorset. At Hod Hill the ramparts were being strengthened when the attack came, yet Vespasian seems to have won a quick surrender. The inhabitants were expelled while, a most unusual move, the legionaries built their own military camp in one corner of the native earthwork. At Maiden Castle, where ammunition dumps of some 54,000 slingstones had been brought from Chesil Beach, resistance was equally vain. After its fall the Romans left behind one of the most grim and telling relics of their conquest: the famous 'war cemetery' by the east gate. After his capture of twenty hillforts in all, Vespasian was able to push on to Exeter.

Having no famous men in command, much less is known of the other two prongs of advance. In the centre, the 14th Legion probably took the line of Watling Street – the road that ran from the east coast of Kent in more or less a straight line to north Wales – as far as its junction (near present-day Leicester) with the great diagonal road, the Fosse Way, which ran from Exeter to Lincoln – thus opening up the heavily forested, sparsely populated Midlands. For the thrust to the north, the 9th Legion, skirting the fens and forging the route of Ermine Street which ran from near Pevensey in East Sussex north to York, presently established its fortress at Lincoln. During these years of easy conquest, the base and centre of administration remained at Colchester, while Richborough was developed as a supply port, soon to be glorified by the triumphal arch that stood as a symbolic entry to *Britannia* at the beginning of Watling Street.

It seems certain that Claudius intended to limit the province to lowland England, hoping only to establish friendly protectorates with the more pastoral and less civilized tribes of Wales and the north. With this intent, by AD 47 a frontier had been fortified along the Fosse Way. Its nature as a frontier is at once suggested by the faithfulness with which this road follows the direct line from south-west to north-east, never deviating more than a few miles on either side.

With Caratacus, a brilliant leader, active in Wales, the policy of containing the province behind the Fosse Way was bound to fail. He had the support of the Silures of south-east Wales and of the Ordovices, whose tribal lands covered the greater part of central and north Wales. The stubborn Brigantes of Yorkshire included elements that were hostile to Rome, though their queen, Cartimandua, was pro-Roman. The resistance fighters, among whom the Silures were the most formidable, were soon raiding and threatening the frontier, and the Roman command saw that these hill tribes would have to be conquered and held down. So the advance was continued westward, a legionary base against the Silures was built at Gloucester *(Glevum)*, while Watling Street was extended to a well-chosen site at Wroxeter *(Viroconium)* to command central Wales.

Caratacus, determined to confront the Romans, moved from the south into Ordovican territory and massed his forces in a strongly protected position among the mountains of Snowdonia. The challenge was accepted, and in a pitched battle in AD 51, Caratacus's forces were defeated and his family captured. He himself rode for Brigantia, rashly hopeful of rousing the dissidents there. Cartimandua, mindful of her alliance, promptly handed him over to his foes to be sent to Rome and put on public display as a prisoner. There, he put his well-known question: 'Why do you, with all these grand possessions, still covet our poor huts?'

Welsh resistance did not by any means cease with the capture of the Catuvellaunian king. The Silures were raiding far and wide and even won a victory over a legionary force. In Brigantia, Venutius, enraged by his wife Cartimandua's betrayal of Caratacus, took over the leadership of the resistance and, with due caution, bided his time for a major uprising. The Romans evidently now determined that Wales must be conquered: strong governors were sent to Britain and, by the end of the 50s, the Silures had been at least temporarily subdued.

The Roman command's next objective was Anglesey *(Mona)*. There were four reasons for this: it was rich in copper, its fertile soil made it a granary for the still hostile Ordovices, it harboured refugee resistance fighters and, equally important, it had become a power centre for the famous Celtic priesthood of the Druids. The Romans were normally tolerant of the gods and religious practices of their subject peoples, but the frightful rites of human sacrifice that the Druids perpetrated in their sacred groves determined the Romans to crush them in Britain as they had already done in Gaul.

An extraordinarily vivid account of the attack has been left to us by the Roman historian, Tacitus. As the fleet of Roman troop carriers reached the Menai Straits, the army was horrified by the spectacle on the far shore. The Britons were working themselves into a fighting frenzy: women dressed in black and brandishing torches went like Furies among the men while, behind this multitude, the Druids stood, arms uplifted, calling down curses upon Rome and her soldiers. For a moment, the soldiers hesitated, filled with dread. Then discipline took command once more, the boats were beached, the cavalry swam ashore and soon their disorganized opponents were ruthlessly cut down in a carnage more dreadful than the frenzy had been. The Romans, under the command of the governor Suetonius Paulinus, destroyed the Druids' sacred groves (said to have been red with the blood of former Roman prisoners) and built a garrison fort intended to play its part in the pacification of Wales. But immediately such ideas had to be abandoned for news was brought to the high command (under Suetonius Paulinus) of the outbreak of Boudicca's rebellion.

Before this second bloody event of the year AD 61 is described it should be made clear that while the military fronts were being pushed towards the highland zone of Wales and the north, the civil province was being developed in its wake. By that year Colchester had been made a *colonia* for time-expired army veterans; *Verulamium* had been founded as a Roman town beside the old *oppidum* of the Catuvellauni and had shops and probably public buildings; London had become a boomtown in the hands of thriving merchants; tribal towns were growing at Canterbury, Chelmsford, Silchester and elsewhere, while the client-kingdoms of Cogidubnus, with Chichester as his capital, and of the Icenian king Prasutagus, were a civilizing influence as allies of Rome. Giving the province a unity Britain had never known before was a network of waterways and good roads built for the military but now serving imperial and local administration, trade and the transport of raw materials. They could also, of course, be used to quell any small outbreaks of trouble that might occur even in this civil area.

There was, however, growing discontent and hardship in the young province. Romanization, whether public or private, cost money, and many of the British aristocracy were in the hands of Roman money-lenders, while the Procurator as chief tax gatherer was making unjustified demands. The abuse of power and maladministration was no doubt partly due to lack of supervision, the governors and their best men generally being far away campaigning.

The spark to fire this tinder was provided by the death of Prasutagus of the East Anglian Iceni. He had no male heirs and, in any case, it was imperial policy to do away with client-kingdoms. Officials and soldiers arrived to take the royal property and reduce the kingdom to provincial status, which also meant disarming. In the process, the widowed Boudicca was flogged and her daughters raped. The justly enraged queen led the revolt, her own people joined by the Trinovantes and other rebels, and a wild, heroic British fighting force swept against the hated Colchester *colonia*, which fell within two days.

Temple and town were destroyed, the population was slaughtered and frightful cruelty was shown to those to be sacrificed in the sacred groves. A legion coming to the rescue was badly mauled, only the cavalry escaping. Suetonius Paulinus dashed back from Anglesey, but there was no time to move troops (one legion even refused to move) and he abandoned both London and *Verulamium* to share the fate of Colchester. In all three towns, archaeology has exposed the burned layer that still commemorates the day when they were given to the flames by British freedom fighters. According to Tacitus, 70,000 men, women and children died in the sackings.

Over-confidence eventually led to Boudicca's defeat by a force far smaller than her own ill-organized tribal contingents. Tens of thousands of British warriors were killed, and tradition has it that the queen took poison. Paulinus set about exacting a fearful punishment: Icenian territory was laid waste and much of the province put under military rule, with garrisons at new forts such as The Lunt at Baginton in Warwickshire.

A new Procurator, Classicianus, himself a provincial, saw that Suetonius Paulinus had gone too far in crushing the wretched Britons, whose past grievances the former well understood. It was largely through his good offices that Paulinus was tactfully withdrawn and a governor appointed with a policy of reconciliation. Classicianus himself, meanwhile, was able to reform the fiscal abuses and liberalize the system. He must have died in office, and part of the broken tombstone of this true champion of the British is now a precious exhibit in the British Museum.

Gradually, the province recovered. Colchester, identified with the imperial cult, had to be rebuilt, and it was at this time that the true provincial capital and the central administration moved to London, so well-sited at the lowest crossing place of the Thames and ideal for sea-borne trade. It soon became, and was to remain, the hub of the lowland road system. For some unknown reason, *Verulamium* was not to be rebuilt for some 15 years. There had been no time for recovery – which was intended to be followed by a further advance against Wales – before the province was caught up in the disasters of AD 68, when, after the suicide of Nero, the Roman succession led to civil war and the legions in Britain, as elsewhere, were torn by divided loyalties. This 'year of the four emperors' ended with the success of Vespasian, putting the empire in the hands of a good soldier with intimate knowledge of Britain.

Meanwhile, however, fresh rebellion had broken out in the province, Venutius seizing the opportunity to rouse the strong anti-Roman elements within the Brigantes. Under his former wife, Cartimandua, the huge territory of Brigantia, stretching from sea to sea across the north of England, had provided a secure flank for the province; now, in AD 69, Venutius declared open war on Cartimandua. The Romans had to rescue the once-fearsome lady, but they failed to check Venutius, who for a year and more was a growing threat to the province.

In AD 71 Vespasian appointed as governor of *Britannia* Q. Pettilius Cerialis, a friend and kinsman, with orders to crush Venutius and the Brigantian rebellion. This he did, establishing a legionary fortress at York and battling westward, probably along the line of the road to Carlisle where some of his marching camps can be seen. At this time, the up-and-coming Agricola was in command of a legion in the west and was able to lend Cerialis support by assailing the Brigantes on their other flank. 'After a series of battles, some not uncostly', as Tacitus records, Venutius was defeated. He almost certainly made his last stand at Stanwick in North Yorkshire, where the vast earthworks had not been completed before the Roman onslaught; they were, indeed, too extensive to be defensible. Sir Mortimer Wheeler, their excavator, commented, 'Stanwick is at the same time a very notable memorial to a heroic episode of the British resistance and a monument to its futility.' The fate of Venutius is unknown.

So the Brigantes were quelled, though by no means finally pacified, and the high command could return to the long-delayed conquest of Wales. The first campaigns were against the Silures, the Romans probably

opening the attack by sea to occupy the Glamorgan peninsula. In AD 75 they were able to advance their legionary base from Gloucester to a new fortress at Caerleon, and a few years later another legionary fortress was built at Chester *(Deva)*, which led to Wroxeter being demilitarized and becoming a civilian tribal town. Caerleon and Chester were long to remain the military bases for the control of south and north Wales.

By the time Vespasian sent Agricola back to Britain as governor in the summer of AD 78, the resistance of the Silures and Ordovices had been largely broken and a network of forts and military roads established along the coasts and among the mountains. Not completely broken, however, for just before Agricola's arrival, the Ordovices had destroyed a cavalry regiment. Knowing the country well, he was able to mete out quick punishment, completing his utter defeat of the tribe by capturing Anglesey just 18 years after Paulinus had been forced to withdraw from it by Boudicca's rebellion.

The next year Agricola gave to dealing with the persistent unrest of the Brigantes. By the end of the campaigning season, he had brought Wales and the north of England under control. The rest of the military history of his Scottish conquest and what followed is told in the account of Hadrian's Wall (pp. 212–25).

Agricola was a brilliant soldier, but was also an imaginative administrator and, being a Gaul by birth, had an understanding of provincials that contrasted with the arrogance of Roman aristocrats. In his first year in Britain, he put an end to various administrative and fiscal abuses that had again crept in. The next year, he initiated a policy of romanization, both material and intellectual, 'with private encouragement and public aid,' Tacitus wrote. On scores of sites, particularly towns with their excellent civic amenities, and the more luxurious villas, archaeology has brought us material proof of the well-to-do Briton's readiness to adopt the ways of civilization. Of them all, perhaps the villa at Lullingstone in Kent gives the most vivid impression of the sophisticated, romanized lifestyle of the British élite. Trade, too, was adding to the number of households that could afford luxuries. One has to recall, however, that many small peasant communities continued to live very much as they had done since the late Bronze Age. Tacitus tells how Agricola encouraged the growth of towns, how he saw to it that 'the sons of leading men were educated in the liberal arts

Lullingstone Villa, Kent. Fourth-century mosaic of the abduction of Europa in the dining room

and stated his opinion that the natural ability of the Britons was superior to the studied industry of the Gauls'.

Monuments

Any account of the monuments left by four centuries of Roman rule must first make a distinction between the civil and military areas. In the early days of conquest military camps and forts were built even in lowland England, but by the time Wales was under control and the northern frontier established the army had been withdrawn from the rest of the province. Many of the military bases were left to decay while others, like Wroxeter, became civil towns.

Roads

The life and government of the province very largely depended on that marvellous network of communications, the Roman roads. The system was originally laid out and built by the legionary engineers and was essentially determined by their military needs. Once the army had been withdrawn, the roads outside Wales and Scotland were at the service of traders, merchants, government and army officials and the important imperial posting service. For the latter, enjoyed by imperial messengers and high officials, relays of horses were kept at short intervals along the roads, with an inn every 30 to 50 kilometres.

Roman roads do normally run in a straight line across level country, but where the terrain was not quite level, sightings were taken from one high point to another and the road was built in a series of short straight sections. In more mountainous country, the engineers were quite prepared to follow the curves of a valley or the irregularities of a ridge. In peaceful times, minor roads were built for carrying raw materials (such as iron ore in the Sussex Weald) or for linking towns and settlements. Other than the motorways, our main roads often follow the line of Roman ones. This in itself testifies to the skill of the Roman engineers who worked without map or compass and often had to cut through dense forest.

Highways were usually laid on a raised bank, known as the *agger*, made of material dug from broad ditches on one or both sides of the road. Often today, these ditches have filled up again, while the *agger* is clearly visible. The roadway itself was most commonly metalled with gravel, small stones or flints well rammed down on a foundation of large stones, and strongly cambered. The metalled surface of highways was likely to be about eight metres wide, though for lesser roads it could be as little as four metres. Sections cut through it have shown that, just as today, it had to be frequently renewed. Altogether some 9600 kilometres of Roman roads have been reliably identified and serve as witness to a system far more effective in every way than anything known in Britain until the turnpikes of the late eighteenth century.

Towns and town buildings

Towns were, of course, as important as roads in the deliberate imposition of the Roman way of life, particularly its culture and civilized habits. The Romans had naturally absorbed from the Greeks and other Mediterranean peoples the conviction that city life was an absolute essential of all civilization, and they therefore hastened to secure its development in Britain. As with the roads, the siting of many towns was determined by military considerations. Since the Belgic invasions, there had been a tendency for large settlements to be low-lying, usually beside rivers, and with the Roman conquest the descent from the hilltops was greatly speeded.

There are four main classes of Roman provincial towns. Those that had the highest status were the *coloniae*, chartered foundations where Roman veterans were granted building plots within the town limits and land holdings without. These *coloniae*, expensively laid out and furnished with public buildings, were few in number, and all were associated with legionary fortresses. The earliest were at Colchester, Gloucester and Lincoln, while York was later raised to *colonia* status.

Far more numerous were the cantonal capitals, the administrative and marketing centres of the old tribal areas. Their development and its costs were largely in the hands of the native Celtic aristocracy, the owners of large estates who became the elected town councillors or decurions. It is not known how many such tribal leaders lived in the

towns – it is not inconceivable that some may have had town-houses only for winter use as did eighteenth- and nineteenth-century aristocrats. Very often the cantonal capital had its tribal name as a suffix, for example *Venta Icenorum* ('of the Iceni', now Caistor-by-Norwich), *Calleva Atrebatum* (Silchester), *Venta Belgarum* (Winchester), *Venta Silurum* (Caerwent).

Towns of this class, though subject to the provincial government, were left to the immediate management of their local élite, who planned them and provided public amenities as they thought fit, which accounts for their striking variety. If a tribal capital grew in size or importance, it might be promoted to the rank of *municipium*, the inhabitants being granted additional rights. On the Continent, these *municipia* are familiar, but in Britain, only *Verulamium* was almost certainly granted this status, though other towns, including London, may have attained it.

The two remaining types of town were smaller and more varied in origin and function. One consisted of minor tribal centres for strictly local marketing, industry and administration, or of posting stations on the highways. The second type comprised settlements – *vici* – that grew up outside military establishments, as they did on Hadrian's Wall.

London, so rapidly advanced to being the provincial capital, is in many ways anomalous. It was from the first a mercantile city, owing its prosperity to its natural advantages as a port and hub of the road system. There is no direct evidence for its official status, but it may well have been promoted first to a *municipium*, then a *colonia*. It was the largest of all British towns, enclosing about 134 hectares.

It is a common misconception that all Roman towns were designed to a standard plan and enclosed within rectangular walls. On the contrary, most civil towns were of quite irregular outline, often roughly oval (Cirencester) or many-sided as can be seen at Silchester. Lincoln is an exception: built exactly upon the defences of the legionary fortress, it is indeed rectangular in plan. In addition, in the early days of the province, most towns did not have any walls at all. A few had defensive earthworks in the first century AD but the great majority remained open until towards the end of the second century, when it became the style to enclose the existing town with a stout bank and ditch. During the two following centuries, some (but not all) towns could afford to add walls, typically of mortared rubble with ashlar facing and bonding layers of red tiles. In the dangerous fourth century, bastions might be added. The gateways, often four in number, through which the principal roads entered the city, were strong and architecturally dignified with their arches and towers. Some had single or twin carriageways running between footways.

Though irregular in outline, the streets of Roman towns were laid out on the grid plan dividing groups of buildings into standard blocks or *insulae*. Some blocks with frontages on the main streets might have rows of shops and taverns, long and narrow with gabled fronts, with craftsmen and shopkeepers living on the upper floors. These premises were usually close-set but detached; occasionally, however, as at *Verulamium*, some ambitious developer would install a continuous row of shops sheltering behind an arcade. Other blocks would have modest private houses built on much the same long, narrow-fronted plan, and still others were far more spaciously laid-out dwellings, some much like country villas. The dwellings of the British tribal nobility, the large estate owners and top officials were sometimes so grand as to be built round an arcaded courtyard. Many towns had inns maintained for the use of official travellers; those identified at Silchester and Caerwent had public and private rooms, a courtyard and bath-house.

All these premises had latrines and an adequate sewerage and water supply. Wells were used, but running water was brought in by aqueducts, usually in open leats but sometimes piped.

Here, in the residential and shopping streets, was the private setting of the civilized urban life the Romans wished to impose. Yet it was in the public buildings that the Roman imperial stamp was most conspicuous, the break with Celtic tradition most complete. In these buildings, government, public health, entertainment and worship were provided. Apart from the city walls, the public buildings have left most for us to see – though, in general, the remains are poor.

Forums and basilicas

At the centre of each town and of its public life were the forum and the adjoining basilica. The forum was the civic centre and market place, often with a market square surrounded by a colonnade lined with administrative offices and shops. The basilica, a great aisled hall as long as 100 metres with columns some eight metres high, occupied the whole of one side. Along the side of the basilica, away from the forum, was a line of offices or 'chambers', perhaps including a more dignified room that was the council chamber of the cantonal administration. The basilica served as the local law court and was used by the governor on circuit with his assize, but might also be employed as a merchants' exchange or public hall.

Public baths

Every town was also provided with public baths, often quite extensive buildings with an open or closed gymnasium for sport and exercises as well as all the facilities for the Turkish manner of bathing. They must have served as a kind of civic club for young and old alike. Rather surprisingly, women might be admitted (although at an early hour), while in the grander establishments they had their own suites of baths, as at the Jewry Wall at Leicester. The finest example of town baths can be seen at Wroxeter.

The patrons first made use of the gymnasium to work up a mild sweat, then removed their clothes in a large unrobing-room before passing into the *frigidarium*, then to the moderately warmed *tepidarium* and on into the intensely hot *caldarium*. This was situated next to the furnace, and steam was created by sprinkling water on the floor. Sweating profusely, the bather was cleansed with oil and a bronze scraper before using the hot plunge bath. He would then make a leisurely return through the suite, finishing with a cold plunge in the *frigidarium* to close his pores. The larger bathing establishments also provided for the more violent regime of dry heat.

The two spas of Roman Britain – Bath *(Aquae Sulis)* and Buxton *(Aquae Arnemeiae)* – can be classified as small towns but owed everything to their curative springs. At Bath the hot spring rose from great depths, was contained by a lead-lined polygonal enclosure and passed into a series of three principal baths of which the Great Bath, at least, was intended for swimming. The presiding deity, the goddess Sulis-Minerva, had a temple nearby. With its baths, the largest of their kind in western Europe, its museum and the marvellous pediment from the destroyed temple, *Aquae Sulis* is as well worth visiting as any Roman town. At Buxton, however, almost nothing Roman has survived.

Theatres and amphitheatres

Town life was also made attractive to the Britons by a liberal provision for entertainment, much of it of a crudely, or even brutally, popular kind.

The Romans had originally borrowed from the Greeks their idea both of drama and of the building in which it was staged. The typical theatre was a D-shaped building open to the sky with a stage along the straight side, and a semicircular space, the 'orchestra', in front of it, enclosed by rising tiers of seats.

Little is known of what was offered to the public in the provincial theatres of the empire. There seem to have been few new plays, the more usual fare being scenes from old favourites chosen to give good parts to popular actors. Audiences also appreciated the pantomimes, in which themes from mythology were performed by masked dancers, to the accompaniment of music and a chanted chorus. If the pantomimes were far from exalted, the public could find bawdy enjoyment and horseplay in the mimes, with their scenes from everyday life and topical allusions. In contrast, theatres were also used for religious festivals.

Few theatre buildings are known in Britain. Three – at *Verulamium,* Canterbury and near Colchester – have been discovered by excavation, two others are known to have existed, while finds of actual masks and of wall-paintings depicting them suggest that there may have been many more. The only Roman theatre on view in Britain is a striking feature within the city of *Verulamium,* where it was closely associated with a temple.

Originally circular in form, the *Verulamium* orchestra could also serve as an arena for spectacles, and there is evidence that it did so. It was therefore halfway to being an amphitheatre – a form of building invented by the Romans to accommodate some of their very un-Greek ideas for popular amusement. Amphitheatres were probably far more often provided for the townsfolk than were theatres. Our provincial examples can be regarded as the humblest versions of Vespasian's Colosseum in Rome and were probably used for very similar purposes.

The amphitheatres were elliptical buildings with central arenas wholly enclosed by tiered seats, often no more than plank benches supported on earthen banks. The banks and the entrances through them were stoutly revetted with timber, sometimes later replaced by good stone masonry. Seating of this kind is very capacious and it seems certain that all the inhabitants of the town and its neighbourhood could be accommodated at one time.

All our known British amphitheatres, save that of Caerwent, stand outside their town walls. The amphitheatres were sited on the

Caerleon, Wales. The excavated and restored Roman military amphitheatre (ludus)

city outskirts because of the large amount of land they occupied. When the walls were built or extended subsequently, the amphitheatres were excluded for obvious reasons of economy.

Town amphitheatres have been identified at Cirencester, Dorchester (Dorset), Silchester, Chichester, Carmarthen and Caerwent, the first four being well worth a visit. Inscriptions record others at York and Leicester and there must have been many more. In truth, however, the best idea of what they were like can be had from the fully excavated and restored monument at Caerleon. This is an example of the military type of amphitheatre known as a *ludus*, which had the relatively larger area that was needed for weapon training and other martial exercises.

Beyond a gladiator's helmet found in Suffolk, some graffiti and gladiatorial scenes on pottery and glass vessels, there is no local evidence of what shows the amphitheatres presented. Probably few British towns could afford spectacular displays, but it is assumed that there were occasional gladiatorial combats as well as contests between men and animals and probably games held on fixed days of the calendar. The most brutal 'entertainment' likely to have been staged was the execution of criminals, who were tied to wheeled stakes to be mauled to death by wild beasts.

Roman figure from Bath
(David Cripps)

Temples

The classic Roman temple stood on a high stone platform (podium), the façade, with its triangular pediment supported by free-standing columns, approached by a flight of steps; behind was the rectangular shrine, or *cella*, housing the image of the god or goddess. The only remains of such buildings that can be seen are those of the Temple of Claudius at Colchester and of Sulis-Minerva at Bath. There were, however, many others with classical features, such as the example at Wroxeter with a *cella* inside a colonnaded court, and the unusual temple with a triangular court adjoining Watling Street in *Verulamium*. The late Roman temple of Nodens (a Celtic god) in the pilgrimage centre at Lydney in Gloucestershire has a basilican plan.

By far the commonest type of temple in Britain and other Celtic lands is known as the Romano-Celtic. It seems to have been of native origin; indeed, a simple Iron Age version was found during construction at Heathrow airport. Alike in town or country, they consisted of a high, rectangular, tower-like shrine with a portico or veranda on all four sides; there were also circular and polygonal variants. A fragment of an urban Romano-Celtic temple is to be seen within a porticoed court near the *Verulamium* theatre. Numbers of others have been identified, but like the two at Richborough and three at Silchester, they are no longer visible. The site of a rural temple of this kind is kept open within the ramparts of Maiden Castle.

As well as the temples dedicated to Roman and Celtic divinities, a few were raised in Britain to serve Eastern faiths. Isis, Serapis and Sol Invictus had their followers, but the only one to have left us visible remains of his temple is Mithras, the Zoroastrian god of light, whose worship seems to have reached Britain by the late second century AD. Mithraism was a moralistic faith, with close-knit bodies of worshippers who practised a complicated ritual and sought to attain salvation through seven grades of initiation, each demanding physical and psychological ordeals.

Mithraea are relatively small, long and narrow buildings wholly or partly underground in the semblance of a cave. Four military examples are known in Britain, three on

Hadrian's Wall and one at Caernarvon, while the richest, no doubt supported by London merchants, was the civilian temple in the Wallbrook. The extraordinary collection of sculptures from this *mithraeum* includes a forceful head of the god complete with Phrygian cap, probably from the standard bull-slaying icon of the cult.

Christianity must have been well organized in Britain by the early fourth century, yet the remains it has left are surprisingly sparse: the foundations of a small church within the walls of Silchester, a few traces of Christian iconography, and the little chapel in the Lullingstone villa.

Public monuments

In addition to buildings to serve the inhabitants' physical and spiritual needs, every city with claims to civilization had its public monuments, and the most expressive of Roman pomp and pride were the triumphal arches. They must surely have been set up in all *coloniae, municipia* and other important towns, yet the only examples to have been identified are three at *Verulamium*, all of them on the line of Watling Street. A much grander version of the ceremonial arch was the unique monument at Richborough set up towards the end of the first century AD to celebrate the conquests of Britain and as the symbolic gateway into the province. Set on a massive platform it was probably a four-way arch some 15 metres high, cased with Carrara marble and adorned with bronze statuary.

Finally, main streets and squares would certainly have had their statues of emperors and important officials. A fragment of a life-sized bronze equestrian statue came to light in Lincoln, while a fine bronze head of Hadrian was taken from the Thames near London Bridge.

Rural villas

The rural life of Roman Britain is most clearly brought before our eyes by the many remains of its villas. The Latin word *villa* meant, quite simply, a farm. Moreover, it should not be limited in use to the more luxurious houses of the wealthy estate owners, but can properly be applied to any farmhouse, however humble, built in a more or less romanized style.

Of the 600 or 700 villas known in Britain, the great majority lie south-east of a line from Exeter to the mouth of the Trent, although there are a few in the Welsh Marches, the Vale of York, County Durham and the toe of Cornwall. The younger Pliny wrote that the gentry selected sites for their houses that commanded sunshine and fine views: the Cotswolds, for example, were evidently found as desirable as they are today.

Four types of villa plans are usually distinguished: the cottage, the corridor house, the courtyard house and the aisled house. There is great variety within each type. Very often, improvements were added over the centuries until an original 'cottage' might be incorporated in a handsome corridor or courtyard design. The usual building material for all types was half-timbering with a clay-daub filling, plastered and supported on stone foundations; all seem to have been single-storeyed and roofed with tile or slate. Only the very poorest villas were without underfloor heating, and most had a separate bath-house suite. Mosaic floors were common, though often of simple design.

The simple cottage could be expected to have one or two rooms on either side of a central passageway. In the corridor house, the number of rooms in line was increased, probably with a large room at each end linked by a veranda along the front, perhaps also with a central dining-room floored in mosaic. This corridor plan could be elaborated in a variety of ways, most commonly by an extension of the wings to produce what can be recognized as the average kind of Romano-British country house. They were warm and comfortable but hardly luxurious, and the estates they served were seldom large. A good example is the main dwelling at Brading, Isle of Wight; this and many other villas had additional buildings for farm use or quarters for workers, ranged round a simple court or farmyard.

A courtyard house had a court surrounded by buildings designed as an architectural whole and opening on to a continuous corridor round all four sides. These were the grand centres of the Celtic aristocracy's large estates. The North Leigh villa in Oxfordshire is representative of the form, with a single large courtyard (entered through a main gate with porter's lodge). The villa at Chedworth in the Cotswolds had two courts, the inner one probably kept as a formal garden, and so did the Bignor villa in West Sussex, famous for its mosaics, where the plan had to be adapted to changes in ground level.

The aisled villa, more primitive and essentially unclassical in style, was probably derived from a north European type of farmhouse. In its simplest form, it was a barn-like building, rectangular and divided into nave and aisles by two lines of posts supporting the roof. Although many were smaller, these houses could be over 40 metres in length, frequently with an entrance in one of the long sides. The elaboration of the basic rectangular plan had many variants, sometimes part of the original construction, often later additions. Separate rooms might be made by partitioning nave and aisles or by cutting off a suite along one or more sides. In this way, Roman amenities such as mosaic and tessellated pavements, underfloor heating and, rarely, baths were introduced.

The aisled villa had clear social implications: it would not have been inhabited by the wealthy or highly cultured. The simplest, unpartitioned houses would probably be occupied by a poor farmer's household, together with their animals, and even in the most elaborate, the prosperous farmer was living under one roof with his workers and stock. At Brading, the aisled house was an outbuilding of a grander villa and probably was assigned to farm workers or a tenant.

While nearly all Romano-British villas fall into the four categories described, there were interesting exceptions. Lullingstone

Rockbourne Villa, Hampshire. Part of the hypocaust

was one. In the fourth century, it was dominated by an apsidal dining-hall and reception-room (both with fine classical mosaics), which suggests that it may have been used as a pleasure-house. At different times, it also had a shrine for a local water-goddess, a circular temple and family mausoleum and, finally, a Christian chapel, possibly the earliest known in western Europe.

The most extraordinary villa of Roman Britain was, undoubtedly, that at Fishbourne, just outside Chichester. Its early date, huge size, the elaborate courts, formal gardens and sumptuous interior decoration all add to its unique distinction. Perhaps a Roman gift to the royal house of Cogidubnus, if not to the king himself, it is the only villa in Britain that is wholly exotic – an imported Italian palace.

Fortifications

Visible traces of fortifications, raised by the army according to strictly laid-down guidelines, are numerous in Britain, faint and unexciting though many of them are. They range from temporary marching camps to the large fortresses where legions were stationed over long periods of time.

To understand them, the fundamental division of the Roman army between the legions and the auxiliary troops has to be remembered. The legions, each about 6000 strong (of whom about 5200 were fighting men), were composed of Roman citizens extraordinarily well-equipped and trained. They were organized into ten cohorts, usually composed of 64 centuries (each with 80 – not 100 – heavily armed foot soldiers) with an additional 120 mounted men. Every legion was commanded by a Roman senator aided by tribunes, but the fighting leadership was given by the centurions.

In contrast, the auxiliaries were seldom Roman citizens, but were recruited from the more war-like peoples within the empire, winning their citizenship on discharge after 25 years' service. They were divided into infantry cohorts and cavalry wings *(alae)*, each nominally either 500 or 1000 strong. The cavalry units were only brought up to 1000 men for special duties at critical points: one such was stationed on Hadrian's Wall.

It has been said that 'the legions were relatively civilized, highly trained and expensive;

Overleaf: *Corbridge* (Corstopitum), *Hadrian's Wall, Northumberland. The Roman town of* Corstopitum *served as a military supply base and depot, as well as a settlement for trade, relaxation and retirement*

Caerleon Legionary Fort, Wales

the auxiliaries relatively barbarous, rough and cheap,' and this fact led the high command, when garrisoning a province, to station the auxiliaries along the frontiers, where life was rough and dangerous, holding the legions in their permanent bases well to the rear, ready to crush any enemy force that might break through. This policy was fully observed in Britain: Wales was controlled by a network of forts supported by legions at Caerleon and Chester, while in the north, a continuously fortified frontier was strongly manned by infantry and cavalry units in no less than 16 forts, backed by the legionary fortress at York.

For convenience, the legionary stations are called fortresses (over 20 hectares) to distinguish them from the smaller forts of the auxiliaries (up to 3¼ hectares). In spite of the very great difference in size, fortresses and forts were very much alike in both form and the layout of the internal buildings. They were rigidly rectangular with rounded corners, the proportions varying from about that of a playing card to a more nearly square outline.

The ramparts were fronted by one or more ditches and were pierced by four gateways, usually with twin towers. The greater part of their interior space was occupied by barracks – long, narrow buildings fronted with verandas, each with quarters for the centurion at the outer end. In a fortress, the regulation number of barrack blocks was 64.

While barracks and stores filled both ends of the fort, a broad strip running between them was occupied by the major buildings: the headquarters *(principia)* with its offices, regimental shrine, strong-room and colonnaded forecourt in the centre, flanked on

ever, frequently retained behind the walls. Later there was a tendency for walls to be higher and external bastions to be added.

It is, of course, the ruined masonry dating from the second century onwards that most often survives for us to discover. The legionary fortress that on excavation provided the clearest and most complete picture of its class is Inchtuthill in Tayside, built by Agricola to command the Tay and abandoned after a few years when its legion was withdrawn. It proved to be a diagram come to life, with its 64 barracks and complete range of principal buildings, all within stout defences.

The other three great fortresses – York, Chester and Caerleon – have inevitably been largely destroyed or masked by the later cities. York has the most attractive remains. The south-west wall, which in the fourth century overlooked the River Ouse with eight massive towers, survives in part, conspicuously in the famous multangular tower at the west corner. Equally worth seeing is the internal tower of the east angle, together with a stretch of wall still standing to rampart-walk height in this same stretch, where the Roman work is visible below the medieval, there is another surviving internal tower. Finally, part of the headquarters building of the fortress has been discovered by recent excavations and can be seen in the undercroft of the Minster.

At Chester, the early fortress was rebuilt in stone during the second century AD (from quarries still visible south of the river), and it is remains of this period that can be seen here and there throughout the city. On the north and east sides, the medieval walls followed the line of the Roman walls and incorporated some courses of it, including an internal tower in the north wall. A section of the Roman quay walls can still be seen in the grounds of the racecourse below the city.

Caerleon, on the banks of the Usk, is only partly overlain by the sprawling little modern town, and much of the fortress is exposed to view. An inscription records that the rebuilding of the defences and internal buildings in stone was undertaken in about AD 100, but it appears not to have been quickly completed. The headquarters building has been excavated and so have officers' houses and a hospital. Among the sites left open to view, the most rewarding are the fine military amphitheatre (ludus) already mentioned and the north-west corner of the fortress. This has been laid out to show the stone wall backed by an earthen rampart and,

one side by the commandant's spacious house and on the other most often by granaries. In a fortress, there might also be officers' houses, a hospital, drill hall and construction shop. A roadway ran round inside the ramparts, and the two principal roads coming from the gates crossed in the region of the headquarters building. Bath-houses and amphitheatres were always outside the walls.

Time brought some changes to fortresses and forts, and by far the most important, improving both their appearance and their military strength, was initiated at the beginning of the second century AD. The early ramparts had been earthworks revetted with timber, the gates wooden and the internal buildings half-timbered; now woodwork was replaced by good stone masonry, at least for the fortifications and the principal buildings. The earthen rampart with its walk was, how-

within this, lines of barrack blocks of standard plan. Here, perhaps better than anywhere south of Hadrian's Wall, one can study the quarters in which the legionaries lived.

The above accounts give some idea of the three centres where the main military power of the Roman army in Britain was concentrated for centuries, and of the fourth fortress, Inchtuthill, which was used only fleetingly. The best of the auxiliary forts are described with Hadrian's Wall, and a few others in Wales and Scotland find their due place in the Gazetteer.

It is an astonishing fact that Roman troops on the move through hostile country built strong defensive works wherever they stopped, even for a single night. Each of these marching camps consisted of a v-shaped ditch and a bank, strongly reinforced with a palisade, each man carrying two rough stakes for this. According to the rule book, the camps were to be rectangular, with four gates, just as in permanent forts, but sometimes the terrain determined a less regular plan. (Roman camps can always be distinguished from prehistoric earthworks by their perfectly straight sides.) The force was accommodated in leather tents with the commander's pitched in the centre, taking the place of the headquarters house of the forts.

Totally unlike all the fortresses, forts and camps raised for the conquest and control of the province are the forts of the Saxon Shore, built round the English coasts from Norfolk to Hampshire. These coastal defences, which were partly naval bases, were made necessary by attacks from Saxons and other northern barbarians from the third century AD onward, and provide our most massive Roman ruins. All but one were built close to the sea; indeed, one is now beneath it. Among them, a few (Burgh Castle, Portchester, Pevensey) have been well preserved through being incorporated in medieval castles. Most, though not quite all, have in common high walls of flint or pebble with bonding courses of tile and external bastions, and in size they range from about two to four hectares.

In Norfolk, Brancaster is exceptional for having been stone-faced and without bastions. Pevensey, in East Sussex, is a large and very impressive fort with bonded walls up to 8.5 metres high and eight solid bastions surviving. An ideal example of a Saxon Shorefort is Portchester in Hampshire. The walls, standing to nearly six metres, once had four hollow bastions on each side and one at each corner, but two on the sea side have been washed away. It has well-preserved gates with guard-chambers on the east and west, and posterns in the north and south walls. Its general appearance cannot have changed very much since Roman times.

These forts raised against the North Sea raiders were to be abandoned as the empire collapsed. All seemed hopeless, yet out of the darkness and confusion those small peoples, the English, Welsh and Scots, were to emerge with a great history before them.

THE
GAZETTEER

How to use the gazetteer

The gazetteer is arranged by regions, beginning in the South-east of England and continuing north. Hadrian's Wall has its own section, as befits such a splendid and extensive monument.

A general survey of the prehistory and archaeology of each region opens its section. Thereafter, the counties within it are ordered alphabetically.

The site entries give the name of the site, its archaeological age, the nearest town and the Ordnance Survey map reference. These are followed by brief street directions, if applicable, together with information on opening times (while these were correct at the time of going to press, the authors and publisher can take no responsibility for any changes). The body of the entry highlights the importance of the site, explains its plan and use, and notes any interesting artifacts found there.

To locate sites within a specific area, consult the maps beginning on page 304.

THE SOUTH-EAST

The South-east region comprises the counties of Kent, Surrey, and East and West Sussex. It is now so dominated by London's millions of citizens – for their homes, business and holidays – that it takes an effort to realize that, throughout prehistoric times, its contacts were of a totally different kind. Even after Britain became an island, the South-east, as the promontory approaching closest to the Continent, was open to trade and immigration from overseas, particularly from the Rhinelands to the opposing Thames estuary and by way of the southern-flowing rivers of Kent and Sussex. Equally important – and indeed, throughout the New Stone and Bronze Ages, rather more important – were the thoroughfares across the chalk downs for commerce of all kinds with prosperous and populous Wessex.

The noble ridges of the North and South Downs, direct extensions of the Wessex chalk by way of the Hampshire Downs, are the dominant physical features of the region. They are, in fact, the remaining root of a vast dome of chalk that once covered the whole central area of the Weald; when it collapsed and was carried away, it left exposed the older formations – an outer rim of greensand enclosing the flat claylands of the Vales of Kent and Sussex, rising again at the centre in the so-called Forest Ridges, largely composed of sandstones and including such sandy wastes as Ashdown Forest. The whole of the Wealden area, particularly the expanses of the claylands, once supported the great oak forest of *Anderida* and for this reason tended to be shunned by the Weald's inhabitants, other than a few hunters, until the latest Iron Age and Roman times. There was also considerable woodland on the heavy clay deposits on the North Downs, making farming difficult. The relatively open chalk of the South Downs was attractive for both pasture and arable, and it is to the South Downs that visitors should take themselves if they want to find New Stone Age monuments thick on the ground.

For sites dating from the Old and Middle Stone Ages, the picture is quite a different one, but these, of course, generally involve flint implements only and are not to be visited. Old Stone Age men hunted the plentiful game in the Thames Valley during the second and third interglacials of the Ice Age. Some account of them has already been given (p. 18).

Since the South-east is a deprived area so far as limestone and other cave-forming rocks are concerned, it must also be poor in the cave dwellings of later Old Stone Age people to be seen in the west and north. There is, however, one quite notable exception at Oldbury Hill,

where two shallow sandstone caves afforded shelter to hunters during the last onset of the ice about 35,000 years ago (p. 66).

As for the hunters, fishers and fowlers of the Middle Stone Age (p. 18), they too frequented the Thames Valley where the long, narrow flint axes they used for tree-felling and making dugout canoes are so common as to be known as 'Thames picks'. Other groups sought small game, berries and nuts on the lighter soils of the greensand of Surrey and Sussex, and also the Forest Ridges of the Weald. Very many areas that yield their tiny flint implements are known in west Surrey, while at some of the greensand sites, excavations have uncovered traces of the sunken floors of flimsy huts. One such hut, or pit dwelling, by Abinger Common, Surrey (p. 68), has been preserved, and certainly deserves a visit.

With the opening of the New Stone Age after 4000 BC, it seems that some of the farming immigrants may have travelled with their livestock directly across the Channel to the Kentish coast and the Stour valley. The greater number probably spread along the chalk from Wessex and were soon settled on the South Downs, more thickly to the eastern part since the extreme west, like the North Downs in their entirety, was more densely wooded.

During the earlier part of the period, after about 3500 BC, the farming communities followed much the same activities as they had in Wessex: they raised causewayed camps and earthen and chambered long barrows and sank flint mines.

The four causewayed camps of the South-east are all in East and West Sussex: (*from west to east*) The Trundle (p. 76) inside the Iron Age hillfort near the lovely Goodwood racecourse; Barkhale on Bignor Hill, a large but now inconspicuous example with a single ring; Whitehawk on the downs above Brighton with four rings but also inconspicuous; and Combe Hill (p. 72) behind Eastbourne. Excavations at Whitehawk revealed quantities of bones of cattle, sheep, goats and pigs and also human bones, some showing little care for their disposal and some in a context that strongly suggested some form of cannibalism.

There are some 13 surviving earthen long barrows in the region, all save one on the Sussex Downs. Of these, nine are to the east between Whitehawk and Combe Hill, the others near The Trundle, so that here, as in Wessex, barrows and causewayed camps were closely associated. There is known to have been a long barrow on the Hog's Back, the narrow chalk ridge running west from

Guildford in Surrey, but it has been levelled. The thirteenth earthen barrow is Julliberrie's Grave, isolated on the North Downs above Chilham in Kent.

While the causewayed camps and earthen long barrows of the South-east have their counterparts in Wessex, the history of chambered tombs appears to be quite distinct. Often called the Medway group, since they stand on either side of that river below the southern scarp of the North Downs, there are five sarsen stone megalithic tombs, three of them in long barrows. These tombs were well known to the old antiquaries and have attracted many legends. To the east are Kit's Coty and the Countless Stones; to the west, Addington Park and The Chestnuts stand close together, and the Coldrum long barrow is a mile to the north. The plans of these monuments have convinced most archaeologists that this form is of German or Scandinavian origin, the oldest examples dating back before 3000 BC.

The South-east takes the lead over Wessex in the remaining category of early New Stone Age monuments: the flint mines. On the South Downs no fewer than five groups can be seen with a total of more than 500 shafts – so great was the need for implements to clear and cultivate the downland. Not only are they the most numerous in the country, they are also the oldest – although they continued to be worked into the Bronze Age; radiocarbon analysis gives a date of about 3300 BC. Sample shafts have been excavated in all groups, but unhappily none has been kept open. Blackpatch (p. 69) near Patching, Harrow Hill (p. 74) near Angmering and Cissbury near Findon (p. 72), all in West Sussex are worth seeing – especially Cissbury, where hundreds of sunken pit heads are visible inside and outside the ramparts of the Iron Age fort.

Though the farming communities continued to thrive in the South-east through the later New Stone Age, they did not build henge sanctuaries such as are found in Wessex. One would dearly like to know what differences in religious ideas and practices this absence signifies.

The Beaker Folk settled in the South-east, principally, it seems, in eastern Kent, along the Thames and the Medway and on the South Downs, but their presence is not as strong as might be expected if the Rhine and Low Countries were indeed the homelands of the British immigrants. Most of the vessels found in the region are of a gently curving form rarely found elsewhere.

There are virtually no remains left by the Beaker Folk to attract visitors – although, of course, there may be burials, in addition to the very few that are known, still lying under bowl barrows, or these have been plundered in the unrecorded past. The following centuries of the Bronze Age (c. 1700 – 1400 BC) have more to offer. Just as the people of the Wessex chieftains' graves spread westward (p. 33), so too they extended their range eastward, though hardly beyond the river Arun in West Sussex or Dorking in Surrey. In this westerly part of the region, there are numbers of bell and disc barrows of the Wessex type as well as a good supply of indeterminate bowl barrows.

On the South Downs, the line of bell and bowl barrows – the Devil's Humps of Bow Hill (p. 73), north-west of Chichester – is well worth seeing, while a little to the north, near Treyford, there are five large bell barrows: the Devil's Jumps (p. 73), perhaps the finest group in the county. Further east, set in the lovely holiday country round Alfriston, East Sussex, there is an abundance of round barrows (long ones, too) – as many as 50 strung out by the ridgeway between Firle and Alfriston.

The west Surrey round barrows are nearly all to be found, not on the North Downs, but on sandy heaths to the north and south of the chalk, such as Reigate Heath (p. 69) and Frensham Common (p. 69). An interesting rarity is the triple bell barrow on Crooksbury Common (p. 68) near Farnham.

Grave goods in these Bronze Age barrows of the South-east show that the privileged dead were relations, even if rather poor relations, of the Wessex chieftains. They include beads and other ornamental possessions in gold, amber, faïence, jet and bronze. A unique barrow on the coastal plain at Hove, long ago destroyed, covered a warrior buried in an oak trunk coffin with his dagger, battle-axe and a wonderful handled cup of red amber.

For the late Bronze Age, from about 1000 BC, the Sussex Downs are exceptionally rich in the sites of the settled farmsteads and villages of that time, the outlines of their round huts, compounds, fields and pathways showing in the turf. Some 15 in all have been explored and added much to archaeological knowledge. The two most important – Plumpton Plain near Falmer and Itford Hill near Beddingham, north of Newhaven, both in East Sussex – are badly overgrown but can be recommended to enthusiasts. These conservative forms of settlement provided the background to a time of considerable prosperity in the South-east: numbers of gold bracelets and torques of late Bronze Age styles have come to light in Kent and East and West Sussex and specialized bronze tools and weapons, imported as well as British-made, were in plentiful supply.

In the South-east as elsewhere, hillforts are the conspicuous field monuments of the Iron Age. In this region, there are some 50 in all, many of them on the Sussex Downs or on the greensand hills of west Kent and Surrey; Bigbury (p. 64) is the sole notable example in the whole of east Kent. They range in size from half to one hectare to the 50 hectares of Oldbury (p. 66), near Sevenoaks, most of them contour forts but some of the promontory type. The region lacks spectacular many-ramparted examples to rival those of Wessex, but the chain of forts along the South Downs, each commanding a well-defined block of downland, is striking enough, and for those who like seascapes, sea air and walking on fine turf, they are delightful monuments to visit. From the Trundle (p. 76) at the west end by way of Cissbury (p. 72) and tree-crowned Chanctonbury Ring (p. 71) to the powerful ramparts of The Caburn at the eastern extremity, they offer a perfect route for what used to be known as a 'walking tour'. The best of the hillforts on the greensand are Oldbury in Kent and, in Surrey, Hascombe Hill (p. 69) and Anstiebury just to the east of Leith Hill.

During the last century BC and right up to the Roman conquest of AD 43, the South-east was very much involved in the invasions and dynastic struggles of the Belgic peoples (p. 37), in particular the rivalry between the Catuvellauni and the Atrebates. The principal *oppidum* (p. 37) of the Belgic Atrebates seems to have been in the Selsey–Chichester region; while much of it may now be below the sea, the dykes to the north of Chichester (p. 71) were probably a part of its defences. Bigbury, near Canterbury, the storming of which was described by Julius Caesar (p. 43), was a Belgic stronghold within the tribal lands of the Cantiaci, and there seems to have been a minor *oppidum* on the site of Canterbury and another at Rochester. Archaeologically, however, the glory of the Belgic South-east is in the rich Kentish cremation graves of Aylesford and Swarling. As these were flat cemeteries there is nothing to be seen of them, out of doors, but their elegant pottery and ornamental bronzes (now in the British Museum, London) give an idea of the high culture of the Belgic élite in the decades before the Roman conquest.

After the Roman conquest, the South-east became a most prosperous part of the province, knowing peace from the first since both the Cantiaci of Kent and the Atrebates were avowed allies of Rome. Villas soon took the place of the old Celtic huts, farmhouses on the sunnier slopes of the South Downs enjoyed Roman amenities and the three cantonal capitals and two principal ports, well served by the road system and escaping the Boudiccan revolt, were thriving centres of a highly romanized way of life. The general prosperity depended in part on corn growing and on the iron-working of the Weald – which had been initiated by the Britons but was now greatly developed.

It is not surprising, then, that there are many Roman remains in the region. Not very much survives above ground at Canterbury, Rochester and Chichester, but Roman walls can be traced and also the foundations of a few houses and public buildings. Chichester (p. 71) has the supreme added attraction of the nearby Fishbourne Palace (p. 73), the finest building of its kind in the western provinces of the empire.

In contrast with the towns, the ports of Richborough (p. 66) and Dover (p. 65) have much to offer the visitor. Richborough, indeed, with its long and varied history as the landing place and base for the Claudian invasion, the gateway to the province and as a fort of the Saxon Shore, is the most interesting Roman site south of Hadrian's Wall. At Dover, which succeeded Richborough as the chief port, the famous lighthouse is a magnet, making it easy to imagine the days when this natural harbour was busy with cross-Channel shipping and a base for the Roman fleet. The 'painted house', with its surviving murals, is another attractive ruin.

Of the many country villas in the region, Lullingstone (p. 66) in the Darent valley and Bignor (p. 69) set among the Sussex Downs are by far the most rewarding. The latter commands a splendid view of Stane Street crossing the high downs on its way to Chichester. Another surviving stretch of Roman road is to be seen at Holtye (p. 75), near East Grinstead, a secondary road probably built to take loads of Wealden iron ore to London.

Following upon all these vestiges of civilian life come the forts of the Saxon Shore dating from the time when this South-east region was very vulnerable to barbarian attack. Including the fortifications of Richborough and Dover, five were built, of which Pevensey Castle (p. 75) is by far the most striking, with its bastioned walls still standing over 8 metres high. Raised in the latter part of the third century, it fell, according to the *Anglo-Saxon Chronicle*, in AD 491 when

'Aelle the South Saxon killed all who were inside, and there was not even a single Briton left alive.'

GREATER LONDON

Caesar's Camp Fort *Iron Age*
Wimbledon Common **176(TQ:224711)**
1km NE of junction of A3 and A238. Can be approached by the Causeway and Camp Road from the A219 to W side of the golf course.

A roughly circular fort with a single rampart and ditch enclosing 4.3ha. It was originally a strong earthwork, with a ditch some 4m deep and a massive bank faced at the front and back with stout timbers. It seems to have been built in the 5th century BC.

Keston Tombs *Roman*
Warbank, Bromley **177(TQ:415634)**
6km S of Bromley. By the A233 on the bend S of its junction with B265. Take the road to the Keston Foreign Bird Farm. Open on application to the manager of the bird farm. Telephone Farnborough (0689) 52351.

This interesting funerary group has been several times explored and was fully excavated and restored in 1967. There are 2 principal tombs: the larger is circular, 8.8m in diameter, with a flint and rubble wall supported by 6 buttresses. This was probably sur-

mounted by a mound from 6 to 9m high; the smaller tomb is rectangular, 4.6 by 3.6m, and contained a pit which may have held the stone coffin known to have been removed in the 19th century. It was probably roofed with tiles. Between bastions of the circular tomb a tile-built cist contained an ornamented lead cremation casket. Also outside the tombs were a dozen other burials, 3 of them in urns. A Roman villa stood further down the slope of the hill.

Londinium *Roman*
176/7(TQ:513281)
Defined by the line of the Roman and medieval city walls. London, at the lowest bridging point on the Thames, became the capital of the province and residence of the governor after the Boudiccan rebellion. By the 2nd century, a palace had been built for the governor (on the river W of Suffolk Lane), and a forum with the largest basilica in Britain (E of Cornhill and Lombard St); both have been excavated but are no longer visible. A squarish, stone-walled fort was built at Cripplegate, probably for a ceremonial garrison for the governor. Its later incorporation in

Keston Tombs. The two principal tombs of the Roman cemetery. The circular foundation supported a lofty mound

the city wall accounts for the oddly projecting angle at this point. The walls were raised at the end of the 2nd century, with bastions and riverside defences added in the 4th century.

Visitors would do well to start with a visit to the Museum of London in Aldersgate St where there are well-displayed collections and where guidebooks are available. A useful map can also be bought at the church of All-Hallows-by-the-Tower.

The city walls

Tower of London   A section of wall with a semi-circular bastion on Roman foundations can be seen behind the Wardrobe Tower.
Tower Hill   North of Tower Hill, in Wakefield Gardens, is a stretch of wall, its Roman base built of ragstone with tile-bonding courses. A cast of the inscription of the procurator Classicianus (p. 45) is on view.
Coopers Row   In a courtyard behind Midland House, 8–10 Coopers Row, another section of wall with a Roman base of squared ragstone blocks can be seen by leaning over the railings. From the NE corner of the courtyard, a good view of the outside of the wall can be had through an arch.
St Alphage Churchyard   The N wall of this churchyard (N of London Wall and E of Wood St) is formed by the Roman wall. On the E side, it is double where the Cripplegate garrison fort was incorporated into the city wall.

Noble St   On the W side of this street, the visitor can look down on the walls of the Cripplegate fort with its internal towers. The corner of the fort is visible at the S end.
Old St, West Gate   This entrance to the Cripplegate fort is on view where it is preserved below modern London Wall. Permission to view can be obtained from the Museum of London.

Roman buildings

All-Hallows-by-the-Tower   near Tower Hill Underground Station   In the crypt are the walls of a Roman house with red tessellated floors. Various Roman remains and a good model of Londinium are also on view. Permission to visit must be obtained from the verger.
Temple of Mithras *   This famous temple, now in front of Temple Court in Queen Victoria St, was moved from its original site below Bucklersbury House some 55m to the east. The move has inevitably affected the construction but the plan is sufficiently correct. The fascinating finds from the temple, including a head of Mithras, a carving of the bull-slaying and other cult objects, are on display in the Museum of London and the Guildhall Museum.
Bank of England Mosaic   A 2nd-century mosaic floor with formal decorative designs has been laid at the foot of the staircase at the Threadneedle St entrance to the bank. It has been much restored.

——— KENT ———

Addington Park Chambered
Long Barrow   *New Stone Age*
Addington   **188(TQ: 653591)**
Cut NW/SE by minor road from Wrotham Heath to Addington. Permission needed from owner at Rose Alba. Small fee. See also The Chestnuts Chambered Tomb.

A rectangular barrow, 61 by 11m, orientated NE/SW, it had a kerb of sarsens up to 1.5m high; large stones at the NE end may indicate a chamber. The outline of the tomb can be seen. The only known finds are 'rough pottery'.

Bigbury Hillfort (Bigberry)   *Iron Age*
Harbledown   **179(TR:116576)**
Just S of A2. Footpath from the Upper Harbledown road. The Pilgrim's Way to Canterbury passes through the E entrance.

This 10ha enclosure, now tree-covered, had a single rampart only 2.5m high, and a ditch 5m wide, with a counterscarp bank where necessary. The W entrance is now damaged, but the E is strong, with extra defences. To the N is a 3.2ha annexe that may have been a cattle enclosure. Finds include Iron Age pottery, agricultural implements, firedogs, chariot and horse gear, and a chain, 5.5m long, with slave-collars and a padlock. Finds in Maidstone and Canterbury museums.

The site is thought to be a fort attacked by Julius Caesar and his 7th Legion in 54 BC, when the troops

found the entrances blocked with tree trunks, and had to build a causeway across the ditch.

The Chestnuts Chambered Tomb *New Stone Age*
Addington   **188(TQ:652592)**
Near The Chestnuts house, N of minor road from Wrotham Heath to Addington. Close to Addington Park barrow (qv).

This D-shaped mound, much damaged through the ages, has been partly restored. Orientated E/W, it was at least 15 by 20m. The earthen barrow had a trapezoid stone chamber, divided by a septal stone, at the E end, entered through a façade of sarsens. The 2 capstones and some of the orthostats are massive, up to 10 tons in weight. Inside were the cremated remains of 10 people, including at least one child. Finds from the New Stone Age to the early Bronze Age, housed in Maidstone Museum, indicate that the tomb was in use for a long period. The site was occupied earlier by Middle Stone Age flint-knappers, and there is also evidence for Romano-British settlement here.

Coldrum Chambered Tomb*   *New Stone Age*
ENE of Trottiscliffe   **188(TQ:654607)**
By bridle road from Trottiscliffe. National Trust.

This long mound, originally 21 by 17m, and orientated E/W, has almost disappeared, but the impressive rectangular chamber at its E end still survives: it comprises 4 large sarsen stones, and used to be divided by another. It contained the remains of about 22 people

Coldrum Chambered Tomb. The megalithic chamber at the east end of the long barrow can be seen in the distance, sarsen blocks enclosing the barrow in the foreground. New Stone Age, perhaps as early as 3000 BC

of both sexes and different ages, on paving at the NW side. One skull was on a carefully made stone shelf. Some had suffered from rheumatoid arthritis; and their physical similarities suggest that some were closely related. Finds in Maidstone Museum. The site is now a monument to Benjamin Harrison, a Kentish prehistorian.

Dover Lighthouse and Town House
Roman
Dover Castle   **179(TR:326418)**

Dubris was the site of an 0.8ha fort of the 2nd century, the HQ of the Romans' British fleet (the *Classis Britannica*). Its walls, still up to 3m high, now lie buried under the town centre, around Cannon Street. The town itself developed in the late 1st century AD, and a Saxon Shore fort was built *c.* 270, partly overlapping the earlier fort. A large Roman house, perhaps that of the fort commander, is now open to the public, below New St, and features the biggest area of Roman wall-paintings visible *in situ* in Britain. There is a new museum here (signposted; guidebook available).

The other major Roman feature is the famous *pharos* (lighthouse) on the hill, within the castle, by the church of St Mary-in-Castro. It is the only one still standing in Britain; its twin on the other side of the harbour is merely a heap of masonry. Probably built in the 1st century, it was originally about 25m high, with flame at the top by night, and smoke by day. The bottom 13m are Roman, the rest medieval. The exterior is octagonal, the walls (of rubble encased in stone) 4m wide, and the interior was a 4m square. Guidebook available.

Julliberrie's Grave
Long Barrow   *New Stone Age*
Just SE of Chilham   **179(TR:077532)**
0.4km SE of A252 and A28. On hillside S of Chilham Mill.

An earthen barrow, 44m long, 15m wide and 2m high, orientated NW/SE, it was built of chalk over a turf core. It is now overgrown and stands in a clump of trees. A polished flint axe from the barrow was probably imported from Scandinavia or northern Germany, *c.* 2500 BC. No structures or primary burials are known. A pit near one end contained large nodules of flint and some worked flint.

The site is also called the Giant's Grave (the giant Julabes), and is also thought to be that of Julius Laberius Durus, a Roman tribune killed by the Britons; in fact, 4 Romano-British burials have been found in its ditch. Finds in Chilham Castle.

Kit's Coty House
Chambered Tomb   *New Stone Age*
NE of Aylesford   **188(TQ:745608)**
By footpath between A229 and side road to Aylesford. HBMCE. Signposted.

The mound, 55m long and orientated E/W, has gone, but the impressive stones of its chamber survive at its E end, behind iron fencing. There are 3 uprights, the tallest 2.4m high, and a huge capstone 4 by 2.7m. 'Coty' means house. There are tales that this site and Lower Kit's Coty (*qv*) are the tombs of two contending Kentish kings, or that they were built by witches who lived on Blue Bell Hill. Finally, there is a strange story to the effect that if, at the full moon, one places a personal object on the capstone and walks round it 3 times, the object will disappear.

Lower Kit's Coty House (Countless Stones) Chambered Tomb

New Stone Age
Aylesford **188(TQ:744604)**
Near Great Tottington Farm. HBMCE.

Located 457m to the s of Kit's Coty (*qv*), this jumbled mass of about 20 sarsen stones is now protected by a railing and has trees growing on it. The mound has gone, and the tomb was demolished in the 18th century to obtain road material. There is a tradition that the stones cannot be counted, and the numbers chalked on them show that the story is still prevalent.

Lullingstone Villa *

Roman
Lullingstone **177(TQ:529651)**
w of A225, sw of Eynsford village. HBMCE standard hours. Site museum, guidebook available.

One of the most important villas in Britain, it was occupied for centuries. It began as a simple house in the 1st century AD, at the end of the 2nd it was remodelled, it was neglected for much of the 3rd, it was rebuilt more than once in the 4th, and was finally burned down and abandoned early in the 5th. Some walls still survive to a height of over 2m. The villa is important for its 4th-century floor mosaics, the finest in the country: they include one of Bellerophon spearing the Chimera, surrounded by dolphins and figures of the four seasons; and, in the impressive apsidal dining-room, one of Europa and the bull, with a quotation from Virgil's *Aeneid*.

During a partial reconstruction in the 350s, 4 interconnecting rooms seem to have been cut off to serve as a house-church for the public. The walls of 2 rooms were decorated with Christian motifs: a huge *Chi-Rho* monogram and a row of 6 praying figures. This wall plaster, restored, is now in the British Museum, together with 2 (family?) portrait busts from an earlier pagan shrine at the villa. There was also a shrine dedicated to a local water nymph.

Plan of Lullingstone Villa, Kent (after I. Longworth)

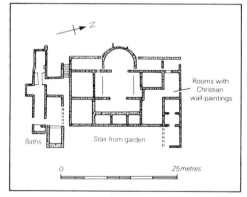

Rooms with Christian wall-paintings

Baths   Stair from garden

0   25 metres

Oldbury Hill Hillfort

Iron Age
sw of Ightham **188(TQ:582561)**
Just N of A25.

This 50ha hillfort, now tree-covered, is protected by a steep cliff to the E and by a single bank and ditch elsewhere, doubled in places. There seem to be 2

phases of construction: in c.100 BC, a small rampart and v-shaped ditch were built, with entrances on the s and NE. In the face of threats in either 50 BC or AD 43, the bank was enlarged and the ditch recut: caches of slingstones have been found. The NE entrance's timber gate seems to have been destroyed by fire. Finds in Maidstone Museum.

Oldbury Hill Rock Shelters

Old Stone Age
Ightham **188(TQ:584565)**
W of Manor Farm on Oldbury Hill. National Trust.

In the steep slopes below the E side of the hillfort (*see above*) and 400m s of the NE entrance are 2 sandstone hollows, now masked by vegetation. Excavations here found 40 well-made hand-axes and hundreds of flakes and tools indicating that the site was occupied during the period of Neanderthal man; it seems to have been occupied, or to have served as a workshop, for a long time. Finds in Maidstone Museum.

Reculver Fort of the Saxon Shore

Roman
Just E of Herne Bay **179(TR:227693)**
Path from Ethelbert Inn, Reculver village. HBMCE. Always open. Booklet.

The 3.2ha fort of *Regulbium* guarded the Thames estuary. Its massive walls, over 2m thick, backed by an earth rampart, formed a square with rounded corners, and extra defence was provided by deep ditches. Half has been eroded away by the sea since the 18th century: the church, a Saxon foundation, now at the cliff edge, stands in the fort's centre. The fort was built c. AD 210, and abandoned c. 360. It was garrisoned by land units.

Richborough Amphitheatre

Roman
Ash **179(TR:321598)**
On hill s of Richborough Castle.

Across the road, in a hillside 800m s of the fortress (*see below*) is a large depression, 61 by 51m, which is the site of the amphitheatre that served the fortress and the town.

Richborough Castle Fortresses and Monument *

Roman
NE of Ash **179(TR:325602)**
NNW of Sandwich, on minor road NW of A256. HBMCE. Standard hours. Booklet.

The important fort of *Rutupiae* was erected at the point where the first landings were made in AD 43: as such, it was a bridgehead and supply base, and constituted the 'main entry' to Britain. It was a safe harbour, and also the location of the best oyster beds, but because of silting it is now 5km inland.

The original wooden buildings were demolished in c. 85, and a huge triumphal arch was set up to commemorate the conquest. It was a '4-way' arch, faced with fine marble and decorated with bronze statues. It must have been over 10m high, but only its huge concrete cross-shaped foundation now survives. By the end of the 3rd century it had been dismantled, and the 2ha Saxon Shore fort built round it: its walls, originally up to 8m high, constitute the main visible

***Kit's Coty House Chambered Tomb**. New Stone Age*

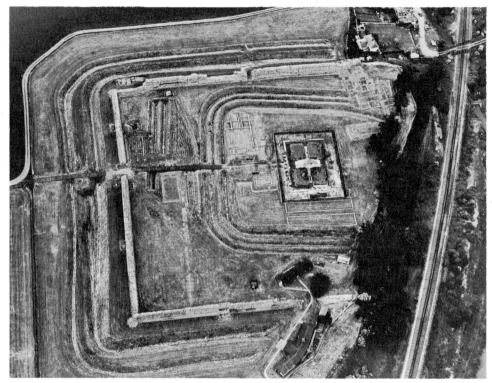

Richborough Castle Fortresses and Monument. *An aerial view of the complex Roman site at the beginning of Watling Street. It is enclosed by triple ditches of the 3rd century and outside them the massive defences of the Fort of the Saxon Shore* (Cambridge University Collection of Air Photographs)

feature today. There were rectangular bastions at intervals, and circular corner towers, and a double ditch outside. A Christian church was built in the abandoned fort *c.* 400; and legend says that St Augustine landed at Richborough in 597. There is a small museum by the fort entrance.

**Stutfall Castle Fort of the
Saxon Shore** *Roman*
Just s of Lympne **179(TR:117342)**

Footpath from Lympne to the Royal Military Canal cuts across the site.

The fort of *Portus Lemanis* was of the same size as Reculver *(qv)* but, in contrast to that site, it has been abandoned by the sea, and now overlooks Romney Marsh. Sections of the walls can be seen down the hillside. An altar to Neptune found in the main gateway (and now in the British Museum) may indicate that this was the HQ of the British fleet at some point in the mid-2nd century.

SURREY

**Abinger Common Pit
Dwelling** *Middle Stone Age*
Abinger Common **187(TQ:112459)**
s of A25, e of B2126, in field of Abinger Manor House. Key from owners at reasonable times.

This shallow v-shaped pit, dug into the greensand, has now been preserved and covered by a wooden hut, with a small museum on site, behind the house. The pit, 4.3m long, 3.2m wide and about 0.9m deep, contained 1056 microlithic implements, with thousands more scattered outside. It has been interpreted as a shelter rather than a workplace; a ledge on the e

side may have been a sleeping place, and 2 postholes beyond the nw end may have supported some sort of roof. There is also a possible hearth at that end, and 2 more certain ones outside. The site is not much to look at, but is an important and rare visible relic of this remote period.

**Crooksbury Common Triple
Bell Barrow** *Bronze Age*
nw of Elstead **186(SU:894449)**
se of Farnham, to e of Common in woodland.

The 3 mounds, enclosed by a single ditch with an

external bank, vary in height from 2 to 3m, and in diameter from 9 to 18m. Nothing is known of their contents.

Farley Heath Romano-British
Temple *Roman*
s of Albury **187(TQ:052449)**
By minor road across Heath.

The foundations of this building can be seen on the Heath, and comprise a square *cella* (shrine) with a veranda around it, the whole enclosed by a polygonal wall. Finds in the British Museum, including British gold coins, and a decorated bronze strip covered with crudely drawn figures of Celtic gods.

Frensham Common Bowl
Barrows *Bronze Age*
Frensham **186(SU:854407)**
By footpath NW from Rushmoor to Frensham. National Trust.

A fine linear cemetery of 4 mounds running N/S along the crest of a hill, they are up to 1.5m in height and 13 to 23m across. Nothing is known of their contents.

Hascombe Hill Hillfort *Iron Age*
Just SE of Hascombe, near **186(TQ:004386)**
Godalming
E of B2130; footpath through woodland from inn at Hascombe.

In a fine location at the SW end of a sandy spur, this little promontory fort of 2.3ha was protected by artificially steepened scarping on 3 sides, with a ditch below the crest, and, at the more vulnerable NE, by a single rampart, over 12m wide, and a ditch 6m wide

and almost 3m deep. An out-turned entrance in the centre had a passage 24m long. Probably dating to the 1st century BC, the fort may be a response to either tribal warfare or Caesar's invasion. Finds in Guildford Museum.

Reigate Heath Round Barrows *Bronze Age*
Just w of Reigate **187(TQ:237504)**
Just s of A25, on heath between A25 and windmill.

The 4 big bowl barrows, opened in 1809, were found to contain 2 cremations. Nothing is known of the contents of the 3 smaller mounds. Height varies from 0·3 to 2.5m, and diameter from 8 to 33m.

Titsey Park Villa *Roman*
Titsey **187(TQ:404545)**
N of M25, E of B269, in Titsey Park. Permission needed from South Lodge.

This villa, discovered and excavated in the last century, had 2 parallel corridors on N and s, which communicated with a central set of rooms, and joined smaller rooms at the ends of the building. Evidence from coins suggests it was occupied from AD 166 to 180. Later, in 320, the w end was used by a fuller, and water and heating systems were installed.

Wisley Common Bell Barrow *Bronze Age*
Wisley **187(TQ:079592)**
Just w of A3, SE of Byfleet, in woodland.

A large mound, damaged in places, it still stands 3m high and 44m across. The 'platform' it appears to stand on is, in fact, the Bronze Age land-surface that has since eroded away around it. No primary burial has yet been found, but a cremation was discovered high in the mound.

——SUSSEX—— (EAST AND WEST)

Bevis's Thumb Long Barrow *New Stone Age*
sw of North Marden **197(SU:788155)**
Between B2146 (to w) and B2141 (to E). On Telegraph Hill, by minor road between East Marden and Compton Park.

Also known as Solomon's or Baverse's Thumb, this mound, 64 by 18.3m and 1.8m high, is orientated E/W, and had flanking ditches N and s.

Bignor Villa * *Roman*
Bignor **197(SU:988147)**
Signposted from Bignor village, between A29 (to E) and A285 (to w). Open daily 1 March–31 October, except Mondays. Also Bank Holidays, Mondays in August and Sundays in November. Guidebook available.

This villa, pleasantly situated by Bignor Hill and facing s, was only 0.4km from Stane St (*qv*). It began in the late 2nd century as a small rectangular 5-roomed timber house but, after a fire, was rebuilt in stone, with a front corridor. It reached the height of its prosperity in the 4th century, when it was a courtyard house with N and s wings, one of the largest villas in Britain at that time. It was abandoned early in the 5th century, and fell into decay.

It is nicely presented with small thatched huts protecting individual rooms, stone and concrete marking other outlines, and a small site museum. Its mosaics include some of the most beautiful known in Britain, with figures including Medusa heads, Ganymede carried off by Zeus as an eagle, and Venus with cupids dressed as gladiators. One room has a sunken hexagonal water basin.

Blackpatch Flint Mines *New Stone Age*
NE of Patching **198(TQ:094089)**
w of footpath from A280, passing Myrtle Grove Farm. 1.6km SE of Harrow Hill (qv).

Although there is little to see now, this site was clearly of great importance for a long time. The small hollows and mounds on the hillside are the visible traces of 100 flint mines: those excavated show that shafts were sunk to the desired layer 3.4m below, and then 5m galleries radiated out. After the pits were exhausted, they were backfilled. Some shafts were used for burials or as deposits for cremations, and barrows were built over them. An antler pick has been radiocarbon-dated to 3140 BC. Finds in Worthing Museum.

Activity continued here into the Bronze age, and

Bignor Villa*. A vigorous dolphin, part of a much larger mosaic with seasons, birds and flowers. The Bignor mosaics are among the finest in Britain.*

Bignor Villa*. Venus with diadem and nimbus; a line of cupids playing is visible beyond*

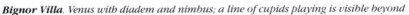

some round huts of that period have been excavated here recently.

Caburn Hillfort
Iron Age
w of Glynde   **198(TQ:444089)**
N of minor road from Lewes E to Glynde from A27, and footpath from Ranscombe Farm.

A circular fort of 1.4ha, its location on top of Mt Caburn affords fine views of the surrounding area. It has a massive timber-laced outer rampart, a smaller inner rampart, and a ditch between. The site seems to have begun as a farming settlement with a palisade *c.* 500 BC; a single earth rampart and a V-shaped ditch were added *c.* 150 BC. In the face of the Roman advance, the defences were strengthened and the outer rampart built, but the fort was sacked and its gate burned. The main entrance was on the NE. Finds at the fort include storage pits for grain, traces of metalwork (crucibles and iron slag), weaving equipment and iron objects. At least 150 pits have been explored: some even had dog turds in them. Some 457m to the w is the single rampart of Ranscombe Camp, which may be an unfinished fort. Finds in Lewes Museum and Salisbury and South Wiltshire Museum.

Chanctonbury Ring Hillfort and Dykes
Iron Age & Roman
ESE of Washington   **198(TQ:139121)**
E of A24, s of A283. Footpath through woodland from Lock's Farm, Washington.

A small pear-shaped fort of 1.4ha, dating to 400–300 BC, it has a single rampart of dump construction, and an external ditch, with some extra defences to the w and E, and a simple entrance gap on the SW. The approaches along the spur on w and SE are barred by cross-dykes, 400m away. The fort has been made even more conspicuous by beech trees planted in it in the 18th century: it is said that if one runs round it 7 times, the Devil will come out of the trees! Among the trees can be seen the traces of a small rectangular Romano-Celtic temple, as at Maiden Castle (p. 85) of the 1st or 2nd century AD. It has a rectangular *cella* (shrine), 7 by 5m, with walls of flint and mortar, and a rectangular outer enclosure. Finds in Lewes Museum.

Chichester
Roman   **197(SU:861047)**
The market town of *Noviomagus Regentium* probably replaced an earlier Belgic settlement around Chichester Entrenchments *(see below)*. It began as a military supply base, and, after AD 47, developed into a town, linked to *Londinium* by Stane St *(qv)*, and comprising timber buildings and a statue of Nero. Later, the usual features were added – forum, basilica, baths, temples, earthen amphitheatre – and the town constituted the centre of government of Cogidubnus, the pro-Roman client-king who probably lived in the palace at Fishbourne *(qv)*. In the late 2nd century, the timber buildings were replaced by stone and brick; earthen ramparts and stone gateways were erected (enclosing a 40ha polygon), soon to be changed to a wall of flint and mortar, with bastions added in the late 4th century. The town declined after the Roman withdrawal, but occupation was never interrupted.

There is little to be seen today: remains of one of the bastions survive on the SE; part of a mosaic pavement can be seen in the Cathedral; and the 1st-century dedication slab of the temple of Neptune and Minerva (which mentions the 'great king Cogidubnus') is now set into the wall of the Assembly

Chanctonbury Ring Hillfort and Dykes. There is something magical about this little hillfort, probably built in the 4th century BC. Its clump of trees is a famous landmark

Rooms in North St. Finds in City Museum, in the Guildhall Museum, and the Cathedral Treasury. Traces of the amphitheatre can be seen in Whyke Lane North.

Chichester Entrenchments
Iron Age (?)
Chichester   **197(SU:826083 to 921084)**
Extensive earthworks N of Chichester.

An Iron Age settlement here, probably founded by the Atrebates, preceded the nearby town at Chichester *(see above)*. At that time, the land between Chichester and Selsey formed a peninsula bounded by the river Lavant and other water courses, and thus the complex series of earthworks effectively cut off an area of many square kilometres. The northernmost outer earthwork is called the Devil's Ditch and can be traced for almost 10km eastward to Boxgrove Common; it has an external v-shaped ditch. the eastern end is particularly well preserved, but recent excavation has shown some work here to be medieval.

Cissbury Hillfort and
Flint Mines *
New Stone/Iron Ages
SE of Findon, just   **198 (TQ:139080 fort,**
N of Worthing   **137079 mines)**
E of A24. Signposted from Findon village. National Trust.

This great ovoid hillfort of over 24ha probably dates to *c.* 350 BC; its rampart, 9m wide, comprises 60,000 tons of chalk, with an external ditch 6m wide, and faced with a wall of up to 12,000 vertical timbers at least 4m high. There was a minor counterscarp bank, and entrances on the S and E. Finds include weaving equipment, pottery, iron tools and a hoard of hundreds of beach-pebble slingstones. The fort was abandoned before the Romans arrived, and its interior was already under the plough when the defences were renewed against the threat of Saxon invasion.

To the W of the fort and outside its S entrance can be seen the far earlier traces of flint mines. What are now merely overgrown hollows are the remains of about 250 blocked shafts that were sunk down 12m through 6 seams of flint to reach the quality stone; galleries radiated out into this layer. The work was done with antler picks (which have been given radiocarbon dates of *c.* 2700 BC), scapula shovels and chalk lamps. Two shafts were found to contain skeletons: one a young man surrounded by chalk blocks, the other a young woman who seems to have fallen in. Finds from the fort and mines are in Worthing, Brighton and Lewes museums, and the British Museum.

There is a legend that the hill is a lump of earth thrown from the Devil's spade when he dug the Devil's Dyke to the N of Brighton. There is said to be an underground passage from the fort to a now-demolished Hall some miles away, with treasure at the Cissbury end – but anyone who dug for it was sent packing by large snakes who guarded it. The fort itself is supposed to be a fairy dance-floor at midnight on Midsummer's Eve.

Combe Hill Causewayed Camp
New Stone Age
NE of Jevington   **199(TQ:574022)**
Footpath NE from Jevington to Upper Willingdon cuts through the camp.

This 0.6ha camp, in a dominating situation with fine views, comprises 2 concentric arcs of ditch; the inner ditch is at least 4m wide and 1m deep, with at least 16 causeways, while the inner rampart is 0.5m high. No postholes have been found, but many sherds of pottery have been recovered. Finds in Lewes Museum.

Cissbury Hillfort. *Iron Age*

Devil's Dyke Hillfort. A promontory fort of the Iron Age.

Devil's Dyke Hillfort
Iron Age
SSW of Poynings **198(TQ:259111)**
Minor road NW from A2038 on outskirts of Brighton. Bus service. Car park and restaurant.

A 16ha promontory fort with spectacular views, it has a massive bank and ditch at the SW end, while minor earthworks defend the top. One round hut has been found inside, 8.5m across, with pits in its floor containing pebbles, mussel shells, animal bones and Iron Age pottery. A later Iron Age or Romano-British settlement was found outside the fort on the present golf course. The 'dyke' is the valley to the SE, said to have been dug by the Devil in an unfinished attempt to flood the Sussex churches. Two mounds near the fort are supposed to be the tombs of the Devil and his wife.

Devil's Humps Bell and
Bowl Barrows *
Bronze Age
Summit of Bow Hill, **197(SU:820111)**
Stoughton Down
E of Stoughton, W of B2141. Hill paths from Stoughton, Chilgrove et al. Longish walk.

A small linear cemetery (also known as Bow Hill Graves, or King's Graves), it consists of 5 mounds running SE/NW on this ridge. From S to N there are 2 big bell barrows, 3.7m high and up to 40m across; a small pond barrow, and finally 2 big bowl barrows, 3m high and 20–32m across. One barrow contains a cremation with a whetstone. Nothing else is known of these mounds' contents. They are said to be the burial place of Danish chiefs killed in battle, and by running 6 or 7 times round them one can raise the Devil. A twin bell barrow in a single ditch can be seen 1.8km to the SW (SU: 808107).

Devil's Jumps Bell Barrows
Bronze Age
Treyford **197(SU:825173)**
NE of B2141, 1.2km S of Treyford. By minor road, then steep climb by footpath.

A fine linear cemetery of 6 bell barrows, running NW/SE. Two of them are known to have contained cremations. The largest pair, at the centre, are about 4m high and 43m across.

Firle Beacon Long and
Round Barrows
New Stone/Bronze Ages
West Firle **198 (TQ:470060 long barrow)**
2km SE of West Firle, S of A27. Footpath.

The long barrow, 34 by 21m, is 2.6m high and orientated E/W. There may be a collapsed internal structure at the E end. Over 50 round barrows are scattered along the ridge and around the track, most of them 10m across and up to 0.9m high. The long mound is said to be the tomb of the giant of Firle, and a silver coffin is also said to be buried on the hill.

Fishbourne Palace *
Roman
Salthill Road, Chichester **197(SU:841047)**
Signposted along A27. Open every day May–September, 10am–7pm; March, April, October, 10am–4pm; November (Saturdays and Sundays only), 10am–4pm. Closed December–February. Admission fee. Guidebooks.

Discovered in 1960, this luxurious palace may have been that of Cogidubnus, the pro-Roman client-king, and at its height it covered 4ha. It seems to have begun as a military supply base, with timber buildings, and played a part in Vespasian's troop movements against the Isle of Wight and the SW. In c. AD 75, construction of the palace began, round a large formal garden, and with several decorated mosaics. After some alterations and the addition of more

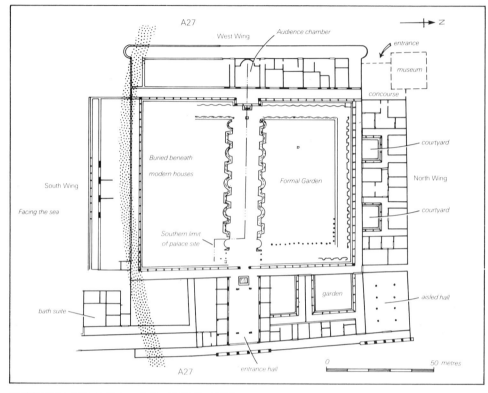

Fishbourne Palace, Sussex (after B. W. Cunliffe)

mosaics, there was a fire in the late 3rd century that caused molten lead to fall from the roof of the N wing on to the mosaic floors. The site was abandoned, the walls pillaged for stone, and a few burials inserted into the rubble.

The palace had fine marble from Italy and Greece, friezes of moulded stucco, an elaborate bath suite, and wall plaster. The mosaics include a winged cupid on a dolphin, sea monsters and a Medusa head.

The s wing is still buried under modern houses, but the site of the E wing is marked out in the grass, while the N is roofed over. There is a fine museum, and half of the formal garden – the only one known from this period north of the Alps – has been laid out with the correct species of plants.

Harrow Hill Flint Mines and Fortlet
New Stone/Iron Ages
NE of Angmering **197(TQ:081100)**
A track WNW from the A280 passes the hill. 1.6km NW of Blackpatch (see above).

Pits and depressions here are the only visible trace of about 160 backfilled shafts. Excavation of one found it to be 6m across and 6.7m deep, with 6 galleries radiating from the base: some of these still had smoke-marks from lamps and tally-marks scratched on the walls. This shaft cut down through 2 seams of flint and exploited the 3rd, though the upper 2 were also attacked a little. The usual tools (antler picks, ox scapulae) were used, and it estimated that one pit

could produce 350 tons of material, most of it probably being traded. One antler pick was dated to 2980 BC.

Some pits are overlain by a small 0.3ha Iron Age enclosure, with a single bank and ditch, which was probably used for cattle slaughtering: there was a stout palisade, a strong gate and no signs of permanent occupation. The skulls of up to 100 oxen were found. Finds in Worthing Museum. It is said that this area was the last home of the fairies in England, but that they left when the flint mines were opened.

High Rocks Hillfort and Rock Shelters
Middle Stone/New Stone/Iron Ages
NW of Frant **188(TQ:561382)**
Just SW of Royal Tunbridge Wells. Footpath NW from A26, S of High Rocks Inn. Small charge.

This damaged promontory fort of 9.7ha is protected by sheer sandstone cliffs at N and w, and a double rampart cuts across the promontory's neck. There are outworks, and an entrance at the SE corner. The outer bank and ditch were probably built in the 1st century BC; the inner, stone-revetted bank was added, with a broad shallow ditch, in the 1st century AD. The interior of the site is under cultivation. Finds in Royal Tunbridge Wells Museum.

The rocks below the fort house a series of rock shelters that seem to have been occupied in the Middle and New Stone Ages; microlithic tools and pot-

The Long Man of Wilmington Hill-figure

sherds have been found, as well as hearths, and there are radiocarbon dates of *c.* 3700 BC.

Hollingbury Hillfort
Iron Age
Brighton **198(TQ:322078)**
W of A27, footpath bordering the golf course leads southward up the hill.

A square fort of 3.5ha, in a commanding position with fine views, it had a single rampart of chalk rubble encased in 2 rows of posts, and a ditch 3m wide. There are entrances on E and W; gateposts and rampart posts are now marked in metal. The fort may have been begun in the 6th or 5th century BC, but dates primarily to the 3rd. Four bowl barrows stand inside the enclosure; one of them contained bronze axes and jewellery (now in the British Museum). Other finds in Brighton Museum.

Holtye Roman Road
Roman
E of Holtye **188(TQ:462388)**
Excavated section S of A264, 6km E of East Grinstead. Sussex Archaeological Trust. Signposted. Always open.

A fenced-off section of a secondary Roman road, 4.6m wide, probably constructed *c.* AD 100 as a link from Watling St to Lewes, it is of great interest because it served an iron-smelting area in the Ashdown Forest, and is mainly composed of iron slag. Compacted down, it resembles a modern road; ruts were made in it by carts heavily laden with iron ore.

Long Man Hill-figure *
Age unknown
S of Wilmington **199(TQ:543035)**
Footpaths E from minor road SW from Wilmington to Litlington. Best seen from minor road leading S from village. Signposted footpath.

Apart from the one at Cerne Abbas (p. 81), this is the only chalk-cut human figure in Britain; thin and unsexed, it is 70m tall and holds two poles of some sort. Its date is unknown, but it was restored in the 1870s. There are many theories as to its identity: Woden, Thor, Beowulf, Mercury, Apollo, King Harold, etc. The best analogies are the stance of a soldier holding 2 standards (on 4th-century coins), and a 7th-century Saxon belt buckle from Kent showing a warrior with a spear in each hand. There is a legend that a Roman is buried in a golden coffin beneath the figure.

Pevensey Castle Fort of the
Saxon Shore *
Roman
Pevensey **199(TQ:644048)**
A259 passes the Castle. HBMCE. Guidebook.

The impressive 3.2ha fort of *Anderida* was built in the late 3rd or early 4th century AD; at that time the sea came up to its S/E walls, but the fort, an irregular oval, now stands above marshes. The walls, 3.7m thick, still stand up to 7.6m in height, and their almost complete circuit survives, although a stretch on the N has fallen outwards. Ten (of the original 15?) massive U-shaped bastions remain. The E gate led to a

Above: **Pevensey Castle**. *The east gate of this 4th-century AD Fort of the Saxon Shore. One of the eleven surviving bastions stands to the north*

Left: **Pevensey Castle**. *General view*

small harbour, the N had a postern gate with a curved passage, and on the W side stands the great gateway, 3m wide, with 2 bastions and guard chambers inside. The fort was purely a military installation, and contained wooden huts. The Anglo-Saxons captured it in AD 491 and killed all the Britons inside, according to the *Anglo-Saxon Chronicle*. The military role persisted through history: the Normans built the castle that now dominates the site, and in 1940, pill boxes were inserted; there is a disguised one on the NW bastion, and another in the ruins of the keep's E wall.

Stane Street *Roman*
ESE of A285 **197(from Bignor SU:983139 to Eartham SU:940105)**
Long stretch of Roman road crosses Bignor Hill. National Trust.

One of the main Roman roads in southern Britain, it ran from Chichester to London. One fine stretch can be seen in woods and downland. The *agger,* the metalled road surface, is 9m wide, and made of many layers of chalk and flint, pounded together, and

topped with gravel and flint. This embankment is over 1m high, and on either side, 7.6m away, is a small ditch.

The Trundle Hillfort* *New Stone/Iron Ages*
S of Singleton **197(SU:877110)**
By Goodwood Park racecourse.

This hill dominates a wide area. The Neolithic causewayed camp is an enclosure of 1.2ha, with a maximum diameter of 300m, and has a ditch spiralling round it. The several causeways cross the ditches at irregular intervals. The flexed skeleton of a young woman was found buried in the ditch under a small heap of chalk blocks, and bone from the site has been dated to *c.* 3000 BC.

This site was later enclosed, in *c.* 250 BC, by a 5ha Iron Age fort; the octagonal defences comprise a single rampart and ditch, with a small counterscarp bank, and inturned entrances on E and W. The final phase of rebuilding seems to have been *c.* 50 BC. Finds in Lewes Museum. There is a legend that Aaron's golden calf is buried here.

Wessex has never been a very precisely defined area. The name is, of course, that of a West Saxon kingdom founded at the beginning of the sixth century AD that remained as a distinct but variable entity until the tenth century. Geologically-and, therefore, to some extent archaeologically-it should include the Berkshire Downs and perhaps eastern Somerset, but these areas are peripheral and, for the convenience of the Gazetteer, it will here be limited to the counties of Hampshire, Dorset and Wiltshire.

By far the greater part of the landscape of these areas is one of open downland with its undulating plains, nobly rounded hills curving down into deep, often yew-sprinkled combes and divided by river valleys where the chalk may form steep scarps. Although the chalk seldom rises above 275 metres, it is very much an upland region (as distinct from the highlands to the west) with finely moulded horizons and, it seems, its own pale light and invigorating air.

These Wessex uplands are centred on Salisbury Plain, which is therefore the hub of a radial system of chalk and limestone hills extending over much of England south and east of the Pennines. The longest of the chalk ridges leaves Salisbury Plain as the White Horse Hills and the Chilterns, runs narrowly through Cambridgeshire and Norfolk as the East Anglian Heights and Norfolk Ridge, then rises strongly again beyond the Wash in the Lincolnshire and Yorkshire Wolds. South of the Thames valley, leaving Salisbury Plain by the Hampshire Downs, the chalk thrusts one long finger, the North Downs, to the coast at Dover, and a shorter one, the lovely line of the South Downs, that breaks off in the lofty white cliffs of Beachy Head. Within Wessex itself, a short southern chalk belt runs from Cranborne Chase and the Dorset Downs to the coast by Weymouth and beyond. In addition to these chalk highways, there is the powerful line of limestone uplands known to geologists as the Jurassic Belt, running from the Cotswolds across Oxfordshire and Northamptonshire, then dwindling but rising again in Lincoln Edge and on to the limestone of the North Yorkshire moors.

All these radial uplands, like the central chalk downland itself, would have been lightly wooded in prehistoric times in contrast with heavily forested valleys and lowlands. It could be readily cleared for pasture and arable farming, and allowed free movement of men and of cattle. As well as these land routes, three rivers - the Christchurch Avon, the Bristol Avon and the Thames - offered trade routes to the Bristol Channel, the English Channel and beyond to the North Sea.

The inhabitants of Salisbury Plain and the surrounding downland were thus extraordinarily well placed for trading and other contacts with the rest of Britain, northern Europe and France and (via south Wales) with Ireland. At home they enjoyed some of the best conditions for mixed farming and an abundant supply of flint. They were able to take full advantage of their good fortune, particularly in the earlier Bronze Age, under the leadership of a vigorous élite, so it is not surprising to find that Wessex is rich in monuments of the prehistoric past and, in Avebury, Stonehenge and Silbury Hill, possesses three of the greatest in all Europe. Maiden Castle, too, is sufficient proof that, well into the Iron Age, Wessex rulers commanded exceptional wealth and power.

We now know that the gravels of many lowland valleys were quite populous in prehistoric times. However, partly because in those surroundings earthworks of all kinds were easily flattened, and still more because the valleys were continuously developed in later periods when the uplands were deserted save as pasture, their prehistoric sites can be detected only by air photography and excavation.

Chalk is, in any case, an ideal medium for the study and enjoyment of ancient monuments. No cutting into it can ever be lost, so that archaeologists can easily and with certainty discover all the smallest post holes and ditches, every pit, sacred or profane. And the fact that, once turf has grown over chalk earthworks, they remain stable through thousands of years has endowed them with a unique permanence and visibility.

Then again this sculpturing of the open downland is wonderfully pleasing to the eye. The groups of barrows are solidly satisfying and stand out (as they were intended to do) boldly against the sky, attaining an intense poignancy in the evening light. The rounded hills seem made for their crowning ramparts. In short, Wessex - and, most of all, Wiltshire - can be judged the most rewarding region in all Britain for visitors seeking communion with their ancient past.

There are no visit-worthy sites of the hunting age in Wessex although tools of the Old Stone Age have been found in river gravels, most frequently in Hampshire. Fishers and fowlers of the Middle Stone Age were scattered over much of the region, seldom on the chalk but by the rivers or the coast-notably by the Solent and in the Isle of Wight.

It is with the New Stone Age and the establishment of the farming life that Wessex leaps into prominence, the downland being exceptionally well endowed with monuments of the period, most significantly from its opening phases (p. 19). There are no less than six causewayed camps, all of them on hilltops, on a line running north-west up the western side of the region, from the one that underlies the Iron Age fort of Maiden Castle on to Windmill Hill and Knap Hill near Avebury. The two last are especially notable - Windmill Hill (p. 111) because it is excavated and gave its archaeological name to a phase of New Stone Age culture, and Knap Hill (p. 104) because it is well preserved and has a fine, dominating position above the Vale of Pewsey. The intervening 'camps', all relatively inconspicuous, are near the headwaters of the Stour, Avon and Kennet, suggesting that it was by these rivers that the farmers penetrated the downland.

The same can be said of the roughly contemporary earthen long barrows (p. 21) of Wessex that are concentrated round the same rivers, but also on the Upper Test and Itchen and on the Dorset Downs west of Weymouth. Some 170 have been identified in the three counties, and since only nine have been selected for the Gazetteer, there is plenty of scope for any explorer with a will to take up an Ordnance Survey map and hunt for more - though most will show only in 'low profile'. They are sometimes to be found in pairs.

In contrast with the generally earlier earthen long barrows, the chambered variety are few in Wessex, and those are concentrated on the Marlborough Downs - where the local sarsen stones lay ready to hand. By far the best of them, and the only example to be scientifically excavated, is the West Kennet long barrow (p. 111) at Avebury. It is a typical gallery grave with paired side chambers so very much like some of the Cotswold tombs that there can be little doubt that, if they did not come from the Cotswolds, the builders were strongly influenced from that quarter. Another link is provided by the presence in both areas of the odd device of the false entrance (Lugbury, p. 104, and Giant's Cave, p. 104).

Among other activities of the earlier New Stone Age peoples, flint mining seems to have been surprisingly little developed. Of the small number of sites known, the two most noticeable lie on either side of the county boundary between Wiltshire and Hampshire, north-east of Salisbury. Those tested proved to be simple pits without the galleries of the Sussex mines and Grimes Graves (p. 138). On the other hand, prosperous Wessex farmers obtained polished stone axes, or the material for making them, from western sources ranging from Penwith in Cornwall to Cumbria. This widespread network of trading contacts (discovered by petrological sampling) is the best proof we have that Stone Age communities did not inhabit little enclosed worlds, but were visited by travellers who directly or indirectly brought them information as well as axes from distant and very different realms. Indeed, a few stone implements, including ceremonial axes in jadeite, seem to have come from overseas - from Brittany.

It is in its sacred sites - those amazing creations of primitive religious instincts, where muscle was driven to immense labours by the promptings of the psyche - that Wessex attains its greatest glory. As we have seen (p. 30), these temples and ceremonial ways began to be raised in the late New Stone Age, but, with a long history as holy places, were brought to their highest architectural power in the Stonehenge of the Bronze Age.

Wessex was well supplied with henge sanctuaries, some dozen being known in addition to the great 'cathedrals' of Avebury and Stonehenge. Their history in relation to the late Stone Age people and their development by the Beaker Folk and the Wessex chieftains has already been sketched (pp. 30-34). Of the more notable henges, the earliest foundations are thought to have been the Dorset examples of Knowlton (p. 85) and Maumbury, probably dating from the mid-third millennium. In Wiltshire, the first Stonehenge may have followed in about 2200 BC, while Avebury seems to have been complete save for the Kennet Avenue and the Sanctuary by 2000 BC and Woodhenge at about the same date. Durrington Walls appears to be the latest, its large bank and ditch having been dug early in the second millennium.

It is sometimes not appreciated that, of these principal Wessex henges, great stones were used only at Avebury and Stonehenge: the original Sanctuary at Avebury, the Woodhenge and Durrington Walls all having multiple rings of wooden posts, once accepted as free-standing but now more generally thought to have supported roofs.

One other type of sacred monument has its best exemplars in this Wessex downland where the evidence of the religious life of our forebears is so abundant. This is the *cursus*, a long, narrow enclosure between parallel banks and ditches, probably built as a processional way. One stretches for nearly 3 kilometres, while a second, the finest in the country, is the Dorset Cursus (p. 81), no less than 10.4 kilometres in length.

There is a point on the summit of King Barrow Ridge on the Amesbury road where one can get a full realization of Stonehenge as the centre of religious activities that were both intense and long-lasting. On the downs surrounding the great temple, 300 or more barrows rise in lines and clusters. They cover every phase of time from the Stone Age long barrows to the latest round barrows of the Wessex chieftains. As they were added to century by century, so the temple itself was brought step by step to its final Bronze Age magnificence. Nowhere can barrows be seen better, in all their variety – long, bowl, disc, saucer and pond – than on Winterbourne Stoke Down to the west and Normanton to the east.

Round barrows of these types are abundant in Wessex – 6000 surviving, most of them, of course, on the chalk but also to be found on Hampshire heathland. Nowhere is there so great a concentration as on Salisbury Plain, but the Marlborough Downs have their share and so does the Dorset Ridgeway, while the Hampshire chalklands can show several cemeteries.

Wessex formerly possessed a number of small free-standing stone circles, but most have been destroyed and the few that can be seen are sadly ruined. These are strung along the Dorset coast westward from Corfe Castle – where the Rempstone circle, of which half survives now in dense woodland, is close to the fine Nine Barrows group (p. 86).

In the later Bronze Age, especially after 1000 BC, there may have been an increase in cattle ranching to account for a number of faint embanked enclosures to be seen on the Marlborough Downs, Cranborne Chase and elsewhere, while the network of ditches noted at Quarley Hill (p. 95) and including Grims Ditch may be ranch boundaries. They will appeal only to those with an enthusiasm for ancient farming. It is with the hillfort buildings of the Celtic Iron Age that Wessex regains its archaeological pre-eminence. So many of them survive on the chalk hills that, in some areas, they are a striking feature of the landscape. Most are contour forts – that is to say, with their ramparts following the contours of the hill – and while some are of the

(usually early) single rampart type, for example, Scratchbury (p. 104) and Quarley Hill (p. 95), there are many with multiple defences. Maiden Castle is supreme, but among other outstanding multivallate forts are Badbury Rings, Eggardon, Hambledon and Hod Hill in Dorset, Danebury Ring in Hampshire and Yarnbury Castle in Wiltshire. Ladle Hill (p. 92) has a special attraction for those who like to know 'how things are made', for, having been left half-finished, it reveals how the plan was marked out and the digging assigned to gangs, each with its own section of ditch and bank. The Gazetteer includes 29 of the Wessex hillforts, enough to give a fair sample of the variety of their designs and history.

Undoubtedly the earliest Roman building in Wessex is the camp in the corner of Hod Hill – since it dates from AD 43-4. After the rapid subjection of the Durotriges that it symbolizes, the region became a peaceful and fairly prosperous part of the Roman province, with cantonal capitals of modest size at Silchester, Winchester and Dorchester (Dorset). Although much has been discovered of the layout and history of the two latter towns, there is little to be seen of either save in their museums and at the Dorchester amphitheatre and aqueduct (p. 86). In Silchester (p. 95), on the other hand, Wessex has one of the most striking urban remains in the entire province, with the circuit of its walls still standing and the plan of all its roads and buildings known from excavation.

Silchester was an important road centre (*see map*, p. 96), but no more can be said of the system beyond mentioning the section known as Ackling Dyke and the Old Sarum – Dorchester road that can be seen and walked between Oakley Down and the Badbury Rings hillfort.

Individual buildings worth a visit are the large courtyard villa at Rockbourne (p. 95), the Brading and Newport villas in the Isle of Wight and the meagre remains of temples at Jordan Hill, Weymouth (p. 84) and on the summit of Maiden Castle.

Bokerley Dyke (p. 81) is a strong earthwork running between Cranborne Chase and Salisbury Plain, built, it seems, during the fourth century AD to control the Ackling Dyke highway. By far the best preserved and most enjoyable monument left by the Roman engineers is Portchester Castle, dramatically set on its headland jutting into Portsmouth harbour. This is the westernmost of the forts of the Saxon Shore (p. 58), its bastioned walls still standing four square, little changed since the days when they were built against the Saxon raiders.

Finally, in the Cerne Abbas Giant (p. 81) the Wessex chalk displays a hill figure unique in its enormous size, its method of execution and its unashamed phallicism. It was almost certainly cut during Roman times, and the Giant, brandishing his knobbed club, may represent Hercules, but a Hercules who also served a local fertility cult. It is an amazing proof of the continuity of country life and ways that the villagers should have defended this outline against the encroaching grass through more than 15 centuries.

DORSET

Abbotsbury Hillfort *Iron Age?*
194(SY:555866)
NW of Abbotsbury, just N of B3157. Park area.

A triangular fort of almost 2ha, it has a double bank with a ditch in between, with extra defences on the w and se. There are about 9 hut circles inside the fort, and also a round barrow, 12m across, just inside the s defences. A square earthwork on the sw, surrounded by a ditch that cuts through both banks, *may* be the base of a Roman signal station.

Badbury Rings Hillfort *Iron Age?*
NE of Shapwick **195(ST:964030)**
NW of Wimborne Minster, immediately NE of B3082. Signposted.

This conspicuous ovoid fort of 7.3ha, now tree-covered, is in a dominating location and has massive double banks and ditches, with a smaller external bank/ditch. The nearby picnic area has caused a certain amount of erosion of these defences. There is an inturned entrance on the e, and a complex gateway on the w. In the environs of the fort, there are field systems (to s and w) and Bronze Age barrows, and 4 Roman roads converge immediately to the n. The fort is unexcavated.

Aubrey said that a sword was found here by villagers who used it as a 'cheese-toster' [*sic*]; and the fort is one of several identified as Mt Badon, where Arthur defeated the Saxons in 518. There is a legend that he lives on as a raven in the wood, and that a gold coffin is buried here.

Badbury Rings. *Iron Age hillfort with two and three lines of ramparts* (Cambridge University Collection of Air Photographs)

Cerne Giant. This Romano-British (?) hill-figure probably represents Hercules

Black Down, Hardy Monument Round Barrows (Ridgeway Barrows)
Bronze Age
NE of Portesham   **194(SY:613876)**
SW of Dorchester, not far W of Maiden Castle (qv).
Many barrows in area (see also Poor Lot). Via
routes to the monument.

There is a great concentration of barrows along the Ridgeway here: near the monument to Sir Thomas Hardy (Nelson's flag captain at Trafalgar), there are 9 bowl barrows and 1 bell barrow, which contained several cremations. The linear cemetery, 1.6km to the SE (Bronkham Hill, SY:623873), comprises 30 barrows – mostly bowls, but also 4 bells and a double-bowl. Finds in Dorset County Museum, Dorchester.

Bokerley Dyke
Roman
Cranborne Chase   **184(SU:022198 – 063168)**
SW of Salisbury, on both sides of A354.

This impressive earthwork, which may date from the 4th century AD, runs for 5.6km between Cranborne Chase and Salisbury Plain. The bank, 10.7m wide, is still 2m high, while the V-shaped ditch on the NE is of similar width, and 3m deep.

Cerne Giant Hill-figure *
Romano-British(?)
Cerne Abbas   **194(ST:667016)**
Just E of A352: good view from A352 just N of
village. Abbey St, Cerne, through churchyard, left
through wood, a steep climb. National Trust.

Unlike the Long Man of Wilmington (p. 75), this chalk-cut figure, 55m high, is more than a mere outline: the face, ribs and genitalia are also depicted; indeed, since the 18th century, the erect phallus has incorporated what used to be the navel, and thus its length has increased by over 1.5m. The conspicuous genitalia may indicate some sort of fertility cult, and certainly, until recent years, maypole dancing took place on Mayday in the small rectangular enclosure, just above the figure, known as the Trendle or Frying Pan. It is said that women who wished to conceive used to spend the night on the figure, and belief in its power to impregnate seems to have persisted through the centuries. Even the local monastery did not obliterate the genitalia, and the figure is still scoured every 7 years. The date of the giant is unknown but, with its great club, 36.5m long, it is generally thought to represent Hercules, and thus may date from the 2nd century AD, a time when the emperor Commodus revived worship of this god, and posed as his incarnation. There is also a legend that a real giant was killed on the hill, and the figure was traced around his body.

Chalbury Hillfort
Iron Age
Just SE of Bincombe   **194(SY:695838)**
Near Jordan Hill (qv). Many barrows in the area.

A pear-shaped fort of 3.4ha on a very steep hill dominating Weymouth Bay, it has a single bank, 6m thick, of rubble encased in drystone, and a flat-bottomed ditch, with an entrance-gap on the SE. Over 70 hut-circles are known inside, with storage pits. Excavation uncovered a scatter of disarticulated human remains, which indicates exposure of the dead. There are also 2 Bronze Age round barrows at the centre, one of which contained a cremation. The fort probably dates from the 5th century BC.

Dorset Cursus
New Stone Age
    195/184(ST:970125 to SU:040191)
Runs from Bokerley Down SW to Thickthorn Down
(qv); E of A354. Many barrows in the area.

Eggardon Hillfort. A large, powerful hillfort that once protected a crowded Iron Age settlement

One of the largest prehistoric monuments in Britain, it is the largest known *cursus*, a type of structure unique to Britain. The name was coined by Stukeley in the 18th century, since he saw a resemblance with a racecourse. It runs for 9.7km, and comprises a parallel pair of banks and external ditches, about 90m apart, though in reality it is 2 shorter cursuses joined together. There are about 200,000 cubic metres of chalk rubble in the banks, quarried out of the ditches. Unfortunately the monument is now largely ploughed out, and most of its length is only visible from the air. The best parts to see are those to the E and W of the B3081 at Bottlebush, and the squared-off end on the SW (ST:971123) where it incorporates the 2 Thickthorn Down barrows (*qv*). It also incorporates a number of such barrows in its banks, and at Gussage Hill a long barrow crosses its track, so there may be some association with a cult of the dead. There have been suggestions of astronomical alignments. Excavation of the ditch has shown that it is 3m wide at the top, 2m at the bottom, and 1.2m deep with a flat bottom and steep sides. The lowest pottery in its fill dates from the early Neolithic.

Eggardon Hillfort *Iron Age*
SE of Powerstock **194(SY:541948)**
Lane through Whetley and King's Farm passes NE side. N of A35. Signposted.
An impressive 8ha hillfort in a spectacular setting, it has 3 banks and 2 ditches, with entrances on the SE (inturned) and NW, the easier approaches. The 500 depressions inside the fort were probably huts and storage pits. There is a henge monument nearby (SY:546946) with a small round barrow at its centre, and entrances on NW and SE.

Hambledon Hillfort and
Causewayed Camp* *New Stone/Iron Ages*
Between Child Okeford (to W) and Iwerne
Courtney (to E) **194(ST:845126)**
W of A350. Footpath and climb from Monk's House on Okeford-Iwerne road and other tracks. Near Hod Hill (qv).
After Maiden Castle (*qv*), this is the most impressive hillfort in Dorset. An area of 12.5ha is enclosed by 2 ramparts and ditches, with an outer counterscarp bank. There are inturned entrances on the N, SW and SE. The fort grew in 3 stages, starting at the N end (4.9ha), then taking in the centre and finally the S – the crossbanks that mark these stages can still be seen. The earliest stage probably dates from the 3rd century BC, the last from between 50 BC and the Roman invasion. Several hundred depressions inside may be hut platforms, denoting a dense population, but a lot of flint-digging took place here in the 19th century. Also inside the fort, at the highest point, is a New Stone Age long barrow, 70m in length.
To the SE of the fort is a massive fortified New Stone Age complex, the scene of recent excavations. It seems to have been a great ritual centre, and radiocarbon-dates of 2900–2600 BC have been obtained. The causewayed camp, of 8ha, has a single line of causewayed ditch with an inner bank. The ditch contained a great deal of human skeletal material, including crouched infant burials, and skulls placed at intervals. The labour involved in constructing the camp has been estimated at 40–45,000 man hours.
There is another enclosure of 1ha, 800m SE of the camp, with an even more massive ditch that contained a lot of charcoal, implying a burned superstructure of timber, and human skulls had been

placed round its circuit, as at the camp, except that, here, the heads had been severed before being put there. There were several timber structures inside the enclosure, which also had a timber-lined entrance passage. The fortifications were renewed periodically, but the enclosure was finally sacked – an intact skeleton was found with an arrowhead in its chest.

The camp may have been an open-air cemetery, where corpses were exposed, while the other enclosure might have been occupied by farmers, who also herded cattle.

There is a second long barrow near the camp. Nothing is known of its contents or those of the other barrow. Finds in Dorset County Museum, Dorchester.

Hengistbury Head Promontory Fort
Bournemouth/Christchurch   *Bronze/Iron Ages*   **195(SZ:164910)**
Footpaths from Southborne.

Although Hengistbury is the location of a large open-air site dating from the end of the Old Stone Age (10550 BC) and the Middle Stone Age (7800 BC), with many flint tools and traces of fire, and also of some Bronze Age activity (7 bowl barrows on the Head, and 2 more to the NW), it is best known for its great promontory fort on the S side of Christchurch harbour.

This stronghold was defended by the 'Double Dykes', 457m long, across the neck of the headland; it used to be much bigger, but sea-erosion has reduced

it to 70ha. The inner bank is 3.7m high, and its ditch over 12m wide and 3.7m deep. The outer defences are smaller.

Excavation, which still continues, has shown that this was a warehouse and trading centre, with spacious anchorage, and controlled the rivers that led into Wessex. It was begun in the 8th – 6th century BC, and the occupants exploited the promontory's ironstone. It was largely abandoned until the 1st century BC, when trade was revitalized. It was a centre for importation: a vast amount of pottery, imported from France and the Mediterranean, has been found, including amphorae bringing wine from southern Italy. In addition, there was saltmaking and a remarkably advanced metal industry (copper and iron), and coins were minted locally. Thousands have been found here, mostly of the Durotriges tribe, and of the Dobunni. Gold coins and bracelets have been found on the beach. The site was occupied into the Roman period. Finds in Red House Museum, Christchurch.

Hod Hill Hillfort *
NW of Stourpaine   *Iron Age/Roman*   **194(ST:857106)**
Just W of A350. Bridlepath from E of Hanford House or footpath from Stourpaine. Just SE of Hambledon Hill (qv).

A rectangular fort of 21ha, it has a double bank and ditch, except on the W where the steep descent to the river Stour made only single defences necessary. There are inturned entrances at the NE and SW corners. It was probably begun in the 5th century BC (radiocarbon date: 460 BC), and was densely occup-

Hengistbury Head Promontory Fort. View from the Iron Age promontory fort that defended what is now Portsmouth Harbour

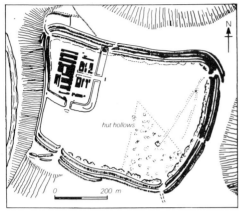

Hod Hill, Dorset (after J. Dyer)

ied – hundreds of round hut depressions and pits following street lines have been detected, and many can still be seen in the SE corner – until it was taken by Vespasian's troops in AD 43. The latter's *ballista* attack seems to have been concentrated on a large hut on the SE, surrounded by a rectangular palisade: piles of slingstones were found by its doors.

The Romans then built a fort of their own in the NW corner, the highest point of the hill, to take advantage of the views and the access to the river, for which they made a small gate in the Iron Age rampart. Their fort, of 4.4ha, used the original defences on the N and W, and had 2 main gates on the S and W. It was garrisoned by about 600 legionaries and 250 cavalry, and was occupied until AD 51. Finds in the British Museum.

Jordan Hill Temple   *Roman*
Weymouth   **194(SY:698821)**
Footpath E from A353. HBMCE. Always open. Near Chalbury (qv).

On a hill overlooking Weymouth Bay, this Romano-Celtic temple, 76m square, has walls over 1m thick. In its SE corner there is an enigmatic shaft, almost 4m deep; at the bottom was a stone cist containing a sword, a spearhead and 2 urns. The shaft had been filled with 16 distinct layers of ash and charcoal, each containing the remains of a bird (buzzards, crows, starlings, ravens) and a coin, and separated from the next by roofing slabs. The coins show that the building was in use in the 4th and early 5th centuries. Presumably the layers are the result of sacrifices, buried in a consecrated area. Outside the temple, almost 100 burials were found in the 19th century, and between the temple and the cliff are the walls of another small structure – a shrine or a signal station.

Knowlton Circles
NW of Woodlands

New Stone Age
195(SU:025100)

From carpark by central circle, Lumber Lane, off B3078. HBMCE.

There are 3 henges here in (almost) a straight

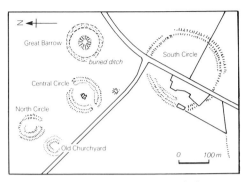

Knowlton Circles, Dorset (after J. Dyer)

alignment NW/SE. Only the central circle is now clearly visible. Little can be seen of the one to the N (84m across), while the southern circle was 229m across and is bisected by the B3078. The central circle is 97.5m across, with an earth bank, still 3.7m high in places, and an internal ditch 10.7m wide, with entrances on the NE and SW. The presence of a 12th-century church at its centre shows that the site continued as a sanctuary. Between the central and S circles is the tree-covered Great Barrow, 6m high and 38m across – its position is thus identical to that at the Thornborough Henges (p. 211). There are other round barrows in the vicinity.

Maiden Castle Hillfort *
Winterborne Monkton

New Stone Age/ Iron Age/Roman
194(SY:669884)

SW of Dorchester. Between B3159 (to W) and A354 (to E). Signposted. HBMCE. Bookstall. Always open.

One of the biggest and most impressive sites in Britain, it has an inner circumference of 2.5km and its enormous ramparts enclose 18ha.

The earliest occupation known here was a 8ha causewayed camp at the E end, dating from *c.* 3000 to *c.* 2000 BC, with 2 causewayed ditches, 15m apart. Then a massive earth bank, 0.5km long, was built NW/SE down the length of the ridge; burials were found at its E end, but little is now visible of this earthwork.

Between 350 and 70 BC, the Iron Age defences were developed, the first phase being a 6.5ha fort on the site of the Neolithic camp, subsequently extended to 18ha. The huge ramparts and ditches were constructed *c.* 150 BC, and strengthened *c.* 75 BC, when the great entrances on the W and E were remodelled. Maiden Castle became a flourishing town, although little is known of Iron Age life here – no doubt new excavations will reveal a great deal about this.

In AD 43 Vespasian and the 2nd Legion attacked the weaker E entrance. Over 50,000 slingstones from Chesil Beach were found here (a sling would have had a downhill range of 140m from here) but the Roman attack was victorious. In the museum in Dorchester can be seen the spine of a defender with a Roman *ballista* bolt embedded in it. In a war cemetery found just outside the gate, each of the 30 Britons was accompanied by a mug and some food, such as a shoulder of lamb.

Knowlton Circles. This is the central henge of the three at Knowlton. A medieval church was built within the pagan sanctuary

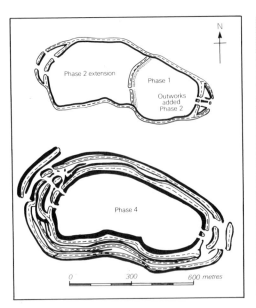

Maiden Castle, Dorset, showing its development from the earliest site (after Sir Mortimer Wheeler)

Right: *Maiden Castle Hillfort*. The 4th-century AD Romano-Celtic temple built at the north-east end of the great hillfort

By AD 70 the Britons had been resettled in *Durnovaria* (Dorchester), the new Roman town, and the fort was deserted. In the late 4th century, a small Romano-Celtic temple, 12m square, was built in the NE part of the fort, where its foundations can still be seen. It has a square *cella* (shrine) at the centre, surrounded by a veranda. There was a 2-roomed (priest's?) house just to the N. Some 4th-century coins have been found, including gold specimens. Some of the Bronze Age barrows visible from the fort contained gold ornaments and a small amber cup. Finds in Dorset County Museum, Dorchester.

Maumbury Rings Henge and Amphitheatre
Dorchester
New Stone Age/Roman
194(SY:690899)
On A354 to Weymouth (just E of the road).
This site began as a circular henge with a single entrance on the NE. Its enormous bank was up to 3.4m high; the irregular internal ditch, no longer visible, was not continuous, but rather a series of 45 shafts, some over 10m deep and 4m across. These huge pits were deliberately filled, and bones, tools and chalk phalluses have been found here.

In Roman times, this site was used as the amphitheatre for Dorchester: its external diameter was over 100m, and a 3m thickness of chalk was removed inside to lower the floor and make an oval area 58 by 48m. Finally, the site was used in the 17th century as a civil war gun emplacement (opposite the entrance), and Mary Channing was strangled and burned in the arena in 1766 for poisoning her husband. The same entrance gap remained in use throughout all these periods. Finds in Dorset County Museum, Dorchester.

Nine Barrows Long and Round Barrows
E of Corfe Castle
New Stone/Bronze Ages
195(SY:995816)
Footpath through trees SE from B3351, then climb to ridge top (Ailwood Downs).
This linear cemetery on the crest of a ridge comprises 1 long and 17 bowl barrows. The long mound, 34m long, 1.8m high and orientated E/W, is best seen from the S. The round mounds vary in size. Contents unknown. They are supposed to be the graves of 9 kings killed in battle.

Oakley Down Round Barrows
N of Wimborne St Giles
Bronze Age
184(SU:018173)
By sharp bend of A354 NNW of Wimborne St Giles. To N of Knowlton (qv).
A splendid Bronze Age cemetery of at least 29 closely packed mounds, it produced a wealth of finds in the last century: pottery, bronze daggers, beads of shale and amber, flint arrowheads, etc. Bowl, bell and disc barrows are to be seen here. Finds in Devizes Museum.

The edge of 2 disc barrows is cut by Ackling Dyke, a Roman road that ran from Old Sarum (p. 104) to Badbury Rings (*qv*) and Dorchester, and also round the edge of Silbury Hill (p. 104) and across the Dorset Cursus (*qv*). Its side ditches can be seen in places (best at SU:016163).

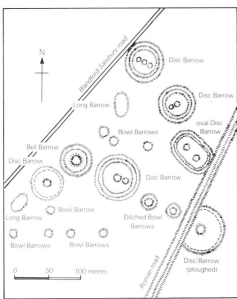

Pilsdon Pen Hillfort
N of Pilsdon

Iron Age
193(ST:413013)

Immediately N of B3164. Steep walk up.

This 3ha oval fort at the end of a spur, with spectacular views, has a double bank and ditch with counterscarp, and entrances on N, SE and SW. It probably dates from the 1st century BC. Excavation has found a number of huts (one of which contained a crucible with traces of gold, and may therefore have been a goldsmith's workshop) and a large rectangular timber building at the centre, which was later replaced by a banked enclosure: it may have been some sort of shrine, as at South Cadbury (p. 129). A Roman *ballista* bolt was found here. The tumuli inside the fort were probably caused by 18th-century rabbit-breeding. Finds in Dorset County Museum, Dorchester.

Pimperne Long Barrow *
NE of Pimperne

New Stone Age
195(ST:918105)

Immediately N of A354; bridleway opposite entrance to Blandford Camp.

This huge parallel-sided mound, on the crest of a ridge, is 100m long, 2.7m high, and orientated NW/SE. It has berms and side ditches, but nothing is known of its contents.

***Oakley Down Barrows**, Dorset, (after J. Dyer)*

Poor Lot Barrows *Bronze Age*
Kingston Russell **194(SY:589907)**
Immediately s of A35 in triangle between Kingston
Russell (to NW), Littlebredy (to s) and
Winterbourne Abbas (to E). Close to Black Down
(qv).
Of these 44 mounds, 24 are bowl barrows; there
are 7 bells, 8 discs and 5 ponds. Those s of the road
form 2 lines, but only 2 have been excavated. Finds in
Dorset County Museum, Dorchester. There are 2
long barrows just to the SW (SY:580905).

Poundbury Hillfort and
Aqueduct *Iron Age/Roman*
Dorchester **194(SY:683912)**
On the NW edge of the town, by Poundbury Road
and the river Frome.
A rectangular fort of 5.5ha, it has a double bank
and ditch, and commands the ford across the river as
well as an approach to Maiden Castle. Excavation has
indicated 3 main phases: first, there was a Middle
Bronze Age enclosure system. This was followed in
the 4th century BC by an enclosure that partly followed the earlier works, with a timber-faced bank
and a deep V-shaped ditch. After c. 50 BC, the bank was
strengthened and enlarged with a limestone revetment and a capping of chalk blocks, and the outer
dump bank with V-shaped ditch was added. The
inner rampart is still massive. There was an entrance
on the E, and just outside it is an extensive Romano-
British cemetery of the mid-4th century AD: some
footbones here had traces of leprosy. Finds in Dorset
County Museum, Dorchester.
The outer defences were damaged on the N and E
by the Roman aqueduct (and by the 1855 railway
tunnel) that carried water 19km from the river to
Dorchester. It followed the s side of the valley as
a chalk-cut, clay-lined channel, 1.5m wide and
0.9m deep, and was probably capable of providing
over 55 million litres per day. It is best seen
between SU:671917 and 674914, where it forms a
terrace.

Rawlsbury Camp Hillfort *Iron Age?*
Stoke Wake **194(ST:767058)**
On Bulbarrow Hill, lane SE of the village.
A small pear-shaped contour fort of 1.6ha, with
superb views, it has a double bank and ditch, which
bend away from each other on the N and s to form
enclosures 20m across; there is an entrance passage
on the E, and hut depressions can be seen inside the
fort. Undated.

Thickthorn Down Long Barrows *New Stone Age*
Just NW of Gussage St Michael **195(ST:971123)**
SE of A354. By Dorset Cursus (qv).
These barrows are located at the SW end of the cursus. The larger NW mound has not been excavated,
but is 46m long and 2m high, with a U-shaped ditch.
The smaller SE mound is over 30m long, 2m high, and
is also surrounded by a U-shaped ditch, but a causeway on the SE had 3 postholes. No primary burials
were found inside, though a strange structure of turf
and chalk rubble was discovered. Three intrusive
Beaker burials were found on the SW, while the
ditches contained pottery and 2 chalk phalluses.
Finds in Dorset County Museum, Dorchester.
There is a legend that a gold or silver coffin is
buried in the SE mound.

HAMPSHIRE

Beacon Hill Hillfort *Iron Age*
WSW of Kingsclere **174(SU:458573)**
s of Newbury, just w of A34. In Country Park with
car park and picnic area. Just NW of Ladle Hill
(qv). Signposted.
A contour fort of 5ha in a splendid location, it has
an hour-glass shape enclosed by a single bank and
ditch, with a counterscarp bank and an inturned
entrance on the SE. Inside, there are about 20 hut hollows, and some storage pits have been excavated; animal bones and pottery have been found. On clear
days, Ladle Hill can be seen to the E. One corner of the
fort contains the fenced-off grave of Lord Carnarvon,
patron of the Tutankhamen excavations, who used to
own the site and who lived in the nearby Highclere
Castle.

Beacon Hill. An hour-glass-shaped Iron Age
hillfort with single rampart

Buckland Rings Fort *Iron Age*
Lymington **196(SZ:315968)**
Between A337 (to E) and road to Buckland (to W).

A strong rectangular enclosure of 2.8ha, it has double ramparts and external v-shaped ditches, with a counterscarp bank, and probably dates to the 1st century BC. Both ramparts seem to have been strengthened with timbers. An entrance on the NE was approached by a hollow way, and had a gate 3m wide. The defences were either destroyed by the Romans or dismantled on their instructions. Finds in Winchester City Museum.

Bury Hill Hillfort *Iron Age*
Upper Clatford **185(SU:345435)**
Just SW of Andover. E of A343. Signposted.

The first phase of this fort probably dates to the 6th or 5th century BC, and comprised an oval enclosure of 8.9ha with a single chalk bank and ditch, and an entrance on the SE. Later, in the 3rd or 2nd century BC, a smaller oval was built inside this, with double chalk banks and a v-shaped ditch in between, 6m deep. Occupation continued after the Roman invasion, well into the 1st century AD. Two female skeletons have been found in the site. Finds in Winchester City Museum.

**Butser Hillfort and
Experimental Farm** *Iron Age?*
SW of Petersfield **197(SU:712201)**
Minor road W from A3 around Oxenbourne Down. In Country Park.

A flat-topped hill of 32ha, it is protected by earthworks across a neck of high ground to the SW: first, a low bank and a ditch 9m wide; and, further to the SW, two more cross-dykes. There are many Celtic fields, ancient trackways and round barrows in this area. At Little Butser (SU:719207) is an experimental Iron Age farm; two round houses have been built, and experiments are carried out in growing crops, breeding animals, storing food, clearing vegetation, cooking, making pottery, etc. It is open daily except Mondays and there is a small entrance fee. Guidebooks and cards available.

Danebury Ring Hillfort *   *Iron Age*
NE of Nether Wallop   **185(SU:323377)**
*N of A30, s of A343; approach road and car park
provided in Country Park. Signposted.*

Excavation in recent years has revealed something
of the complex history of this impressive ovoid fort of
5.3ha, which seems to have been continuously
occupied for 500 years. Its defences (a double bank
and ditch) are now covered in beech trees; the inner
rampart is up to 5m high, and about 18m wide at its
base. The earliest features found on the site were
some (early Bronze Age?) ritual pits, some of which
contained dismembered dogs. The fort was begun in
the 6th or 5th century BC, and comprised a number of
circular houses with storage pits. In the 4th century,
it was replanned, and 2 parallel streets were laid out,
with rectangular 4- and 6-post structures along
them, which backed on to areas of storage pits. These
post structures were in rows over 90m long, and
were rebuilt many times. The 'streets' had flint-cob-
ble metalling that was also replaced several times.
The ramparts and the gateway were strengthened
between 400 and 100 BC. By the 2nd century, the placing of storage pits no longer respected the streets or
the building lines. Occupation on a large scale seems
to have ceased c. 100 BC: the E gateway had just been
refortified, but was soon burned down, and the fort
was abandoned. There was some final use of the site
as a farmstead around the time of the invasion of AD
43.

The fort contained thousands of pits. Excavation
has produced abundant pottery, grain, animal bones,
evidence of weaving and iron-smelting and of shale
and salt distribution, and a hoard of 21 sword-shaped
currency bars. Human bones were scattered widely
across the fort, and piled up, dismembered, in pits:
clearly a simple form of disposal of the dead was in
operation. The fort's population has been estimated
at 200–300.

Three long barrows of the New Stone Age can be
seen nearby at SU:320383. Finds will be displayed at
a Danebury Museum attached to Andover Museum.

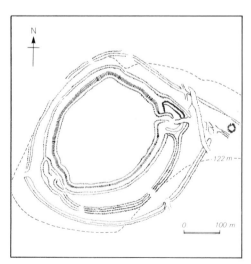

***Danebury Ring**, Hampshire (after B. W. Cunliffe)*
Right: ***Danebury Ring Hillfort**. Iron Age*

Ladle Hill Hillfort
Iron Age?
Just sw of Sydmonton   **174(SU:478568)**
E of A34. Steep climb from the N or by easier paths from the E. Just SE of Beacon Hill (qv) *and sw of Silchester* (qv).

An unfinished but roughly rectangular fort of 2.8ha, its ditch was clearly being dug by a number of different gangs at the time work was halted. Its date is unknown. There is a disc barrow, 52m across, to the N (with a hole in the top to show it has been robbed) and other ploughed-out barrows in the area.

Lamborough Long Barrow
New Stone Age
E of Cheriton, w of Bramdean   **185(SU:593284)**
Just N of A272 and minor road from Cheriton to Bramdean.

An unexcavated long barrow, 67m long, 33.5m wide and orientated E/W, it is 2.1m high at the E end. The broad and deep flanking ditches yielded a single sherd of late New Stone Age pottery (now in Winchester City Museum).

Old Winchester Hill
Iron Age?
E of Meonstoke   **185(SU:641206)**
E of the A32. From car park on minor road SE of Warnford.

This unexcavated ovoid contour fort, with superb views (as far as the Isle of Wight), has a bank, ditch and counterscarp bank, with particularly strong defence on the SE. The rampart is still 2m high, and there are inturned entrances on the W and E. A number of bowl barrows stand inside the fort, with others around the entrances. There is a legend that this was the original spot chosen on which to build Winchester, but whenever the materials were gathered, they were moved mysteriously; so the town was built 17km to the NW.

Popham Beacons Round Barrows
Bronze Age
s of Overton   **185(SU:525439)**
Immediately N of A30, at junction with road N to Steventon. E of railway.

A linear cemetery of 5 barrows on high ground: the central mound is a saucer barrow, almost 50m across, which is overlapped to the N by a bell barrow (with a bowl barrow beyond), and to the s by a bowl (with a bell beyond). Unexcavated.

Portchester Castle Fort of the Saxon Shore *
Roman
Portchester   **196(SU:625046)**
Portsmouth. s of A27. HBMCE. standard hours. Signposted. Guidebook.

Portus Adurni, the finest of the shore forts, is located on a promontory jutting into Portsmouth harbour, and covers 3.6ha. Its outer walls, 186 by 189m, and over 5m high, are the most complete Roman walls in northern Europe; only the gateways are medieval. It is still possible to see the junctions between the work of different gangs of builders. The 14 D-shaped bastions are hollow (and therefore had timber floors, and could only support light catapults), and the external ditch can be seen. The sea still washes up to the s wall.

It is thought to have been built in the late 3rd century AD, but by 300 the troops had been withdrawn

and the military buildings demolished. A civilian population moved in until *c.* 340, living in timber buildings and with resurfaced roads. It was then garrisoned until 370, and then abandoned again. Ger-

man mercenary troops occupied it in sunken huts during the 5th and 6th centuries. The Normans placed their keep within the walls, and a Romanesque church was built in the SE corner.

Ladle Hill. The unfinished Iron Age hillfort can be seen at the centre (Cambridge University Collection of Air Photographs)

Quarley Hill Hillfort
Iron Age?
sw of Quarley   **184(SU:262423)**
Climb s from road between B3084 and Grateley.

An ovoid hillfort of 3.5ha, in a commanding position, it began as an enclosure with a simple timber palisade. Later the defences that survive today were built: an unfinished dump rampart, 2m high, a wide v-shaped ditch, 4m deep, and a slight counterscarp bank. There were entrances on the sw and ne, the latter also unfinished. A number of linear earthworks that meet on this hill may be the relics of cattle ranching in the late Bronze Age. Finds in Winchester City Museum.

Rockbourne Villa
Roman
se of Rockbourne   **184(SU:120170)**
On e edge of West Park. s of village on Fordingbridge road. e of Bokerley Dyke (p. 81) Guidebook.

Over 70 rooms have been found in this extensive courtyard villa, discovered in 1942, and more probably remain to be uncovered. The house began as a timber construction in the 1st century AD, and this was replaced by a stone villa in the 2nd. It flourished in the 3rd and 4th centuries. Visitors can see a mosaic floor, and some hypocaust; there is also an interesting site museum. Two rather battered milestones were used as building material. Over 22kg of coins were found in a hoard here in 1967: 7714 *antoniniani* and 3 *denarii*.

St Catherine's Hill Hillfort
Iron Age
Immediately se of Winchester   **185(SU:484276)**
e of A33. Roman road goes past to the se.

This fort, preceded by an unfortified settlement in the early Iron Age, probably dates to *c.* 400 BC. A single chalk dump rampart, 2.4m high and 12m wide at its base, encloses an oval area of 9.3ha. There is a wide external ditch, and a low counterscarp bank, with an inturned entrance on the ne. Excavation suggests that there were 4 periods of construction, but the fort was sacked (perhaps by the Belgae) in *c.* 50 BC, and abandoned. The site's name is derived from the chapel on this hill. Finds in Winchester City Museum.

Silchester Romano-British Town *
Roman
Silchester   **175(SU:640625)**
e of Silchester Common. Roads to St Mary's church within the Roman walls. HBMCE. Guidebook at museum.

The town of *Calleva Atrebatum* was the capital of the *civitas* of the Atrebates. Built shortly after the Roman invasion, it originally had timber buildings, replaced in stone by the end of the 2nd century. It has not been built over, but most of it is now under the plough. The present walls, 6.7m high, date from the 3rd century, and enclose a 43ha hexagon. They are still impressive in places, and an almost complete circuit survives, with 2 of the 4 gates well preserved on N and s. The town, which stood at the junction of

Left (top): **Portchester Castle Fort of the Saxon Shore**, *showing the outer walls and D-shaped bastions*

Left (below): *Aerial view of* **Portchester Castle Fort of the Saxon Shore** (Cambridge University)

Below: **Rockbourne Villa**. Coarsely worked but elegantly designed mosaic in the villa

Above: **Silchester Romano-British Town**. *The walls of the Roman town were built in the 3rd century* AD. *Flint rubble was faced with worked flints and bonded with stone slabs*

Below: *Plan of the Romano-British town,* **Silchester** (Calleva Atrebatum), *Hampshire (after R. G. Collingwood)*

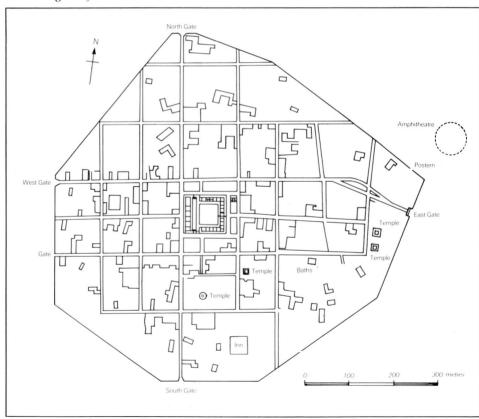

several important roads, had the usual grid of streets and a forum, basilica and baths - the latter were 128m w of the present church; but although it covered a similar area to Roman Colchester (p. 134), it only contained about 180 houses. Large areas must have been left unoccupied, or were occupied by wooden huts. There were 3 temples, 2 of which lie beneath the church: a small column serves as a sundial base in the churchyard. On the s side of the forum was an early (4th-century?) Christian church.

Evidence from coins suggests that, despite being sacked (and having some quarters burned) in the late 3rd century, the town flourished into the 5th or even 6th century, after which it was abandoned. The many finds are in Reading Museum and in a small museum near the rectory, and some objects, including the famous bronze 'Silchester eagle', are at Stratfield Saye, the home of the Dukes of Wellington.

The town's oval amphitheatre (SU:644626) is outside on the NE; its exterior can be seen from Pitfield Lane, the interior from Wall Lane.

ISLE OF WIGHT

Afton Down Long and
Round Barrows   *New Stone/Bronze Ages*
Afton   **196(SZ:352857)**
Just NE of Freshwater Bay, immediately N of A3055. At w end of golf course. National Trust.

This group of 24 barrows includes a long barrow, 34.7m long, 0.9m high, and orientated E/W. Most of the round barrows are bowls (17), but there are 4 bell barrows, and 2 disc barrows, one of which is used as a golf green. Excavation in 1817 produced nothing of significance in the long barrow, but several cremations in the round barrows. Finds in Carisbrooke Castle Museum.

Brading Villa *   *Roman*
sw of Morton   **196(SZ:599863)**
w of A3055. Small charge. Guidebook.

This villa, discovered in 1879, was founded c. AD 300, and flourished until the early 5th century as the centre of a rich agricultural estate. One of the finest villas open to the public, it had a courtyard of 55 sq m, and detached farm buildings on the N and s; the E side was open to the sea, which was closer in that period. The w wing is roofed and open to view, and houses the site museum. Its mosaics, some of the best in Britain, include figures such as Orpheus, Bacchus with gladiators, and Perseus holding Medusa's head.

Chillerton Down Fort   *Iron Age?*
Chillerton, Gatcombe   **196(SZ:483842)**
On hill just w of Chillerton, off minor roads w of A3020. Strip lynchets to the SE.

This 10ha promontory fort is protected by steep slopes on the N, s and E, while 5 mounds of earth, up to 3m high, form an irregular rampart cutting off the promontory. The defences are therefore unfinished, but there is a ditch at the sw, and an entrance at the NW end.

Five Barrows Round-Barrow
Cemetery   *Bronze Age*
Shalcombe   **196(SZ:390852)**
Just w of B3399.

A linear cemetery of 8 mounds in a fine location. A series of 6 bowl barrows is flanked by a 2.7m high bell barrow to the w, and a disc barrow, over 35m across, to the E.

Newport Villa   *Roman*
Newport   **196(SZ:500880)**
Cypress Road, off A3056. Small charge.

A small villa by the river Medina, it was of the corridor type with projecting wings. Part of it, including bath suite, hypocaust and mosaics, can be visited, and there is a small site museum. The villa was probably occupied from the late 2nd to the late 4th century AD.

WILTSHIRE

Aldbourne Four Barrows
(Sugar Hill Barrow Cemetery)   *Bronze Age*
NW of Aldbourne   **174(SU:249773)**
Just E of A419. Track running N from Aldbourne church.

There are 3 bell and 1 bowl barrows in this group; 2 more bowls can be seen 0.8km to the NW on top of Sugar Hill, and 2 more, ploughed out, to the sw. Excavations in this group in the last century produced cremations, together with grave goods such as beads, pottery and a dagger. Finds in the British Museum.

Avebury Sanctuary
Complex *   *New Stone Age*
Avebury   **173(SU:103699)**
Part of village lies within the henge monument. Tourist amenities.

John Aubrey (p. 9) declared the Avebury sanctuary to surpass 'the much renowned Stonehenge, as a cathedral does a parish church'. In this, he was showing a partiality for his own discovery for, although Avebury covers a far larger area than its rival and is a most impressive place, it has no true architecture, its sarsen stones standing singly and quite unworked. It is, in fact, a relatively primitive circle-henge on an unprecedented scale.

In atmosphere, the 2 famous sanctuaries are quite unlike, for while Stonehenge's Salisbury Plain makes a bald, stark setting, now invaded by tourism, the surroundings of Avebury, despite through traffic, are far more sequestered, with trees and the little village partly inside the ring.

What is perhaps Avebury's dominant feature - the great circular earthwork - encloses 11.5ha, the bank measuring 427m across and about 5m high, with an

Avebury Sanctuary Complex. *The West Kennet Avenue running towards the Sanctuary on Overton Hill*

internal quarry ditch that was once as much as 9m deep and steep-sided. When all was in pure white chalk it must have been an awe-inspiring spectacle. As a henge, Avebury is most unusual in having 4 original entrances through bank and ditch – now used by the A361 and the village street.

Set about 6.7m inside the ditch is the outer circle of at least 98 massive sarsen boulders, very rugged and variable in shape and size – the tallest standing near the N entrance is 4.4m in height. Many of the stones were removed, some for village buildings, but enough survive, particularly in the SW sector, to give an idea of the original grandeur. Here and elsewhere in the monument, the sockets of missing stones are marked with concrete blocks.

Inside this circle are the remains of two smaller stone rings – to N and S – the southern being the better preserved. This was 52m in diameter and seems to have had 29 stones with a tall pillar stone ('The Obelisk') at the centre. The northern inner circle was slightly smaller, perhaps with 27 stones. Inside it again was a small circle surrounding a most interesting centrepiece: 3 huge sarsens forming a triangular structure known as The Cove – a name now sometimes used at other megalithic sites. One of the 3 stones fell in the 18th century and is now missing.

The other striking feature of the Avebury complex, a later addition, is the West Kennet Avenue, running on a sinuous course from the S entrance to Overton Hill, 2.4km to the E. It consisted of 100 pairs of sarsens facing one another at a distance of about 15m, each pair consisting of a relatively tall, narrow stone opposite a broad, squatter one. It is thought probable that

Above: ***Avebury Sanctuary Complex***. *The two largest stones of the great circle*

Below: ***Avebury***, *Wiltshire (after J. Dyer)*

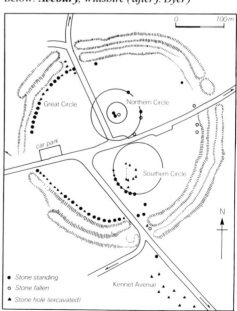

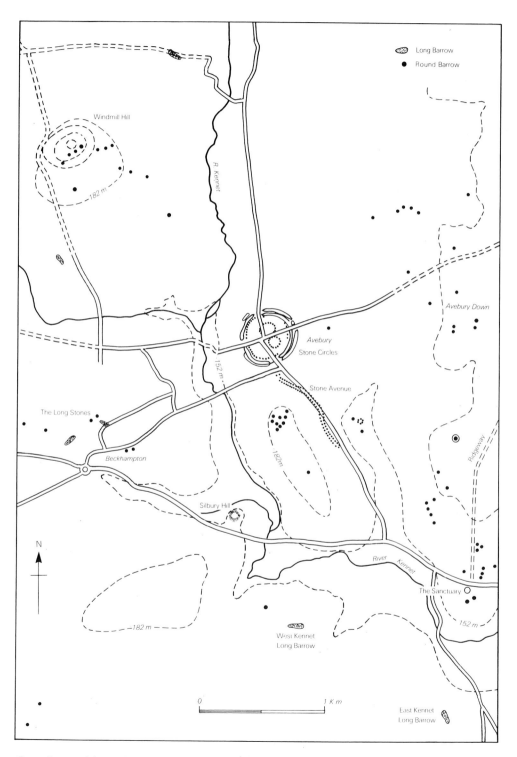

General map of the Avebury region (after J. Dyer)

Long Barrow

Round Barrow

Windmill Hill

R Kennet

182 m

Avebury Down

Avebury
Stone Circles

Stone Avenue

The Long Stones

Ridgeway

Beckhampton

182 m

Silbury Hill

N

River Kennet

The Sanctuary

152 m

182 m

West Kennet
Long Barrow

East Kennet
Long Barrow

0   1 K m

these are male and female symbols. Beaker burials were found at the foot of 4 of the stones.

This avenue has been restored at its N end adjoining the main temple. Towards its s end, at West Kennet village, it bends SE and climbs the hill beside the A4 to Overton Hill, ending in the site known as The Sanctuary. (For an account of its destruction, see p. 10).

The Sanctuary, beside the Ridgeway above the river Kennet, appears first to have been a round wooden house, probably used for ritual purposes at the end of the New Stone Age. Its position was indicated by 6 concentric rings of postholes, now marked by concrete pillars. It is possible that this was not a building but circles of free-standing posts. The wooden construction was succeeded by a double circle of sarsen stones, now marked by rectangular concrete blocks, the outer one about 40m in diameter. Against one of the stones of the inner circle was the grave of a young man with a beaker beside him. There is a group of round barrows, perhaps later in date, to the north of The Sanctuary.

In Stukeley's day (p. 10), a second avenue led from the w entrance of the Avebury temple to the Longstones w of Beckhampton (SU:089693). Two of these now survive; a crouched Beaker burial was found beside one of them.

The Avebury temple must date from the second half of the 3rd millennium BC, perhaps to a few centuries before the construction of Stonehenge I. The Avenues and the stone circles of The Sanctuary were certainly the work of the Beaker Folk,

who probably added them early in the following millennium.

Barbury Castle Hillfort
Iron Age
s of Wroughton **173(SU:149763)**
From the Ridgeway or road s from B4005 towards Burderop Down. Signposted.

An impressive egg-shaped fort of 4.7ha, on the edge of the Marlborough Downs, it has 2 strong ramparts and deep ditches, with an inturned entrance on the w, and an eastern entrance with a curved outer earthwork. From the air, traces of huts and storage pits can be seen inside the fort, and Iron Age jewellery and chariot fittings have been found. Finds in Devizes Museum. The Ridgeway follows the edge of the downs, passing just N of (and below) the fort on its way to Avebury (*qv*).

Battlesbury Hillfort
Iron Age
Warminster **184(ST:898456)**
N of A36; from Sack Hill, 2.4km E of Warminster. Just s of Bratton Castle (qv) and 1.6km NW of Scratchbury (qv).

This ovoid fort of 9.7ha, dominating the Wylye valley, has a double rampart with a ditch in between, and triple defences on the more vulnerable w side. There are entrances on the E and NW, with outworks. Skeletons of men, women and children found outside the E entrance may represent a war cemetery. Storage pits inside the fort have yielded pottery, querns, whetstones, slingstones, animal bones and iron tools. Finds in Devizes Museum.

Barbury Castle Hillfort. *Iron Age*

Bratton Castle Hillfort
New Stone/Iron Ages
SW of Bratton **184(ST:901516)**
Just s of B3098, above Westbury White Horse. Just N of Battlesbury (qv). HBMCE.

A rectangular hillfort of 10ha with superb views, it has a single bank and ditch, but double defences on the more vulnerable E. The entrances at the S and NE have outworks, and the modern road runs through them. Querns and slingstones have been found in the fort, which also contains a New Stone Age long barrow, 70m long and 3.7m high at its E end, where charred human skeletons were found.

The white horse below the fort used to face the other way, but was remodelled in 1778. It may have originated in 878 to celebrate a victory by King Alfred.

Cow Down Round Barrows
Bronze Age
SW of Collingbourne Ducis **184(SU:229515)**
Just sw of junction of A338 and A342. SE of Snail Down (qv).

Thanks to ploughing, vegetation and vehicle tracks, this linear cemetery is not in the best of condition. It comprised 12 bowl barrows and a disc barrow in 2 lines running SW/NE. Many cremations were found in them. Finds in Devizes Museum.

Durrington Walls Henge and Woodhenge Monuments
New Stone Age
Durrington **184(SU:150437; Woodhenge 152432)**
A345 from Netheravon s to Amesbury runs through Durrington Walls. Woodhenge is just w of A345 and the river Avon.

Durrington Walls is an enormous henge, 520m across and 12ha in area. Its flat-bottomed ditch was 6m deep, over 18m wide at the top, and the external bank may have been 27m wide, and is still 1m high. There are entrances on the SE and NW; hundreds of deer-antler picks have been found, including many by the SE entrance, and it has been estimated that the henge must have involved 900,000 man-hours of work. Radiocarbon dates average 1950–2000 BC. Excavation of part of the henge revealed a timber structure just inside the SE entrance, comprising 6 concentric rings of postholes, which was rebuilt several times; its door faced the henge entrance. Further N was another circle of posts and an avenue of postholes leading from it through a horn-shaped façade of timbers. There were no doubt many more such structures inside this henge, and just the larger of the 2 that are known must have used up 3.5ha of natural oak forest. Both of them may have been roofed buildings like the one at Woodhenge. There is little to be seen of the site today. Finds in Salisbury and South Wiltshire Museums.

Woodhenge, 91m to the S, was discovered from the air in 1928. Its ditch, almost 50m in diameter and 1.8m deep, has an external bank, and an entry on the NE. Inside are 6 concentric oval settings of postholes, which are now marked by concrete pillars. It may have been a roofed building with an open centre, or perhaps just a series of decorated posts. A small cairn now marks the spot where a grave was found containing a 3-year-old girl who died of a fractured skull. Some postholes contained useless chalk axes. The site, whose name was given in jest, has produced radiocarbon dates of *c.* 1830 BC, and is therefore slightly later than Durrington Walls. Finds in Devizes Museum.

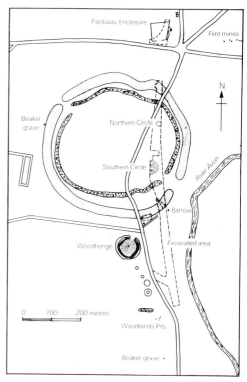

Durrington Walls, Wiltshire (after G. Wainwright)

Figsbury Rings Hillfort
Iron Age
Winterbourne **184(SU:188338)**
Track N from A30. Signposted. National Trust.

This circular fort of 6ha has a single rampart, still up to 4m high and 12.8m wide, and an external v-shaped ditch, over 10m wide and over 4m deep. There are entrances on w and E. An indication inside the fort is clearly unfinished, but it is not known whether it is earlier or later than the fort, which probably dates to the 5th or 4th century BC. It may have been dug to obtain more chalk for the rampart. A second ditch inside. A Bronze Age sword was found here in 1704. Finds in Devizes Museum.

Fyfield and Overton Downs Celtic Fields
Iron Age
Fyfield region **173(SU:142710)**
N of A4, NW of Marlborough. Downs lie within Nature Conservancy Council reserve. National Trust.

In this landscape, one can still see many great sarsen stones, like those used in the prehistoric monuments, scattered over the chalk downs. Rectangular 'Celtic fields' can also be seen, with lynchet banks up to 3m high; and at SU:128715 there is a sarsen that was used for polishing stone axes.

At SU:129706 is the Overton Down experimental earthwork, built in 1960 to study the efficacy of prehistoric tools, and the effects of time and weathering on the mound itself and on materials buried inside it. There are plans to cut through the mound after 2, 4, 8, 16, 32, 64, etc. years.

Giant's Cave Chambered Long Barrow
New Stone Age
SW of Luckington **173(ST:821829)**
W of B4040. SE corner of Badminton Park on Badminton-to-Luckington road.

This trapezoid mound, already ruined in the 17th century, is over 37m long and orientated E/W. It has a limestone revetment, and a V-shaped forecourt at the E end that is a false portal. Two burial chambers were found in the N side, and 2 in the S. The NE chamber contained 3 men, a woman and a child; the NW had 3 men, 2 women and a child at the end of a long passage; the SW had one man, 3 women and 3 children; and the SE had one woman. A fire had been lit in its passage. Another long barrow, in even worse condition, can be seen 225m to the SE (ST:821828).

Knap Hill Causewayed Camp
New Stone Age
NE of Alton Priors **173(SU:121636)**
Footpath from Alton Priors-to-Marlborough road. Nature Conservancy Council.

This pear-shaped camp of 1.6ha, 164m across, is most visible from the road to the N. It occupies a prominent position on a steep scarp above the Vale of Pewsey. It has a single ditch, up to 2.7m deep and 3.5m wide, crossed by 5 causeways; the inner bank is now barely visible. The bottom of the ditch's fill has been radiocarbon-dated to 2760 BC and the upper levels (which contained Beaker sherds) to 1840 BC. There is a round barrow inside, and another outside. There may have been some Iron Age activity here, and there is a small Romano-British enclosure in the NE part of the camp. Legends speak of a treasure on Knap Hill. Finds in Devizes Museum.

Lugbury Long Barrow
New Stone Age
NE of Nettleton **173(ST:831786)**
S of M4. Footpath S from B4039 to Nettleton Green.

This mound, which is over 66m long and orientated E/W, was excavated in the last century. It has a prominent false portal comprising a huge central stone flanked by 2 others; there are 4 chambers on the SE side – no longer visible – 3 of which contained a total of 26 skeletons of all ages, including 10 children. There is a strange legend of a golden wheelbarrow being buried here.

Normanton Down Barrows*
New Stone/Bronze Ages
Wilsford **184(SU:118413)**
S of A303. Near Winterbourne Stoke barrows (qv). From A303, green lane (ancient trackway) to Druid's Lodge on A360. 0.8km SW of Stonehenge (qv). Part HBMCE.

This barrow cemetery, possibly the most important in England and the closest to Stonehenge, stretches for over 1km in a line E/W, and comprises 26 mounds: one long, 12 bowls, 7 discs, 4 bells and 2 saucers. All were opened in the 18th and 19th centuries. The long barrow, 36m long, had 4 skeletons in it at the E end, and a possible mortuary enclosure adjoins it to the S. The mound's ditch has produced material radiocarbon-dated to 2560 BC. Several of the round barrows yielded gold objects, daggers, faïence beads and necklaces of shale and amber. The most spectacular finds, from Bush Barrow (7th from the W), comprised 3 daggers, an axe, a shield, a lozenge-shaped gold plaque on the body's chest, and a remarkable sceptre, or mace, with a fossil rock for a head and bone mounts decorating its shaft. This tomb's occupant was probably a Wessex chieftain, and his grave goods are now in the British Museum, but there are replicas in Devizes Museum, along with the finds from the other mounds.

Oldbury Castle Hillfort
Iron Age
ESE of Calne **173(SU:049693)**
Footpath S from A4 opposite Yatesbury turning.

A triangular fort of 8ha, near the 19th-century Lansdowne obelisk and the 18th-century White Horse of Cherhill, it has 2 strong ramparts and ditches, and 2 entrances on N and SE: the latter is inturned and has extra defences. Another bank crossing the fort from NW to SE suggests that it was extended in size at some time. Storage pits in the fort contained Iron Age pottery. Finds in Devizes Museum.

Old Sarum Hillfort and Castle Mound
Iron Age/Roman/ Medieval
Stratford sub Castle **184(SU:137327)**
Immediately W of A345, 2.4km N of Salisbury centre. HBMCE. standard hours. Guidebook.

Salisbury's predecessor is an oval early Iron Age fort of 11.9ha, with superb views; it has a massive single bank and ditch, and an entrance on the E. Subsequently it was used by the Romans (a building and pottery have been found) and it may be the posting station known as *Sorviodunum*. Finally, the Normans occupied it: the site is dominated by their motte (castle mound), and the outline of their cathedral is marked out in the turf.

Scratchbury Camp Hillfort
Iron Age
N of Norton Bavant **184(ST:912443)**
N of the A36 and the railway. Close to Battlesbury (qv) and Bratton Castle (qv).

A contour fort of 15ha, it has a bank, ditch and counterscarp, with entrances on E, NE and NW. The small round earthwork inside may be an earlier enclosure, as at Yarnbury (qv) and is dated to 350 BC. Seven barrows inside the fort contained cremations, and grave goods of bronze and amber. Strip lynchets can be seen on the hills round the fort. Finds (from barrows) in Salisbury and South Wiltshire Museum and (from fort) Devizes Museum.

Silbury Hill*
New Stone Age
S of Avebury **173(SU:100685)**
Immediately N of A4 between West Kennet (to E) and Beckhampton (to W). HBMCE.

This is the largest man-made prehistoric mound in Europe, comprising 354,000 cu m of chalk. It was built on a sloping spur, so the lowest 7.6m are solid and undisturbed. The base covers 2.2ha, the mound is almost 40m high, and its flat top is over 30m across. Estimates of the labour required are 18 million man-hours – that is, it took 500 workers at least 10 years. Plant remains from its core have yielded a radiocarbon date of 2145 BC.

All efforts to discover its function have failed and few objects have been found: in 1776, Cornish tin miners were brought here to dig a shaft down from the centre of the top, and nothing was found; in 1849 a tunnel was dug to the centre from the base, and side galleries were opened up, but again nothing was found. Finally, in 1968 – 70, a BBC-sponsored tunnel was again dug at the base. Despite the lack of 'finds', this work did provide the date, and showed that the mound was probably built in 4 phases.

Silbury Hill. *The largest artificial mound of prehistoric Europe*

The Roman road from *Cunetio* (Mildenhall, Wilts.) to *Aquae Sulis* (Bath, *qv*) made a detour round its base. There are many theories about the mound's function (e.g. that it was a giant sundial), but most believe that it contains a rich burial. There is a legend that King Sil is buried here, wearing golden armour and sitting on horseback, or in a golden coffin; or that there is a life-size gold figure buried here. Finds in Devizes Museum.

Snail Down Round Barrows   *Bronze Age*
sw of Collingbourne Ducis and
Collingbourne Kingston   **184(SU:218521)**
Path s from A342. Ministry of Defence. Not far from Cow Down (qv *).*

This impressive early Bronze Age cemetery is frequently inaccessible as it is on MoD land – on a firing range – and, in any case, has been badly damaged by tanks. It originally comprised about 30 barrows

forming a rough semicircle; all of the main round types are represented, and they contained both burials and cremations, together with grave goods of the Wessex culture. One bell barrow has been radiocarbondated to 1540 BC. Excavation has revealed evidence of buzzard droppings next to a possible exposure platform. The cemetery seems to have been in use for c. 200 years, and in fact some of the mounds overlie late New Stone Age/Beaker occupation. Finds in Devizes Museum.

Stonehenge Sanctuary ✱   *New Stone/Bronze Ages*
Amesbury   184(SU:123422)
3.2km w of Amesbury by A344, just beyond junction with A303.

Stonehenge, the sanctuary that stands in noble ruin on Salisbury Plain, is a unique work of megalithic architecture, the greatest creation of prehistoric man in all Europe, yet present-day visitors often confess to disappointment. This response is largely due to the blighting effect of mass tourism. There are still many who can remember when one could wander freely among the stones with grassy turf underfoot, but now visitors are barred from the temple area and get what impression they can from a distance. It may not be much comfort to frustrated visitors to know that a full reform of the present arrangements has been promised.

Disappointment is also due to the fact that we are now all familiar with the scale of colossal buildings, hence the frequent plaint: 'Stonehenge is so small.' One must try to imagine the small-scale human world of those who came to it at the time of its completion: to them, the size of Stonehenge would have been as amazing as the first sight of Manhattan to prewar Europeans.

The Stonehenge sanctuary has a constructional history spanning some 7 centuries, roughly the same as that of Westminster Abbey. While it has attracted antiquarian interest since the 16th century (pp. 9 – 10), it was not until Professor R. J. C. Atkinson's excavations of the 1950s that the long story of development and change was pieced together. The following simplified outline is based on his division of the building into three periods.

Stonehenge I was laid out in late New Stone Age times, in about 2200 BC, when Salisbury Plain was already the centre of a prosperous farming people, their main wealth being in cattle and sheep. It consisted of a precisely circular bank at least 1.83m high and a quarry ditch outside it with a much smaller bank round its outer lip. The entrance to this earthwork was to the NE, and outside it, at a distance of some 24m, a massive sarsen block was erected. This is the Heel Stone, now beside the A344, the only unmasoned sarsen in the entire monument. Just

inside the bank, 56 pits were roughly dug in the chalk, then, it seems, very soon refilled, many with cremated human remains in and near them. The present ring of flat concrete markers over these 'Aubrey Holes' (p. 9) gives an appearance of regularity quite alien to the original jagged pits.

This earliest Stonehenge, now so inconspicuous that visitors often ignore it, was a fairly typical 'henge' except that, at 292m across, it is unusually large. It is also uncommon for the principal bank to be inside the ditch.

The second phase – *Stonehenge II* – saw the sanctuary enriched by an undertaking unparalleled in our prehistory. Eighty tall, thin blocks of volcanic rock, now known as the 'bluestones', mostly of diorite but a few of rhyolite and weighing up to 4 tons apiece, were brought from the Preseli mountains of Dyfed to be erected inside the henge in two concentric circles – a distance, as the crow flies, of 217km. The most likely route for the transport of the stones is down from Preseli to Milford Haven (where a chunk of micaceous sandstone, now the 'Altar Stone', was added to their number) along the Welsh coast by raft or dugouts, up the Severn estuary to the Bristol Avon and the Frome, overland to the Wylye and so on via the Wiltshire Avon to their final destination. The other addition made at this time was the 'Avenue', defined by parallel banks with outer ditches, that

Above: **Stonehenge Sanctuary**. *The south-east side of the outer circle with a blue stone and trilithons showing within*

Previous page: **Stonehenge Sanctuary** at dusk

Below: **Stonehenge**, *Wiltshire*

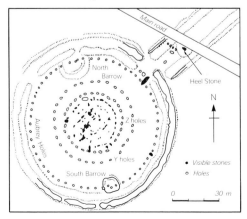

runs from the sanctuary entrance, taking in the Heel Stone, straight down the slope until it swings E and SE (now visible only by air photography) to reach the Avon near West Amesbury House. It is believed that the bluestones were landed at this point and that the Avenue was a ceremonial way made for their final triumphant entry to Stonehenge.

It is very probable that the Beaker Folk were behind this extraordinary enterprise: they knew the Welsh coastal route to Ireland from their interest in gold and other metals, and there is other evidence that they were associated with the bluestone circles. Only a tremendous religious compulsion could have inspired it, and Professor Atkinson's guess is that, for them, Preseli had become a holy mountain, its strange rocks holy stones. The long journey may be dated to the 17th century BC.

With *Stonehenge III*, even more powerful and ambitious rulers now evidently took command and the presence of their richly furnished barrows clustering round Stonehenge makes it almost certain that those responsible for bringing the temple to its final grandeur were the Wessex chieftains (p. 32).

Large numbers of naturally eroded sarsens (grey wethers) still lie on the Marlborough Downs some 38km N of Stonehenge, and it was from here that 80 colossal blocks, weighing from 20 to 50 tons, were to be brought to Stonehenge. Probably roughed out on the spot to the desired shape, they would have been lashed to sledges or cradles and hauled over rollers – perhaps to an assembly point at the Avebury sanctuary. From there, the route was full of difficulties, particularly crossing over the south scarp of the Vale of Pewsey – perhaps at Redhorn Hill. It has been calculated that it would have taken over 1000 men 7 weeks to transport one block and that the total undertaking would have needed 10 years.

On the site, the bluestone circles had been dismantled and the ground levelled, and there was now the tremendous task of shaping the rough sarsens with stone mauls. Again it has been calculated that it would take 50 masons, working a 70-hour week, 2 years and 9 months to shape and smooth both faces of all the uprights and lintels – a perfectionist aim unknown elsewhere in megalithic architecture.

The 30 uprights (about 26 tons each) of the great outer circle at Stonehenge were tipped into and pulled upright in holes 1.22 - 1.52m deep, carefully adjusted to level their tops for the reception of the lintels. These tops were then worked down to leave projecting tenons. Both long sides of the lintels were curved to fit the diameter of the circle, an amazing refinement, and their ends interlocked with tongue-and-groove joints; mortices were sunk on their undersides to fit over the tenons of the uprights. With these devices, the circle was given an overall stability that, in part at least, has withstood the passage, and the human onslaughts, of some 3500 years.

Even more effort went into the inner horseshoe setting of the 5 trilithons, each with 2 uprights supporting a single lintel – again secured with mortice and tenon. These rose in height from the 6m of the outer pair to the 7.3m of the giant central trilithon – though now only 2 trilithons survive intact.

The bluestones, still holy, had to be fitted into the new temple but their disposal was subject to changes of intent. The tallest 22 were shaped and erected inside the sarsen horseshoe on some plan that involved both trilithons and edge-to-edge jointing. The remaining unhewn stones were to be erected in 2 rings outside the sarsen circle, but this was not carried out – instead, the trilithon structure was dismantled and all the bluestones rearranged according to the present plan: a simple horseshoe inside the sarsen trilithons and a circle outside them. Very many of them have been plundered. The Altar Stone, now fallen, seems to have stood at the centre of the bluestone horseshoe.

Since Professor Atkinson's excavations, the dating of Stonehenge has been in dispute. Drawing upon the then accepted date for the Wessex chieftains and their known trading contacts with the Mediterranean, he assigned the sarsen temple to about 1500 BC and bravely suggested that its unique architectural refinement was designed by a Mycenaean Greek architect in the employ either of a supreme Wessex chieftain or of 'some voyaging Mycenaean prince'. Then came the early dates of the adjusted radiocarbon system (p. 14) and dreams of Mycenaeans had to be abandoned: Stonehenge was standing long before their day. More recently, however, further readjustments are making Atkinson's dates look quite possible again, and now some prehistorians are happy to date Stonehenge III to the 15th century BC, and the dagger carved on one of the sarsens can once again be recognized as possibly of Mycenaean type.

There is no reason to doubt that, from the time of Stonehenge II if not before, the temple was aligned on the midsummer sunrise, and perhaps in reverse on the midwinter sunset, or that these events would have been the occasion of great festivals. To these almost certain facts, fancies have been added. The axis is far too inaccurate for precise dates to be based on the eastward creep of sunrise. Nor does the midsummer sun rise exactly over the Heel Stone – and in prehistoric times it would have been even further to the W. In fact, the first gleam will not be exactly over the stone until AD 3260. It is quite possible that the circle was used for observations of the moon or major planets – but there is nothing to prove it.

Stonehenge is at the heart of an area containing many religious monuments: numbers of long and round barrows crown the surrounding downs, notably the King Barrows to the E and Normanton Down (*qv*) to the S. The Stonehenge Cursus, an embanked processional avenue with a long barrow at the E end, runs for nearly 3km to the N of the temple.

Tilshead Old Ditch

Long Barrow *New Stone Age*
SW of Tilshead **184(SU:023468)**
SW of A360. Visible from road from Tilshead SW to Chitterne. Ministry of Defence. Controlled entry.

This fine earthen mound is the longest in England, being 120m in length and 3.4m high, and it has large side ditches. Two primary burials were found here, one of which was a small woman with a cleft skull, on a funeral pyre and under a cairn of flints. Three secondary burials were also found. A second long barrow can be seen by the road at Tilshead Lodge (SU:021475) and the Tilshead White Barrow at SU:033468.

West Kennet Chambered
Long Barrow *
New Stone Age
s of Avebury
173(SU:104677)
s of A4, 0.4km from Silbury Hill (qv). Signposted.
HBMCE. Torch needed. Leaflet available at Avebury.

This great wedge-shaped mound, one of the largest such barrows in Britain, is impressively sited on a hill overlooking Silbury Hill. It is over 100m long, orientated E/W, and 3m high at the E end, where the great restored façade of upright sarsens can be seen, in front of a concave forecourt. Behind this is a passage, now easily accessible, with 2 small chambers on either side. The interior roof is 2.3m high, and the chambers are each roofed by a large capstone and crude corbelling. Several upright stones at the chamber entrances (especially the SW chamber) were used as whetstones for axes. Most of the tomb's stones are local sarsens, but some of the drystone oolite came from up to 32km away.

In 1685 a doctor from Marlborough dug up bones here to use for medicine. Excavation in 1956 found a further 46 burials of all ages from babies to old people: all those over 30 had arthritis, some adults had spina bifida and spondylolisthesis (a congenital spine defect), and the remains displayed many abscesses and fractures. Some skulls and long bones had deliberately been removed. The remains were found disarticulated in the side chambers, mixed with pottery and flints.

After being used for about 1000 years, the tomb was filled to the roof with earth and stones, mixed with potsherds, beads and bone tools. It was at this point (the late 3rd millennium BC) that the entrance was blocked with the great slabs. Finds in Devizes Museum. There is a tradition that, at Midsummer's Day sunrise, a 'ghostly priest with a large white hound' is supposed to visit the site.

Windmill Hill Causewayed Camp *New Stone Age*
SW of Winterbourne Monkton
173(SU:087714)
W of A361 at East Farm, or N from A4 by road from Avebury Trusloe. National Trust. Long walk.

This camp, which gave its name to the earliest Neolithic culture in England, is the largest of its kind, covering 8.5ha, and with a diameter of 360m. It com-

Windmill Hill, Wiltshire (after A. Keiller),
showing the excavated ditches in black

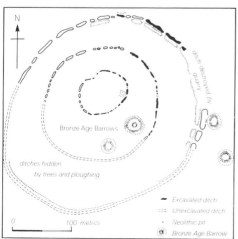

prised 3 irregular concentric ditches, broken by a number of causeways. It has been estimated that 120,000 man-hours would have been required for this work, but it was not a defensive site: rather, a regional focus. The ditches were deliberately filled – the site itself was kept clear – and much pottery (from over 1300 vessels), flints, animal bones and other refuse have been found buried in them, together with hearths, chalk figurines, balls and phalluses as well as human remains, especially long bones. The bottom of the ditch fill has been radiocarbon-dated to 2580 BC, and its upper part (Beaker period) to 1540 BC. The hill was also occupied c. 2960 BC, before the earthworks. Later, a Bronze Age bell barrow was built between the inner and centre ditches, and others form a small cemetery to the E. Finds in Alexander Keiller Museum, Avebury, and Devizes Museum. Little can be seen of the camp from the ground.

Winkelbury Hill Hillfort
Iron Age
Berwick St John
184(ST:952218)
s of Berwick St John.

A triangular promontory fort at the end of a long, narrow, steep-sided spur, it seems to have developed over 3 phases. First, in the early Iron Age (5th–4th century BC), 5ha of the spur were cut off by 2 ramparts and ditches, wide apart. Later, c. 250 BC, a rampart was planned around the edge of the escarpment, but was never finished. Finally, c. 50 BC, a curved rampart and ditch were built, with an entrance at the E end, reducing the fort to an oval of 1.8ha at the end of the spur. Finds in Salisbury and South Wiltshire Museum.

Winterbourne Stoke
Barrows
New Stone/Bronze Ages
NE of Winterbourne Stoke
184(SU:101417)
Around the junction of A303 and A360. Near Normanton Down Barrows (qv). National Trust.

A fine cemetery of barrows in 2 almost parallel rows, it has a long barrow close to the road junction, and the later round mounds are clearly aligned on it. The long barrow, 72m long and 3m high, had a primary male burial at the higher end, and 6 other intrusive burials (a man, a woman and 4 children). To the NE are a bowl, a bell, a pond, another bell and 6 bowl barrows. A parallel line to the W features a bowl, 2 discs, a bowl and 2 ponds. To the NW, on the E side of the A360, is a group of 5 bowls and 2 saucers. Some of the round mounds contained tree-trunk coffins, others cremations, and the Wessex culture grave goods include bronze daggers, beakers, cups, urns and beads. Finds in Devizes Museum.

Yarnbury Castle Fort *
Iron Age
N of Steeple Longford
184(SU:035404)
N of A303, 3.2km W of Winterbourne Stoke. Farm track.

This impressive 1st-century BC fort of 10.5ha is roughly circular, and has 2 enormous banks, 7.6m high, and correspondingly deep ditches, with traces of a 3rd external rampart. There is a formidable inturned entrance on the E, 9m wide, which has complex outworks. Inside the fort is an earlier (7th–5th century?) circular enclosure of 4ha that had a timber-revetted rampart and a deep v-shaped ditch with an entrance on the W. Until 1916 a sheep fair was held by the E entrance, on this early enclosure; the hollows visible here may therefore be traces of the fair. A small triangular enclosure outside the fort on the W may be Roman. Finds in Devizes Museum.

THE SOUTH-WEST

The South-west-comprising Avon, Cornwall, Devon and Somerset-cannot be called a mountainous region, yet it is very much a part of the highland zone of Britain, its structure, its scenery and its natural resources all being founded upon ancient rocks. Although it has no peaks, several areas of Cornwall, Devon and western Somerset are over 300m above the sea, and parts of Dartmoor are over 600. A land offering contrasting scenery of wild, bare uplands, meadows and lush green valleys is bounded by fine rocky cliffs with coves and bays. No one in the peninsula lives very far from the sea, and from early times, its inhabitants have been much affected by maritime movements and trade.

The oldest rock occurs round the promontories of the Lizard in Cornwall and Start Point in Devon, but most of the peninsula consists of Devonian and Carboniferous rocks which, at from 200 to 300 million years old, are geologically middle-aged. What, however, was to have the greatest effect on the landscape and on human settlement was the violent rucking up of the earth's crust that followed Carboniferous (Coal Measure) time. Its effects are preserved in dramatic folding of the rock strata such as can be seen at Hartland Point on the north coast of Devon, but more significantly in the upsurge of molten volcanic rocks, particularly of the great masses of granite forming Dartmoor, Bodmin Moor, Hensbarrow, Land's End and on to the Isles of Scilly. The emanations from the granite produced veins of minerals among the surrounding fractured rocks, roughly in the order of tin nearest to the granite, then copper, zinc, lead and iron. The intense heat of the granite also changed the nature of adjoining rocks, toughening them and making them crystalline.

Here, then, was the source of much of the subsequent prosperity of the South-west. The toughened rocks were to prove ideal for the polished stone axes of the New Stone Age and were to be widely traded (p. 19), while tin and copper brought wealth through the Bronze Age (and thereafter); the Romans exploited the lead of the Mendips. It can be assumed that tin was given in exchange for the splendid gold neck ornaments (*lunulae*) from Ireland dating from the early Bronze Age and now to be seen in Truro museum. The Greek historian, Diodorus, writing in the first century BC, described how the tin was dug, smelted, made into ingots shaped like knuckle bones, and carted to St Michael's Mount whence it was carried by sea and land to the Mediterranean.

The north-east of the peninsula is dominated by Exmoor and the parallel ridges of the Quantocks and Mendips which, though thrown up by the same upheavals, are very different from the granite heights. Exmoor and the forested Quantocks with their heathery summits consist of Devonian sandstone, while the Mendips are totally different again-typical limestone country of bare, pale uplands with scars of naked rock, and channels and caverns where water has dissolved the stone. Cheddar Gorge itself is a long, twisting cavern with its roof fallen in. Between the ridges of the Quantocks and Mendips lie the fen and marshes of the Somerset Levels, significant in that, until recent times, they helped to cut off the peninsula from the rest of southern England. One of the most surprising discoveries of south-western archaeology is the stout corduroy timber trackways that, in the late Bronze Age, men laid across the surface of the marsh.

Its natural attractions of sea, cliffs and sharply varied, unspoiled landscapes make the South-west holiday country. So it is fortunate that to these appeals of nature another can be added: abundant remains of early peoples. There are no such grandiose monuments as those of neighbouring Wessex, but all periods from the Old Stone Age to Roman times are well represented, and in the wilder regions, especially Dartmoor and Bodmin Moor, the wealth of settlements with stone huts, compounds and little fields brings the living conditions of Bronze and Iron Age folk very close.

The South-west is exceptionally well-endowed with cave dwellings of the Old Stone Age, most of them in the limestone of the Mendips, but including the fascinating Hyena Den by Wookey Hole (p. 129) in central Somerset, and Kents Cavern (p. 127), Torquay-the last already occupied far back into the Ice Age (p. 16).

The peninsula began to be settled early in the New Stone Age by farmers making landfalls along the south coast. The causewayed camp at Hembury (p. 127) represents this early settlement. It is, however, the later megalithic tombs that are the best memorial to the age in the South-west. The very finest of them, the elaborate chambered long barrow of Stoney Littleton (p. 115) in Avon, is a southern outlier of the Cotswold group. Of the rest, mostly sited between south-west Devon and Land's End, none is equal to this great gallery grave, but several are striking and picturesque, their denuded chambers, often with huge capstones, standing out in the bare countryside. They include short gallery graves in long mounds, such as towering Trethevy (p. 125) and Lanyon Quoit (p. 121), but in that extremity of England, Penwith, where they are plentiful, the chambers are usually set in round cairns.

Towards the end of the New Stone ·Age, a few henge sanctuaries were built in the South-west–Castilly being the most typical; the Stripple Stones (p. 125) in the middle of Bodmin Moor, because they are embanked, can be called a henge, but may well be of later date. Then there is that most remarkable sacred site of Stanton Drew in Avon (p. 115), with its three stone circles with avenues and a 'cove', which can be likened to the one at Avebury.

The truth is that the Stripple Stones and Stanton Drew expose the difficulty there is in dividing the late Stone Age monuments from those stone circles, stone rows and menhirs that are such a conspicuous feature of the moorlands of the South-west. These, since they are directly related to round barrows, undoubtedly date from the Bronze Age.

The Beaker Folk spread into the peninsula in numbers, though rather late in their history, and it seems that here as elsewhere in southern England they joined with the megalith builders and together their descendants were responsible for raising the stone settings that pattern the moors. Among the best groups of stone rows and avenues leading to round cairns are those of Shovel Down (p. 128) and Merrivale (p. 128), both on Dartmoor.

While small stone circles may accompany the linear settings, a number of free-standing stone circles, large and small, can be seen on Dartmoor and Bodmin Moor, a few on Exmoor and more again in that open-air museum, the Penwith promontory.

In the South-west, the single graves of the Beaker Folk were commonly below small mounds. Most of the larger round barrows of the region were raised after about 1550 BC by a new dominant class, probably a branch of the élite families of the Wessex Chieftains' graves (p. 32). The simple bowl form was preferred for these barrows, but there are a few of the bell and disc varieties. The possessions buried with the dead cannot quite rival those of the Wessex chiefs, yet they reveal considerable wealth, due no doubt to the profits of the tin trade, in ornamental objects of gold, amber, faïence and jet-like Kimmeridge shale. It was at this time that the Irish gold *lunulae* reached Cornwall.

Led by this vigorous aristocracy with its widespread trading connections, descendants of the Stone Age and Beaker peoples were to form a stable society of farmers that changed very little, though improving its equipment, down to the end of the Bronze Age. To this period belong those remains so characteristic of the South-west: settlements marked by 'hut circles' and associated cattle pens. Some of these were quite large villages, and it is easy to imagine the clustering huts when their stone walls supported conical roofs of thatch or turf. They might be open or, like well-known Grimspound (p. 126), protected by stout defences. Such settlements are best seen in the western and southern valleys of Dartmoor.

As in the rest of Britain, fortifications are the principal monuments of the Celtic Iron Age. Celtic-speaking invaders were arriving by the fifth century BC, but they did not at first greatly change the lifestyle of the Bronze Age settlement. It was not until the third century that the Celtic tribesmen, later to be unified under the name of the Dumnonii, began to develop their more bellicose tendencies and constructed hillforts.

It was at about this time, however, that a further incursion of Celts arrived from France, most probably from Brittany, and, in time, effectively Celticized the entire peninsula. Nearly all their settlements, even small homesteads, were fortified, and they raised most of the hill and promontory forts that figure so largely in the Gazetteer. These include really large strongholds such as Hembury (p. 127) and Ham Hill (p. 128) and the distinctive many-ramparted promontory forts of the north Cornish coast, among them the great fort on Trevelgue Head (p. 125) and other smaller but equally strong cliff castles.

For an appreciation of the everyday life of this time, one should go to the Glastonbury Museum and the Somerset County Museum in Taunton where finds from the Glastonbury and Meare lakeside villages can be seen. In the boggy ground the perishable possessions of the villagers were preserved–wood, leather and textiles–as well as quantities of iron tools complete with wooden handles. Pottery and shapely wooden vessels were incised with curvilinear Celtic designs linking them with a school of ornamental metalwork centred on this same region of Somerset.

Many of the Celtic forts and settlements, notably Ham Hill, flourished well into Roman times. This is not surprising since, unlike their neighbours the Durotriges of Dorset, the Dumnonii did not put up much resistance to the Roman conquerors. After the fall of the Dorset hillforts (p. 44), the 2nd Augustan Legion under Vespasian drove on as far as the Exe, the tribal leaders submitted and by AD 48 the conquest of the South-west was virtually complete. A few years later a town was founded at Exeter and became *Isca Dumnoniorum*, the Dumnonian capital, a branch from the Fosse Way (p. 44) linking it with the main road system. Roman merchants began to exploit Mendip lead and silver.

Isca Dumnoniorum went through the usual development of wooden buildings being replaced by stone and town walls being added by the end of the second century, but outside the capital, the canton was to remain relatively backward and little Romanized. There were some villas and other signs of civilized Roman life in east Devon, but in the western peninsula, domestic building is represented only by one rather uncouth little villa at Magor near Camborne. For military architecture, we have to go to Martinhoe (p. 128) and Old Burrow on the Exmoor coast: a pair of stoutly ramparted fortlets probably built for operations against the Silures of South Wales (p. 44).

By far the most interesting monuments to visit are again a speciality of Penwith. These are the villages of 'courtyard' houses of which the best preserved are Chysauster (p. 120) and Carn Euny (p. 116) where, in addition to the curious stone-built dwellings with their outbuildings and fields, there are examples of the unique underground passages known as *fogous*. These very distinctive villages began to be built just before the Roman conquest, but were inhabited until the end of the fourth century. For the rest, most of the Dumnonii maintained their farming life with little change from the prehistoric past except that they made a limited use of coinage and might acquire some Samian ware to set above their own simple crockery.

The administration of the canton from *Isca Dumnoniorum* was beginning to crumble even before the Roman withdrawal from Britain, but there was to follow an age of Celtic twilight before the Saxons completed their conquest of the western peninsula in the ninth and tenth centuries AD. During this time, many of the Dumnonii migrated to Brittany, which is why the Cornish language, a living tongue until recent times, is so closely akin to Breton.

AVON

Aveline's Hole Cave
Dwelling *Old Stone Age*
sw of Burrington **182(ST:476587)**
Beside B3134 in Burrington Combe just beyond 'Rock of Ages'.
This cave was probably a base camp, at the end of the Ice Age, from which its occupants exploited the Mendips. About 400 artifacts have been found – mostly flint tools, but also a barbed bone harpoon – together with 60 seashells for a necklace. The outer chamber was found to contain at least 50 humans, including 2 who were crushed by a roof fall; most of the remains are now lost, but some human bone has given a radiocarbon date of 7164 BC, which is probably associated with occupation in the Middle Stone Age. Finds in University of Bristol Speleological Society Museum.

Bath Roman Baths and *Roman*
Mosaics * **172(ST:751647)**
Baths and museum open in summer, Monday- Saturday 9am-5pm and Sundays 11am-5pm. Admission fee.
The remains of *Aquae Sulis* constitute one of the most impressive Roman monuments in Western Europe, and certainly the best known in Britain after Hadrian's Wall. This small town of only 9.3ha was located at the point where the Fosse Way crossed the Avon, and where there were hot mineral springs.

Being a spa, it had many hostels, but at the end of the 2nd century AD a rampart and ditch were built and, later, a stone wall.

The Great Bath was built in the late 1st century AD and is still a tremendous sight, although now open to the sky. It is 22m long, 8.8m wide and 1.5m deep, surrounded by a colonnade, and has a lead-lined bottom. There is a stone 'diving board' at one end.

The water comes from a deep natural spring at 49°C, and has been found beneficial to rheumatic and scrofulous complaints. There were a number of smaller baths, with water at different temperatures: e.g. one can see a circular bath with hypocaust. The drainage system gradually broke down as the water table rose, causing serious flooding. Finally, the site was abandoned and marsh took over.

The baths were associated with the cult of Sul(is) Minerva, a Celtic goddess, whose Medusa-like head in the famous 'Gorgonhead' sculpture from the temple pediment (now in the Bath Roman Museum) seems to have been combined with that of the Avon water-god. The museum also houses many other interesting finds, including votive offerings by hopeful or grateful bathers. A replica of the temple portico can be seen in the Sydney Gardens behind the Museum of Art, and mosaics can be seen in the basement of the Royal Mineral Water Hospital (enquire at entrance).

Dolebury Hillfort
Iron Age
Just SE of Churchill **182(ST:450590)**
Just E of A38. By footpath between houses on A38 S of Churchill Gate.

This rectangular fort of 7.3ha, in a dominating location with superb views, has a fallen rampart of limestone, with a ditch and counterscarp all around except on the S. There is an inturned entrance on the W. An annexe of 0.4ha at the E end provides additional defence at the easier approach. The site was later used for lead-mining and as a rabbit warren, which may account for the banks inside it. Finds included Iron Age and Romano-British material.

Keynsham Villas and Museum
Roman
(Somerdale) Keynsham **172 (ST:656690 house**
Museum open daily. **& 645693 villa)**

To the west, in a cemetery N of the A4, are the remains of a large villa that is cut by the road. It had up to 50 rooms around a rectangular courtyard, and contained coloured wall plaster and some mosaics. Architectural fragments can be seen to the W of the cemetery chapel, but the best mosaics are now in the museum in the factory, to the E.

Here, a small rectangular house was found in 1922 when the J. S. Fry factory (now Cadbury's) was built. It was 10.7 by 15.5m, and had 6 main rooms including a bath suite. It has now been moved 320m to a position opposite the entrance lodge, where there is a museum.

Stanton Drew Stone Circles
New Stone Age
Stanton Drew **172(ST:601634)**
Signposted in the village. Two circles HBMCE, closed Sundays, admission fee, leaflet; access through Court Farm. Third circle reached through farm.

This site has the biggest stone circle in Britain after Avebury (p. 97), and the site as a whole is a sanctuary comparable to Avebury. It comprises 3 stone circles and a 'cove' of 3 stones.

The central ring – a true circle 113m across – has 27 of its original 30 stones, though only 3 are still upright. It is flanked by 2 ellipses: that to the NE is 30m across, and has 8 stones, 4 of them standing; that to the SW has 11 fallen stones, and is on private land. All of these stones are massive unshaped blocks of sandstone, limestone or conglomerate, and come from a variety of sources. To the NE of the central and NE rings are the remains of 2 stone avenues that joined together just beyond the NE ring and probably continued on to the river Chew. Across the river, and 360m NNE of the great circle, is a fallen sarsen stone, 2.1m long, called Hautville's Quoit.

The 'cove', beyond the SW ring, is by the Druid's Arms Inn and the churchyard; 2 of its stones are still standing. There are 2 alignments at the site: the first involves the cove and the central and NE rings; the second involves the SW and central rings and Hautville's Quoit.

'Stanton' means 'stones farm' (or village), while Drew was the name of a 13th-century family here. The stones are said to be countless, and it is not possible to move them; if one tries, one is struck dead on the spot – or at least becomes very ill! According to tradition, they are a wedding party turned to stone because, thanks to the Devil's hypnotic fiddle-playing, they danced into Sunday morning. The 3 stones of the cove are supposed to be the parson, bride and bridegroom.

Stokeleigh Promontory Fort
Iron Age
NE of Long Ashton **172(ST:559733)**
Immediately NW of Clifton Suspension Bridge. Overlooks Clifton Gorge. National Trust.

This triangular fort of 3ha was protected by the Avon Gorge on the NE, by the Nightingale valley on the S, and by a triple curving rampart at the landward side. It is now covered by beech woods. The outer bank is slight, but the massive inner bank of dumped limestone is up to 9m high. There was an entrance gap at the NW corner. Excavation has shown that it was built in the late 3rd century BC, and occupied till the mid-1st century AD. There was some further use in the 3rd, but the site was abandoned by AD 400.

Stoney Littleton Chambered
Long Barrow
New Stone Age
SW of Wellow **172(ST:559733)**
Signposted. Key from farm. Small fee. HBMCE. Leaflet. Torch needed. 0.8km uphill walk across fields.

One of the finest such barrows in Britain, it is a wedge-shaped mound 32m long, and orientated NW/SE. The broad SE end has a funnel-shaped forecourt, and the entrance is noteworthy for its enormous lintel, and for the fine ammonite impression in one door jamb. A narrow passage, only 1.2m high in places and 14.6m long, has 3 pairs of chambers leading off it, and ends at a terminal chamber. All of the interior is of drystone, with a corbelled roof. The total number of burials here is unknown, but some burned human bones have been found in the chambers. Finds, and two skulls, are in the Bristol City Museum. The tomb was restored in 1858.

Worlebury Camp Hillfort
Iron Age
Weston-super-Mare **182(ST:315625)**
By road from Weston or Worlebury. Signposted.

This impressive fort of 4ha was defended by sea cliffs at N and W, by a single rampart and ditch on the steep S side, and by 2 stone ramparts – still over 3m high – and no less than 5 ditches on the vulnerable, level E side. Inside, and especially on the E, can be seen the traces of nearly 100 rock-cut storage pits, some of them 1.5m deep. Finds here include pottery, charred grain and iron spearheads. Skeletons were found in 18 pits and, in the site as a whole, about 100 people have been found. Some bore signs of violence, such as sword cuts on the skulls, which show that the fort was attacked, by Belgic invaders or the Romans. Finds in Weston-super-Mare Museum and Somerset County Museum, Taunton.

***Stanton Drew Stone Circles**, Somerset (after L. V. Linsell)*

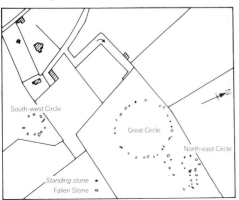

CORNWALL

Carn Brea Hillfort
New Stone/Iron Ages
sw of Redruth
203(SW:685407)
Road N to the hilltop from Carnkie. Lies between castle and Sir Francis Basset monument.

The earliest occupation on this granite ridge was a Neolithic enclosed village at the E end, which has been given radiocarbon dates of 3109 – 2687 BC. Some huts were found in it, and hundreds of arrowheads, many of them broken, indicating that the site was attacked.

The great Iron Age hillfort, probably dating from the early 1st century AD, covers 15ha, and was apparently built in 3 stages. It had 2 strong ramparts round the s and single defences on the N, still well preserved here and there, which were faced with stone slabs; the simple entrance had guard chambers. Several hut circles have been traced inside; the occupants probably traded in tin and copper ores, and a hoard of Kentish Celtic gold coins was found here in the 18th century. A 12th-century medieval castle now caps the E summit, and to the w is the Basset monument. Finds in Truro Museum and the Ashmolean Museum (Oxford).

Carn Euny Village and Fogou
Iron Age
sw of Sancreed
203(SW:403288)
Five-minute walk NNW from Brane. Just E of lane. Many tumuli and standing stones in vicinity, including Chapel Euny (qv). HBMCE. Signposted. Admission fee. Leaflet.

Although there was some New Stone and Bronze Age occupation here, the site is a remarkable restored Iron Age village, where timber huts were replaced by stone by the 1st century BC. One can see courtyard houses, like those at Chysauster (*qv*), with floors of clay and beaten rock, containing hearths, postholes and drains with stone covers. There is also a deep clay-lined pit for grain. The occupants were clearly farmers, stockbreeders and perhaps traders in tin. The site was occupied into the 1st century AD.

The most striking structure, which is in the centre of the village (not a typical position), is the *fogou*, an underground passage 20m long. This souterrain was built by lining a deep, wide trench with stone slabs, and then putting a corbelled roof over it, which was then covered with earth to form a low mound. One end is joined to a hut, the other has a narrow passage and a doorway. This *fogou* is unique in having a circular side-chamber (with a corbelled roof) at one end. Opinions differ as to the function of these structures – cattleshed, cold-store, hiding place or ritual – and, of course, they could have served all these purposes. Finds in Penzance and Truro museums.

Carn Gluze (or Gloose) Barrow
Bronze Age
St Just
203(SW:355312)
Lane wsw from St Just. Signposted from mine chimney. HBMCE.

Also known as Ballowal Barrow, this complex structure is an oval, double-walled cairn, 11m by 9m, built over a T-shaped pit cut 2m down into the rock, with rough steps leading into it, and with 4 small stone cists around it: these contained small Middle Bronze Age pots. The walls of the cairn are still 3.6m high; it had another ring of stone cists around it, one

of which can be seen, and a wall 1.5m high was built round the whole thing. Finally, an entrance grave was inserted on the SW; it had a paved floor covering burned human bones and Middle Bronze age pottery. Finds in Truro Museum and the British Museum. According to tradition, the fairies dance here.

Castle Dore Hillfort
Iron Age & later
w of Golant
200(SX:103548)
NE of Tywardreath. Just E of B3269, between Lostwithiel and Fowey.

A fine small circular fort of 0.5ha, it has double banks of earth, stone and turf – still up to 2m high, though overgrown – and v-shaped ditches, with a wide entrance on the E. It is thought to have been built c. 200 BC, but the elaborate inturned wooden gateways were installed c. 50 BC. Hut circles are known inside the fort. It was abandoned at the end of the 2nd century, but reoccupied in the 5th, when 2 great rectangular timber halls were built. Legend associates the site with King Mark of Cornwall, and with the story of Tristan and Isolde. Finds in Truro Museum.

Chapel Euny Chambered Barrow
(Brane Entrance Grave)
Bronze Age
Just sw of Brane
203(SW:402282)
From Brane hamlet to Brane Farm for entry pass. National Trust. Near Carn Euny (qv).

A typical example of this region's entrance graves, it comprises a mound 6m in diameter and 2m high, with a kerb of stones and a stone-lined passage on the SE leading to a chamber. The latter is 2m by 1m, still 2m high, and roofed by 2 big capstones.

Chun Castle Hillfort *
Iron Age
s of Morvah
203(SW:405339)
Signposted sw from Bosullow Common. 100m E of Chun Quoit (qv).

This small round fort, 85m across, is impressive despite the extensive robbing of its stone for such projects as the paving of Penzance streets. Dating to the 3rd/2nd century BC, it has a double drystone rampart of granite, still up to 2.7m high in places, with external ditches. The entrance on the sw is flanked by stone gateposts. Inside, several round Iron Age huts underlie rectangular 6th-century AD huts. There is a blocked-up well on the NW. Smelting pits in the fort have produced tin slag (one cake weighed 5.4kg). Features resembling pulpits in the main rampart are the traces of Methodist services here in the last century. Finds in Truro and Penzance museums.

Chun Quoit Chambered Tomb *
New Stone Age
Morvah
203(SW:402340)
Just w of Chun Castle (qv). Many settlements and standing stones in vicinity. Close to Lanyon Quoit (qv). Uphill walk.

A splendid sight on open moorland, this chamber, 1.8m square, of 4 huge slabs capped with a stone 2.4m square, is all that remains of the tomb. Its round barrow was 10.7m across.

Carn Euny Village and fogou. *Iron Age settlement*

Chun Castle Hillfort. *Iron Age fort with circular and rectangular huts*

Above: *Chysauster Village*. *Iron Age and Roman village: a courtyard house*

Right: *The Hurlers Stone Circles*. *Bronze Age*

Chysauster Village *   *Iron Age/Romano-British*
N of Madron   **203(SW:472350)**
N of Penzance, SW of Nancledra. Signposted NW from Badgers Cross. Rough climb. HBMCE. standard hours. Admission fee. Leaflet. Many tumuli and standing stones in vicinity.

A compact and well-preserved Iron Age village, it has 4 pairs of courtyard houses along a street, with entrances facing away from the prevailing wind, and a couple of outliers. The houses are small ovals, built of stone; they are about 27m long, with passages up to 6.7m long leading into open courtyards 8–9m across. There are tiny rooms in the thickness of the wall, and the main room has a socket hole, covered by a flat stone. Presumably this held the post that supported some sort of roof. The floors are well paved, and there are open hearths, covered drains and stone grinding-basins. Hand-grinders and pottery have been found, and each house had a terraced garden. There is a ruined *fogou* (souterrain) just to the S.

Chysauster, which dates from 100 BC to the 3rd century AD, was overgrown until excavated in the last century; and Methodist preachers used it for their open-air services. Finds in Penzance and Truro museums, and the British Museum.

Halligye Fogou *   *Iron Age*
S of Mawgan   **203(SW:714239)**
From B3293 by side road NE from Garras. Footpath uphill from edge of wood. Torch needed.

The finest *fogou* (souterrain) in Cornwall, it was associated with a small fortified homestead, now disappeared, which dated from the 1st century BC to the 3rd century AD. Part of the *fogou* was under the inner of the homestead's 2 ramparts, and its exit in the ditch therefore constituted a 'secret entrance'. It is T-shaped, 16.5m long, with walls and roof of stone slabs. One stone just inside the passage may have been a device to trip strangers.

Harlyn Bay Cemetery *Iron Age*
Harlyn Bay **200(SW:877753)**
s of road through Harlyn. Small admission charge.
Open during the day except Fridays and Saturdays.

This site is of importance because Iron Age burials are rare, and over 100 were found here in 1900, buried under 4.6m of drifted sand. Each was a cist, a rectangular hole lined with upright slabs of slate; a crouched skeleton lay in each accompanied by Iron Age jewellery (bronze rings, pins, etc.) of the 4th and 3rd centuries BC. The bodies were covered by slate slabs. Five graves were preserved under glass, and there was a small private museum, but in recent years the graves have been covered over, and the museum closed. There is a legend that this stretch of road is haunted.

The Hurlers Stone Circles *Bronze Age*
Just w of Minions **201(SX:258714)**
NW of village. Track from carpark. HBMCE.

Three circles of granite stones stand, almost touching, in a line NE/SW on Bodmin Moor. The s circle, 32m across, has 9 surviving stones; the central egg-shaped ring, 41m across, has 17, with a fallen stone in its centre; and the N circle, 33.5m across, has 13 stones. Each circle originally had 25 – 30 stones, all carefully dressed and erected so that their tops were more or less level. the central ring had a 'floor' of granite crystals, and the N one was paved with granite slabs; they were joined by a paved pathway, 2m wide. There are 2 standing stones, the Pipers, 120m wSw of the central ring; and over 20 round barrows exist within a radius of 2km, including (0.4km NE of the N circle) Rillaton Barrow (SX:260719), on the summit of a ridge, which contained the famous gold cup, now in the British Museum.

The site's name comes from a legend that the stones in the circles are men turned to stone for hurling a ball on the Lord's Day. The stones are supposed to be uncountable.

Lanyon Quoit Chambered
Long Barrow *New Stone Age*
NW of Madron **203(SW:430337)**
NW of Penzance. Immediately E of minor road NW from Madron. Signposted. Behind high wall. Close to Chun Quoit (qv). National Trust.

Also known as Giant's Quoit or Giant's Table, since a giant's bones are said to have been found in it, the tomb is next to the road. Its mound, 27m long, has gone, and the stones of the chamber at its N end collapsed during a storm in 1815. It was restored in 1824, but one of the uprights broke, and only 3 were re-used.

Lanyon Quoit Chambered Long Barrow. *Exposed chamber of the New Stone Age barrow*

Trethevy Quoit Chambered Tomb. New Stone Age

Merry Maidens Stone Circle
Bronze Age
SE of St Buryan   **203(SW:433245)**
Just s of B3315. Lay-by 0.8km to E of it. Other standing stones in vicinity.

This superb true circle, 24.4m in diameter, of 19 regularly spaced blocks of local granite, each about 1.2m high, has a well-defined entrance on the NE; they were dressed to make their tops level and flat. The site's name (like its Cornish name, *Dans Maen*, 'stone dance') is derived from the tale that these are 19 maidens turned to stone for dancing on a Sunday. The pipers were also petrified, and can now be seen as 2 stones, 4/4.5m high, some 400m to the NE (SW:435248); they may be aligned with the circle, but cannot be seen from it, and there is no archaeologically proved connection. There is a legend that the circle's stones cannot be moved; attempts to do so have failed, and the cattle used for the purpose have fallen down and died.

Just to the SW (SW:430244) is the Tregiffian burial chamber, which contained cremations and an urn, and is worth visiting for the big cup-marked stone by the entrance (the original is in the Museum of the Royal Institution of Cornwall, Truro, but a replica can be seen at the site).

Mulfra Quoit Chambered Tomb
New Stone Age
N of Madron   **203(SW:452353)**
Footpath w from the Penzance-Porthmeor road. Short uphill walk.

Also known as Giant's Quoit, this small rectangular chamber on the moors has a fallen capstone which leans against its 3 supports. There are traces of a round mound, 12m across.

Porthmeor Village
Romano-British
SW of Zennor   **203(SW:434371)**
Path s from B3306. Permission from Porthmeor Farm.

Dating to the 1st to the 5th centuries AD, this collection of 7 circular huts and 2 courtyard houses is surrounded by a wall. Lower down the hill is a second enclosure with one courtyard house and a fine *fogou* (now roofless) that has a passage 5.8m long, 1.5m wide, that leads to a curved corridor, some 7.3m long.

Rough Tor Hut Circles, Hillfort, Stone Circle *
Bronze/Iron Ages
NE of St Breward   **200(SX:141815)**
Bodmin Moor. Road ESE from Camelford, signposted Rough Tor. Part National Trust.

This summit was incorporated in the defences of a small hillfort that had double stone walls on the w, but only a single wall on the steep E side. Inside it can be seen the traces of hut circles: others, with small enclosures and fields, can be seen scattered for 0.8km along a track on the NW slope. Undated, but probably Late Bronze Age/Iron Age, 1000-700 BC. Nearly (SX:144800) is the ellipse of Fernacre, comprising about 52 small granite stones, 39 of them still standing.

The Rumps Cliff Fort
Iron Age
Pentire Point, NW of St Minver   **200(SW:934810)**
N of Trebetherick. Road from Pentireglaze to Pentire Farm. Then signposted path. National Trust.

A fine promontory fort of 2.4ha, with superb coastal views, it has 2 headlands with a shallow bay in between in the area protected by its triple ramparts and ditches. The central defences are still impressive: the rampart had front and rear stone revetments, and the ditch was broad and deep. There were 2 strongly defended entrances. Some round huts have been found inside, and pottery suggests occupation in the 1st century BC and the 1st century AD. Trade is shown by fragments of wine amphorae from the Mediterranean.

Stripple Stones Henge
New Stone Age?
NE of Blisland   **200(SX:144752)**
Bodmin Moor, Hawks Tor. SW of St Breward. Minor track NW from A30 towards Bradford, and footpath up past Trippet Stones.

This ruined circle henge (NW of Bodmin Moor) has an outer bank, 68m in diameter, and an internal ditch. Inside is an irregular circle of 15 stones, 44.6m across; only 4 are still standing, since their holes are shallow, and there is a large fallen slab at the centre.

The entrance, on the SW, faces the Trippet Stones, 1.2km away (SX:131750), which have 8 upright and 4 fallen granite slabs, the remains of a circle of 33m diameter, said to be maidens turned to stone for dancing on the Sabbath.

Treen or Treryn Dinas
Cliff Fort
Iron Age?
E of St Levan   **203(SX:398220)**
Footpath SE from Treen, signposted to Logan Rock. National Trust.

Also known as Giant's Castle, this promontory is defended by massive outer and inner ramparts, with 3 smaller banks in between. Two hut foundations can be seen just inside the entrance; unexcavated. According to tradition, the key is kept by a giant in a holed rock called the Giant's Lock. Inside the fort is Logan Rock, a large rocking stone.

Trethevy Quoit Chambered
Tomb*
New Stone Age
Just NE of St Cleer   **201(SX:259688)**
N of Tremar. Take lane N from Tremar to Darite; behind cottages. HBMCE.

Also known as the Giant's House, this is the most impressive portal dolmen in the region. Its oval mound has disappeared since the last century, but the chamber survives, 4.6m high, divided by a huge cross stone, with a fragment broken off to leave space for a body to be inserted. The massive capstone, 3.7m long, has a hole through it, and rests on 7 uprights.

Trevelgue Head Cliff Fort
Iron Age
Newquay   **200(SW:825630)**
NW of St Columb Porth. Footpath beside putting green.

This superb promontory fort with fine views must have been virtually impregnable since it was defended by 6 ramparts and ditches. In addition, the sea cut into the promontory and made it into a tidal island; there are triple defences to either side of this sea-cleft. Traces of circular huts can be seen on the promontory, which was already important in the

Trevelgue Head Cliff Fort. Iron Age

Bronze Age (bronze-smelting, and 2 large round barrows). It was occupied until the early Middle Ages, and Mediterranean amphorae have been found in a Roman hut inside. Finds in Truro Museum.

Warbstow Bury Hillfort
Iron Age?
Warbstow **190(SX:202908)**
E & s of A39, NE of B3262.

This fort has extensive views all around except to the sw, and consists of a double bank with a ditch in between, and an extra intermediate bank on the flatter, more vulnerable sw. The inner rampart is 4.4m high, and has entrances on the NW and SE. A long low mound can be seen w of the fort's centre.

Zennor Quoit Chambered Tomb *
New Stone Age
Zennor **203(SW:469380)**
Footpath s from B3306 opposite house called 'Eagles Nest'.

This tomb's mound, 12m across, has now gone, but the chamber remains, a rectangle of 5 stones, plus a huge fallen capstone, 5.5m across. There was a straight façade at the E, 2 uprights with a gap between leading to a small antechamber. Also known as Giant's Quoit, it is said to have been erected by a giant, and to be immovable. It is also said that, if the stones are moved, they will return of their own accord.

DEVON

Blackbury Castle Hillfort
Iron Age
sw of Southleigh **192(SY:187924)**
Immediately s of road that goes SE from the B3174 to join the A3052 at Hangman's Stone. HBMCE.

An oval fort of 2.6ha, located near the coast, it has a single dump rampart and a v-shaped ditch. The entrance on the s had a roadway 61m long, and a strong gate with big postholes. The roadway leads to a triangular outer enclosure that may have been for corralling animals. There is sparse evidence of occupation, but one hut was found to contain many slingstones. Finds in Rougemont House Museum, Exeter.

Broad Down Barrows *
Bronze Age
sw of Farway **192(SY:147963 to 174937)**
Along B3174 between Hare and Hounds (to NW) and Broad Down (to SE).

A remarkable linear cemetery of about 60 bowl barrows, although many are now destroyed or overgrown. Their dimensions vary, and they cluster in groups. Some are known to have contained cremations. There is a possible henge at SY:161955 in dense woods – it is a low circular earthwork, 61m across, with an external ditch but no visible entrance. Finds in Rougemont House Museum, Exeter.

Chapman Barrows and Long Stone
Bronze Age
N of Challacombe **180(SS:695435; Long Stone 705431)**
E of lane from Parracombe on to Parracombe Common. There are many other tumuli, but circles and standing stones in the area.

A fine linear cemetery of 10 mounds goes N/W across the end of the ridge; their dimensions vary. The Long Stone, 450m to the SE, is a thin (15cm) slab, 2.7m high. According to tradition, fiery dragons are often seen here.

Clovelly Dykes
Iron Age?
sw of Clovelly **190(SS:311235)**
N of A39 and w of the B3237 turning into Clovelly. Permission from East Dyke Farm.

This complex of widely spaced enclosures is located at the junction of 3 ridgeways. It is thought to be an Iron Age stock-rearing site.

Corringdon Ball Chambered Long Barrow
New Stone Age
NW of South Brent, Dartmoor **202(SX:669614)**
Footpaths from South Brent. Many other stone rows, settlements and cairns in this area.

This pear-shaped mound, 40m long and 20m wide, is orientated SE/NW, and has a ruined stone chamber of large stones at the wider and higher SE end. The Corringdon Ball stone rows stand 0.4km to the w (SX:666612) and comprise small stones, now overgrown. One row, 152m long, is aligned on a mound of stones, and to the SE of this is a ruined ring barrow which has 2 triple rows aligned on it.

Countisbury Promontory Fort
Iron Age?
E of Lynton, Exmoor **180(SS:741493)**
On Wind Hill, 1.6km E of Lynton, above Lynmouth Bay.

This promontory, 1.6km in length, is defended by the sea to the N, the river Lyn to the s, and on the E by a huge rampart, 9m high and 0.4km long, with an external ditch. There is a single entrance.

Exeter City Walls
Roman
Exeter **192(SX:923925)**

The first installation here was a 15ha legionary fortress for Vespasian's 2nd Legion, and dates from 55 – 60 AD. Work on the town, *Isca Dumnoniorum*, began in c. 75. The cantonal town of the Dumnonii, the Roman capital of the sw region, it covered 37ha, and had a grid of streets, stone houses, a forum and basilica, baths, and defensive walls: the town wall, of dark purplish stone, dates to the late 2nd century, and was 3m thick and 6m high. Fragments of it can be seen at the base of medieval walls, especially around Northernhay and Southernhay. Finds can be seen in the Rougemont House Museum in Castle Street.

The town, located on the Fosse Way, was in decline by the late 4th century, but occupation persisted until the 7th.

Grimspound Walled Settlement
Bronze Age
w of Manaton, Dartmoor **191(SX:701809)**
Signposted on track turning s from B3212 at Shapley Common; cairns, hut circles, settlements and field systems, and stone rows in the area.

Named after Grim, a mythical figure, this enclosure of 1.6ha seems to have been a cattle-farming set-

Clovelly Dykes. *The wide-spaced banks of this hillfort were probably designed for the control of cattle*
(Cambridge University Collection of Air Photographs)

tlement, and probably dates from 1000–800 BC. The outer granite wall has been restored, and is now 3m wide and over 1m high. Inside can be seen the remains of over 20 stone hut circles (in the centre and on the s), of some supposed cattle pens (on the w) and some 'storage huts' (on the N). The living-huts have stone door jambs, hearths or cooking holes, and a stone in the centre as the base for a roofpost. Some had raised areas that may be sleeping benches. The enclosure has an entrance on the SE, with a paved approach, and a spring at its lower end.

Hembury Hillfort * *New Stone/Iron Ages/Roman*
NE of Payhembury **192(ST:113031)**
Immediately N of A373, NW of Honiton. Short steep path.

This plateau, dominating much lowland terrain as far as Dartmoor, was first occupied by a Neolithic causewayed camp at its s tip: there are 8 stretches of flat-bottomed causewayed ditch, about 2m deep, with traces of a rampart on the s side, and of an oval hut inside. Hearths have been found, and pits with cereals, querns, pottery and 600 scrapers. Radiocarbon-dating suggests a brief occupation (3330–3150 BC). Nothing of the period is visible at the site.

After a long period of abandonment, the triangular 3ha Iron Age fort was built: it started with 2 palisades and a small fort, later replaced by triple banks/ditches to the N and w, but only double on the E. There are entrances to the w and N, each gateway approached by a long passage. Later, 2 banks were built across the centre, and the N part seems to have been used for human occupation, the s as a cattle pound. No huts have been found, but many slingstones were discovered. According to legend, the defence of the hillfort was left to the women, who welcomed the enemy, took them to bed and stabbed them.

Recent excavation in the E part revealed that the Roman military used about half the fort, which was probably empty when they arrived in *c.* AD 50. It was a useful site, being near the Fosse Way, and they rebuilt the w gate and erected some big timber structures. Ironworking took place, but after a brief occupation, the buildings were dismantled, with upright posts being sawn off at ground level.

Finds in Rougemont House Museum, Exeter.

Kents Cavern
Cave-dwelling *Old Stone Age*
Torquay **202(SX:934641)**
Ilsham Road, signposted off Babbacombe Road.

One of the most important inhabited caves of this period in Britain, it had remains of the Lower Palaeolithic (pre-Neanderthal) period, the Middle Palaeolithic (Neanderthal period) and, especially, the Upper Palaeolithic, as well as traces of periodic use from the Middle Stone Age to medieval times. Bones were found of animals such as mammoths, woolly rhinos, cave bears, hyenas and lions. The earliest use can be estimated at 100,000 BC, but the Upper Palaeolithic material has been radiocarbon-dated to 26770/26210 BC and 12325/10230 BC. During these periods it was a base camp, and the horse was the main animal used at the end of the Ice Age. From here, the occupants could exploit both the Teign and Dart valleys. Tools of this period comprised hundreds of flint implements–including 'laurel leaf' blades–and 3 harpoons, a bone needle and an ivory rod. Excavation was begun in the 1820s by a Catholic priest, but he could not publish his results until much later because they clashed with contemporary religious belief. Finds in Museum of the Torquay Natural History Society (Babbacombe Road), and in the Natural History Museum, London.

Lakehead Hill Stone Cists   *Bronze Age*
NE of Princetown   **191(SX:644774)**
Take B3212 NE from Princetown, and minor road SE
to Bellever; then up footpath w through woodland.
There are other cairns and settlements in the area.
   There are 3 stone cists here: at SX:645776 is a great
stone rectangle above ground, surrounded by a cairn
circle, 7.6m across, of 6 stones; a row of 11 stones
curves 13m down the hill to the E. This monument
was restored in 1895. At SX:643777 is another rectangular cist, while that at the main reference above
is at the centre of a kerb circle, 6m across.
   On the N of a clearing in woodland (SX:644782) is
a pound enclosing hut circles.

Martinhoe Fortlet   *Roman*
Martinhoe, Exmoor   **180(SS:663494)**
N from village towards sea, or steep cliff path
between Woody Bay and Heddon's Mouth.
   There was a Roman signal station at the cliff edge
here, facing the Bristol Channel, but little can be
seen today. The fortlet was designed for a *centuria* of
80 men, who would have policed the Silures in South
Wales, and dates from AD 60-75. It had double ramparts and ditches, with the entrance on the N facing
the sea. An outer rampart and ditch, 21m beyond
these, had an entrance facing S. Excavation found
wooden barrack blocks, field ovens and a furnace.
The fort was probably abandoned when the
Caerleon fortress made it redundant. Finds in Athen-
aeum Museum, Barnstaple.

Merrivale Stone Rows and
Other Monuments*   *Bronze Age*
Princetown, Dartmoor   **191(SX:553746)**
NW of Princetown, immediately s of B3357, just E of
Merrivale village. Within sight of road.
   Three of Dartmoor's 60 stone rows can be seen
here: 2 doubles running E/W, and a single. That nearest the road is 180m long, and contains about 160
small stones, with a blocking stone at the E end. The
second, 27m further S, is a 264m row of over 200
stones, and also has a blocking stone on the E. Halfway along its length is a round cairn in a circle, 3.6m
across. To the SE of it is a large stone cist, and W of that
is a cairn from which the 3rd row, of a few stones,
runs 43m to the SW.
   South of the rows, and 360m S of the road, is a circle, 19m across, of 11 surviving small stones. Near it
can be seen a 3.2m standing stone. The site is also
known as Potato Market or Plague Market, because
trading took place here when the plague raged in
Tavistock.

Prestonbury Castle Hillfort   *Iron Age?*
Drewsteignton, Dartmoor   **191(SX:746900)**
s of minor road from Drewsteignton SE to Preston.
   A strategic fort dominating the Teign (together
with that across the valley at Cranbrook Castle,
SX:738890), it is an oval of 1.2ha with strong triple
defences, an entrance on the E, and 2 annexes on the
NE. Unexcavated. Cranbrook is far bigger (5.3ha), but
has a single rampart and ditch, with entrances on SW
and SE, and is also undated.

Shovel Down Stone Rows   *Bronze Age*
SW of Gidleigh, Dartmoor   **191(SX:660860)**
Road w from Chagford to Teigncombe and
Batworthy. Footpath up Shovel Down.
   This area is a complex of stone circles, rows, cairns
and standing stones. On the N, near Batworthy, can be
seen 2 double rows of small stones, which lead to (or
from) a cairn with a cist at its centre. From here,
another double row runs 120m SE to another cairn,
and has a blocking stone at its S end. The tallest stone,
known as the Longstone, is 3.2m high. Further S,
another double row leads to a standing stone, 1.5m
high, which is all that remains of a trio called the
Three Boys. Another 100m to the SE is a stone cist.

SOMERSET

Cheddar Cave Dwellings   *Old Stone Age*
Cheddar   **182(ST:466539)**
By B3135 along the Cheddar Gorge.
   Cheddar Gorge contains several caves known to
have been occupied by humans towards the end of
the last Ice Age. *Soldier's Hole*, in the SE face and 46m
above the floor of the gorge, had flint work of the
'Solutrean' period, c. 30,000 BC. It was also used in the
New Stone and Bronze Ages and Roman period. *Flint
Jack's Cave* (ST:463538) at the SW end of the gorge
had a quantity of flint work. But the major site is
Gough's Cave, probably a base camp for exploiting
the Mendips, which yielded over 7000 flint blades,
and 2 perforated 'batons', one of them made from a
human arm bone, and an incised bone that may have
been a tally stick. These finds date from c. 25,000 -
10,000 BC, but the famous skeleton of 'Cheddar Man',
found in 1903, has been radiocarbon-dated to only
7130 BC. There was also occupation in Iron Age and
Roman times. Finds from here and Soldier's Hole are
in the small site museum; those from Flint Jack's Cave
are in the Weston-super-Mare Museum and the British Museum.

Cow Castle Hillfort   *Iron Age?*
SE of Simonsbath   **180(SS:795374)**
Take minor road SW from Simonsbath to Blue Gate,
then track ESE to Horsen Farm, and footpath to ford
0.4km SE of fort. Or footpath SE from Simonsbath
along river Barle. 2km walk.
   This isolated oval fort of 1.2ha is beautifully situated on a hill overlooking the junction of the Barle
and White Water. It has a single stone rampart, still
almost 2m high, and 2 possible entrances on the NE
(where traces of an outer rampart can be seen) and
the SE (a small upright stone here may be part of a
gateway). It is said to have been built by fairies for
protection against the earth spirits.

Ham Hill Hillfort*   *Iron Age/Roman*
s of Stoke Sub Hamdon   **193(ST:484164)**
Minor road SE from Stoke sub Hamdon to
Odcombe runs through the fort.
   There was occupation here in the Bronze Age, but
by AD 43 this vast L-shaped fort of 85ha (with a circumference of 4.8km) was probably a great tribal
centre of the Durotriges. It has double bank/ditches,

South Cadbury Castle. The site was occupied in Stone Age and Saxon times, but the ramparts are principally Iron Age

with extra defences on the NE and SW, and inturned entrances on the SE and NE. There is a rectangular annexe on the S, a triangular one on the N. Finds include chariot parts, currency bars, coins, an infant burial in a stone cist, and a cremation in a pit including an iron dagger. The NW corner had a possible war cemetery, and certainly Roman military equipment has been found on the site. There was a large Roman villa just to the E. The fort has been much damaged by quarrying for the fine, honey-coloured 'Ham limestone', used in thousands of buildings. Finds in Somerset County Museum, Taunton, and the British Museum.

South Cadbury Castle
Hillfort*   *New Stone Age/Saxon*
South Cadbury   **183(ST:628252)**
Just SW of South Cadbury church. National Trust.

This trapezoidal hill is occupied by a large 7.2ha fort that dominates the countryside, and is defended not only by very sheer slopes but also by 4 – and, in places, 5 – steep ramparts.

The first occupation here occurred in the New Stone Age, and has been radiocarbon-dated to 3350 – 2510 BC. Pottery, arrowheads and stone axes have been found. After 800 BC, there was a Late Bronze Age settlement here (pottery, loom weights, etc.), and then an unfortified Iron Age settlement by the late 7th or early 6th century BC.

The first defences date to c. 500 BC, and were complete by the end of the 2nd century BC. The rampart was strengthened with timbers and limestone blocks, and there were entrances on the SW, NE and E. The defences seem to have been rebuilt or modified at least 5 times. It was a town, with many large round and rectangular huts, storage pits, a 'shrine' and evidence of textiles and metalworking.

When the Romans under Vespasian arrived in AD 43, it was taken and occupied. The remains of a mas-

sacre (the dismembered skeletons of 30 men, women and children) were found scattered around the SW gateway: some had been gnawed by scavengers. In c. 70, the Romans broke down the walls and burned the gates, and the site was abandoned.

Finally, it was refortified in c. 470, and a large wooden hall was built. It is from this period that the site's association with King Arthur may date; already in the 16th century, Leland said that this was Camelot. There are many legends: that the hill is hollow and Arthur and his knights sleep within, awaiting the time when England needs them; that every 7th year, on Midsummer's Eve they come out to water their horses; and that on nights with a full moon they ride round the hill on silver-shod horses. It is also said that fairies lived here until the installation of bells in South Cadbury church drove them away.

Finds in Somerset County Museum, Taunton.

Wookey Hole Cave-
dwellings*   *Old Stone Age/Roman*
Wookey Hole, NW of Wells   **182(ST:532479)**
Signposted from N end of village. Open summer 9am-dusk; winter 10am-noon and 1.30-5pm. Floodlit. Privately owned. Museum on site.

Wookey Hole cave itself had Late Iron Age and post-Roman occupation in its 1st chamber: a skeleton was found with a dagger, a billhook and a stalagmite ball. But *Hyena Den*, a small cave 55m to the SE (ST:531480) was occupied by humans in the Middle Palaeolithic (Neanderthal period) and Upper Palaeolithic – i.e. c. 35,000 – 12,000 BC. Excavations in 1852 found flint implements, including 6 handaxes, and bones of cave lions and bears, hyenas, mammoths, bison, woolly rhinos and elks. The cave seems to have been occupied alternately by humans and hyenas during the last Ice Age. Finds in Wells Museum, and Manchester and Oxford University museums.

EAST ANGLIA

East Anglia, accepted as covering Cambridgeshire, Essex, Norfolk and Suffolk, is a large region poor in surviving prehistoric monuments. The scarcity is due to both natural and historical causes. In post-glacial times, very large areas became densely forested, while the rising sea level that followed the melting of the ice flooded some previously habitable land, laying down silts or causing peat formation and so destroying archaeological sites. A dramatic reminder of encroachment by the sea since the New Stone Age is the 'submerged forest' off the Norfolk coast where, at very low tides, dark tree stumps are uncovered.

Another very simple, natural reason for the lack of striking monuments is, of course, the lack of building stone, and the fact that the area of chalk, where earthworks are likely to survive, is very small. Had sarsens been available, for example, it is most probable that the Arminghall henge (p. 135) would still be marked by at least the ruins of a fine stone setting.

As for the human destruction of monuments, this has resulted from the intense cultivation that has been carried out more or less continuously since the Middle Ages. This has been accompanied by drastic efforts at drainage and water control: almost all the waterways in the fenlands are artificial, and it is now known that the Norfolk Broads are submerged peat-cuttings. Aerial photography has shown how many prehistoric sites have been completely obliterated.

The most important natural features of the region determining the settlement by prehistoric people are the forested clay lands, which covered most of Essex and ran in a broad belt up the centre of Suffolk and Norfolk, with lighter, more cultivable soils, including the Breckland heaths, on either side, and, most significant, the narrow ridge of chalk that runs by way of the Gog Magog Hills of Cambridgeshire and the East Anglian Heights to reach the coast in the variegated cliffs of Hunstanton. This open chalk belt, roughly followed by the ancient tracks recognized as the Icknield Way, is important for the preservation of monuments, but still more because it formed a direct link with the Thames Valley and Wessex.

East Anglia is of outstanding interest for the archaeology of the Old Stone Age, particularly of the early hunters of second interglacial times (p. 16). Their flint hand-axes and other implements have been found in numbers in the Brandon, Mildenhall area and round Norwich, while a contemporary culture has been named the Clactonian after finds at Clacton-on-Sea. At this site, a roughly pointed wooden spear had been preserved – at some 250,000

years, the oldest wooden implement in Britain.

The last phases of the Old Stone Age are hardly represented in East Anglia, but during the Middle Stone Age, before the spread of forests, it provided ideal conditions for fishing and fowling, and at many places in Norfolk and Suffolk and under the fenland peat in Cambridgeshire, their various types of tiny flints, axes and 'Thames picks' (p. 18) have come to light. One famous find, an antler fish spear, was trawled up from the seabed off Norfolk, a relic from the time before 6000 BC when East Anglia was still linked with Denmark by freshwater fenland.

All this vast stretch of history, however, must be tracked down in museums. It is only from the New Stone Age that a few monuments survive in the field, and these are poor enough with the one great exception, the Grimes Graves flint mines. Though all is uncertain, it is likely that some of the farming peoples came by sea, perhaps from the Low Countries, and some by land following the chalk from Wessex. Their early settlement areas were on Breckland and other light soils, but these sites are known from pottery and flints and hold nothing at all for the visitor.

The few religious monuments worth looking for, and that barely, are the Arminghall henge (p. 135) and three long barrows, two close together at West Rudham (p. 140) and Harley in north-west Norfolk, just to the east of the Icknield Way, and the third on Broome Heath, Ditchingham (together with round barrows, but all in a bad way) in the Waveney Valley.

The Grimes Graves flint mines (p. 138) have already been discussed in the historical introduction, both as an industrial site and for the unique shrine for the goddess of fertility found in one of the reputed 366 shafts. Grimes Graves is in Breckland, where sandy soil overlies the chalk supporting what the writer remembers as glorious open heathland, but which is now heavily conifered. Mining appears to have started later here than in Sussex, and since the site is not far from the Icknield Way, it can be assumed that the enterprise was introduced from the south.

Round about 2000 BC the Beaker peoples spread over much of East Anglia, some of them perhaps coming directly from the Low Countries or Germany. Beaker burials below mounds are known, but since there is nothing distinctive about them, they must take their place among other round barrows – with which the region is well endowed.

Of one prehistoric fact there is no doubt at all: just as in the South-west and South-east, in the early Bronze Age a branch of the Wessex élite (p. 32) extended their rule into East Anglia, following the chalk right up to north-west Norfolk. Their bell, disc and rare saucer barrows, all near the Icknield Way, are unmistakable and some, such as one at Little Cressingham (p. 138), cover burials almost as rich in grave goods as those of the Wessex chieftains. Examples of Wessex types find a place in the Gazetteer-at Seven Hills in Breckland (p. 138), near Bircham (p. 135) and Weasenham in north-west Norfolk, as well as Little Cressingham. Mention should perhaps also be made of Chippenham in Cambridgeshire and of a southern outlier at Martlesham in south-east Suffolk.

As elsewhere, barrow building continued through the middle Bronze Age, the dead being cremated and the remains placed in urns. Some 250 round barrows in all have been counted in Norfolk, 100 in Suffolk, most of them on heathland and other light soils, some in groups or pairs, some singly, and few worth a detour. A very much smaller number survive in east Cambridgeshire and in Essex - but everywhere the destruction has been relentless.

During this time and the succeeding late Bronze Age, there is good archaeological evidence that East Anglia enjoyed a moderate prosperity with mixed farming supporting a mounting population prosperous enough to share in the general adoption of ever more specialized bronze tools and weapons, distant though the region was from sources of the metal. The wealthiest possessed ornaments of Irish gold and fine bronze shields and swords - some of the best having been found in the peat of the Cambridgeshire fens. There are, however, no conspicuous field monuments from this period, and even for the Iron Age, the expected forts are exceptionally few - partly though not entirely because nature had provided so few suitable hills.

The first iron-using Celts were settling by 500 BC, those to the west in Breckland and round the edge of the fens (at that time too wet to be habitable) differing from those in the Ipswich area. The more war-like tribesmen of the second phase arrived from northern France during the third century BC and were probably forebears of the ruling aristocracy of the Trinovantes of Essex and the Iceni of Norfolk and Cambridgeshire. The first rampart of the Wandlebury hillfort (p. 132) on the Gog Magog Hills dates from about this time and may conceivably have been an early tribal centre of the Iceni. Although no Icenian capital is known to compare with Camulodunum (Colchester) of the Trinovantes, the tribal aristocracy appears to have been exceptionally opulent: a hoard at Snettisham, near the Norfolk coast of the Wash, with further finds close by, has yielded 50 gold and electrum torques and arm rings, many of them massive and of magnificent design, while from other sites have come handsome horse and chariot fittings. (Originals are in the British Museum, but copies can be seen in the Norwich Castle Museum.) Most of these treasures were made in the region during the last century BC and could have been worn by the immediate ancestors of Queen Boudicca and her royal husband.

The century and a half before the Roman conquest was dominated by the invasions of the Belgic peoples, their aggressive expansion against neighbouring tribes, and political dealings with Rome (pp. 37-9). The Iceni felt the Belgic pressure and it is possible that they added the outer defences of Wandlebury against it. Warham Camp (p. 139), the best-preserved fort in the region, was built as BC became AD, but its purpose there near the north coast is obscure. The main Belgic attack was against the Trinovantes, and when at last Cunobelin crushed them and transferred his capital to their oppidum of Camulodunum behind the great Lexden Dykes (p. 135), Essex and the adjoining Trinovantian territory of south Suffolk were brought from relative obscurity to be the centre of power in Britain and, following from that, briefly supported the capital of the Roman province.

Colchester was certainly the first place in the province to have a great classical building - the temple of Claudius - and even after the capital was moved to London, it remained the most important town and road centre in the region. The circuit of its walls can still be traced and the Roman collections in the Colchester and Essex Museum are remarkable. After the terrible events of the Boudiccan revolt, when the Trinovantes were the chief allies of the Iceni and Colchester was sacked, the harrowing of the tribal lands in punishment was so severe that East Anglia lagged behind in romanization and prosperity.

Not indefinitely, however: the Romans soon started the drainage of the fens, turning much of them into rich cornlands. The Car Dyke (p. 132) was cut both for drainage and to carry grain to feed the northern garrisons. The cantonal capital of Caistor-by-Norwich (Venta Icenorum) at Caistor St Edmund seems to have been founded by about AD 70, to be followed by the town and port at Caister-by-Yarmouth (p. 136).

In the countryside, Iron Age huts gave way to timber-built farmhouses and more fully romanized villas, while the cultivation of the forested clay lands began; here, too, potters made use of the abundance of clay and wood. The road network was good and was soon carrying goods such as Samian ware, glass and wine pouring in from the Continent. The most important regional roads were the Great Road from London to Colchester and on to Caistor, and a branch from the Great Road at Chelmsford which, north of Ixworth, becomes the Peddars' Way (p. 138) - the fine *agger* of which can be followed in long stretches as it runs up to the coast near Hunstanton. Another road worth visiting is the continuation of the *Via Devana* running past Wandlebury hillfort on the Gog Magog Hills above Cambridge – almost certainly heading for Colchester. The ancient Icknield Way remained in use, romanized in parts.

The East Anglian coast was wide open to barbarian attack and, by the end of the third century, had its forts of the Saxon Shore. There is little to see at Brancaster, the Walton fort (Felixstowe) fell into the sea and that on Bradwell Point (p. 134) was badly ruined, but Burgh Castle (p. 135), overlooking the harbour of Caister, can repay a visit.

Although Caistor-by-Norwich was in decline before the end of the fourth century, rural life remained prosperous. Indeed someone, presumably a wealthy villa owner, buried the sumptuous, ornate, Mediterranean-made table silver found at Mildenhall in Breckland. This East Anglian treasure is by far the richest in all Britain: one must go to the British Museum to see it.

CAMBRIDGESHIRE

Belsar's Hill Fort　　　　　　　*Iron Age*
Willingham　　　　　　　　　**154(TL:423703)**
From road E of Willingham, a footpath NE to Aldreth runs through fort.

This ovoid fort, built on an island on the edge of the fens, was joined by a causeway through the marshland to the Isle of Ely, 14km to the NE. It has a single bank and ditch with entrances on the W and E.

Car Dyke Canal　　　　　　　　　*Roman*
Waterbeach Airfield　　　　　　　**154(TL:485664)**
Best stretch of the Canal runs along E side of A10 where it passes the airfield.

This big dyke stretches for 12km from the river Cam at Waterbeach to the Old West River. It is thought to be of the early 2nd century AD, and excavation revealed that it is 2m deep and flat-bottomed, with sides sloping outwards. Believed to be a Roman transport canal, it is one of the many wide canals built to drain and exploit the marshland.

Chesterton Town　　　　　　　　*Roman*
E of Water Newton　　　　　　　**142(TL:122968)**
Just visible in fields between the A1 and the river Nene. Ermine Street crosses site.

The small town of *Durobrivae* comprised an 18ha polygonal area straddling Ermine Street, and surrounded by a wall, rampart and ditch. Metalled lanes led away from the road, with stone houses along them. This was an industrial centre, with a school of mosaicists and large-scale pottery manufacture: the Castor potteries nearby were part of the Nene Valley area's pottery industry, and large kilns have been found that could probably contain 600 vessels per firing. The industry was in full production by the end of the 2nd century AD. A hoard of 30 superb 4th-century silver objects was found here in 1975, some

bearing the Christian *Chi-Rho* monogram. Aerial photography has revealed a fort beside the town; but little can be seen of the town today except for the surrounding earthworks, and Ermine Street's *agger* heading NW from the bend in the A1.

Moulton Hills (Arm's Hills)
Round Barrows　　　　　　　　*Roman*
Bourn　　　　　　　　　　　　**153(TL:326571)**
On N side of Bourn on high banks above road at Crow End and Caxton road junction.

This trio of mounds straddles the road. They are up to 25m across and 2.4m high, with wide surrounding ditches. Roadworks have damaged them. There were traces of Roman occupation on the land surface beneath the adjacent pair, and these 2 barrows contained cremations and Romano-British potsherds, as well as a coin of Aurelius (2nd century AD).

Wandlebury Hillfort/
Gog Magog Road　　　*Iron Age/Roman*
NE of Stapleford　　　　　　　**154(TL:493533)**
N side of A1307, on hill above golf course on Gog Magog Hills, 6km S of Cambridge.

A circular, tree-covered fort of 6ha, it has 2 banks and ditches with a counterscarp, and an entry on the SE. Some sections of the defences are still impressive, but landscaping in the 18th century damaged others. Excavation has shown that there were 2 main building phases, and the pottery suggests a date of 5th/4th century BC for the first, with the extensive refortification occurring in the late 1st century BC or early 1st century AD - possibly a reaction by the Iceni to the Belgic expansion. Shallow storage pits have been found, some of which contained graves: one was the upper half of a 6-year-old whose legs had been removed before the flesh rotted. Finds in Cambridge

Car Dyke Canal. *This Roman canal was probably used for transporting grain and other goods*

University Museum of Archaeology and Ethnology.

There is a legend that if a warrior enters the fort by moonlight and shouts 'Knight to knight, come forth!' he will immediately be faced by an armed warrior who charges on horseback until one of them is dismounted.

The Gog Magog Road is a stretch of the *Via Devana* that runs past the fort as a green road.

133

ESSEX

Ambresbury Banks Fort   *Iron Age?*
Epping Forest   **167(TL:438004)**
Immediately E of B1393, just SW of Epping.

A beautifully located lowland plateau fort of 4.5ha, it comprises a rectangle enclosed by a single bank, still up to 2m high, and a v-shaped ditch, 3m deep and over 6m wide; there are traces of a counterscarp bank here and there. A stream was included at the south as a water supply. The site is undated, but is said to be the site of Boudicca's battle against Suetonius Paulinus in AD 61.

Bartlow Hills Barrows *   *Roman*
N of Ashdon   **154(TL:586448)**
Footpath signposted on Bartlow-to-Ashdon road.

Despite the track of a now-defunct railway, and a number of tunnels dug into them over the years, these still constitute the finest group of Roman barrows in Britain. Only 4 remain of an original 9, but they are still impressive, being up to 12m high. They used to stand in 2 parallel rows of 5 small barrows (now disappeared) and 4 large. Finds made in the last century were destroyed by fire. It is known that the mounds contained stone coffins, cremations and various vessels and grave goods; there are some finds in Saffron Walden Museum. There is some evidence for a villa nearby.

Bradwell Fort   *Roman*
Bradwell-on-Sea   **168(TM:031081)**
3km NE of Bradwell along Roman road, on extremity of Bradwell Point.

Othona was one of the Roman forts of the Saxon shore built at the end of the 3rd century; it controlled the mouth of the Blackwater. Little of it now survives: a circular bastion at the NW corner and an internal tower to the S. In 654, St Cedd built a little chapel on the wall with material from the fort: the walls can be seen in section inside the chapel, and there are fine stretches of the wall adjoining it.

Colchester *   *Iron Age/Roman*
      168(TL:995253)

The original Iron Age *oppidum* here, *Camulodunum*, capital of the Trinovantes, was captured *c.* 10 BC by the Catuvellauni, led by Tasciovanus. Later the Trinovantes took over again, but by AD 10 the whole of SE England was being ruled from here by Cunobelin, Tasciovanus' son, who died in AD 42. It comprised a promontory of 34 sq. km, with the Roman

Bartlow Hills Barrows. Roman

river and the Colne protecting it on 3 sides. To the w there was a series of dykes defending the 5km gap between the rivers. These dykes–v-shaped ditches with internal banks–can till be seen: e.g. Gryme's Dyke (TL:956267 to 956214) and Lexden Dyke (TL: 974246). The capital itself consisted of groups of timber and wattle/daub huts, but it was nevertheless wealthy: the Colne estuary provided access for traders from the Continent, and the town imported fine pottery and glass from Gaul and Italy. Gold, silver and bronze coins were struck here. Finds in Colchester and Essex Museum.

Camulodunum was of primary importance to the invading Romans in AD 43, as shown by the fact that Claudius himself entered the town in triumph. Two areas of Belgic settlement were allowed to continue, but a legionary fortress was immediately constructed nearby; a few years later, its defences were removed and, in c. 49, a *colonia* was built for veterans to the E of it, on the hilltop: *Colonia Claudia Victricensis*. It had no town wall, and was dominated by a huge temple dedicated to Claudius, a senate house, a theatre and a collection of timber-framed houses and shops. The rectangular temple, 32m long, had a portico of 8 columns; its podium, owing to a lack of local stone, was hollow, with big vaults filled with sand.

The *colonia*, with its probable population of at least 10,000, expropriated vast areas of farming land, and the local inhabitants developed crippling debts to Roman merchants and moneylenders. These were major causes of Boudicca's revolt in AD 60: the town was besieged, the inhabitants took refuge in the temple and were massacred together with the infantry of the 9th Legion, and the town was burned down. By 110 the rebuilt city of 44ha had walls 4km in circumference, with 6 gates and 2 posterns. The massive main (w) gate, the Balkerne Gate, is the most impressive relic of the Roman town, although part of it lies beneath the Hole in Wall Inn on Balkerne Hill: there are fine sections of wall, and the remains of 2 arch-

ways, while part of the ruins still stand up to 6m in height.

Much of the wall's circuit can still be walked (in about an hour). The Norman castle is built on and around the great temple's podium, and the vaults can be visited: a relic of the oldest fine classic building in Britain. The museum in the castle contains a remarkable collection of Roman antiquities, including sculptures from the tombs that lined the road to London, such as a famous sphinx.

Loughton Hillfort
Iron Age?
Epping Forest **167(TQ:418975)**
In the Forest, E of A104 and 0.8km NW of Loughton church.

An ovoid, lowland fort of 2.6ha, it has a single bank and ditch, with a number of gaps. There may have been a water supply in the SE part of the site. Steep slopes on the w added to the defences.

Mersea Mount Barrow
Roman
West Mersea, Mersea Island **168(TM:023145)**
Just E of B1025, at Barrow Hill farm.

This large Romano-British mound, 34m across and nearly 7m high, has a brick vault at the centre that contained a cremation in a glass bowl inside a lead casket. According to legend, it is the tomb of a centurion, and is haunted by his ghost. In 1912, a passage was built to give access to the burial chamber (key obtainable from a house nearby). Finds in Colchester and Essex Museum.

Wallbury Hillfort
Iron Age
SW of Great Hallingbury **167(TL:492178)**
S of Bishop's Stortford, on spur above river Stort, between river and A1060.

An ovoid fort of 12.5ha, it has 2 tree-covered banks and ditches, but only a single set of defences to the w, where steep slopes gave extra protection. The original entry was probably on the E. Iron Age pottery has been found around the site.

NORFOLK

Arminghall Henge
New Stone Age
Bixley **134(TG:240060)**
Just s of Norwich, w of road from Trowse Newton to Caistor St Edmund.

The visible traces (a depression in the ground and a low bank) of this site are scant testimony to its importance as a sacred site: it was a Class I henge, with a double ditch and a wide gravel bank in between, about 38m in total diameter, and a single entrance on the SW. In the centre, by the present pylon, was a horseshoe-setting of 8 posts, facing SW (the midwinter sunset), 14.6m across. The posts were each almost a metre across, from oak trees of more than a century's growth, and must have weighed 7 tons, and they were placed 4.9m apart. The remains of one have been radiocarbon-dated to 2490 BC. There is no sign of a central post, and the structure was probably unroofed. One of the earliest henges, it seems to be a prototype of a stone circle (no stone was available in the area) and resembles Woodhenge (p. 103). Aerial photography, which first discovered the site, revealed that abundant round

barrows accumulated in its vicinity; and there are several flint mines around here, including Grimes Graves (*qv*). Finds in Norwich Castle Museum.

Bircham Common Round Barrows
Bronze Age
SE of Great Bircham **132(TF:775316)**
On either side of minor road SE to West Rudham.

Of this line of 4 barrows, which runs NW/SE on arable land, only the northernmost (TF:775316), isolated by the road, is accessible. It is an overgrown bell barrow, 27m across, but its ditch and bank are gone. It contained a potsherd. Across the road are 2 bowl barrows and a big bell barrow that contained a cremation together with flints, a bronze awl and gold-covered beads.

Burgh Castle Fort of the Saxon Shore *
Roman
Burgh Castle **134(TG:475046)**
Signposted at w end of Burgh Castle village. Near Great Yarmouth. HBMCE standard hours. Guidebook available.

Burgh Castle Fort of the Saxon Shore. The walls of this late-3rd-century Fort of the Saxon Shore are of rubble faced with flint and bonded with tile. The bastions were added later, and this one has become detached

The 2ha fort of *Gariannonum*, which dates to *c.* AD 275, controlled the Waveney river inland from Great Yarmouth. After construction had began, the plans were changed, and massive external semicircular bastions were added to the walls, being bonded to them only above the 2m level. Their flat tops have sockets in the centre for the positioning of catapults. A cavalry unit from the Yugoslavia area was stationed here. The fort was destroyed in the mid-4th century. St Fursa built a monastery within the walls in 630, which lasted until the 9th century; finally, a typical Norman motte was built in the sw corner, but it was removed in 1839.

The wall on the w has now gone, but the stone foundations of a riverside quay were found here recently. The other 3 walls remain impressive, standing up to 5m, almost their original height. It is possible to discern the junction-points where different gangs of workers met.

Caister-by-Yarmouth Town and Port   *Roman*
Caister-on-Sea   **134(TG:517123)**
On A1064 on w outskirts of the resort. HBMCE standard hours.

A small town with a sheltered harbour, it was founded *c.* AD 125 and commanded 2 river mouths and the terminus of the Fen Causeway that led to the important potteries and industrial area of the Nene valley. It traded with the Rhineland (being at the shortest crossing-point to the Rhine's mouth) for glass, fineware and lava millstones. The earliest settlement had a simple rampart and palisade, but as trade flourished, a massive flint wall was constructed *c.* 150. There was a forum and basilica in the town centre, and a large house just inside the s gate, which may have been a boarding-house for seamen. Occupation lasted until the 5th century, and resumed from the 7th to the 9th. Outside the s gate was a cemetery of over 150 burials, a dozen of which were roofed with ship's timbers and iron nails, and date from the late 7th century. Little can now be seen of the Roman town except for parts of the wall of the s gate and of the 'boarding-house' foundations.

Caistor-by-Norwich Town   *Roman*
Caistor St Edmund   **134(TG:230035)**
E of A140 and of railway, s of Norwich.

The small town of *Venta Icenorum* is most visible from the air. Founded by AD 70, after the Iceni revolt in 60, it was laid out on a grid system, and had a forum, basilica, baths, temples, etc. Timber buildings were replaced by stone in 150. The interior is now farmed, but sections of the town's earthen rampart can be seen on the s, and part of the deep external ditch near the little church. Finds in Norwich Castle Museum.

Caister-by-Yarmouth Town and Port. *Foundations of the seamen's boarding-house in this small 2nd-century Roman town and port*

Grimes Graves Flint Mines*　　*New Stone Age*
NE of Weeting　　　　**144(TL:817898)**
*NW of Thetford, between A1065 (to w) and A134 (to
E). Signposted. HBMCE standard hours. Admission
charge. Publications stall.*

The largest group of flint mines in Britain, it probably covers 38ha: 300 to 400 pits have been found in
the 14ha investigated, and are visible as shallow
depressions in the heath. The shafts are as much as
15m deep, since the miners ignored the inferior
bands of flint nearer the surface and went for the
fine-quality material beneath. Once this layer had
been reached, radiating galleries up to 9m long were
cut into it. The work was done with antler picks
(many may have been found in the shafts) and chalk-cup
lamps provided light. The nodules were hauled up in
bags or baskets and were crudely shaped on the spot,
the waste being used to fill up exhausted pits. It has
been estimated that 20 men could work a mine, with
10 in the galleries and the rest carrying and shaping.
A shaft would have taken about 4 months to dig, and
each gallery 2 months: a single mine might have
yielded 50 tons of material. Most of it was probably
used to make axes, which have been found in huge
numbers. Some open-cast mining took place on the N
where there are exposures of flint. Radiocarbon dating indicates that the main work was done from 2300
to 1800 BC, but occupation continued well into the
Bronze Age; flint knapping was carried out into the
present century for flints used in pistols – an enormous heap of waste flakes can be seen behind the
Flint Knappers Arms in Brandon.

Among the important finds from the site is a
'mother goddess' figurine found at the bottom of one
shaft with a heap of flint blocks with 7 antlers on top,
chalk balls, a realistic carved chalk phallus and a
chalk-cup lamp. One shaft is open to visitors: it is 9m
deep; access is by ladder, and electric light has been
installed. There is an informative diorama of a typical
shaft in Norwich Castle Museum – which also has
finds from the site, as do Ipswich and Thetford
museums and the British Museum (the latter has the
figurine).

Holkham Fort (Camp)　　　　*Iron Age?*
NW of Holkham　　　　**132(TF:875447)**
N of A149.

An ovoid lowland fort of 2ha, it stands on an island
amid tidal saltmarshes and near a creek that used to
be open to the sea. It may have been built by the Iceni
in the face of Belgic expansion. It has a single bank
and ditch, with an extra bank on the SE, and entrance
on the S. Steep slopes provided a natural defence on
the W.

**Little Cressingham Round
Barrows***　　　　　　　*Bronze Age*
SW of Little Cressingham　　**144(TL:861986)**
S of B1108, in Seven Acre plantation. HBMCE.

These 4 mounds, clearly visible from the road,
include a really massive example, Bell Hill (65m
across and over 4m high) to the S. A bowl barrow
(TL:867992), now ploughed out, contained a male
burial with typical 'Wessex Culture' material: gold
plates, an amber necklace with spacer beads, and 2
bronze daggers. Finds in Norwich Castle Museum.

Peddars' Way Road*　　　　　*Roman*
Fring SE to Castle Acre　**132(TF:727356 to 817154)**
E of King's Lynn, w of Harpley.

The name given to a section of the major Roman
road from Chelmsford where it forks NW beyond
Ixworth heading for Holme-on-Sea. Between Castle
Acre and Fring the 11m-wide *agger* offers good
walking.

Seven Hills Round Barrows　　　*Bronze Age*
Thetford　　　　　　　**144(TL:904814)**
*3.2km SE of Thetford, between A1088 (to w) and
A1066 (to N).*

Occupation by the military in both world wars has
done great damage to this necropolis, and only 6 barrows now survive in 2 groups of 3; originally there

were at least 11, forming a linear cemetery E/W. Nothing is known of their contents. The western group comprises 2 bowl barrows and a bell, the eastern group has 3 bowls. They were constructed of sand capped with chalk. The biggest is 2m high and 30m in diameter.

Thetford Castle Hillfort　　　　*Iron Age?*
Thetford　　　　　　　　　**144(TL:875828)**
Earthen ramparts round the Norman motte of the castle.

　The ford where the prehistoric Icknield Way crossed the river was controlled by this bivallate fort

Warham Camp Fort. Iron Age

that is now occupied by a Norman motte, 25m high. The defences are said to have been made by the Devil scraping his shoes after building the Devil's Ditches of the region; and treasures such as golden bells are said to lie beneath the motte.

Warham Camp Fort ∗　　　　*Iron Age*
s of Warham All Saints　　　　**132(TF:944409)**
E of B1105. 4.5km N of Little Walsingham.
Bridlepath W off road running s from Warham All Saints to Wighton.

Warham Camp Fort. *Low-lying Iron Age fort by the river Stiffkey. It dates from the 1st century* BC *and was occupied in Roman times* (Cambridge University Collection of Air Photographs)

This impressive circular plateau fort, the finest monument of its period in the region, encloses 1.4ha with its massive double banks and ditches; the ramparts are still up to 3m high, although 18th-century landscaping destroyed them on the sw, where the entrance probably was. It may have been built by the Iceni at the end of the 1st century BC/early 1st century AD. There was also some Romano-British occupation. Finds in Norwich Castle Museum.

Weasenham Plantation Round Barrows
Bronze Age
Weasenham All Saints **132(TF:853198)**
N of Swaffham. 1.6km s of Weasenham All Saints on A1065.
This must once have been an impressive cemetery,

and contained at least 15 mounds: but cultivation has destroyed many of them. At the w side of the plantation (private land), there are 2 saucer barrows, a bell and a bowl barrow. On the E, the only really visible specimen is a huge bell barrow, 42m across and 2m high, with a ditch and external bank. Two bowl barrows to the s were excavated recently; one contained a cremation in an urn in a central pit; the other had 2 cremations with flint tools and over 350 Beaker sherds. There are 3 other bowl barrows 1km to the E.

West Rudham Long Barrows
New Stone Age
s of west Rudham **132(TF:810253)**
s of A148.
These mounds (on either side of a minor road) are of a type rare in the region, but they have little to show: that to the N of the road (TF:810253) is an overgrown ovoid mound of turf and gravel, 58m long, with a ditch, and orientated s/N. It had a forecourt at the s end, with a pit in it. The barrow to the s of the road (TF:809252) is now merely an unploughed patch.

THE SOUTH MIDLANDS

Launching into the Midlands, one has to deal with regions that are larger, less well defined and, as a whole, poorer in notable prehistoric remains than the south of England. In the South Midlands (comprising Bedfordshire, Berkshire, Buckinghamshire, Gloucestershire, Hereford & Worcester, Hertfordshire, Northamptonshire, Oxfordshire, Warwickshire and West Midlands), most surviving monuments are on the chalk and limestone uplands of the Chilterns and the Cotswolds, and, for the Iron Age, along the border country of Hereford & Worcester. It should be remembered that in populous areas, such as the Thames Valley, hundreds have been destroyed, and the change of a county boundary has robbed Berkshire of her best-known antiquities – Wayland's Smithy, Uffington Castle and that most Berkshire of beasts, the White Horse. These are now in Oxfordshire.

The hunters of the Old and Middle Stone Ages are represented in the region by just one cave dwelling: King Arthur's Cave (p. 157) near the pleasant little town of Ross-on-Wye, where their distinctive tools were found and, below stalagmites, the bones of mammoth and woolly rhinoceros.

For the New Stone Age of the early farmers, there is a quite exceptional concentration of monuments on the Cotswolds. The only habitation site worth mentioning is the remains of an interrupted ditch camp on Crickley Hill (p. 148), but of the Cotswold speciality – chambered long barrows – there are over 90, most of them between Wootton-under-Edge and Stow-on-the-Wold. It has only been possible to describe the dozen finest in the Gazetteer, but many more are worth seeking out by anyone taking a leisurely holiday among these enchanting hills – so well supplied with pleasant inns and hotels.

While the walled, often trapezoidal, mounds of these tombs are fairly constant, the chamber plans vary greatly – the most conspicuous division being between those, like Hetty Pegler's Tump (p. 148), in which the forecourt leads directly into the megalithic chamber, and those, like Belas Knap (p. 146), in which the court is closed by a sham entrance, the actual chambers opening on to the sides of the mound.

The existence of virtually identical chambered long barrows in South Wales (p. 280) proves beyond little doubt that the farmers who built the Cotswold long barrows arrived by way of the Bristol Channel and Severn estuary. A scatter of similar chambered tombs extending south from Gloucestershire appear in the Wessex section and as far as the southern outlier of Stoney Littleton; to the north, there is Arthur's Stone (p. 154) with its huge capstone, while the extreme outlier to the east is Wayland's Smithy (p. 163).

This well-known monument is by the Ridgeway near its approach to the Icknield Way, the ancient thoroughfare that ran along the western slopes of the Chilterns following the chalk onwards to make a link between Wessex and East Anglia. The Chilterns are not as rich in prehistoric remains as might be hoped, partly because much of the chalk has a skin of topsoil supporting woodland, partly because so many monuments, especially barrows, have been destroyed. The importance of the route already in the New Stone Age is, however, sufficiently marked by the White-leaf Barrows (p. 145) above the chalk-cut cross so clearly visible from Princes Risborough station, by the interrupted ditch camp at Maiden Bower (p. 143), by Waulud's Bank enclosed settlement near Luton, and by the long barrow on Therfield Heath (p. 158).

The Cotswolds are strikingly poor in Bronze Age monuments, though two small bowl barrow cemeteries – one by the Air Balloon Inn near the Crickley Hill fort (p. 148), the other just south-west of Snowshill in Gloucestershire – were raised by the Wessex chieftains as they spread on to the limestone. Now it is the Chilterns that have a little more to offer – in the shape of round barrows. There is the Cop bowl barrow near Bledlow Cross (Bucks), which yielded a Cornish greenstone axe, and two bell barrows on Lodge Hill between Bledlow and Saunderton deserve mention, although they did not win a place in the Gazetteer. The finest group on the Chilterns is the Five Knolls barrows (p. 143) on Dunstable Down that includes a triple bell as well as bowl barrows, and possibly two of the pond variety. On again past a few round barrows on Galley Hill (p. 143) and there is a cemetery of ten bowl barrows with the long one on Therfield Heath, survivors of a much larger number, some over the Cambridgeshire border, all now levelled.

One well-known yet unexpected monument of the Bronze Age remains to be mentioned – though some might assign it to the end of the New Stone Age. This is the Rollright stone circle (p. 161), in lonely isolation from the rest of its kind, one of the easternmost of stone-built prehistoric structures. Visitors may be disappointed by the 'leprous' appearance of the close-set uprights but will be delighted by the setting – this is an ideal place for a picnic.

The South Midlands has a good share of Iron Age hillforts, most of them in the Chilterns, the Cotswolds or the border country of Hereford & Worcester. The Chiltern forts that dominate the Gazetteer entries for Buckinghamshire are not striking: many have only a single line of lowish ramparts. Ivinghoe Beacon (p. 145) is of interest for its site and its early date, and Cholesbury (p. 145), enclosing the village church, is of some strength. Then there are the 40 kilometres of Grim's Dyke (Ditch) (p. 144), possibly a tribal boundary, that invites walking.

The Cotswolds hillforts are more attractive and impressive, especially those along the western scarp, commanding marvellous views across the Vale of Evesham and the Severn valley to Wales and the Malverns. Uleybury (p. 154), near Hetty Pegler's Tump, is one of the best; then there is Crickley Hill – near where the exquisite Birdlip mirror was found in the richly furnished grave of some Celtic *grande dame*, probably of the Dobunni, whose tribal area this was. Painswick Beacon (p. 152) has an exceptionally fine view, and Salmonsbury (p. 154), although off the scarp, is worth seeing and only a step from Bourton-on-the-Water.

The extremely confusing earthworks on Minchinhampton Common (p. 152) introduce an interesting historical issue of the 1st century AD. It is known from other evidence that the Belgic Catuvellauni were pressing against the native Dobunni along the eastern Cotswolds, and both here and at Bagendon to the east the defences suggest the Belgic type of *oppidum*.

At a fort further to the north, there may be proof that the Belgae were indeed savage aggressors. This is at Bredon Hill (from which Housman surveyed the 'coloured counties') where the violently hacked about skeletons of many young men were found outside the gate (p. 154). The excavator attributed this massacre to Belgic attack – but it must be admitted that Roman swordsmen may have been responsible.

Though Bredon Hill is a lofty outlier of the Cotswold limestone, it is already over the boundary into Hereford & Worcester. From here, it is only some 20km across the Severn valley to the Malverns – to a different world, for this steep, sudden little range was erected by violent geological buckling that forced up tough, ancient rocks through their younger mantle. The famous and spectacular Herefordshire Beacon (p. 157) encloses an upstanding ridge of these rocks above Little Malvern, while Midsummer Hill to the south (a walk where one can feel on top of the world) is an early fort with the small, rectangular houses that are a distinctive feature of the Welsh Marches.

North and west of the Malverns, there is a concentration of notable hillforts, from Sutton Walls (p. 157) and Credenhill (p. 156) south of Hereford to Croft Ambrey (p. 156) north of Leominster. Many of these forts had a long history, and at Sutton Walls some two dozen mutilated bodies had been thrown into the ditches, victims, it is believed, of a Roman storming. Croft Ambrey is well known to archaeologists for its long, regular rows of rectangular buildings.

Warwickshire is a county which, because so much of it was densely forested, is exceptionally poor in antiquities: for this reason, a few undistinguished Iron Age forts have found a place in the Gazetteer.

The Midlands were, of course, very largely opened up by the Romans who relentlessly cut their highways across them. The road system of the present region is dominated by Watling Street, which on its way from *Verulamium* to Chester crosses the great southwest to north-east line of the Fosse Way at High Cross in Northamptonshire. Akeman Street, linking *Verulamium* with Cirencester by way of Alcester, was of importance in the South Midlands, and so too was Rykneild Street, running due north from Bourton and Alcester.

The region has, in fact, much to show from the centuries of Roman rule, but while these roads linked all parts together, it is difficult to give the same coherence here. It seems best to make a loose division between east and west, picking out the principal sites within each.

In the extreme south-east, *Verulamium*, by St Albans, is probably the most rewarding Roman civil site in Britain, with its great theatre, sections of city wall and the London Gate where Watling Street entered the town. Much that the excavations revealed but is now covered can be appreciated from the excellent site museum. There are also the neighbouring earthworks of the Catuvellauni to be visited by the energetic. Away to the west, there are two exceptionally fine groups of Roman barrows: the Six Hills (p. 158) near Stevenage, within earshot of the A1, and the Thornborough barrows (p. 145) east of Buckingham.

Oxfordshire has the North Leigh villa (p. 161), which grew to be a large courtyard establishment with an elegant dining-room. Mention can also be made of Dorchester-on-Thames; there is not much to be seen save a bank and ditch, but it can serve as a reminder of many such small Roman towns, of which little has remained except the *'chester'.*

Cirencester was a major road centre, and since one of the roads is the Fosse Way (the others are Akeman and Ermine Streets), it is on the edge of the western part of the region. A fort was built here in the early days of the Fosse frontier (p. 44) before it became the site of a large town, the cantonal capital of the Dobunni (*Corinium Dobunnorum*). It is likely that the first citizens moved down from an old tribal centre at Bagendon on the adjacent spur of the Cotswolds. Many of the houses, shops and public buildings have been uncovered but cannot now be seen – the amphitheatre, however, demands inspection as does a section of the rampart and wall. The great attraction is the really excellent museum with reconstructed rooms and many treasures (p. 148).

Corinium must have been the city centre serving some of the civilized villa owners of the Cotswolds – evidently already recognized as ideal residential country. Of their surviving houses, the most rewarding (and most visited) is the elaborate, double courtyard Chedworth villa (p. 146) in an idyllic valley.

Its owners had patronized a school of mosaic artists at *Corinium*, as had those of the even grander villa at Woodchester where, unhappily, the great mosaic is only occasionally uncovered. The Great Witcombe villa (p. 148) is well worth seeing – it, too, has a lovely setting at the western foot of the Cotswolds, where the *colonia* of Gloucester would have been within easy reach.

To the south across the Severn estuary are the various remains in Lydney Park (p. 150), including the unique Roman iron mine and the equally exceptional ruins of a temple and sacred healing establishment.

It might be expected that, considering the years of fighting before the area was pacified, there would be Roman forts to be seen along the Welsh Marches, yet the only site worth mentioning is the town at Kenchester (p. 157) probably established soon after the pacification. (At Gloucester, which was the base of operations, the plans of both legionary fortress and *colonia* are known, but there is virtually nothing on view.) For a fort that certainly was involved in the struggle, one has to look much further east – to The Lunt near Coventry, occupied from about AD 60 to 75. Here there are not only the usual defences and military buildings, but one gateway has been most correctly and solidly reconstructed – the best effort of this kind for all Roman Britain.

BEDFORDSHIRE

Five Knolls Round Barrows *New Stone/Bronze Ages*
Dunstable **166(TL:007210)**
SW outskirts of Dunstable, extreme N of Dunstable Downs, just S of B489 and B451 junction.

Supposedly the burial place of 5 chiefs or kings, this group of 7 round barrows constitutes the finest such cemetery in the region. Beyond the bowl barrow at the S end is a trio of bell barrows enclosed by the same ditch. At the N end of the group is another bowl barrow that contained a female burial with a flint knife, and a secondary Bronze Age cremation in a collared urn.

Over 90 skeletons were discovered near this barrow's surface; about 30 of them, with their hands tied, were executed and probably date to the 5th century AD; gallows victims were added in later centuries. Two pond barrows to the E are unexcavated. Finds are in Luton Museum.

Galley Hill Barrows *New Stone Age/Roman*
Streatley **166(TL:092270)**
N of Luton, 3km SE of Streatley. Footpath ENE from A6 opposite St Margaret's Home.

A pair of small bowl barrows: the S one was robbed in the past and may date to the Iron Age; the N one is kidney-shaped, and contained an empty central pit, but each lobe also covered a pit: one contained the skeleton of a young man with New Stone Age potsherds, the other had over 20 ox jawbones. Fifteen bodies (11 men, 3 women and a boy) were added in the 4th century AD. Finally a gallows stood here 500 years ago, and 6 of its victims were buried at its foot, heads downwards, together with a 'witchcraft deposit' of a horse skull and dice. Finds in Luton Museum.

Maiden Bower Fort *New Stone/Iron Ages*
Houghton Regis **166(SP:997224)**
SW of Houghton Regis. 2km W of Dunstable. Footpath ENE from Sewell. Above chalk quarry.

A small, roughly circular plateau fort of 4.5ha, it has a single rampart (still 2m high in places), a deep v-shaped ditch, and an entrance on the SE. Finds of skeletons and slingstones indicate that fighting took place here in the Iron Age. On the N side, the modern quarry has exposed part of the flat-bottomed ditch of an underlying New Stone Age causewayed camp. The fort's interior is under cultivation. Aerial photography has revealed many 'Celtic fields' around the site, with hut circles and storage pits. Finds in Luton Museum.

Sharpenhoe Clapper Hillfort
N of Streatley   *Iron Age?*   **166(TL:066302)**
Just E of road NNW from Streatley to Sharpenhoe. National Trust.

This small promontory fort, superbly located on a wooded, N-facing spur with fine views, comprises a single large rampart across a neck of land. The ditch is wide but shallow, and there are traces of 2 small exterior banks; all the defences are now damaged. Excavations suggest the rampart is medieval, but below it lie the remains of a timber palisade. There are lynchets outside to the SW.

Waulud's Bank Enclosed Settlement
Luton   *New Stone Age*   **166(TL:062247)**
NW of Luton near Leagrave railway station by source of the river Lea. In public park.

A very large and enigmatic earthwork enclosing over 7ha, it comprises a great chalk bank, still 2.5m high in places, which curves round from the source of the Lea to the river to form a semicircular area; and an external, flat-bottomed ditch up to 9m wide and over 2m deep. No entrances or internal features are known, but New Stone Age pottery and many flint arrowheads of this period and the Bronze Age have been found here. Finds in Luton Museum.

——— BERKSHIRE ———

Caesar's Camp Hillfort
Easthampstead   *Iron Age?*   **175(SU:863657)**
Incorporated in recreation area 2.6km s of Easthampstead between A3095 and A322.

One of the best contour forts in England, this 8ha enclosure – roughly of oak-leaf shape – has strong defences that run along the 122m contour around the valleys. There is a bank, an external ditch and traces of a counterscarp bank, and 4 entrance gaps, 2 of which (N, S) are probably original. Unexcavated, but Iron Age pottery and Roman coins have been found.

Grimsbury Castle Hillfort
Hermitage   *Iron Age*   **174(SU:512723)**
7km NE of Newbury and 1km s of Hermitage. Just E of B4009. Minor road crosses the site. In private woods: access permitted if Country Code observed.

A triangular, multiple enclosure fort of 3.2ha, its earthworks follow the hill's contours and comprise 2 banks of dump construction with a U-shaped ditch in between. To the W is another curving rampart/ditch. There are entrances on N and W, each approached by a hollow way, and another on the SE leading to water. The site is unexcavated, but is probably of at least 2 periods in the Iron Age. It is named after Grim, a mythical figure, and according to legend, a wood nearby has a bottomless pond containing a golden calf.

Grim's Ditch Running Dyke
Aldworth   *Iron Age?*   **174(SU:546785 to 570792)**
Three stretches of dyke to s and SE of Aldworth, on both sides of B4009. Main length runs 1.6km E from Beche Farm.

A boundary rather than a defensive earthwork, the ditch is always on the N side, and the maximum combined height of ditch and bank is only 1.8m. In addition to the Beche Farm section, fine stretches can be seen on Hart Ridge (SU:585775) and at SU:593796. Also known as Devil's Ditch, it is supposed to have been ploughed by the Devil in one night, and two nearby barrows (SU:520883) are the scrapings from his ploughshare.

Inkpen Beacon Long Barrow (Combe Gibbet)
Inkpen   *New Stone Age*   **174(SU:365623)**
2km SE of Inkpen. Reached by bridle path on ridge between Walbury Hill to SE and Inkpen Hill to W.

Clearly visible, owing to the reconstructed Combe Gibbet, this earthen long barrow, 60m long and 2m high, is orientated E/W, the E end being the broader. Flanking ditches, 4.5m wide, are best seen on the N side. To the SE is Walbury Camp, a 33ha hillfort, probably of the Iron Age (SU:374617).

Lambourn Chambered Long Barrow
Lambourn   *New Stone Age*   **174(SU:323834)**
4.5km N of Lambourn, 1.6km W of B4001. s end of Westcot Wood.

Located to the NW of Lambourn Seven Barrows (*qv*), this mound of stacked turves, orientated ENE/WSW, is 80m long, 20m wide, and still 1m high at the E end, but its remains are unspectacular, since the SW end is ploughed; the NE end is in a private wood. Excavation revealed a number of skeletons, and a sarsen stone cist at the E end contained a crouched secondary burial, a female with a necklace of dogwhelk shells. The flanking ditches yielded New Stone Age potsherds, and a radiocarbon date of 3415 BC.

Lambourn Seven Barrows (Round Barrow Cemetery)*
Lambourn   *New Stone/Bronze Ages*   **174(SU:328828)**
4km N of Lambourn, W of B4001, around minor road N to Kingston Lisle.

Just E of Lambourn Long Barrow (*qv*), this is one of the most accessible round-barrow cemeteries in the country: it comprises 40 mounds, of different types and periods; most stand in 2 rows NW/SE, with others scattered between and around them; but only a couple of dozen are readily visible. There are saucer,

bowl and disc barrows, and the cemetery's period of use probably coincides broadly with that of Stonehenge. Beside the road, further N, is a restored bowl barrow that contained 2 cremations; over 100 more were later inserted. Finds in the Ashmolean Museum (Oxford) and the British Museum.

BUCKINGHAMSHIRE

Boddington Hillfort *Iron Age?*
Wendover **165(SP:882080)**
1.6km E of Wendover. Approached through housing estate off A4011.
This 7ha fort, located at the end of an oval spur, has a ditch and a single rampart of dumped chalk, turves and flint, still well preserved in places. There are entrances on SW and NW, but the interior is now wooded.

Bulstrode Fort *Iron Age?*
Gerrards Cross **175(SU:994880)**
Just W of junction of A40 and B416.
A large ovoid fort of 8.5ha, it has a double rampart with ditches. Of the gaps in these defences, at least one (SW) is not original. A pebbled hearth and some other traces of occupation were found in the SW of the site.

Cholesbury Fort *Iron Age*
Cholesbury **165(SP:930072)**
S of Tring. Ramparts enclose Cholesbury church.
An ovoid, tree-covered plateau fort of 4ha, it has 2 banks and a ditch in between, with an extra bank/ditch to the SE and W, and entrances on NE and SW. Pottery of the 2nd/1st centuries BC was found here. Finds in Aylesbury Museum.

Grim's Ditch Linear Earthwork *Iron Age?*
Best section at Great Hampden **165(SP:835022)**
NW of Prestwood. Runs for 40km through the Chilterns. Passes Hampden church.
Another example of an Iron Age (?) dyke, it has a number of large gaps, presumably filled by forest or fences. It may represent a boundary of expansion by the Catuvellauni. Apart from the above stretch, there is a fine length on Pitstone Hill (SP:949142) and another at SP:857020.

Ivinghoe Beacon (Beacon *Late Bronze/Early*
Hill) *Iron Ages*
Ivinghoe **165(SP:960168)**
NE of Ivinghoe. Immediately S of B489, by minor road to Ashridge. National Trust. Picnic area.
This pear-shaped fort of 2.2ha is one of the oldest in England and stands beside the Icknield Way. The defences, now much reduced, comprised a timber-framed rampart of chalk rubble, and a single, broad and deep chalk-cut ditch, with an extra ditch on the S. The entrance on the E was 3m wide and had a passage lined with posts. The fort's interior has traces of round and rectangular huts, and pottery and metalwork indicate that occupation began in the 7th or even 8th century BC. There are barrows around the site. Finds in County Museum, Aylesbury.

Pulpit Hill Hillfort *Iron Age?*
Great Kimble **165(SP:832050)**
SE of Great Kimble, NE of Princes Risborough. Road and track up from road S of Great Kimble church.
A little contour fort of 1.6ha, it encloses a shield-shaped area; the steep slopes on the NW and SW meant that a single bank and ditch sufficed here. On the E, where the approach along the spur was easier, the defences were doubled around the entrance. There are many other banks and ditches in nearby woods, which may date to the Iron Age.

Thornborough Barrows *Roman*
Thornborough **165(SP:732333)**
SW of Thornborough, ESE of Buckingham. Immediately N of A421, a little E of Thornborough bridge.
These 2 large and well-preserved barrows, about 4m high, were opened in the last century. One had probably been robbed earlier; the other had a cremated body on a rough limestone floor and protected by a timber construction. It was accompanied by very rich grave goods – bronze jugs, pottery, amphorae, glassware, etc. – and probably dates to the 2nd century AD. the barrows are located near the junction of 5 Roman roads.

West Wycombe Hillfort *Iron Age?*
West Wycombe **165/175(SP:827949)**
NW of High Wycombe, just N of A40 and W of A4010. Ramparts surround West Wycombe church.
This small round fort of 1.2ha is cut into on the SE by the mausoleum of Sir Francis Dashwood, founder of the 'Hell Fire Club'. Its defences, now covered in trees, comprise 2 banks and a deep ditch in between. The caves below Church Hill are artificial, from a more recent period.

Whiteleaf Barrows *New Stone Age*
E of Monks Risborough **165(SP:822041)**
Above the Whiteleaf chalk-cut cross. Footpath from near its base.
An unimpressive trio of mounds located near a medieval chalk-cut cross; that nearest the cross is a stunted long barrow, and contained a wooden chamber housing the foot of an arthritic middle-aged man, the rest of whose bones were scattered in the forecourt to the E. A cremation was inserted later. Animal bones, hundreds of flints and fragments of pottery were also discovered.
Just to the NE is a possible pond barrow of the Bronze Age and, at the end of the ridge, a small bowl barrow. Finds in the Institute of Archaeology (University of London).

GLOUCESTERSHIRE

Avening Reconstructed
Burial Chambers *New Stone Age*
Avening **162(ST:879984)**
SE of Stroud, E of B4014, and 300m N of Avening
church. Not far from Gatcombe Lodge (qv).

In 1806 a chambered tomb – the original location of which is uncertain – was excavated, and its 3 chambers reassembled in a rectory garden. Three skeletons had been found in one chamber, 8 in another, Two of the chambers still have their capstones, traces of an entrance passage and a porthole entrance.

Belas Knap Chambered
Long Barrow * *New Stone Age*
NW of Charlton Abbots **163(SP:021254)**
S of Winchcombe. Steepish footpath signposted on
road to Charlton Abbots. HBMCE.

Reached by a long and steep uphill path, this trapezoidal cairn – the name Belas Knap means 'beacon mound' – is located at an altitude of 300m, with fine views. It is an impressive monument of drystone walling, over 50m long and up to 18m wide; at the broader N end, 4m high, is a deeply indented, U-shaped forecourt, with 2 forward-projecting hornworks: the 2 uprights and the lintel here appear to be the entrance, but in fact this is a false one, blocked by another stone. There are 4 small, polygonal burial chambers built into the body of the mound, and entered directly through passages from the sides: only one stone remains of the one at the S end of the mound, but the others can still be entered. Excavation revealed at least 38 skeletons in these chambers, with 5 children and a man's skull behind the false

Belas Knap Chambered Long Barrow. New
Stone Age

entry. The mound has been partly restored. Finds in Cheltenham Art Gallery and Museum.

Chedworth Villa * *Roman*
N of Chedworth **163(SP:053135)**
From Fossebridge on A429 (Fosse Way) take
minor road NW to Yarnworth and Withington.
National Trust. Signposted. Shop, visitors' centre,
guidebook. Open mornings and 2-7pm. Closed
Mondays (except bank holidays), January and
1-15 October.

One of the finest villas in Britain, it was discovered by accident in 1864; much of it has been excavated. Located on the lower slopes of a hill, it seems to have been begun early in the 2nd century AD as 3 separate half-timbered wings around a small valley-head, with a stone bath-house. In the 3rd century, these buildings were linked by corridors and verandas, and the villa reached its full development in the 4th, when new reception rooms were added, the bath-house was converted to dry heat, and a spring was reorganized to feed a nymphaeum (a shrine to a water goddess).

The main rooms and mosaics are now inside protective buildings: in the W wing, the dining-room floor has a fine mosaic of the 4 seasons and Bacchus, while adjoining it to the N is a series of private rooms leading to a bath-suite of 5 rooms, with hypocaust below the hot-room. A large portion of the N wing comprises the main bath-suite that originally used damp heat and was later converted to dry heat with cold plunge baths. The villa's NW corner has the nymphaeum, which supplied the fresh water. Some stones from this pool's rim (now in the site museum) carry the *Chi-Rho* monogram, which implies that this shrine was later Christianized.

Above: *Chedworth Villa*. *The hypocaust*

Below: *Chedworth Villa*. *The four seasons mosaic*

Cirencester Town and
Amphitheatre *Roman*
Cirencester **163(SP:025018)**
Amphitheatre by footpath from Cotswold Avenue.
Fragments of basilica SE of The Avenue, and of
walls in the Beeches, Watermoor Gardens and in
the Abbey Gardens.

The rich and flourishing town of *Corinium*
Dobunnorum was founded in the late 1st century AD
as the local tribal capital of the Dobunni. The town's
centre lay over the earlier Roman fort that stood at
the head of a line of communication back to the s
coast. By the 2nd century, it was the largest town in
Britain with perhaps 12,000 inhabitants – a centre of
the wool trade and a market for the many farms of the
region. In the 4th century, it was a major centre for
mosaics, and its 'school' of mosaicists had widespread influence: some of its designs are recogniz-
able at Chedworth (*qv*). Most of the town has been
built over, and few remains are now visible: there is a
short stretch of town wall, N of London Road; the
course of the basilica's walls is outlined in Tower
Street; and, above all, the grass-covered amphitheatre
stands SW of the town, its banks up to 8m high. However, the superb Corinium Museum houses many
treasures, including the famous mosaics, some fine,
coloured wall-plaster, and a Christian word-square
scratched on a painted house-wall.

Crickley Hill Hillfort *New Stone/Iron Ages*
E of Little Witcombe **163(SO:928161)**
SW of Cheltenham, W of Air Balloon Inn at junction
of A417 and A436. National Trust.

One of the earliest defended sites in Britain, it
began as a causewayed camp with 2 lines of interrupted ditches cutting off the low knoll at the promontory's centre; the stone from the ditches was piled
up as a bank behind each. There were 2 narrow
entries, each opposite a causeway, and each with a
gate. Hundreds of arrowheads have been found along
these defences (which presumably enclosed a settlement) and traces of a burned palisade imply a sudden
end to occupation, and perhaps even warfare. This
early phase of the site may span the period 3500–
2500 BC.

After being deserted for centuries, the promontory was again fortified in the 7th or 6th century BC,
with an enclosure twice the size of the earlier one. A
deep rock-cut ditch and a 3m-high drystone wall
were the defences, and a narrow entrance and timber-lined passage led to a roadway between lines of
buildings. These were probably large houses, with
small square storage huts around them; the positions
of the postholes are now set out with blue markers.
About a third of this fort has been excavated, and it
is thought 50–200 people lived in it. After
being occupied for a generation or two, the settlement ended abruptly with houses and gates burned
down.

After several years, the fort was gradually rebuilt,
with a massive pair of stone bastions, and a second
gate in a large outwork. This settlement was quite
different, with a single great round house just behind
the gate, an irregular ring of smaller ones around it,
and clusters of small, square buildings nearby. Once
again, the postholes are now indicated by yellow
markers. The gateway has been dated by radiocarbon
to the late 6th/early 5th century BC. This fort did not
last very long and, like the others, was attacked and
burned.

Gatcombe Lodge Chambered
Long Barrow *New Stone Age*
Gatcombe Park **162(ST:884998)**
SE of Stroud. Immediately W of minor road
from Minchinhampton S to Avening (qv),
in beech trees at N tip of the park. Direct access
restricted.

This fenced-off barrow, now overgrown and
damaged, is orientated NE/SW and is 55m long. Excavation at the E end's forecourt proved it to be a false
portal, but a large burial chamber with a huge capstone was found in the N side; it contained a
crouched skeleton. A large slab near the W end of the
mound may mark another chamber. Nearby is the
'Long Stone', over 2m high and full of holes caused by
weathering, and a second stone forms a stile in a wall.
Mothers used to pass babies through the holes in the
'Long Stone' to ward off whooping cough and rickets;
there is also a legend that the stone runs round the
field at midnight.

Great Witcombe Villa *Roman*
SW of Great Witcombe **163(SO:899142)**
Signposted track S from A417, 400m E of A46
crossing. Key from farm.

Another fine villa in a pleasant location, it resembles Chedworth (*qv*) in that it is built around a courtyard, and it has a bath-suite of 3 rooms in the W wing,
now protected by a roof. There are splendid mosaics
in the suite, with decorations of marine life. The
foundations of other parts of the villa are visible, and
2 rooms have been identified as shrines to water
spirits.

Hetty Pegler's Tump
Chambered Long Barrow
(Uley Tumulus) * *New Stone Age*
N of Uley **162(SO:789001)**
W of B4066, 1.6km N of Uley church.
Signposted. Key from Crawley Hill Farm (2nd
house on right, on way to Uley), 0.8km along
road. Small admission charge. HBMCE leaflet.
Torch needed.

This grassy mound, 36m long, named after the
wife of a 17th-century owner of the field, has a deep
forecourt of drystone walling, a portal of 2 uprights
and a massive lintel, and a 22m passage with 2 pairs of
transepts. The 2 chambers on the N side are now
blocked off, but the S pair can be entered; the end of
the gallery was blocked off to form another chamber.
There may have been at least 23 burials in the tomb,
while outside the entrance 2 skeletons were found
together with the jaws of several boars.

The finds can now be seen in Guy's Hospital
Museum, London.

Leighterton Chambered
Long Barrow *New Stone Age*
SE of Boxwell **162(ST:819913)**
NW of Leighterton, SW of Nailsworth, on road to
Boxwell.

A massive, tree-covered mound, now standing
enclosed by a wall in an arable field, it is 67m long,
6m high at the E end, and orientated E/W. Excavations
almost 300 years ago uncovered 3 chambers at the E
end, containing inhumations, with cremations in
urns by the entrance of each.

These chambers have now disappeared, as has a
standing stone that Aubrey saw at the E end in the
17th century.

Above: ***Hetty Pegler's Tump Chambered Long Barrow***. *The entrance to the chamber still covered by its long barrow*

Below: ***Hetty Pegler's Tump Chambered Long Barrow***. *The burial chamber much as it was left by New Stone Age man. Note the combination of drystone and megalithic walling*

**Lodge Park Chambered
Long Barrow**   *New Stone Age*
Eastington   **163(SP:143126)**
*SE of Eastington and Northleach, in NE corner of
Lodge Park.*

An unexcavated mound, 46m long and aligned NW/
SE. A number of large stones protrude from it. The 2

parallel uprights at the SE end and the fallen capstone
may be a false entrance or a chamber.

**Lydney Hillfort and
Temple Complex ***   *Iron Age/Roman*
Lydney Park   **162(SO:616027)**
1.6km SW of Lydney, in the park. Just N of A48.

Permission needed in writing from the agent at Lydney Park Estate Office.

A promontory fort was built on this steep spur in the 1st century BC; a wide rampart with an external v-shaped ditch protected an area of 1.8ha. The bank was made higher – and 2 more built in front of it – in the late Roman period, and in the 4th century build-

Great Witcombe Villa. Part of the foundations of this Roman villa, which is built around a courtyard

ings were placed inside the fort, protected by a stone wall.

The site was an important Roman iron mine, and

one 15m-long shaft is accessible through a trapdoor just north of the Adam & Eve statues, though a torch is needed. Roman pick-marks can be seen on the walls.

Substantial traces survive of a large temple and its precinct, occupying half the fort, and dedicated to Nodens, a Celtic god of healing and hunting. Its plan is that of a basilica, with a nave and side-chapels, and 3 sanctuaries at the back. It was lavishly furnished with mosaic pavements. Oblique to its back wall is a long building divided into several individual rooms – possibly shops, or used for 'ritual incubation' so that the god could appear in pilgrims' dreams. There was also a suite of baths, overlying a second iron mine. Finds, including many votive offerings, are in a private museum in Lydney Park House.

Lydney Hillfort, *Gloucestershire (after R. E. M. Wheeler)*

Minchinhampton Common *Iron Age*
Minchinhampton **162(SO:857004)**
The Bulwarks curve across Common from the Halfway House Inn.

An enigmatic series of earthworks that probably formed part of the boundaries of a defended territory or *oppidum* covering over 240ha: the main feature, known as The Bulwarks, is a low bank with drystone revetment that curves 2.5km round to SO:870012 across the Common and thus cuts off the steep-sided spur. The bank varies in height up to 1.5m; if the ditch

is internal, then the earthworks may be protecting the 80ha containing Minchinhampton. Pottery implies that the defences date to the late Iron Age, or to immediately after the Roman conquest. Finds in Stroud Museum and the British Museum.

Notgrove Chambered
Long Barrow *New Stone Age*
NW of Notgrove **163(SP:096212)**
w of Bourton-on-the-Water. Immediately s of A436 and E of railway bridge. Signposted. HBMCE.

This barrow was originally a trapezoid, 48m long, orientated E/W, with drystone walling all around. It had a curved forecourt on the E, from which a narrow passage led to an antechamber and on to 2 pairs of transept-chambers, each built of megaliths and drystone. The end of the passage constitutes a fifth chamber. The interior is now open to the sky. Excavation found that fires had been lit in the forecourt, and that the chambers contained the remains of at least 6 adults and 3 children, as well as animal bones. To the w of the passage was a small, closed polygonal chamber under its own small, circular cairn, which was later incorporated into the mound: it contained the crouched skeleton of an elderly man, and that of a young woman lay above the 'dome'. There is a legend that a golden coffin is buried in the barrow. Finds in Cheltenham Art Gallery and Museum.

Nympsfield Chambered
Long Barrow *** *New Stone Age*
s of Frocester **162(SO:794013)**
sw of Stroud, w of B4066 to Uley/Dursley, at edge of wood. Picnic area.

An ovoid mound, 27m long, and orientated E/W, it was restored in 1976. The horned forecourt of drystone at the E end has a short entrance passage leading through a square antechamber, past a chamber on either side, to a terminal chamber. The interior is now open to the elements. Fires had been lit in the forecourt, and many pig bones were found in the material blocking the entrance. The remains of 23 people were found inside, together with pottery, flint and bone tools, and pieces of ochre. Some human bones bore traces of burning; and many of the people seem to have had abscesses, septic teeth and inflamed gums. Finds in Stroud Museum.

Painswick Beacon *Iron Age?*
Painswick **162(SO:869121)**
2km N of Painswick on road linking A46 with B4073.

This fort, much damaged inside by the building of a golf course and quarrying, has impressive double banks and ditches (with a counterscarp bank) on most sides, but is defended by steep slopes on the NW. The strong inturned entrance is on the NW, while an enigmatic deep, circular hollow in the fort's centre is probably not a well but may have had some ritual purpose.

Randwick Chambered
Long Barrow *New Stone Age*
w of Randwick **162(SO:825069)**
NW of Stroud. In woodland NW of Randwick church. National Trust.

A trapezoidal cairn, it is now 35m long because quarrying has removed the sw end. Originally it was 20m longer, and surrounded by drystone walling. There was a shallow horned forecourt, and a square

Above: ***Nympsfield Chambered Long Barrow***. *Slab-built chamber of the New Stone Age long barrow*

Below: ***Painswick Beacon***. *Iron Age hillfort*

burial chamber containing the fragmented bones of at least 4 people – though only a few pieces of skull were present, and no thigh bones at all. The mound was divided by axial and lateral lines of drystone walling, forming a series of compartments. Finds in Gloucester City Museum.

Salmonsbury Fort
Iron Age
Bourton-on-the-Water **163(SP:175208)**
Short road off E side of Bourton-on-the-Water. In angle between Windrush and Dikler rivers.

This unimpressive rectangular lowland fort of 22.7ha had 2 gravel banks revetted with drystone (though only the inner bank survives on the NW) and 2 V-shaped ditches. Extra defence was provided by the rivers. Of the 2 original entries, that on the NE is still in good condition. Excavation revealed circular huts inside, and pits nearby were filled with rubbish and the remains of 2 infants. A crouched female skeleton was found in another pit, and a man in a shallow grave. Pottery indicated occupation from the 3rd to 1st centuries BC, the ramparts being built in the 2nd, and a hoard of 147 currency bars was found in the site. Finds in the Ashmolean Museum (Oxford), Cheltenham Art Gallery and Museum and Gloucester City Museum.

Uleybury Hillfort *
Iron Age?
Uley **162(ST:785990)**
0.8km NW of Uley. Footpaths from the B4066 at West Hill, Uley and Crawley.

This fine promontory fort with superb views covers a 13ha rectangle on a flat spur. The natural defence of steep slopes on all sides except the N was supplemented by 2 banks and ditches. Of 3 possible entrances, the most important was probably that in the N corner, with 3 extra lines of defence outside it, now damaged. A crouched burial, a rubbish pit and 2 Iron Age currency bars were found in recent excava-

tions, while surface finds include a gold coin (now in Gloucester City Museum) of the Dobunni, the local Iron Age tribe.

West Tump Chambered
Long Barrow
New Stone Age
w of Brimpsfield **163(SO:912132)**
1.6km SW of Birdlip in Buckle Wood. NE of Stroud.

A tree-covered mound enclosed by drystone walling, it is 45m long and orientated NW/SE. A horned forecourt at the broad SE end has a false entrance with 2 uprights; 4 skeletons were found in the forecourt. A short, narrow passage near the NW end of the S side leads to a burial chamber in which at least 20 skeletons were found – including a young woman on a semicircle of 5 flat stones, next to the remains of a baby. Finds in Cheltenham Art Gallery and Museum.

Windmill Tump Chambered
Long Barrow
New Stone Age
SW of Rodmarton **163(ST:932973)**
NE of Tetbury, 0.8km N of A433. In fields S of Rodmarton-to-Cherington road.

Another tree-covered mound, now surrounded by a modern wall, it is 70m long, orientated E/W, and contains at least 5000 tons of stone. The drystone forecourt at the E end has a false entrance comprising 2 uprights and a blocking stone. There are 2 rectangular burial chambers beyond it, but they were reached by passages and porthole entrances from either side: these were filled in after excavation and thus cannot be visited. The N chamber had a huge 8-ton capstone, and it contained the crouched skeletons of 10 middle-aged adults and 3 small children, together with potsherds and 2 flint arrowheads. The other chamber contained potsherds and human bone. There is a legend of an underground passage and a golden coffin at this site. Finds in the British Museum.

——————HEREFORD & WORCESTER——————

Arthur's Stone Chambered
Long Barrow
New Stone Age
Dorstone **148/161(SO:318431)**
S of Willersley and 1.6km N of Dorstone. S of road to Pen-y-Moor Farm. HBMCE.

This mound was at least 18m long and orientated N/S; its polygonal chamber (9 uprights and a massive 25-ton capstone) and ruined passageway survive. There are legends that this is the tomb either of Arthur himself or of a king or giant he killed. Small cupmarks on a stone nearby to the S are said to be the marks made by the giant's elbows as he fell – or by Arthur as he knelt to pray – or made for the heels of quoits players: hence its name, the Quoit Stone.

Bredon Hill and Conderton
Hillforts *
Iron Age
NE of Bredon **150(SO:958402 & 972384)**
Isolated hill N of Tewkesbury. Lanes and tracks up from Kemerton, Great Comberton and Conderton.

Bredon Hill is a promontory fort, protected by cliffs on 2 sides, and by 2 ramparts and ditches across

the S end; the outer rampart is of drystone and dates to c. 300 BC; the inner, of dumped clay, to 150 BC. Inside were circular huts and storage pits. The fort seems to have been attacked and destroyed early in the 1st century AD, possibly by Belgic raiders before the Roman invasion. The gate was burned, and the remains of over 60 young men were found, cut to pieces, around the inner entrance. It seems that a row of heads or skulls was displayed on poles above the gate.

Conderton is a small ovoid enclosure with superb views; its first phase, c. 300 BC, comprised a single stone rampart with ditch, enclosing 1.2ha. There was a counterscarp bank on the E and W, and entrances on N and S. Rather than a fort, it may simply have been a cattle enclosure. Then, in the 1st century BC, a drystone wall was built across the spur, isolating an area of 0.8ha inside the enclosure. It had an inturned entrance, and seems to have been a village with a

Arthur's Stone Chambered Long Barrow. New Stone Age

Bredon Hill Hillfort. On the hill made famous by A. E. Housman, this Iron Age promontory fort was the scene of a great slaughter - probably by attacking Belgae

number of circular huts and storage pits. Together with the cattle compound, which had continued in use, it was abandoned before the Romans arrived. Finds from both sites in Birmingham City Museum.

Credenhill Hillfort   *Iron Age*
N of Credenhill   **149(SO:451445)**
NW of Hereford. Track N from Credenhill off the A480.

One of the largest and finest contour forts in Britain, it is now tree-covered. A single rampart and ditch enclose 20ha, and the 2 entrances (E and SE) are inturned, with possible guard-chambers. Excavation near the E gateway revealed 3 rows of square and rectangular huts with raised floors. The pathways were 4.5m wide, and the huts 3.5m apart. They seem to

have been rebuilt several times. Storage pits and Iron Age potsherds were also discovered. Finds in Hereford Museum.

Croft Ambrey Hillfort *   *Iron Age*
Croft   **149(SO:444668)**
SW of Ludlow. From Cock Gate on B4362 into Croft Castle Park. Final uphill walk of 1.2km. National Trust.

Occupation of this triangular fort may have begun very early, since carbonized grain from its main quarry ditch has been radiocarbon-dated to 1050 BC. It seems to have started as an enclosure of 2.2ha with sheer slopes to the N, and a small rampart and ditch to S and W. There were rows of 4-post buildings (granaries?) inside. Later it was extended to 3.6ha, with a massive rampart and 2 gates (at SW and E), both with guard-chambers: timber from one guardroom has been radiocarbon-dated to 460 BC. The huts were rebuilt, and stood in rows along streets. There is ample evidence of extensive grain production (charred grain, saddle querns) as well as of stockrear-

The town of *Magnis* formed an irregular hexagon of 8.9ha, and was an important market centre. There were many shops and workshops, houses with fine mosaics, and a bath building. Little is now visible.

King Arthur's Cave Cave-dwelling
Old Stone Age/ Roman
s of Whitchurch **162(SO:545155)**
NE of Monmouth. 1.2km SW of Great Doward. HBMCE. Signposted. Torch needed.
This small cave at the foot of a low cliff, in woodland 90m above the Wye, was first excavated in 1871. Under a thick layer of stalagmite were flint tools of the late Old Stone Age, although some were possibly of the preceding Neanderthal period, and others of the subsequent Middle Stone Age. There were ashes, and bones of many animals such as mammoth, woolly rhino, lion and cave bear. In the last Ice Age, the cave probably served as a repeatedly occupied base camp. The site owes its name to a legend that Arthur, when pursued by enemies, concealed his treasure here, and Merlin's magic ensured that its hiding place would never be found. Finds in Cheltenham Art Gallery and Museum, Gloucester City Museum and University of Bristol Speleological Society Museum.

Midsummer Hill Hillfort
Iron Age
E of Eastnor **150(SO:761375)**
4.8km SSW of Little Malvern, just N of A438. Track N from Hollybush village. National Trust.
An irregular area of 12ha, including 2 hilltops, is enclosed by a stone-faced rampart and a ditch, with a counterscarp bank in places. There are entries on NW and SW; the latter was frequently rebuilt, and had guard-chambers: the first gate here is radiocarbon-dated to 420 BC. The interior has traces of about 250 rectangular huts arranged along streets. Carbonized grain associated with the destruction of the eighth gate is radiocarbon-dated to 50 BC; and the fort was finally burned down in AD 48 when Ostorius Scapula attacked the Decangi. Finds in Birmingham City Museum.

Risbury Hillfort
Iron Age?
Humber **149(SO:542553)**
SE of Leominster. E of road from Stoke Prior to Risbury.
A rectangular lowland fort of 3.6ha, it has massive ramparts, up to 9m high, of dumped clay and stone facing: they are double on the W, triple elsewhere. The original entrance was probably in the W side.

Sutton Walls Hillfort
Iron Age
Sutton St Michael **149(SO:525464)**
N of Hereford. Track N from Sutton St Michael.
One of the scandals of British archaeology, this elongated ovoid fort of 12ha has had much of its interior removed for gravel; this has left a quarry now used as a dump for toxic waste. The first occupation of the site in the early Iron Age did not involve defences. By 100 BC, a v-shaped ditch and an internal bank, revetted with timber and drystone, had been built, and huts were constructed later. Around AD 25, the defences were strengthened; but in AD 48, 24 people were killed–probably by the Romans–and thrown into the ditch: their skeletons bear wounds, and some were decapitated. However, the fort remained occupied until at least the 3rd century. Finds in Hereford Museum.

ing (mostly sheep) and weaving. An annexe of 4.8ha was presumably an animal corral; and occupation seems to have ended c. AD 48. Finds in Hereford and Birmingham City museums.

Herefordshire Beacon Hillfort*
Iron Age
s of Colwall **150(SO:760400)**
1km SW of Little Malvern to s of A449. Climb up from opposite 'British Camp Hotel'.
A steep climb leads to this large contour fort, impressively crowning its ridge, with superb views over a huge area. In the 3rd century BC, it enclosed 3.2ha, but 200 years later was expanded to 13ha; there is a double bank and a ditch in between, with an entrance on each side. Many hut-circles can be traced inside. The dyke and ring motte are medieval. Finds in Hereford Museum.

Kenchester Town
Roman
Kenchester **149(SO:440428)**
NW of Hereford. Just N of A438 on Roman road from Rochester to Caerwent.

——————— HERTFORDSHIRE ———————

Arbury Banks Fort
Ashwell   *Iron Age*
                   153(TL:262387)
NE of Baldock. Among fields 1.2km SW of Ashwell.

An ovoid plateau fort on arable lowland, it has 5.1ha within its double bank and deep v-shaped ditch. Potsherds and the bones of farm animals have been found, while aerial photography indicates that the site had one big round hut, together with other postholes and pits. It was probably a defended farming settlement. Finds in Ashwell Museum.

Ravensburgh Castle
Hillfort
Hexton   *Iron Age*
                  166(TL:099295)
N of Luton, 1.2km S of Hexton. Track from B655 to view W ramparts. For entry, permission needed from Hexton Estate Office.

This tree-covered rectangular fort of 9ha is the largest in eastern England, and may be the *oppidum* that Cassivellaunus defended against Caesar in 54 BC. It has a double bank and ditch on the W, but the natural defence of very steep dry valleys on the other 3 sides needed only a single rampart. There were entrances on NW and SE. The site originated *c.* 400 BC, and the earthworks were renewed in the early 1st century BC. Finds in Letchworth Museum.

Six Hills Barrows
Stevenage   *Roman*
                  166(TL:237237)
S of Stevenage New Town beside the A602.

Standing by the Roman road that lies beneath the Great North Road (A1), these Roman mounds are well-known landmarks; about 3m high, they are mostly about 18m across. Some were opened in 1741, but only fragments of wood and iron are recorded.

Therfield Heath
Barrows
Royston   *New Stone/Bronze Ages*
                  154(TL:342402)
Just SW of Royston, S of A505 beside golf course.

A large barrow cemetery, conspicuous on the skyline overlooking the Icknield Way, a prehistoric trackway. There is a low long barrow of turf and chalk rubble, 33m long, orientated E/W, with a wide berm and ditch around it. It contained 2 cists with ashes, and one disarticulated skeleton. Just to the N stands a group of 10 round barrows, 6 of which are called the 'Five Hills'! They contained a number of inhumations and cremations, and one had 9 disarticulated skeletons.

A kilometre further W is another round barrow (Pen Hills) at one end of an Iron Age boundary ditch (Mile Ditches). Finds in Cambridge University Museum of Archaeology and Ethnology.

Verulamium, Prae Wood
and Beech Bottom Dyke *
St Albans   *Iron Age/Roman*
             166(TL:136073 museum)

The Catuvellaunian *oppidum* here is represented by the many low earthworks of Prae Wood (TL:123068) – overgrown banks and ditches that start to the NW of the gamekeeper's cottage. Two cemeteries have been found here, and abundant pottery, ovens

and coin-moulds in baked clay. The same people were probably responsible for Beech Bottom Dyke (TL:155093), a massive ditch between 2 banks, 27m wide and 9m deep, somewhat resembling that at Wheathampstead (*qv*). This was probably connected to Prae Wood, and defended the area between the Ver and Lea rivers.

The Romans established a fort here, but it was soon replaced by a small town: i.e., 2 rows of shops and hovels strung out along Watling Street. It had grown into a major urban centre by AD 60 when it was destroyed in Boudicca's revolt. The rebuilt town included a monumental forum and basilica, dated to AD 79, but the 1st century AD defensive bank and ditch were removed early in the 2nd century. A fire in *c.* 155 destroyed 21ha, and the new town that arose was doubled in size, with more stone than timber being used; it had 2 triumphal arches and a small theatre. A massive bank and an enormous ditch surrounded the town, with monumental gates on all 4 sides, each of them a double carriageway.

Verulamium was a wealthy market centre, the most important town in Roman Britain, with comfortable houses, fine mosaics, Italian marble and a piped water supply, but by the 4th century the theatre had become a rubbish dump, and the town seems to have flourished only until *c.* 430. Britain's first Christian martyr, St Alban, was executed here in the reign of Diocletian (*c.* 305).

The town has a fine museum, containing magnificent mosaics. The major visible remains are those of the theatre (TL:134074, across the road to the NW), the only one in Britain that can be visited. It had a small raised stage in the centre where animal shows were put on, facilities for performers, and a semicircular bank of raised seats. Guidebook available.

Much of the Roman town lies beneath the playing fields around the museum: St Michael's church is on the site of the forum and basilica in the town centre, while the cathedral walls contain much Roman brickwork. In the centre of the playing fields is a modern building protecting 2 Roman rooms with hypocaust and mosaics. On the S side of the fields is a long stretch of town wall, with a deep ditch in front. Bastions are spaced along the front of the wall, guard-houses behind, and at one end are the foundations of the massive London gate, which had 2 passages for vehicles, 2 for pedestrians and flanking guard-chambers. Near the theatre one can see the remains of some houses and shops: one house had an underground shrine.

Wheathampstead Devil's
Dyke
Wheathampstead   *Iron Age*
             166(TL:187133)
SE outskirts of town, just S of A6129 and the river Lea.

This impressive earthwork, in an area of flat land defended by forest and marshes, was constructed by deepening a natural valley and building a bank on either side. It was once thought to be a fortified Belgic settlement of 36ha – even the HQ of Cassivellaunus that Caesar captured in 54 BC – but it now seems more likely to be part of the discontinuous dyke system that stretched NE/SW between the Lea and Ver rivers with the help of natural obstacles.

Above: **Verulamium**. *This small section of the town wall, dating from about AD 200, shows the construction of flints set in mortar bonded with tiles. There was a huge ditch outside*

Below: **Verulamium**. *The only Roman theatre in Britain that can be visited*

NORTHAMPTONSHIRE

Borough Hill Hillfort *Iron Age*
Daventry **152(SP:588626)**
1.6km E of Daventry. Encloses E end of golf course.
Obstructed to S by BBC radio mast.
This fort of 1.8ha, with 2 strong banks and a ditch in between, had a southern extension of 6.5ha. Excavations revealed a furnace pit, possibly for iron smelting, and a fragment of Iron Age pottery. There used to be a row of Romano-British barrows on the hilltop. Finds in Northampton Museum.

Hunsbury Hill Hillfort *Iron Age*
W of Hardingstone **152(SP:738584)**
3.2km S of Northampton. Reached by bridle path
running S from A45.
Ironstone quarrying in the last century lowered the interior of this fort by 2.4m, and so the defences that enclose its 1.6ha seem more impressive than they did originally. They comprise a roughly circular and tree-covered rampart and deep V-shaped ditch, with counterscarp bank. The rampart, probably constructed in the 4th century BC, was of rubble with timber reinforcement, later replaced by clay. The original entrance was probably that on the SE. The fort may have been preceded by an undefended ironstone-working settlement. The recent quarrying exposed 300 storage pits, but there may only have been half a dozen huts. The finds – weaving artifacts, quernstones, weapons, horse-trappings and pottery – indicate occupation up to AD 50, and are housed in Northampton Museum and the British Museum.

Rainsborough Camp
Hillfort *Iron Age*
Newbottle **151(SP:526348)**
NE of Aynho. Track W; from Camp Farm on Charlton-
to-Croughton road.
A strong, ovoid fort of 2.5ha, with 2 ramparts and ditches, and an inturned entrance on the W; excavation has revealed that this had a timber-lined cobbled passage leading to 2 stone-lined guard-rooms. These were attacked and burned in the 5th century BC; the scorched skull of a middle-aged man was found in one of them. Reconstruction in the late 2nd century BC was incomplete, and the site was later abandoned, though there was some Romano-British occupation here. Radiocarbon dates cluster around 50 BC. Finds in the Ashmolean Museum, Oxford. The drystone walling around the inner rampart is part of the 18th-century landscape gardening.

OXFORDSHIRE

Alfred's Castle Hillfort *Iron Age/Roman*
Ashbury **174(SU:277822)**
3.2km SE of Ashbury on NW edge of Ashdown Park.
By bridle and footpath from B4000.
A small polygonal fort of 0.8ha, it has a single bank and a modest ditch, with an original entrance on the SE. Sarsen stones that used to form the bank's revetment were removed in the 17th century for the building of Ashdown House. The site is probably Iron Age, though it has yielded pottery of later periods. Aerial photography has revealed a 3ha enclosure adjoining it to the N. Legend makes this the place where Alfred's armies gathered before the battle of Ashdown in AD 871.

Chastleton Barrow Fort *Late Bronze/Iron Ages*
SE of Chastleton **163(SP:259283)**
SE of Moreton-in-Marsh. Footpath off A436 NW to
Chastleton.
This small ovoid fort of 1.4ha has a substantial rampart (which used to be faced with stone) but no ditch, and simple entrances on E and NW. Hearths and paving and pottery of the 8th century BC have been found. Finds in the Ashmolean Museum, Oxford.

Cherbury Camp Lowland Fort *Iron Age*
Kingston Bagpuize **164(SU:374963)**
4km WSW of Kingston Bagpuize, S of A420. Approach
from N by way of Lovell's Court Farm.
This fort was built on a low-lying island amid marshy ground: all is now drained and good agricultural land. A metalled track, with wheel ruts 1.5m apart, led along a neck of dry land to an entrance on the E. The fort had 3 ramparts and ditches enclosing an ovoid area of 3.6ha. Occupation may have begun in the 5th century BC and lasted to the 1st century AD. The pottery from the site is now in the Ashmolean Museum, Oxford.

Churn Farm Round Barrow
Cemetery *Bronze Age*
Blewbury **174(SU:515837)**
2.5km SW from A417 at Blewbury. On S side of Churn
Hill and E of Churn Farm.
A row of 4 barrows, all about 1m high and 24–38m across. A cremation was found in one. Further SE (SU:520833) are 2 bell barrows, the larger of which contained a cremation with a bronze dagger.

Dyke Hills Promontory Fort *Iron Age*
Dorchester-on-Thames **164(SU:574937)**
Footpath from S end of Dorchester, near Thames
bridge. 1.2km NE of Sinodun (qv).
The junction of the Thames and the Thame provided natural defences on 3 sides, so that 2 massive banks (still up to 3m high) and a wide ditch in between effectively protected 46ha. It was probably first occupied in the early Iron Age, and aerial photography has revealed abundant huts and pits inside.

Grim's Ditch Running Dyke *Iron Age?*
Mongewell, Crowmarsh **175(SU:608883 to**
Gifford **682868)**
This 8km stretch of dyke runs eastward from the Thames, and may be associated with the Chilterns

Grim's Ditch (p. 144). The best sections are at SU:636606 and 669869.

Hoar Stone Chambered
Barrow *New Stone Age*
Enstone **164(SP:378237)**
In Enstone plantation, s of junction of B4022 and Enstone-to-Fulwell road. Signposted.

The mound has gone, but it is known to have been 1m high in 1824; now protected by a wall, the remains of its u-shaped chamber face E and comprise 3 uprights (up to 2.7m high) and a possible capstone. There are legends that the main stone (the 'Old Soldier') goes down to the village to drink on Midsummer's Eve, and if anyone tries to drag the stones away, they will return of their own accord.

Lyneham Chambered
Long Barrow *New Stone Age*
Lyneham **164(SP:297211)**
2.8km NE of Shipton railway station, immediately w of A361.

This mound, over 50m long, is orientated NE/SW and stands in an arable field. Excavation revealed 2 chambers on the SE side containing human and animal remains. At the overgrown NE end is a standing stone 1.8m high and almost as wide: it may have formed part of a false portal. Just to the NE (SP:299214) is Lyneham Camp, an Iron Age enclosure of 2ha – possibly a cattle corral.

North Leigh Villa *Roman*
North Leigh (East End) **164(SP:397154)**
2km NE of Witney. Signposted. HBMCE.

A huge villa of courtyard type, with many rooms, and with servants' quarters and baths taking up 2 wings. There is also a complex of farm outbuildings. Having been excavated early in the 19th century, it was left open to damage for a long time. It seems to have begun as a simple corridor house with a modest bath-house, and then expanded in size and wealth: there are fine mosaics that can be linked to the mosaicist who worked at Chedworth (p. 146) and, in turn, with the Cirencester school of mosaicists (p. 148). The visible remains comprise the outlines of 3 wings; the dining-room mosaic is protected by a roof.

Rollright Stones Stone
Circle and Tomb* *New Stone / Bronze Age*
Great and Little Rollright **151(SP:296308)**
On minor road linking A34 with A44. Small admission fee. HBMCE.

There are 3 sites here. The *King's Men* are 77 stones up to 2m tall, closely grouped in a circle, 31.6m across, on an exposed ridge above the Oxford plain: these blocks of weathered limestone vary in height and shape, and may be the eroded fragments of far fewer monoliths. The entrance was perhaps on the N. The location makes this site rather isolated from all other stone circles.

The *King Stone*, 73m to the NE, stands alone inside an iron fence across the road, and is actually in Warwickshire. It is 2.5m high and 1.5m wide, and may once have formed part of a burial chamber, or be an outlier for the circle: it would have served as a marker visible from the prehistoric trackway that led up past the ring.

Finally, 360m ESE of the circle are the *Whispering Knights*, also within a fence: these 5 large stones constitute the 4 uprights and fallen capstone of a burial chamber whose mound has gone.

All 3 sites are thought to be contemporaneous, *c.* 2000 BC, and many legends are associated with them. The stones are a king and his army who were turned to stone by a witch. The circle's stones cannot be counted – or anyone who counts them 3 times and gets the same total can have a wish. People used to break off bits of the King Stone for charms to ward off the Devil. Infertile women can be cured by touching the stones with bare breasts. The stones go down to

Rollright Stones Tomb Chamber. New Stone Age or Bronze Age

the stream to drink at midnight, or on New Year's Day. According to Stukeley, in the 18th century, young people used to meet near the King Stone for dancing and feasting on Midsummer's Eve. Finally, attempts to remove stones have brought disaster: 20 horses were needed to drag the Whispering Knight capstone downhill to make a bridge over the Little Rollright, but it rolled on to the grass every night – and only one horse was needed to drag it back to its proper place!

Sinodun Hillfort (Castle Hill) *Iron Age?*
Little Wittenham **174(SU:570924)**
2km ssw of Dorchester. Between A423 (to nw) and A4130 (to s). Carpark and footpath by road from Brightwell n to Little Wittenham. 1.2km sw of Dyke Hills (qv).

This fort is in a superb location on a steep hill with extensive views, notably along the Thames. Its ditch and external bank enclose an irregular area of 4ha,

with a simple entrance on the w. The interior has often been ploughed, which may have destroyed an inner bank. It is unexcavated, but pottery of the Romano-British period and possibly the Iron Age has been found. Finds in the Ashmolean Museum, Oxford.

Uffington Castle
Hillfort *Iron Age?*
Uffington **174(SU:299864)**
9km w of Wantage. One-way road signposted 'White Horse' from B4507. e of carpark on hilltop. HBMCE.

An ovoid fort near the Uffington White Horse (qv), it encloses 3.2ha with 2 strong banks and a ditch in between. The entrance was on the nw. The inner bank was faced with sarsen stones, and embodied postholes and chalk rubble in its construction. A silver coin of the (Iron Age) Dobunni tribe was found outside.

__Uffington White Horse Hill-figure__. Iron Age? (© Georg Gerster/John Hillelson Agency)

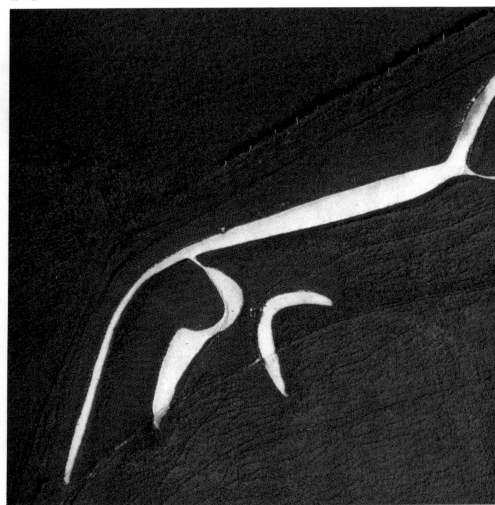

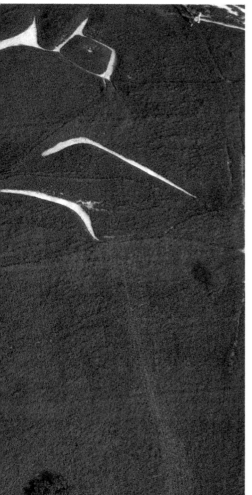

Rollright Stones. *The Stone Circle*

Uffington White Horse
Hill Figure*   *Iron Age?*
Uffington   **174(SU:302866)**
One-way road signposted 'White Horse' from
B4507. Short walk NE from carpark.

Just NE of Uffington fort *(qv)*, the turf on the hill
has been removed to expose the underlying chalk
and depict a figure that is probably a horse, although
it could be a dragon, since the flat hill in the valley
below is called Dragon Hill, and there is a legend that
St George killed the dragon here and that the spot
where the blood spilled is now a patch where nothing grows.

The figure, 110m long and 40m high, is best seen
from a distance. Through its resemblance to an Iron
Age method of depicting horses (on coins, etc.) it is
thought to be of that period, and to represent a tribal
emblem of the Dobunni or Atrebates, although there
are other possibilities: that the Anglo-Saxon leader
Hengist had it cut in the 5th century, or that it commemorates Alfred's victory over the Danes in AD 871.
The earliest known record of it is from the 11th century. At any rate, the figure has been preserved to the
present day, being scoured every 7 years, an occasion
that once gave rise to festivities and sports in the
fort. Many legends are linked with the figure – notably that it is lucky to make a wish while standing on
the eye.

Wayland's Smithy Chambered
Long Barrow*   *New Stone Age*
ENE of Ashbury   **174(SU:281854)**
1.2km NE of B4000. HBMCE.

Beside the Ridgeway, 2km SW of Uffington fort
(qv), this great monument stands in a beech grove.
The first mound was an ovoid, 16.4m long, and comprised a wooden mortuary structure with a stone
floor; it contained 14 bodies, and was enclosed in
sarsen boulders and chalk. No more than 50 years
later *(c. 2820 BC)*, the great wedge-shaped earth
mound was superimposed on it: 55m long and orientated SE/NW, with a sarsen kerb all around it. There are
flanking ditches up to 9m distant. Its S façade is
impressive, being composed of 4 (of an original 6)
great sarsens, 3m high. From here a high passage, 6m

163

Wayland's Smithy Chambered Long Barrow.
New Stone Age

long, leads through an antechamber to a cruciform
burial chamber. The tomb contained 8 people
including a child: there were no grave goods and no
thigh bones. Finds in Reading Museum.

The site is also known as Wayland Smith's Cave: the
Smith (or Volund) was a northern god, associated
with many sites. Here, he is said to have made the Uffington horse's shoes; and it is said that, if a traveller's
horse lost a shoe, he had to leave the animal by the
tomb, place a coin on a stone and, when he returned,
the horse would be shod and the money gone.

——WARWICKSHIRE——
and WEST MIDLANDS

Burrow Hill Hillfort   *Iron Age*
Corley   **140(SP:304850)**
NW of Coventry. Immediately E of B4098 at Corley.

This square fort of 3ha is in a fine position, and has
a single earth and rubble bank with timber-lacing,
and an external ditch, with an outturned entry on the
SW. It probably dates from 50 BC to AD 50.

Chesterton Fort   *Roman*
Chesterton and Kingston   **151(SP:341598)**
*Ramparts on either side of the Fosse Way just NE of
Chesterton Brook.*

A small fort on the Fosse Way, it covered 3.2ha; it is
under plough, but its impressive banks and ditches
still mark its outline.

King Stone, *see* Rollright Stones (Oxfordshire).

The Lunt Fort*   *Roman*
Baginton   **151(SP:345752)**
*On N side of road to Baginton from A45 at junction
with B4115. Coventry Museum Field Centre. Open
weekends 11am–6pm Easter to 1 October.*

This small cavalry fort, one of the early examples
along the Fosse Way frontier, was only rediscovered
in 1960, but has become a most impressive and
rewarding site for the visitor. It was occupied only
from AD 60 to 75, and had an unusual shape caused by
a circular area, 30m across, within the rampart on the
E: this level area, surrounded by a palisade, must have
been an arena or training ground of some kind.

The site is important because of the experimental
reconstruction that has taken place; troops from the
local Royal Engineers Depot built the main eastern
gateway in 2 days, using only equipment available to
their Roman predecessors. The gate's timbers were
placed in the original postholes; above there is a
walkway, and a tower fighting-platform, while on
either side is a 15m length of turf rampart with a palisade on top. A barrack block for 80 men (a 'century')
has also been reconstructed to contain finds.

Meon Hill Hillfort   *Iron Age?*
Quinton   **151(SP:177454)**
*Isolated hill E of A46. Track up past Meon Hall
farm from Lower Quinton-to-Mickleton road.*

This fort has a double rampart and ditch except on

the NW side: here only single defences were needed
thanks to the steep slope. A hoard of 394 currency
bars was found in the centre in the last century. Finds
in Gloucester City Museum, Stratford Museum and
the Ashmolean Museum, Oxford.

Oldbury Hillfort   *Iron Age*
NW of Hartshill   **140(SP:314947)**
*NW of Nuneaton. N of the A47 and of Oldbury
village, enclosing Oldbury Hall.*

A rectangular fort in an impressive position, its single bank (almost 2m high) and ditch enclose 2.8ha. Excavation suggests an early Iron Age date.

Wappenbury Fort
Wappenbury   *Iron Age*
                         151(SP:377693)
NE of Royal Leamington Spa. Village within the ramparts. Footpath W from church.
This much-damaged low-lying fort encloses the

entire modern village; the massive rampart is of gravel and clay, and is best preserved on the NW and E, together with its external ditch. The fort probably controlled fords at its SE and SW corners, and has been dated to the 1st century BC/AD, though there was earlier occupation of the site, in the 4th century BC. Finds in Coventry Museum.

THE NORTH MIDLANDS

Very much like the South Midlands, this is a large region – comprising Cheshire, Derbyshire, Leicestershire, Lincolnshire, Nottinghamshire, Shropshire and Staffordshire – generally rather poor in prehistoric remains but with small concentrations of them largely determined by the geological map. Again as in the South Midlands, the eastern concentration of early sites is on the chalk – of the Lincolnshire Wolds – while in the Marcher country of the west, the many fine hillforts are a direct continuation of those to the south. The great difference between the two regions is that here the best and most concentrated group of the three (the equivalent, as it were, of the Cotswolds) lies near the centre on the Carboniferous limestone of the extremity of the Pennines, south from the Derbyshire Peak, round Buxton and Matlock and across the border into Staffordshire.

The North Midlands has the only Old Stone Age cave-dwellings that can rival, and in many ways surpass, those of the Cheddar Gorge. These are in the narrow limestone ravine of Creswell Crags (p. 170). Here, among a score of caves, the earliest inhabitants can be judged from their implements to have been Neanderthalers; after an interval, they were to be followed, about 30,000 years ago, by hunters of *Homo sapiens sapiens* stock, then abandoned for many millennia before being re-occupied at the end of the Old Stone Age. The gorge has been made a 'Site of Special Scientific Interest' (SSSI), as it indeed is, and visitors are provided with all manner of informative displays, but can only observe the caves through metal grilles.

For the New Stone and Bronze Ages, interest focuses on the Lincolnshire Wolds and the Peak area. The long, narrow strip of the chalk Wolds was well populated during those periods, but has since been so intensively cultivated that a vast number of burial mounds have vanished and most that remain have suffered from the plough. About a dozen earthen long barrows survive, the best grouped at the southern end of the chalk, among them Deadmen's Graves (p. 176) and Giant's Hills (p. 176). Fragments of Beaker ware found in the latter suggest that these Wold barrows are late of their kind.

Of Bronze Age round barrows, fewer than 100 can still be seen on the Wolds – it is difficult to be more accurate since a few of these mounds were raised by the Anglo-Saxons. The two groups of undoubted Bronze Age date that have been given space in the Gazetteer – Bully Hills and Butterbump (p. 176) – are worth finding. These and most other round barrows probably cover cremation urn burials of the full Bronze Age, since the Beaker Folk did not penetrate the area in any numbers.

It cannot be pretended that the antiquities of the Lincolnshire Wolds have much appeal, and the country at its best is no more than pleasant. It is quite otherwise with the Peak region where the hills, moors and wooded valleys are a delight, the ancient monuments abundant, and Buxton and Bakewell most agreeable places in which to stay.

Here the farming communities of the New Stone Age built chambered megalithic tombs. A few were in long barrows – such as Ringham Low (p. 174) and Bridestones (p. 180) – but others of them were passage graves below large round barrows, a form that at once links them with North Wales. Archaeologists had already recognized this relationship with the west before it was most satisfactorily confirmed by the analysis of stone axes, many of which proved to have been traded from the Lake District and North Wales itself. One striking example of the passage graves is Minninglow (p. 174), unhappily much mutilated – partly by Thomas Bateman (p. 10), for it should be remembered that this is Bateman country. Another is Five Wells (p. 172) in which two passage graves are entered from opposite points.

These chambered tombs are of great interest, but the famous monument, pride of this southern Peak district, is the circle henge of Arbor Low, on high ground south-west of Bakewell. The massive bank with two entrances is built from big blocks of limestone chopped from the internal ditch; sadly the 50 large monoliths that form the ring now lie flat round the inner edge of the ditch, as do stones once forming a central 'cove' comparable to that at Avebury. A second henge is the Bull Ring (p. 170), above Dovedale to the north-west.

There are free-standing stone circles here in Peakland. The most worth seeing is Nine Stones Close where four enormous blocks survive below the crag of Hart Hill. Close by is Stanton Moor, which has been described as 'a lost world ... a prehistoric necropolis of cairns, ring cairns, standing stones and stone circles'. Probably all date from the Bronze Age, but this assortment shows how difficult it is to draw a line between true stone circles and ringed burial mounds.

In contrast with the Wolds, Beaker Folk freely penetrated this area and may have been responsible for the development of henges and stone circles. Many were buried

Stanton Moor, Stanton in Peak, Derbyshire.
Standing Stone from the 'prehistoric necropolis'

in the crouched position in pits below round barrows – an example with a well-furnished grave is Green Low (p. 172) on Alsop Moor. The Beaker people mingled with their New Stone Age predecessors to form a somewhat insular and conservative population living in what was essentially a backwater. Numerous though Beaker barrows are, even more of the plentiful Derbyshire round barrows cover cremations of the later Bronze Age.

Moving now to Shropshire, the western area with a striking concentration of ancient monuments, Iron Age hillforts prevail. There are, however, two stone circles surviving, one of which, Mitchell's Fold (p. 177), is well worth visiting on its high, heathland site with a wonderful background of broken hills. There is a round cairn with a standing stone near the circle as well as other round barrows to be seen in the area, though none worthy of a place in the Gazetteer except the group near Ludlow focused on Robin Hood's Butt (p. 178).

Although nearly all stone-built, the hill-forts differ widely in style according to the extraordinary geological complexity of this stretch of the Marches – a favourite training ground for student geologists. A great south-west/north-east crack in the earth's crust – the Church Stretton fault – caused a bewilder-ing variety of hard, ancient rocks to rear up in hills and small ranges with narrow erosion vales between them. The whole is bounded to the south-east by the long line of Wenlock Edge.

Beginning the catalogue of fine hillforts in the south of the county (not too far from the South Midlands' Croft Ambrey), there is Caynham Camp, which, unlike most Shrop-shire hillforts, has been excavated. It has a long history, with many rebuildings, begin-ning it seems at the end of the Bronze Age. To the north, Titterstone Clee is large and conspicuous, while to the west, in a region where almost every hill has its fort, there is the Caer Caradoc hillfort, one of three forts to be associated, quite wrongly, with the gal-lant Caratacus. Beyond Church Stretton, the much more famous Caer Caradoc can be seen from afar, clinging to its rocky ridge. Its builders showed extraordinary tenacity in cutting stone ditches and raising ramparts that made full use of natural crags.

North across the Severn (and not too far from the remarkable industrial museum at Ironbridge), the 400m ridge of The Wrekin, that splendid landmark, is enclosed by the inner and outer ramparts of a long narrow fort. Excavation has shown that it dates back to the fourth century BC, but had a long his-tory, almost certainly becoming the tribal capital of the Cornovii, and only deserted when its surviving inhabitants moved down to the Roman garrison town of Wroxeter a few miles to the west.

Finally, in the extreme north-west of the county, on a glacial esker, is Old Oswestry with immensely complex defences, like those of The Wrekin, developed during the centuries after 400 BC.

These are the best of the northern Marcher hillforts – and very striking they all are. Others are described in the Gazetteer and many more can be found by explorers in this rather strange but fascinating country-side – ideal for walking and rough climbing.

The Roman presence in the North Mid-lands has left its mark, but only one monu-ment of exceptional appeal. Among the important lines of communication, Ermine Street in the east runs up through Ancaster (p. 176) to Lincoln, and then on to Humber-side; the Fosse Way reaches its final destina-tion at Lincoln; Watling Street, after crossing Ryknild Street at Wall (p. 180), turns due west to Wroxeter; the Car Dyke, last seen in Cambridgeshire, can with some difficulty be traced through Lincolnshire. In the northern part of the region, the main roads are begin-ning the Pennine divide, maintained ever since in the eastern and western routes to Scotland. The Roman engineers did, however, drive one road boldly over the southern Pen-nines and this can be seen between Derby and Buxton (where a Roman spa has since vanished), passing by the Stone Age tomb on Minninglow moor.

Villas were not very numerous in this part of the Roman province, nor could many of the owners afford luxury. The most consider-able remains are the cities of Leicester, Lin-coln and Wroxeter. Leicester, cantonal capital of the Coritani, can only show the Jewry Wall (p. 175), a lofty but somewhat dreary piece of masonry surviving from the bi-sexual bath-ing establishment; Great Casterton in the east of Leicestershire deserves to be named as a posting-station on Ermine Street with some surviving earthworks.

It is at Lincoln that our Roman heritage comes to life in the Newport Arch, part of the north gate of the city through which traf-fic still passes. Fragments of the walls, East Gate and outer ditch are also on view. When the legionary base for the northern frontier was advanced to York, this city was built exactly over the old fortress, as a *colonia* for time-expired veterans.

While Roman Leicester and Lincoln can only be glimpsed here and there through the welter of their modern successors, Wroxeter (p. 179) – *Viroconium* – like *Verulamium* and Silchester, is in open country – and open to the spade. Excavation has, in fact, been in progress intermittently since the last century. After it ceased to be a fortress *Viroconium* became a large and prosperous town, one of the places most evidently stimulated by the visit to the province of the Emperor Hadrian – to whom the forum and basilica were dedi-cated in a nobly lettered inscription. It may be true that 'Today the Roman and his trou-ble/Are ashes under Uricon', but archaeolo-gists are at great pains to resuscitate him and his history.

Cheshire, a county poor in ancient monu-ments, has produced the first British 'bog man'. In 1984 peat cutting in the once exten-sive Lindow Moss just to the west of Wilmslow revealed the partially preserved body of a strong, well-nourished man who probably lived in the 6th century BC. He had mousy-coloured head hair, with gingery sideburns, beard and trimmed moustache. It appeared to the excavators that Lindow Man had been felled with an axe, throttled with a violently twisted sinew before having his throat cut.

Among the many Danish bog men a few have ropes or thongs round their necks and historical evidence suggests that strangulation was a feature of ritual sacrifice to a god or goddess – as was committing the body to a bog. This does not deny that the chosen victim might also have been guilty of some offence.

CHESHIRE

Castle Ditch Fort
(Eddisbury Hill)   *Iron Age*
Just NW of Delamere   **117(SJ:553695)**
N of A556, W of B5152. Roman road ran in from SW.
A fort of 4.5ha, with a double rampart and ditch, it was revealed by excavation to have developed over several phases. It began as a simple palisade on the E, dating to the 2nd century BC; later a timber-laced stone rampart and ditch replaced this, and defence was extended to the W. Finally, the outer bank and ditch were built, and the inturned entrances (on S and NW) were strengthened. The fort fell into decay after the Romans dismantled it in the late 1st century.

Chester Fort and Town   *Roman*
Chester   **117(SJ:405663)**
At junction of several Roman roads, including Watling Street.
Deva, at the mouth of the Dee, began as a marching camp and eventually became the 25ha fortress for the 2nd Legion and, in c. AD 88, for the 20th Legion, which moved there from Wroxeter (p. 179). Its rampart had a timber-framed rubble core encased in turf; timber buildings were replaced by stone in c. 102. From Deva, the Romans could patrol the region from North Wales to Lancashire, and also send out sea patrols, but the silting up of the Dee's mouth decreased its

value as a sea base, and was one factor in its abandonment in AD 383.
A large civilian settlement grew up outside, and the large amphitheatre served this as well as the fort, since it could hold 8000 people. Half of the amphitheatre is still under buildings, but remains of the northern part can be seen at Newgate. There are other surviving traces of fortress wall (with bread ovens at Abbey Green); columns and hypocaust can be seen in different parts of the town, as well as part of a quay wall overlooking the racecourse.
Details from the Grosvenor Museum, where finds are housed.

Maiden Castle Fort   *Iron Age*
Just W of Bickerton   **117(SJ:497528)**
S of A534, E of A41.
This small rectangular promontory fort of 0.5ha is protected by sheer, artificially steepened cliffs on the NW, and elsewhere by a double rampart. The outer bank, of sand encased in stone, was probably built in the early Iron Age (radiocarbon dates cluster around 400 BC) while the inner bank, 6.5m thick, was timber-laced, of earth and rubble, and probably dates to the 1st century BC. Its beams were burned at some point. An inturned entrance in the E had a 12m cobbled passage (with wheel ruts) and a gatepost halfway along it.

DERBYSHIRE

Arbor Low Henge and   *New Stone/*
Round Barrows *   *Bronze Ages*
Bakewell   **119(SK:160636)**
8km SW of Bakewell. 1.2km E of Parsley Hay and the A515. Path up from Long Rake Road. HBMCE.
Signposted. Guidebook. Entrance fee at farm.
The most important prehistoric monument of the Peak District, it is known as the 'Stonehenge of Derbyshire', and stands in bleak solitude high in a limestone area with tremendous views. It comprises a classic henge with an oval bank, 76m by 83m, and still 2m high, and 2 entrances on NW and SE, opposite each other but not in line with the centre. It encloses a ditch and a central plateau. The ditch, nearly 2m deep, was cut in solid lime-

stone; about 1500 cubic metres of stone (4000 tons) were removed which would have kept 50 people busy for 6 months. The bank contains boulders weighing up to a ton. On the central plateau is an egg-shaped ring of 50 blocks of white limestone, all now recumbent like the marks on a clockface. It is probable that they were originally erect, but fell owing to the shallowness of the holes in the bedrock. In the centre lie 4 stones, 2 of them very large, which probably formed a U-shaped cove facing SSW, and thus the maximum midsummer setting of the moon. Just to the E of them was an extended male burial (in which the body is laid out flat instead of curled up).
The monument is probably of the late New

Stone Age and early Bronze Age. A tumulus, made of material from the bank, and dating probably to the Bronze Age, adjoins the bank. It contained a cist with a cremation and 2 urns. A long, low earth bank or avenue leads off to the SE, in a 320m curve, and passes near Gib Hill - this Bronze Age mound, still 5m high, has a cist near the top, now open to the sky, which contained an urn and a cremation. Its name derives from the fact that gallows stood on it in more recent times.

Arbor Low closely resembles Cairnpapple (p. 240-1), and also shares many features with Avebury (p. 97-102) and Stanton drew (p. 115). Finds from the site are in Sheffield City Museum, Buxton Museum and the British Museum.

Bull Ring Henge and   *New Stone/*
Round Barrow   *Bronze Ages*
Dove Holes   **119(SK:078783)**
4.8km NNE of Buxton. Just E of A6, and the school in Dove Holes.

This site originally resembled Arbor Low (*qv*) in that it was a henge with 2 entrances, enclosing a stone circle. However, all of its stones are now gone, and the henge has been damaged by quarry-ing. The bank, 75m in diameter, is of limestone rubble, and the interior ditch was 2m deep, and 10m wide. There is a large barrow just to the SW, rather like the position of Gib Hill at Arbor Low.

Castle Naze Promontory
Fort   *Iron Age?*
Chapel-en-le-Frith   **119(SK:054784)**
SW of Chapel-en-le-Frith, on spur of Combs Moss above Combs.

Located at an altitude of 443m, this fort comprises a 3-sided area, defended by sheer cliffs to the N and S. On the E, it is defended by 2 drystone walls and an outer ditch, with an entrance in the centre - though the original entrance is more likely to be the gap between the N end of the walls and the cliff, approached by a hollow way. The inner wall seems to be the earliest feature.

Creswell Crags
Cave-dwellings   *Old Stone Age*
Whitwell   **120(SK:538743)**
On Notts border, S of Whitwell, E of Chesterfield; W of A60, E of A616, around the B6042. Visitors Centre has a slide programme and leaflets. Trail leads

Arbor Low Henge. *A fine circle henge with stones prostrate, c. 2000 BC*

Above: **Creswell Crags Cave-dwelling**. *Cave dwellings of the Old Stone Age above Crags Pond*

Below: **Creswell Crags**, *Derbyshire (after J. Dyer)*

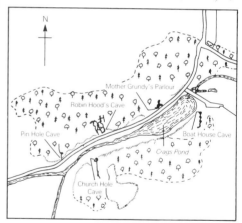

past sites (entry to the caves is barred): allow 1½ hours.

There are a score of caves of archaeological interest in this narrow gorge, with 3 principal phases of occupation: *c.* 41,000 BC, Neanderthal man produced well-made hand-axes and other tools here; in *c.* 28,000-26,000 BC, early modern man made fine flint tools shaped like laurel leaves, and his tools have been found with bones of mammoth, woolly rhino, reindeer and bison. Subsequently, some caves became hyena dens, and, finally, *c.* 11,000-9,000 BC, the 'Creswellians' made flint tools and left a few works of art. There are a number of important caves. *Boat House Cave* is where bones of hyena, horse and bison were 'excavated' with explosives. *Church Hole Cave* contained a huge quantity of bones of Ice Age animals, as well as some stone tools of Neanderthal

man and early modern man. *Pin Hole Cave* contained
the same, and had also served as a hyena den. A nearly
complete duck-egg shell was found by a hearth,
together with remains of others, but the cave is best
known for its engravings – a pointed tool of ivory
with a fish design on it, and an ithyphallic man with
an animal mask and a bow on a piece of reindeer rib.
Some finds are in Sheffield City Museum. In *Robin
Hood's Cave*, the most notable find was an engraving
of a horse head on a bone. Horse bones predomi-
nated in this cave although hare bones were also
abundant, and the remains of a young adult male
were also found. Radiocarbon dating shows that
occupation dates back to at least 28,000 BC, and other
dates in the 9th millennium BC have been obtained.
Finally, *Mother Grundy's Parlour* contained evidence from Neanderthal to New Stone Age times. An
engraving of a reindeer was found, and dates of the
7th, 6th and 5th millennium BC obtained.

It is likely that the last 2 caves were occasional
base camps, from which the nearby plains were
exploited.

End Low, Lean Low and
Parsley Hay Round Barrows
Bronze Age
N of Ashbourne **119(SK:156606)**
*Just sw of Arbor Low (qv). End Low is 1.2km NW of
A515/A5012 junction. Lean Low is just w of A515,
NW of junction with B5054.*

End Low is 20m across and 2m high. In the large
hole at the top, 4m down, a crouched skeleton was
found in 1848, with a bronze dagger and a flint knife.
A child's skeleton lay higher up. Further N, Lean Low
(SK:149623) is a little smaller; it housed a skeleton in
a grave cut into the rock, as well as other burials and a
cremation. Finally, Parsley Hay (SK:144631) had a
skeleton sitting in a rock-cut grave under stone slabs,
with another above, accompanied by a bronze dagger and a granite battle-axe. Finds from these rubble
cairns are in Sheffield City Museum.

Five Wells Chambered
Barrow *
New Stone Age
Taddington **119(SK:124711)**
*Just s of A6, 1.6km w of Taddington, N of footpath sw
to Chelmorton.*

A round cairn of thin limestone slabs, it has 2
wedge-shaped chambers, back to back, each with a
passage leading to it, from the E and w respectively.
Each is now open to the sky, and has 2 portal stones at
its entry. A total of 17 skeletons have been found here,
together with pottery, flint arrowheads and a flint
knife. Finds in Sheffield City Museum.

Green Low Chambered
Barrow
*Late New
Stone Age*
Just NE of Aldwark **119(SK:233580)**
Just s of A5012, 1.6km NW of Grangemill.

A round cairn, 18m across, it had a straight façade
on the s, from the centre of which a tiny passage led
to a chamber, 2m square. This contained an inhumation in a rock-cut pit, together with flints and a
beaker – a typical early Beaker assemblage. The
arthritic skeleton of a man was found among the
cairn's stones, and a pile of disarticulated human
bones was found mixed with those of pig, dog, sheep
and deer. In all, at least 9 people were represented
including several children. Quartzite pebbles were
scattered over the cairn.

Five Wells Chambered Barrow. New Stone Age

Hob Hurst's House and
Beeley Round Barrows
Bronze Age
Beeley **119(SK:287692 & 281668)**
*The first barrow beyond s end of Bunkers Hill
Wood, E of Chatsworth; 3 restored barrows further s
on Beeley Moor.*

Hob Hurst's House (named after a supernatural
being, an unearthly king, Hobthrush, who haunted
woods and other solitary places) is a barrow, 10m
across, and less than a metre high, with a bank and
ditch around it; there also used to be a stone circle
inside the bank.

A stone cist was found at the cairn's centre, in
which a body had been cremated.

On Beeley Moor, there are 3 contiguous cairns, now restored, built on a layer of white sand. They each contained cremations. Finds in Sheffield City Museum.

Mam Tor Hillfort ✗   *Bronze/Iron Ages*
Castleton   **110(SK:128837)**
2.4km w of Castleton above hairpin turn in A625. Also path s from Edale. Near Blue John Cavern. National Trust.

This is not only the largest hillfort in Derbyshire, it also has the earliest radiocarbon dates – 1180 and 1130 BC. Located at an altitude of 500m, it encloses 6ha with a double bank and median ditch. It is probable that an early timber palisade was replaced by the defences now visible. There are entrances on N and S, the weaker N being inturned. A series of hut-circles

has been found inside; those excavated had a double circle of posts. Two Bronze Age round barrows stand in the fort's sw corner. Finds in Manchester University Museum.

Melandra Castle Fort   *Roman*
Longworth   **110(SK:009951)**
E edge of Manchester, NW of Glossop. Between Woolley Bridge (to N) and Gamesley (to S), just s of the river Etherow. w of the A57; track up hill NW of church at Brookfield.

The fort of *Ardotalia*, protected by steep slopes to the N and W, was built *c.* AD 78, and abandoned *c.* AD 140. A clay rampart was reinforced after AD 100 with a stone wall and gateways. The surviving defences are still impressive. A small bath-house stood outside the NW corner.

Nine Ladies, one of Stanton Moor's New Stone Age stone circles

Minninglow Chambered *
Tomb
New Stone Age
Ballidon   **119(SK:209573)**
N of Ballidon, by Roman road. SW of Matlock,
3.6km W of Grangemill, S of A5012.

A large mound, now much damaged, it was robbed from Roman times onward. It contained at least 4 burial chambers; the original chamber at the centre was reached by a drystone passage and enclosed in a small cairn. This mound was then extended, and a second chamber added to the S; both of these chambers have their capstones *in situ*. Later, 2 others were added on the W and SW.

Nine Stones Close Stone
Circle
Bronze Age
Harthill   **119(SK:227627)**
NW of Birchover. On Harthill Moor, NE of Harthill
Crag. 3.2km SW of junction of A6 and B5056, just W
of B5056. See also Stanton Moor.

Four enormous blocks, the largest in Derbyshire, stand on the moor; there were 6 in 1847, but never necessarily 9, since 'nine' may mean 'noon'. There is a tradition that they danced, usually at midday; they are also called the 'Grey Ladies', said to dance at midnight. The southernmost stone, 2m high, has over 1m more below ground. Some think the blocks are the remains of a burial chamber, but they are more likely to be all that is left of a circle, 13m across, although without a bank.

Ringham Low Chambered
Long Barrow
New Stone Age
W of Over Haddon   **119(SK:169664)**
4km E of A515/B5055 junction. E of Ricklow Dale
and N of Lathkill Dale. Part in plantation.

A ruined, long, oval mound, its N end is cut off by a field wall. It had a horned forecourt, 4 or 5 burial chambers, and contained the remains of a score of people, together with animal bones, arrowheads and flint tools. Finds in Sheffield City Museum.

Stanton Moor Stone Circle, Ring
Barrows, Standing Stones *
New Stone Age
Stanton in Peak   **119(SK:249633)**
Spread over moor bounded by roads from
Birchover N to Stanton in Peak, and NE to Stanton
Lees. 1km NE of Nine Stones Close (qv). Signposted.
In the Arbor Low guidebook.

This remote sandstone plateau of 60ha, with extensive views, contains a great number of prehistoric features: in fact it was an early Bronze Age burial ground, and about 70 small cairns were found here. A score have been excavated, and their tally of over 80 cremations suggests that a total of at least 300–400 people were buried on the moor. The cairns also yielded a fine array of collared urns, incense cups, flint and bronze knives, faience beads, battle axes; some finds are in the private Heathcote Museum, Birchover.

Contemporaneous with the cairns are several stone circles. The finest, Nine Ladies, is a little ring, 10m across, of 9 small boulders of millstone grit in a low rubble bank. It is now enclosed by a low, modern stone wall. The bank has entrance gaps on the NE and SW, and 30m to the SW stands an outlying block of millstone grit, the King Stone, also enclosed by a modern wall. The Nine Ladies are said to be a group turned to stone for dancing on the Sabbath, and the outlier is their fiddler. At least 3 more stone circles were known in the vicinity 200 years ago.

Swarkestone Lows
Round Barrows
Bronze Age
Swarkestone   **128(SK:365295)**
S of Derby. 0.8km N of A514/A5132 junction.

These 4 barrows, much damaged by ploughing, were built with turves. The second from the W had a central cremation and 2 intrusive Saxon burials in the berm and ditch. The third from the W had a primary burial in a boat-shaped wooden coffin, with subsequent enlargement into a large bell barrow, with a double ditch round it, to house 3 urn cremations, one of which was radiocarbon-dated to 1395 BC. There were traces of a Beaker habitation site underneath. Finds in Derby Museum.

LEICESTERSHIRE

Bulwarks Hillfort *Iron Age*
Breedon on the Hill **129(SK:406234)**
NE of Ashby de la Zouch, near Breedon village church. Just NW of A453.

A pear-shaped hillfort, the SE half of which has been quarried away in recent times, it used to enclose over 9ha. It had 2 phases: first, a limestone wall, reinforced with timbers, was built. After the timbers decayed, a new wall was built in front, and the bank stabilized with turf. The rampart, and traces of the broad, flat-bottomed ditch, can be seen on the W, and some remnants of the inturned entrance on the W survive next to and under the churchyard wall. Much pottery and other refuse found in the site suggest occupation from the 3rd century BC to the 1st century AD.

Burrough Hill Hillfort *Iron Age*
Burrough on the Hill **129(SK:761119)**
S of Melton Mowbray. 2.4km SE of Great Dalby and the B6047.

A strong trapezoidal fort of 5ha in a fine setting, it may have been the capital of the Coritani. Although abandoned in Roman times, it remained of importance, and fairs and festivals were held here until the 18th century, and even the Grand National was run here in 1873. It is a pleasant and popular beauty spot.

Burrough Hill Hillfort. Iron Age

In Iron Age times, it was occupied for several centuries: protected by sheer slopes on 3 sides, it had strong fortifications on the fourth – a ditch and massive rampart faced with drystone, and an inturned entry at the SE corner, with stone guard-chambers. Excavation of this prominent entrance revealed construction in strong masonry, and a cobbled roadway. No huts have yet been found, but there are many storage pits and finds of pottery, rotary querns and animal bones.

Leicester City *Roman*
Leicester **140(SK:583045)**
Jewry Wall and Museum.

This tribal capital of the Coritani became the 40ha Roman *Ratae Coritanorum*, and was joined to Lincoln (p. 176) by the Fosse Way. There was a Roman fort here just after the conquest. The town had an impressive forum, and several fine mosaics have been found in the city, some still *in situ*, such as a geometric pavement under the railway arches in Bath Lane. The best visible remains of Roman Leicester are a huge piece of wall, over 7m high, at the Jewry Wall site, beside St Nicholas' church – it once formed part of a large public building, most probably the baths. Remains can also be seen of hypocaust and halls. The adjacent museum gives a good view of Leicester's archaeological history, and in particular houses some fine mosaics such as the Peacock Pavement.

LINCOLNSHIRE

Ancaster Town
Ancaster   *Roman*   **130(SK:983435)**
*In break in Lincoln Edge between Sleaford (to E)
and Honington (to W), at junction of A153 and
B6403 (the latter is the Roman Ermine Street, on its
way N to Lincoln).*

A small walled town of 4ha, it may have been a post-ing-station, and was certainly preceded by Iron Age occupation (huts and pits have been found). Nearby was a quarry for Lincolnshire limestone. The visible Roman remains, to the E of the church and N of the A153, comprise walls, probably of the 3rd century AD, buried in a rectangular earthwork enclosing the town. This was just a part of the native settlement strung out along Ermine Street. The rampart and ditch are best seen around Castle Close. A 1st-century fort and a Roman cemetery lie beneath the modern cemetery, and 2 Roman stone coffins are on view by the cemetery path. Finds in Grantham Museum, Lincoln City and County Museum and Nottingham University Museum.

Bully Hills Round Barrows
Tathwell   *Bronze Age*   **122(TF:330827)**
*S of Louth, 1.2km SE of Tathwell, E of minor road SE to
Haugham.*

Lying N of a group of long barrows is this linear cemetery of Bronze Age bowl barrows, which really stand out in the flat Lincolnshire landscape. Six stand together, with the seventh a little way off. Unexcavated.

Butterbump Round Barrows
Willloughby   *Bronze Age*   **122(TF:493724)**
*Under plough, 2.4km E of Willoughby and 0.8km SE
of Bonthorpe.*

These 12 barrows were originally probably even more numerous. Only one has been excavated in recent times: it contained a cremation in a pit, covered by wooden planks, and radiocarbon-dated to 1750 BC. It was associated with a perforated whetstone and a bronze dagger in a wooden sheath. Seven secondary burials had been inserted into the cairn.

Deadmen's Graves
Long Barrows
Claxby   *New Stone Age?*   **122(TF:444719)**
*NE of Partney, 0.8km NW of Claxby. Visible on skyline
from road below. Not far from Giant's Hills (qv).*

A pair of similar long barrows, they have both been damaged, and lie on an E/W axis above a steep, narrow valley with lynchets on its S side.

Giant's Hills
Long Barrow
Skendleby   *New Stone Age?*   **122(TF:429712)**
*3.2km NE of Partney, 1.2km NW of Skendleby, W of
A1028. Near Deadmen's Graves (qv).*

A barrow, 65m long and 23m wide, orientated SE/NW, covered a long wooden enclosure containing a platform of chalk blocks on which were found the disarticulated remains of at least 7 adults and a child. There were side ditches, and a continuous façade of split timbers. At the NW end of the barrow stood a line of 8 posts, perhaps corresponding to the 8 burials. The mound's interior was divided up by short sections of hurdling; bones of ox, sheep and red deer were found, and an antler from the ditch has been radiocarbon-dated to 2460/2370 BC. Finds in the British Museum. A second, ploughed-out barrow lies 225m to the S.

Honington Hillfort (Camp)
Honington   *Iron Age?*   **130(SK:954424)**
*NE of Grantham. 1.2km SE of Honington near
junction of A153 and A607.*

Located on a low limestone plateau, this rectangular enclosure of 0.5ha has a double bank and ditch, with a counterscarp bank, and a simple entrance on the E. Roman coins have been found in the site.

Horncastle Town
Horncastle   *Roman*   **122(TF:258696)**
*On SW foot of Wolds at junction of A158 and A153.
Underlies present market town.*

The small walled centre of *Banovalum*, now on the river Bain, probably had some bearing on Roman coastal defence since it was then accessible to shipping through the system of waterways connecting Lincoln to the sea. Parts of the town wall can be seen – in the branch library in Wharf Road, at the SW angle of St Mary's churchyard and, especially, in Dog Kennel Yard, off Lawrence Street, where the remains of a bastion can also be seen. These walls probably date to the 3rd or 4th century AD.

Lincoln Town and Legionary
Fort
Lincoln   *Roman*   **121(SK:975714)**
The 9th Legion was quartered here from c. AD 50, and then, at the end of that century, it became *Colonia Lindum*, a *colonia* for demobilized veterans who occupied the evacuated 17ha fortress. Small and rigidly planned, it was very similar to the *colonia* at Gloucester. In the 2nd century its size more than doubled, and by the early 3rd, it had spread downhill. The prosperous town had fine, lavishly decorated buildings, incorporating marble from Greece and Italy, and mosaic pavements. Colonnades lined the streets in front of large buildings, and there was terracing for structures down the hillside. A sophisticated system of pipes and an aqueduct ensured a good water supply – part of the aqueduct's embankment can be seen outside the town. Sewers have also been found, as at York (p. 211), with lateral sewers and house drains.

Several large stretches of wall can still be seen: in Bishop's Palace Garden, in Orchard Street and by the cathedral, in front of the Eastgate Hotel, where there is a semicircular bastion from the East Gate. The most striking remains are those of the Newport Arch: a simple, single span over Bailgate, through which traffic still passes, with a smaller arch for pedestrians beside it. In Roman times, the arch would have been taller, since the modern road is 2.5m higher. Objects in Lincoln City and County Museum.

NOTTINGHAMSHIRE

Oxton Camp Hillfort
Oxton
On Robin Hood Hill, 2km NNE of Oxton and the junction of A6097 and B6386.

Iron Age?
120(SK:635532)

A small, 0.6 ha triangular fort with 3 banks and ditches on the E, but only a single rampart, ditch and counterscarp bank on the W. There are entrances on the NW and SE-the former has a large mound, 6m high, outside known as Robin Hood's Pot. It is probably a round barrow, although when it was excavated it was found to contain roman coins and a Saxon burial.

SHROPSHIRE

Bury Ditches Hillfort
Lydbury North
E of A488, NE of Clun and SW of Lydbury North. Just w of minor road s from Lower Down to Clunton. Steep climb through woodland.

Iron Age?
137(SO:327836)

A small (2.5ha), tree-covered, oval fort, it was probably built in 2 phases: first, a double bank, with median ditch; later it was strengthened on the NW by 2 more banks and a median ditch. There are 2 complex entrances, on NE and S, with inturned passages and guard-chambers. There is a legend that the site contains a pot of fairy gold attached to which is a thread of gold wire that will lead someone to the spot.

Bury Walls Promontory Fort
Weston-under-Redcastle
NNE of Shrewsbury. 6.4km E of Wem and E of A49 in fine country above headwaters of the river Roden. Approach from Bury Farm.

Iron Age?
126(SJ:576275)

A fine 5.5ha rectangular fort, it was protected by univallate defences on its 3 steep sides, while the gentler N side has 2 banks and ditches, of which the inner is one of the biggest in Britain, standing 11m above its ditch. There is an inturned entrance cut into the rock at the NE corner; a spring inside, at the NW corner, and another just outside the gate, ensured a water supply. There are also traces of circular huts inside.

Caer Caradoc Hillfort *
Church Stretton
Conspicuous on skyline 2.8km NE of Church Stretton and E of A49. Trackway up E face of hill to SE entrance of fort.

Iron Age?
137(SO:477953)

A long, narrow, 2.5ha fort of the Cornovii, impressively sited on its ridge, it is protected by steep slopes, and has an inner bank and quarry ditch, and an outer ditch and counterscarp bank. A man-made track leads up to an inturned entrance on the SE, with guard-chambers.

Caer Caradoc Hillfort
Knighton
E of A488, s of Clun, 4km NE of Knighton.

Iron Age?
137(SO:310758)

This fine, 1ha, oval hillfort, with tremendous views, has deep internal quarry ditches, and double banks/ditches. There are inturned entrances on E and w - the latter, being easily accessible, has guard-chambers and also an extra bank and ditch outside. There are traces of huts inside the fort. Undated.

Caynham Camp Hillfort
Caynham
3.6km SE of Ludlow on a ridge above a tributary of the river Teme.

Iron Age
137(SO:545737)

A rectangular, 4ha hillfort, it has a double rampart and ditch, except on the N where steep slopes make only a single rampart necessary. Excavation suggests 4 phases of development, starting with a timber-laced rampart and a rock-cut ditch; these defences were subsequently refashioned, enlarged and strengthened. The original main inturned entrance is on the E. Aerial photography has indicated the presence of postholes and storage pits. Abundant carbonized wheat has been found. Finds in Birmingham University and City Museum and Art Gallery.

Mitchell's Fold Stone Circle
Chirbury
E of Chirbury and the A490. In clearing among bracken in heathland on lower slopes of Stapeley Hill.

Bronze Age
137(SO:304983)

Also known as Medgel's or Medgley's Fold (after a giant who used to milk his cows in this enclosure), this conspicuous monument is in a superb setting on high, dry heathland with a good view westward to Wales. There are 16 unworked dolerite stones, up to 1.8m tall, and 10 of them are still erect. There used to be more, as is shown by their irregular spacing. They form a flattened circle of 26/28m diameter. There may have been a central stone, and 70m to the SW is a stone called 'the altar' on a cairn. About 2km to the NE is a similar flattened circle, the Hoarstones (SO:324999), with a centre stone, but it is far less impressive, and lies, overgrown, in a marshy field.

Old Oswestry Hillfort *
Oswestry
1.6km N of Oswestry, w of A483. HBMCE. Signposted.

Iron Age
126(SJ:296310)

This impressive, 5.3ha fort had a long and complicated development. The first installation of round wooden huts was undefended. Subsequently there were at least 3 phases of defence, with banks and ditches being replaced or strengthened; there were also up to 7 ramparts. The later inhabitants had huts with thick stone walls. It is thought that occupation began in the 6th century BC, but was abandoned after the Roman conquest.

Robin Hood's Butt Round Barrow
(Old Field Round Barrow) *Bronze Age*
Bromfield **137(SO:490779)**
Just w of B4365, 3.6km nw of Ludlow by A49.

A circular mound, 27m across and 4m high, contained the skeleton of a young teenager and a bronze knife: the body may have been burned *in situ*. Four other barrows on the racecourse (SO:495776) were found in the 19th century to contain cremations, but have now been flattened.

Titterstone Clee Hillfort *Iron Age*
Bitterley **137(SO:592779)**
ENE of Ludlow on lofty Clee Hill. 2.4km E of Bitterley, N of A4117.

An isolated hillfort, located at an altitude of 533m, it is one of the highest and largest (28.8ha) in Britain. It has a single bank of earth and rubble, and no ditch. There is an important inturned entrance on the s, and a minor one on the N. Excavation suggests that the fort developed in 2 phases: the rampart was origin-

The Wrekin Hillfort *
Wellington
Iron Age
127(SJ:630083)
3.5km sw of Wellington by turning s from A5.

A major hillfort of 8ha, isolated on a long, narrow ridge, it has tremendous views. Thought to have been the tribal capital of the Cornovii, who were later resettled at Wroxeter *(qv)*, it has an inner enclosure of 2.8ha that was protected by a main rampart, 6m wide, strengthened by cutting the hillside below to steepen it artificially, and with inturned entrances on the NE and sw. An outer bank, occasionally doubled, surrounds this, with an inturned entry on the NE. There were rows of small, square buildings between the inner and outer enclosures, and storage pits have yielded pottery of 300 BC. A possible Bronze Age round barrow stands at the sw end. Some of the final drystone walling seems to have been built badly, in a hurry, perhaps in the face of a Roman advance.

The Wrekin, Shropshire (after J. Dyer)

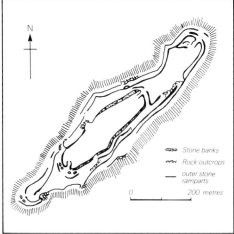

Wroxeter Town and Legionary Fortress *
Wroxeter
Roman
126(SJ:565088)
8km se of Shrewsbury, and due w of The Wrekin (qv), s of A5, round the B4380. HBMCE.
Guidebook available. Signposted.

This garrison town of the 14th Legion was founded in AD 58 when the Legion was moved up from Wall (p. 180) to help with policing the Welsh tribes. After the 14th Legion left Britain in AD 69, the 20th took its place here, but was then moved to Chester. So, after 30 years in a military role, Wroxeter became a civil settlement, the tribal centre of the Cornovii - hence the name *Viroconium Cornoviorum*. It seems to have been bigger and wealthier than other similar capitals, and was, at one point, the fourth largest city in Roman Britain, covering 73ha. It had a large forum, and one of the most imposing bath complexes in Britain. A planned street system divided the town into spacious rectangular blocks, many occupied by the large, opulent residences of tribal magnates - their sumptuous houses often had over 20 rooms on the ground floor, and some had private baths and flush toilets. An aqueduct ensured a good water supply.

Old Oswestry Hillfort. *It is thought that occupation of this Iron Age hillfort may have begun in the 6th century BC. It was abandoned after the Roman conquest*

ally faced with timber and later by drystone walling; the s entrance was originally timber-lined, and later, trapezoidal stone guard-chambers were built behind it. There are traces of hut-circles on the E, while the sw has been damaged by quarrying.

This defended centre for wealthy tribal members lost its forum and town hall to fire in 286, and they were never rebuilt. The baths lasted until the 350s, but the principal site remained derelict, with only timber shacks and workshops on it. The city was gradually abandoned in the 5th/6th centuries, and later quarried for stone by medieval builders. Much of it is known from aerial photographs, and part now lies beneath the modern village.

The most impressive visible remains are: a large section of wall that formed part of the entrance to the baths from the exercise hall; beside it, the layout of part of the bath complex; and, to the north, across the road, a length of the forum colonnade. Other remains can be seen in the site museum. The Victoria & Albert Museum in London houses the site's fine inscription dedicating the city hall and forum to Hadrian in AD 129/30.

STAFFORDSHIRE

Berth Hill Hillfort *Iron Age?*
Maer **127(SJ:788391)**
NE of Market Drayton. Immediately N of A51, 1.2km N of Maer.
A small (3.6ha), triangular, tree-covered fort on a spur, with a double bank and intermediate ditch. The weaker NNE side has an extra bank and ditch. An inturned entrance on the W is approached by a hollow way, while a simpler entrance on the NE is approached by a track. A spring inside the fort provided a water supply.

Bridestones Chambered
Long Barrow
Congleton *New Stone Age*
118(SJ:906622)
4.8km E of Congleton, S of A54 and just N of road joining A527 at Dane in Shaw to A523 at Ryecroft Gate.
The mound, now destroyed, was 90m long. The chamber, now overgrown, had a broken porthole stone dividing it in 2, and just wide enough for a corpse. Two small side chambers were destroyed in the 18th century; the E end of the chamber had a semicircular forecourt. Nothing is known about the contents.

Castle Ring Hillfort *Iron Age?*
Cannock **128(SK:045128)**
S of Rugeley. On high ground overlooking Cannock Chase from the E. N of Cannock Wood and NW of Park Gate. Entry through E side by the Lodge. Signposted.
Well situated at the highest point of Cannock Chase (244m) with superb views all round, this pentagonal fort of 3.4ha has defences that vary with the topography: from 2 banks and ditches with a counterscarp bank on N and W, to 5 banks and 4 ditches on the flatter S/SE. The original entrance was on the E – the others now visible are recent.

Ilam Tops Low
Round Barrow *Bronze Age*
Ilam Moor **119(SK:136527)**
S edge of Peak National Park, on high ridge W of Dove Dale. NW of Ashbourne, N of A52, W of A515.
In a group of round cairns on this ridge, containing cremations, burials, beakers, etc., there is one that is the most conspicuous. This mound, of alternating layers of earth and stones, covered a pit, cut into the rock, containing remains of a bull on a bed of charcoal. Above this was a mixture of human bones (adult and child), a crushed beaker and a bronze awl.

Long Low Round Barrows *New Stone Age*
Wetton **119(SK:122539)**
NW of Ashbourne, just NW of Ilam Tops (qv). 2km SE of Wetton at end of road leading from village. SE of Thor's Cave (qv).
A pair of limestone mounds, connected by a wide, low bank with a facing of upright limestone slabs, this unique monument is supposed to be the scene of high revels by fairies on Christmas Eve. The larger N mound, now much robbed of its material, had a large stone chamber containing 13 skeletons and 3 leaf arrowheads. The S mound had traces of a cremation. Finds in Sheffield City Museum.

Thor's Cave *Old Stone/Iron Ages/*
Cave-dwellings *Roman*
Wetton **119(SK:098549)**
High above E bank of river Manifold, NE of Grindon and SW of Wetton. Reached from road W from A515 at Alsop-en-le-Dale.
A huge opening, overlooking the river and facing NW, it was used towards the end of the Old Stone Age – sparse material has been found – and more intensively in the Iron Age and Roman period, from c. 200 BC to AD 300. Finds in Derby Museum and Sheffield City Museum.

Wall Town *Roman*
Wall **139(SK:100065)**
SW of Lichfield, just N of A5 between its junction with A461 (to W) and A5127 (to E). HBMCE. Signposted. Guidebook.
Letocetum began as the garrison fort of the 14th Legion before it moved to Wroxeter (p. 179) in c. AD 58. It seems to have been a posting-station, providing a hostel and horses for travellers, and was a prosperous settlement owing to its location on a major road (Watling Street). It covered 8 – 12ha. Remains of the *mansio* (imperial posting hostel) have been found, but are not visible; whereas the complex bath-house, one of the most complete in Britain, has been consolidated and preserved. The site museum also has material from the small Roman farmstead at nearby Shenstone.

THE NORTH OF ENGLAND

This region – comprising Cumbria, Durham, Humberside, Lancashire, Northumberland and Yorkshire (north, south and west) – is, of course, dominated by the Pennine range with its millstone grit and mountain limestone spine dividing the eastern and western coalfields. In general, this massive central block is short of prehistoric field monuments as conditions, except in some of its valleys, were too harsh for much settlement. On the other hand, little survives in Lancashire either, or in the low-lying vales of York and Pickering. The concentrations of such remains are on the chalk of the Humberside Wolds, on the limestone of the North Yorkshire moors, in southern Cumbria and the area south-east of Penrith and far away in the Cheviot country of Northumberland.

The Wolds are to be seen both geologically and archaeologically as a continuation of those south of the Wash, while the northern moors (including the Hambledon and Cleveland hills) form the end of the Jurassic belt curving up from Dorset and forming a corridor for the passage of people and ideas. Looking so different with its heather carpet, the moorland limestone is, in fact, almost identical with that of the Cotswolds. Cumbria, with its far older rocks, has much in common with north Wales – including a broad belt of volcanic intrusions that provides the most spectacular scenery of the Lake District and also raw materials for stone-axe factories such as Pike of Stickle (p. 191) in Langdale. There is also a lava flow round the Cheviots, though much of the high ground there is of sandstone.

Before making an historical tour of the monuments, it will be well to pick out certain distinctive features of the archaeology of this northern region. The first is negative: among the vast number of burial mounds, and despite the good supply of suitable stone, there are no chambered barrows, no megalithic gallery or passage graves. This suggests how definite and particular was the cult that inspired such funerary architecture.

In contrast with this lack of megalithic chambers, the region is rich in stone circles, Cumbria exceptionally so, a further proof that the people who wanted mausoleums for their dead and the people who wanted sacred rings for their ceremonies, though they both employed megaliths, had little to do with one another.

A lesser peculiarity of the New Stone Age in this region is all but limited to Yorkshire. This is the custom of leaving a narrow trench at one end of a long barrow, putting in dismembered bodies, covering them with limestone pieces and cremating them *in situ* before the mound was closed. Other distinctions are the Bronze Age rock carvings and the Iron Age chariot burials, but these must be described more fully in due course.

To return to historical beginnings, hunters of the Old Stone Age hardly ventured so far to the north even in the warm intervals of the Ice Age. The only field monument worth a mention is the Victoria Cave, Settle (p. 211), which was briefly inhabited some 10,000 years ago. For the Middle Stone Age, Star Carr (p. 18) is the most informative site in all Britain, but, alas, there is now nothing to be seen of this lakeside settlement. These hunters and fishing folk, who are also known to have been in Holderness, had spread across the swampy North Sea area from Denmark, while other groups whose ultimate homeland was probably France hunted the moors and even put up their flimsy shelters on the Pennine hills.

When the New Stone Age farmers arrived, then, they found only a tiny population before them. As usual they settled the chalk and the limestone country for preference, where we recognize their presence mainly from long barrows. Some dozen have survived on the Humberside and Yorkshire Wolds, but, just as in Lincolnshire, they have been miserably reduced by ploughing. Another dozen long barrows can be recognized on the limestone of the North Yorkshire moors, scattered but most of them round the periphery. The largest – Scambridge (p. 210) – had a cremation trench containing at least 14 bodies. This was one of the many Yorkshire barrows opened by the good Canon Greenwell (p. 12). Another long barrow, near Scarborough, was exceptional in being well furnished – with flint axes, knives, arrowheads and also boars' tusks. There seems little doubt that the practice of burial in long barrows had already been brought to this region from southern England quite early in the New Stone Age: one Wold barrow has a radiocarbon date of 3000 BC and others may well be earlier. On the Wolds, there are two round barrows dating from the New Stone Age, one of them the huge Duggleby barrow with its extraordinary assortment of interments (p. 204). It is assumed that these are relatively late, probably well after 2500 BC.

Note should also be taken of an undoubted Stone Age long barrow among the fells of Northumberland, the delightfully named Devil's Lapful.

The North of England has a large number of sacred sites, many of them attractive places to visit. The most striking are the stone circles of Cumbria and the henges of North Yorkshire, but to these should be added the gigantic standing stone (menhir) at Rudston in Humberside (p. 194) and the monumental trio of such stones, the Devil's Arrows (p. 203), at Boroughbridge. Cumbria can also show two henges – King Arthur's Round Table and Mayburgh (p. 189) – and there are some small stone circles (Duddo and Goatstones) and a henge (Coupland) in the far north of Northumberland.

Of the Cumbrian circles, Castlerigg (p. 185) above Keswick is one of the most accessible yet delightful of ancient monuments: a peaceful spot and the circle a noble one, commanding a prospect as lovely as any in the Lake District. Long Meg and Her Daughters away to the north of Penrith is another fine and interesting circle, while there are a number of more remote places with a rich assortment of circles, avenues and cairns, such as Moor Divock (p. 191) and Brats Hill.

The Yorkshire henges at Thornborough (p. 211) and on Hutton Moor (p. 205) are six in number, all concentrated between the rivers Ure and Swale, and are surrounded by round barrows in what must have been a most sacred area dedicated to religious rites and ceremonies. The great ring earthworks, with ditches outside as well as inside the banks, were massive in their day – and those at Thornborough were whitened with gypsum crystals brought from the Ure. Now they are plough-worn but still impressive.

Archaeologists have been much exercised in trying to date these sanctuaries. While henges are classified as dating from the late New Stone Age and free-standing stone circles assigned to the Bronze Age, in the North of England it seems that some of the circles may be among the earliest of their class and the henges among the latest of theirs. Thus it may well be that the Castlerigg stones were already standing before the Thornborough henges were dug, and it should be safe to say that the former date from 2200 – 1700 BC – though many very small circles were probably later.

There is no question about the Bronze Age date of hundreds of the round barrows to be seen throughout the region. The Beaker Folk had penetrated all areas, including the far north, but their round barrows are relatively much more numerous on the Wolds than on the North Yorkshire moors – where there are enormous numbers of later Bronze Age burial mounds. In West Yorkshire, the main concentration of Bronze Age barrows is between the Aire and the Wharfe on Rumbolds and Ilkley moors – already on the trade route for Irish bronzes via the Aire Gap.

In several Yorkshire round barrows, the dead have been placed in oak coffins, the wood preserved in wet peat; at Loose Howe (p. 210), water gushed out of the coffin when it was moved. Not far from here, on Danby Rigg, is one of the best examples of a still unexplained phenomenon: round cairns among numbers of little cairns that appear to be without burials or any ritual features.

The rock carvings – mostly cup-and-ring designs that are such a notable feature of the Bronze Age in this region – are widespread, and searchers may always find new examples. They are best seen on Ilkley Moor (p. 205), where they seem to confirm the connection with Ireland, and in the Doddington moor region in Northumberland (p. 196), but there are many more. The same motifs are sometimes carved on monuments, for instance on Long Meg herself, and on the kerbstones of round barrows.

The North of England is not noted for its Iron Age hillforts, for although there are innumerable small ones, particularly between Hadrian's Wall and the Scottish border, there are few of striking size or strength. There is a number of defended settlements with walls enclosing clusters of round huts and these tend to grade into the small forts. In Northumberland, strong stock enclosures may be attached to forts – suggestive of early days of cattle rustling.

Almondbury on the outskirts of Huddersfield is one of the larger forts of the region and also one of the earliest in its foundation – which was seemingly at the end of the Bronze Age. The earthworks were then developed through stages to reach their present impressive size by the 1st century BC. Later they were adapted to the needs of a medieval castle. Wincobank at Sheffield (p. 211) wins a place in the Gazetteer principally because it, too, is a quickly accessible suburban hillfort.

In North Yorkshire, Ingleborough (p. 210) is a noble site, a mountain of 716m, its summit capped with a flat spread of millstone grit above its limestone bulk. It is defended by natural crags, but these are reinforced by a powerful wall built of blocks of millstone grit – unhappily much mutilated. Round huts can be traced on the level green sward of the interior. Ingleborough must have been a great Brigantian stronghold, and it is reasonable to imagine the tribesmen defending it desperately against Roman attack.

The other famous North Yorkshire site is

Stanwick (p. 210), where the extended earth-works attributed to Venutius give it the look of a Belgic *oppidum*.

North Yorkshire can show enclosed farming settlements such as Grassington (p. 205) and the neat farmstead of Staple Howe (p. 210), but these are perhaps even better represented in Cumbria where Burwens (p. 185), Ewe Close (p. 186) and Holme Bank all merit their place in the Gazetteer. Villages of this kind often persisted into Roman times.

Cumbria also possesses some minor hill-forts (e.g., Carrock Fell, p. 185), but there are more to be enjoyed, together with unspoilt Cheviot country, at the extremity of England. Lordenshaws (p. 197) is near Rothbury, a small but multi-ramparted fort with round huts inside – and groups of cup-marked stones not far away. All the other forts selected for the Gazetteer are round about Wooler near the headwaters of the Breamish and Till. Dod Law (p. 196) is worth exploring, and nearby are many cup-and-ring rock carvings; Humbleton Hill is a fair-sized fort with stout stone walls; Old Bewick, a complex promontory fort – and here again there are rock carvings. The largest, most impressive and interesting of the group is Yeavering Bell, where a single, strong stone rampart encloses a twin-topped hill. Inside, the floors of some 130 timber huts were scooped into the hill slopes and there were probably more in the central saddle. It must have been a powerful tribal stronghold (p. 200).

One cannot leave the Iron Age of the region without mentioning the unique pride of Humberside archaeology – its chariot burials, even if as field monuments they make a wretched showing. These burials almost beyond question represent the ruling élite of the Celtic tribe of the Parisii who took possession of Humberside from about 300 BC, coming most probably from the Marne region of France. This is the clearest instance of the warrior-led invasions discussed earlier (p. 36). Such graves were first discovered in the Arras and Danes Graves cemeteries (p. 193) where they lay among hundreds of others, mostly of humbler folk, all covered by small round barrows. Of the three burials at Arras, one was of a woman, one of an old man, and the third a man with a shield; all contained dismantled chariots, but only the old man was allowed his pair of horses. Recently it was suggested that, since the dead were unarmed, the vehicles were ordinary carts used to convey the bodies to the cemetery. In 1984, three more chariot burials were found in quarries at Wetwang – one of a wealthy lady with her mirror and engraved workbox, her chariot enriched with coral knobs, another of a man with a long sword and no fewer than seven spears. The chariots have had their status restored.

In the Roman period, the North of England was, of course, the principal military zone of the province. Hadrian's Wall and its history have their own section (pp. 212-225) and here only Roman remains apart from that famous frontier need be described. So overwhelmingly do military works prevail that only two civil sites find a place in the Gazetteer: the villa at Rudston (p. 194) and the town at Aldborough (p. 200). Almost all other sites are of forts, very many of them dating from Agricola's campaigns, usually later rebuilt in stone. Strategically, they related to the highways to the north on either side of the Pennines and the roads running between them over the Pennine passes.

York, the legionary headquarters, is the principal fortress of the region, and with patience there is still much to see there (p. 211). North-west of it, on the A1, is Aldborough, which became one of the cantonal capitals of the Brigantes. The remains (including mosaics) are considerable, which is more than can be said of Malton (p. 210) to the west, although that was an important fort and road centre. To the north again lie the four Cawthorn camps (p. 202), thought to have been built in part as military exercises. From there, Wade's Causeway can be traced to its fine exposure on Wheeldale Moor.

Since the recent boundary changes, County Durham now contains the two most regular strategic lines of forts. These are Piercebridge (p. 193), Binchester (p. 191), Lanchester and Ebchester along the Roman road to Corbridge on Hadrian's Wall, and westward from Piercebridge the close-set line of second-century forts on the Stainmore Pass: Greta Bridge (p. 191), Bowes fort and signal station (p. 191), Rey Cross (p. 193) at the summit and, just in Cumbria, Maiden Castle overlooking the Eden valley. In the valley is Brough-by-Bainbridge (p. 201), and at Temple Sowerby, before the Roman road joined the Carlisle highway at Penrith, is one of only two Roman milestones still *in situ*.

From Penrith, a Roman road ran to Ambleside (p. 184) then on up the dramatic Wrystone Pass to Hardknott fort (p. 187), superbly set above the Dudden, and so on down Eskdale to the Roman naval base at Ravenglass (p. 191).

CUMBRIA

Ambleside Fort
Roman
Ambleside   **90(NY:372034)**
ssw of the town, s of road connecting A591 and A593. Near head of Windermere.

The fort of *Galava* was originally built of clay and timber; the remains visible today – albeit very overgrown – are those of the stone fort built in the 2nd century AD and occupied until the 4th. Two gates, some angle towers and some central buildings were left exposed after excavations earlier this century.

Brats Hill Stone Circles
Bronze Age?
Burnmoor, Miterdale   **89(NY:173023)**
1km steep climb by footpath up Gill Bank, N from Boot village, Eskdale.

The great circle of Brats Hill, just below the knoll, is flattened on the N side, and is 32 by 26m. There are 42 stones, of which only 8 are still upright. In its sw sector, the circle contains 5 low cairns that covered cremations, animal bones and antlers. Some scholars believe the monument has good solar alignments, with a low outlier stone (NW) quite close to the line on the midsummer solstice. The site is undated.

There are 4 other circles on this plateau: 2 stand 130m NW of Brats Hill at White Moss, and 2 others 450m to the N at Low Longrigg; all contain cairns. It is possible that these circles are aligned to various constellations.

Brougham Fort
Roman
90(NY:538289)
Beside Brougham Castle on the s bank of river Eamont, 1.6km SE of Penrith, s of Roman road (A66).

The fort of *Brocavum* stood on the road to Carlisle, and had a substantial civil settlement beside it. A 12th-century castle stands on the site, but some Roman ramparts survive as grassy banks, and there are some inscribed Roman stones in the castle keep.

Burwens Settlement   *Iron Age/Romano-British*
Crosby Ravensworth   **91(NY:621123)**
s of Crosby Ravensworth, at Crosby Lodge. Just w of minor road from Crosby Ravensworth s to Orton.

Of the many settlements in this area (*see* Ewe Close), this is one of the best preserved. It stands on a gentle, N-facing slope, and is surrounded by a rectangular wall; a 'village street' leads SE from the entrance on the NW, and there are a number of hut-circles, some with courtyards. There are traces of fields for over 1ha to the N and E.

Carrock Fell Hillfort   *Iron Age?*
Mungrisdale   **90(NY:343337)**
Very steep climb to SE slopes of Caldbeck Fells. w of track from Mosedale N to Calebreck. Inside bend of the river Caldew.

This oval fort, reached after a stiff and difficult ascent, is well protected by sheer crags to the SW. A drystone wall–fine stone-facing survives in places–enclosed some 2ha. The eastern end has a cairn with its central cist uncovered, and there are hundreds of other cairns on the N slope of the fell by the Caldbeck.

Castle Crag Hillfort   *Iron Age?*
Shoulthwaite   **90(NY:295186)**
SE of Keswick. Footpath up through woodland, from NW end of Thirlmere.

A small, oval hillfort, it stands in a woodland clearing on the E side of Castlerigg Fell, and dominates the steep slopes of Shoulthwaite Gill. The site has certainly been modified by humans, though perhaps not entirely constructed. A stone/earth rampart, over 2m high, survives to the E and S, with an entry on the E; and 2 ditches, with a bank between them, to the SE.

Castlerigg (The Carles)   *New Stone/*
Stone Circle ✻   *Bronze Ages*
E of Keswick   **90(NY:292237)**
s of minor road branching right off A66 at Chestnut Hill, Keswick, near Goosewell Farm. Alongside lane. Signposted.

Set dramatically in a natural amphitheatre of hills, with marvellous views of Lakeland, this pear-shaped circle, 30m in diameter, comprises 38 stones, 5 of which have fallen; only a few exceed 1.5m in height.

Castlerigg Stone Circle. New Stone Age/Bronze Age

There are faint traces of a bank, and there is a wide entry on the N, marked by a pair of massive stones at the nearest point to the river Greta. An enigmatic and unique rectangle of 10 stones stands inside the circle, touching its eastern edge: excavations in 1882 found only charcoal here.

This may be one of the earliest circles in Britain; it is located by a pass to Borrowdale, and near fine sources of stone for axes. There are many theories concerning astronomical alignments involving the circle, the rectangle and an outlier stone, but only one or two simple alignments are considered feasible.

Ewe Close Walled
Settlement   *Iron Age*
Crosby Ravensworth   **91(NY:609135)**
w of road from Crosby Ravensworth s to Orton. On Roman road from Brougham to Low Borrowbridge. Near Burwens Settlement (qv).

A large (0.5ha) enclosure on the NE side of a hill, it comprises 2 groups of huts with paddocks. The w group has a big round hut in the centre, with a paved floor, and all the huts have thick stone walls. The village was also occupied in Roman times and another similar village, Ewe Locks, is 640m to the s.

Grey Croft Stone Circle   *Bronze Age*
Seascale   **89(NY:034024)**
Just NW of Seascale, by Newmill Beck. Small road leaves B5344 at edge of Seascale, and heads NW to Calder Bridge. Circle lies just to W.

This oval, in the shadow of Sellafield (Windscale), originally comprised 12 huge boulders of volcanic lava. It was buried in the last century, but was excavated and restored in 1949, when 10 stones were re-erected. A low, oval cairn at the centre contained a cremation, and there is a small outlier stone to the N. Some simple astronomical alignments are possible.

***Hardknott Castle Fort.** A lonely Roman fort of about AD 100*

Hardknott Castle Fort ✱   *Roman*
Hardknott Pass   **89(NY:218014)**
N of very steep road from Eskdale over pass, running E to join A593 near Ambleside. Small car-park.

The 1.2ha fort of *Mediobogdum* is very remote, but in a superb and dramatic situation at the head of the pass, surrounded by spectacular scenery. It was built in the late 1st century AD to control the pass and

Above: ***King Arthur's Round Table***. *Sacred henge with enclosing bank* c. *2000 BC*

Below: ***Mayburgh Henge Standing Stone***. *New Stone Age*

to improve communications with the Cumbrian coast; its most important feature is the large (1.2ha) parade ground to the NE which, through an impressive feat of engineering, was levelled out of a boggy hillside; it has a big tribunal on its N side. The fort had double gates on its 3 exposed sides (S, E, W) and a bath-house outside to the S. Occupation did not last beyond the 2nd century.

Holme Bank Walled Settlement
Iron Age?
Urswick **97(SD:276734)**
On slope overlooking Little Urswick. To ESE of Little Urswick, and N of Scales.

This enclosure was surrounded by a stone wall strengthened by massive orthostats, up to 4m long and 1m high. The entrance was on the E, and the interior, bisected by an earthen bank, contained 2 huts. Another hut with a paddock lay 22m to the NW.

King Arthur's Round Table and Mayburgh Henges
New Stone Age
Yanwath/Eamont Bridge **90(NY:519285 & 523284)**
S of Penrith. King Arthur's Round Table is E of the A6, by the river Lowther. Mayburgh Henge, to W of A6, is just S of river Eamont.

King Arthur's Round Table is a circle, 90m across, enclosed by a ditch inside a bank with 2 opposing entrances: one survives on the SE. The site was much mutilated in the last century, but the bank is still up to 1.5m high. A cremation took place in the centre of the site. Mayburgh Henge, better preserved, is in a lovely setting. It is 65m across, with a single entry on the E, facing the other site. Its great tree-covered bank, up to 6m high, must contain over 5 million cobblestones; there is no ditch. A large standing stone in the centre is the only survivor of a foursome, while another 4 originally stood inside the entrance.

The sites are thought to date to c. 2500 – 1700 BC.

Long Meg and Her Daughters *
Bronze Age
NW of Hunsonby, SW of Glassonby **91(NY:571373)**
3km N of Langwathby; the farm lane passes through it. Signposted. Always open.

The largest stone circle in the area, and one of the biggest in Britain; of an original 70 stones, only 59 survive, of which 27 – the 'daughters' – are standing. Long Meg is a massive sandstone outlier to the SW, 18m from the circle, and bears faint spiral carvings on the side facing the circle (best seen in evening sunlight). According to legend, these rocks are all witches turned to stone.

Traces of an earth bank on the W side may make this a circle henge; its entry is on the SW, near Long Meg. An estimate of 42,000 man-hours' work has been made for erecting the stones. Long Meg makes

Long Meg and Her Daughters. A large Bronze Age stone circle: Long Meg is an outlier with spiral carvings

Moor Divock Stone Circle*. Bronze Age*

the site very visible from the w, and there is a possible alignment on the midwinter sunset.

Moor Divock Stone Circles, Rows and Barrows
Askham Fell *Bronze Age*
90(NY:497220)
Along 1.6km of moorland sw of Askham, and adjoining High Street (Roman road).

On a wide, exposed plateau is a complex of small circles, avenues, ring cairns and barrows. These little stone rings with burial cairns, on the spurs and terraces of the lower fells, represent almost the end of the stone circle tradition. Parallel lines of stones connect the circles.

Pike of Stickle Axe Factory
Langdale *New Stone Age*
90(NY:272072)
sw slopes of the Langdale Pikes. Steep tracks n up from B5343 from Skelwith Bridge, where it ends at Middle Fell Farm.

Between the head of the Pike of Stickle (600m) and the foot of the scree (150m) stretches a Neolithic axe factory, full of discarded flakes and broken implements. The rock—a grey-green, fine-grained volcanic tuff—was ideal for axes, which were traded as 'blanks' as far as Cornwall, Scotland and, above all, Wessex. Chipping floors here have been dated to the 3rd millennium BC. Finds in Carlisle Museum and Art Gallery, British Museum, etc.

Raiset Pike Long Barrow
Crosby Garrett *New Stone Age*
91(NY:684073)
w of Crosby Garrett Fell, se of Sunbiggin Tarn and Tarn Moor. Between track going ene from Raisbeck and track joining it, going nw from Newbiggin-on-Lune.

A 55m long barrow damaged by early excavation, it covered a mortuary building that housed abundant wood and the disarticulated bodies of 3 adults and 3 children. A flue trench, with a 2m standing stone at one end, was the means by which the wood and bodies could be burned inside the barrow. Other burned

disarticulated bodies—including many children—were found to the NW of the stone.

Ravenglass Fort
Ravenglass *Roman*
96(SD:088958)
On Esk estuary, sw of A595 near Ravenglass. Site cut by railway, along coast.

The fort of *Glannoventa* guarded the port; a road went n from here up Eskdale to Hardknott (qv). Little remains of the fort, but part of a bath-house was preserved, as it was incorporated into a medieval building: traces of colour survive in some niches; walls are up to 4m high; traces of doors and windows can be seen.

Shap Stone Circles
Near Shap and the A6 *Bronze Age*
1. *Shap Centre, or Gunnerkeld, just e of the M6, ne of Shap:* **90(NY:568178).**
2. *Shap North, or Wilson Scar, w of A6 and M6, nw of Shap:* **90(NY:550184).**
3. *Shap South, or Kemp Howe, s of Shap, just e of A6, w of railway:* **90(NY:567133).**

Gunnerkeld, most easily seen from the south-bound carriageway of the M6, comprises 2 concentric ovals enclosing a mound and cist. The inner oval, 18m across, is the more complete; only 3 of the 18 stones of the outer (28m across) still survive. *Wilson Scar* is a small circle, 15m across and comprising 32 small stones. *Kemp Howe* is near the railway line and the river Lowther. Only 6 massive stones now remain of the 24m circle; and 8 stones survive of a splayed 3km avenue heading nw to Skellow Hill Barrow and the huge Thunder Stone (NY:552157) over a kilometre away.

Temple Sowerby Milestone
Temple Sowerby *Roman*
91(NY:620265)
On Roman road (A66) se of Temple Sowerby and nw of Kirkby Thore (site of the Roman fort of Brauoniacum). n side of road, in iron cage; lay-by.

One of only 2 Roman milestones in Britain still standing in their original position (the other is at Chesterholm, Hadrian's Wall, p. 221), it still stands nearly 1.5m high.

DURHAM

Binchester Fort *
Bishop Auckland *Roman*
93(NZ:210312)
On Dere Street (Roman road), near crossing of river Wear, just n of Bishop Auckland. n of A689, w of A688 to Spennymoor.

A large cavalry fort providing rearward support for Hadrian's Wall, it was occupied from AD 79 to 122, then abandoned until c. 160. *Vinovia* had sumptuous baths with a spectacular hypocaust, built c. 350. Defences were rebuilt in the early 4th century; later, part of the commandant's house was split into smaller units, some of which were used for iron-working and cattle-slaughtering. Ramparts can still be seen in the N and E.

Bowes Fort
Bowes *Roman*
92(NY:994134)
Just w of Bowes, by river Greta, on A66 (Roman road).

The fort of *Lavatris* controlled the eastern end of the Stainmore Pass. Much of its stonework was used

for the church, which stands inside it, and the Norman castle, and what remains is very overgrown. It covered 1.7ha, was built in the early 3rd century, and occupied until the late 4th century. The ditches are still visible except where obliterated by the castle moat. There was a small aqueduct and an exterior bath-house to the se. Further w, near the Bowes Moor Hotel (NY:929125) and at the mouth of the Pass, are the remains (a rectangular ditch and turf rampart) of a 2nd-century signal station.

Greta Bridge Fort
Greta Bridge *Roman*
92(NZ:087132)
Just s of A66 (Roman road), turning to Brignall.

The fort of *Maglona* is now partly covered by the Morritt Arms Hotel, but some earthworks can be seen in a field nearby: these constitute the southern defences, and comprise an earthen rampart and 2 ditches. The fort itself is undated and more or less unexcavated, but the *vicus* was occupied from the early 2nd to the end of the 3rd century.

Piercebridge Fort *Roman*
Piercebridge 93(NZ:210157)
w of Darlington, just s of A67 to Barnard
Castle. By Dere Street (Roman road) crossing of
river Tees.

This large fort (4.4ha), with massive stone walls backed by an earth rampart, had rectangular towers, flanking the gates and perhaps designed for artillery. Built in the early 4th century, it housed a taskforce of heavy cavalry.

The commander's house had hypocausts, wall plaster and a private bath-house: remains of these are still visible. Dere Street crossed the Tees on a stone/timber bridge here.

Left (above): **Binchester Fort**. *Tile columns of the hypocaust in the fine bathhouse of the Roman fort*

Left (below): **Piercebridge Fort**. *Foundations of the 4th-century barrack blocks of the Roman fort*

Rey Cross Fort
(Marching Camp) *Roman*
Bowes 92(NY:900124)
Far out in the country, w of Bowes. Site cut by the
A66 (Roman road).

This fort on the Stainmore Pass, at an altitude of 400m, owed its existence to the push by the Romans N through the Pennines to Carlisle (AD 72/3). The ramparts surrounded a temporary marching camp that held an entire legion under field conditions – i.e., in tents rather than barracks. Part of the western defences has been quarried away, and some of the N rampart has disappeared into a bog. No ditch was dug owing to underlying bedrock.

——— HUMBERSIDE ———

Arras Round Barrow Cemetery *Iron Age*
Market Weighton 106(SE:907417)
A1079 from Beverley to Market Weighton cuts
through site, a few km E of Market Weighton.

This cemetery, now split by the road, has been almost completely levelled by ploughing; 3 mounds are visible out of an original total of 100 small barrows, each up to 9m in diameter and no more than 1m high. They were excavated in 1815; each covered a single, usually crouched body in a pit dug into the chalk. A few barrows lay in large, square, ditched enclosures, a feature that links these burials to others on the Continent; it is thought that they are the graves of immigrants from N France. Three were buried with dismantled 2-wheeled chariots, one of them with 2 horses. A few personal ornaments have been found, and food offerings, but no weapons or pottery. Dating is vague: the 'Arras culture' may correspond to the 4th to 2nd centuries BC. (*See also* Danes Graves, Scorborough and p. 183.)

Danes' Dyke *Iron Age*
Flamborough 101(TA:216694, s end)
NE of Bridlington. Massive dyke cuts off
Flamborough Head. Nature trail from cliffs inland.
The B1255 cuts the dyke 1km from the s end.

A massive defensive earthwork, 4km long, from coast to coast, cuts off 8 sq. km of the peninsula; it is up to 5m high, and its ditch is 18m wide. There are traces of a second bank outside the ditch. The dyke is thought to date to *c.* 300 BC–AD 100, and has no connection with the Danes.

Danes Graves Round
Barrow Cemetery *Iron Age*
Great Driffield 101(TA:018633)
Just s of Roman road from Kilham West Field to
Bridlington. Tumuli are just s of Westfield Farm;
track SE from road; all E of the B1249 between
Great Kendale and Langtoft.

The cemetery is now overgrown and almost unapproachable because of an abattoir. A few mounds survive, but originally there were about 500 small round barrows up to 1m high and up to 9m in diameter. There was one chariot burial, like those at Arras (*qv*), but most graves were poorer than those at Arras: simple, crouched burials with a coarse, plain pot. A few food offerings and personal ornaments are known. Finds are in the British Museum. Dating is vague: 4th to 2nd century BC.

Rudston Standing Stone *
Rudston   *Late New Stone/ Bronze Ages*   **101(TA:097677)**

w of Bridlington. In village churchyard, just by the B1253 from Rudston to Bridlington. N of Roman road from Kilham to Bridlington.

A 26-ton monolith of gritstone, hauled from Cayton Bay, 16km away, it towers to 7.8m in the churchyard. The tallest standing stone in Britain, it is thought to date to *c.* 2000 BC. There are some slabs of a megalithic cist by the churchyard wall. This area also has 2 long barrows, and 3 cursuses converge on the end of the chalk ridge where the pillar stands: the squared-off end of one is still visible from the ground as a 1m bank (TA:099658).

A major roman villa existed near the village on both sides of the Kilham – Rudston road; nothing is visible on the site, but its important and unique mosaics are on show in the Mortimer Archaeological and Transport Museum, Hull.

Scorborough Round Barrow Cemetery
Just N of Leconfield   *Iron Age*   **106(TA:017453)**

In field SE of Scorborough Hall; near the A164 from Beverley/Leconfield to Great Driffield.

Rudston Standing Stone. *Later New Stone Age/Bronze Age*

Another cemetery of the 'Arras culture' (*see also* Arras and Danes Graves). At least 120 small barrows survive, mostly up to 5m across and 0.3m high. Two are square. A few have been excavated, and contained crouched burials and no grave goods. Nevertheless, it is the finest surviving monument of the Arras culture, and one of the best-preserved barrow cemeteries in Britain since, being on heavy clay, it has never been ploughed.

Willy Howe Round Barrow *
NE of Thwing   *Late New Stone/ Bronze Ages*   **101(TA:063724)**

Halfway between Wold Newton (to w) and Burton Fleming (to E). Track leads from road between Wold Newton and Burton Fleming, s to Willy Howe Farm. Tumulus is to E (on left).

This very large barrow, 7.3m high and 39.6m across, was explored in the last century. Because its size and construction are analogous with that of Duggleby Howe (p. 204), this suggests a date of *c.* 2200–1700 BC. A 'grave pit' was found, but no burials or datable objects.

LANCASHIRE

Bleasdale Circle or Palisade Barrow
Bleasdale   *Bronze Age*   **102(SD:577460)**

N of Preston and Blackburn, 9km E of Garstang, 0.4km NE of Bleasdale church.

This turf barrow, 1m high, supported a free-standing timber circle, 11m in diameter, comprising 11 oak posts, whose positions are now marked with concrete pillars. In the centre was a grave containing urns with cremations. A ditch round the barrow held a line of birch poles with, to the SE, an entrance marked by 2 large posts. This entry was close to the edge of an outer palisade circle, 45m in diameter. One oak pole has been radiocarbon-dated to 1810 BC. Finds in Preston Museum.

Castercliff Camp Hillfort
Nelson   *Late Bronze/Iron Ages*   **103(SD:885384)**

2km SSW of Colne and 1.2km ESE of Bott Lane Station, Nelson. Just NE of Marsden Hall, SE of the A6068.

This oval hillfort of 0.8ha was probably built in 2 phases; a first, inner bank, 30cm high, with no ditch, was followed by a massive bank with ditch and counterscarp. The defences were never completed on the N side, where stretches of unconnected ditch survive.

There were entrances on E and w, the latter with a series of outworks. Many stones in the bank show traces of burning, which may represent destruction or an attempt at vitrification. The fort has been radiocarbon-dated to 510 BC.

Pikestones Chambered Long Barrow
Anglezarke   *New Stone Age*   **109(SD:627172)**

SW edge of Anglezarke Moor, NNW of Horwich and NNE of Yarrow Reservoir.

A long cairn, 45 by 18m, it had a long and narrow burial chamber of 5 stones at the N end. To the s was a circular drystone structure, while the cairn's northern end has a double drystone revetment wall.

Warton Crag Hillfort
Warton   *Iron Age?*   **97(SD:492728)**

2.4km NNW of Carnforth, 0.8km w of Warton, at s end of Warton Crag.

This triangular fort of 6ha was protected by sheer slopes to the SW and SE, and by 3 widely spaced ramparts to the N. The best preserved is the inner defence, which had an entrance near the E end, but no ditch. The middle bank is 45m N of this, while the outer, 60m further N, is now overgrown and hard to distinguish.

NORTHUMBERLAND

Chew Green Fortlet and Camps
Brownhart Law   *Roman*   **80(NT:788085)**

By river Coquet; just inside county boundary, s of Brownhart Law. On Dere Street (Roman road), a visible section of which runs s to High Rochester

(qv). Access through Redesdale army camp (permission required from duty officer).

This complex of 4 temporary Roman forts and fortlets constituted a staging post for troops going N. The first was built *c.* AD 80 for a full legion. The ramparts

are still clearly visible. Five km to the N is the native hillfort of Woden Law (NT:768125). Other camps lie on either side of the track/Roman road at NT:815057.

Dod Law Rock Carvings *   *Bronze Age?*
Doddington   **75(NU:004317)**
Scattered over moor to E of B6525 running N from Wooler to Doddington and beyond.

This major concentration of rock carvings, on outcrops in a small area of high moorland, includes cup-and-ring marks, and unusual designs – e.g., some irregular multiple squares enclosing cupmarks bear a superficial resemblance to Iron Age fort plans. The visit is best started by Shepherd's House. The most important decorated slab lies on level ground between the camps and behind the house (NU:005317). There are also many carvings among the Dod Law Forts *(qv).*

Dod Law Forts (Camps)   *Iron Age*
Doddington   **75(NU:004317 west; 006317 middle; 008316 east)**
See directions for Dod Law Rock carvings above.

The E camp is an oval enclosure with a single bank and ditch. The one on the W is a D-shaped farmstead, with wide and high double ramparts, enclosing a number of large huts, 5m across. The middle camp, also D-shaped, has a single bank and ditch with traces of a second bank on the N. No huts have been found, and it may have been a stock-enclosure.

Five Round Barrows and Five
Kings Standing Stones   *Bronze Age*
Holystone   **81(NT:953020, 955015)**
Barrows on Holystone Common above and to W of river Coquet, just S of Holystone. Standing stones a little to the S on Dues Hill.

There are not 5 but 9 well-preserved cairns (of an original 14) on the Common. Their sizes vary greatly, and they contained inhumations and/or cremations. Finds – pots, bone pins, flint tools – in the British Museum. There are not 5 but 4 standing stones – one of which is fallen – on Dues Hill, each about 2m high.

Great Hetha Fort and
Hetha Burn Settlements   *Bronze/Iron Ages*
Hethpool   **74(NT:885274 fort; 881275/878276**
SW of Hethpool, W of Wooler.   **settlements)**

This small oval fort has a pair of massive concentric stone ramparts with an inturned entrance on the E. The numerous hollows in the enclosure are the sites of timber huts. The fort was protected by steep slopes on all sides except the SW. Just to the N is the fort of Little Hetha while, at the foot of the hill, stands the Hethpool Stone Circle (NT:892278): 8 fallen stones form a rough horseshoe.

On the NW slope of the hill, below the main fort, are the 2 rectangular settlements of Hetha Burn, comprising a series of hut-platforms levelled out of the hillside. Low walls of turf and stone can still be seen. This site may date to the late Iron Age.

Greaves Ash Hut-circles
and Enclosure *   *Iron Age/Roman*
W of Ingram on river Breamish   **81(NT:965164)**
W of A697. Near Linhope Spout waterfall, 2.5km uphill from Linhope hamlet, NE of Linhope.

On a S-facing slope above the river is the biggest known group of stone hut-circles: there are about 40

of them, covering 8ha, in 2 enclosures. They are about 6m across, and had paved floors. Field and paddock boundaries can also be seen in the vicinity. The earliest site is the hillfort at the W end, with 2 ramparts; it was later overlain by one of the hut-enclosures.

High Rochester Fort   *Roman*
Rochester   **80(NY:833987)**
Just N of Rochester and the A68. Dere Street (Roman road) runs through it, N/S.

The fort of *Bremenium* has the most substantial Roman remains N of Hadrian's Wall: a strong W gate with walls up to 2m high, and other walls in the NW corner. Along Dere Street, 750m from the E wall, are a number of large tombs, including one fine circular example ('The Roman Well').

The fort, a forward defence from which scouts and cavalry could patrol the Scottish lowlands, was, under Severus, the most northerly in the empire. During

rebuilding, c. AD 140, it was provided with solid platforms to carry big catapults with an arc of fire covering the valleys to the s and w, as well as Dere Street. Some ammunition (stone balls) is still visible.

Most of the surviving walls date to the final reconstruction in the early 4th century AD; the fort was burned and sacked in the Pictish uprising of AD 342, and abandoned. Forward defences were then pulled back to Risingham (*qv*).

More Roman camps lie to the NW (NY:828988, etc.) and SE; several along the road. Another Roman road runs E from the fort. Inscriptions and reliefs in University Museum of Antiquities, Newcastle.

Humbleton Hill Hillfort *   *Iron Age*
Wooler   **75(NT:967283)**
Just w of Wooler, overlooking the rivers Till and Glen, and Wooler Water. Pleasant walk of 1.6km w from Wooler. The hill is s of the A697.

Humbleton Hill Hillfort. One of the hut circles within the strong stone-walled Iron Age fort overlooking the river Till

This fort, protected by steep slopes on nearly all sides, has a walled enclosure at the centre, with an entry on the NE, and annexes to the E and NW. All of these enclosures contain hut-circles.

Lordenshaws Hillfort   *Romano-British*
Hesleyhurst   **81(NZ:054993)**
s of Rothbury, to the w of the B6342 at Hesleyhurst. On spur near river Coquet. Reached by a 730m walk from a lane.

This small (0.3ha) fort, impressively situated high in Rothbury Forest and overlooking some fine scenery, comprises 3 ramparts and ditches, still well preserved in places, enclosing a number of hut-circles. There are passage entrances to the E and w.

Above: **Lordenshaws Hillfort**. *A good example of a cup-marked stone, presumably of Bronze Age date*

Right: **Lordenshaws Hillfort**. *Romano-British*

On the way up to the fort, and some 270m sw of its centre, are 2 rock outcrops with cup-and-ring marks and grooves (probably Bronze Age), one on each side of the collapsed deer park wall. To the NE of the fort (NZ:056993) are 6 cairns.

Old Bewick Hillfort *Iron Age*
Bewick **75(NU:075216)**
On w-facing hill above river Breamish, E of Wooperton and the A697, N of the B6346 and Harehope Hall.
This strong fort comprised a circular double rampart and ditch on the edge of a steep escarpment. Later, a second enclosure was added on the E, and finally the whole was enclosed by a rampart and ditch to the N. There are possible hut-circles in the earliest site. Just SE of the fort are a series of rocks with cup-and-ring marks (Bronze Age). Ring-marked stone in Alnwick Castle Museum.

Risingham Fort *Roman*
West Woodburn **80(NY:891862)**
Just w of A68 and just E of Dere Street (Roman road). S of river Rede and West Woodburn.
The fort of *Habitancum*, like High Rochester (*qv*), was a forward post for Hadrian's Wall. Built *c.* AD 140, lost and abandoned after the 180s, it was rebuilt *c.* 205 to house a cohort of 800 men and to act as a base for scouts and cavalry. It was reconstructed to face w in the early 4th century, received severe fire damage *c.* 350, and was finally abandoned *c.* AD 367. The s gate was very strong, having towers with 7-sided fronts. The fort was close to the important Redesdale iron deposits, and over a ton of coal was found in the bathhouse.

Roughting Linn Rock Carving *Bronze Age*
Ford **75(NT:984367)**
15km s of Berwick, 5km N of Doddington. Close by the fort (see below). Approaching from NE, it is 3km along lane from B6525, on right in a clearing amid gorse and silver birch. Not visible from road; not signposted.
The largest inscribed rock in the county – 18m long, 12m wide, 3m high – this spectacular expanse of sandstone is profusely decorated with over 60

Roughting Linn rock carving. Fine specimen of the mysterious cup-and-ring carvings on the largest inscribed rock in the county. Bronze Age

carvings: mostly cup-marks, grooves, concentric circles and some exceptional motifs such as 'boxed U's' and a cup/ring with 9 rays.

Roughting Linn Fort *
Ford
Iron Age
75(NT:984367)
5.6km NNW of Doddington, NW of the B6525.
Just SW of the Linn (waterfall) is a rectangular promontory fort; the easy eastern approach was guarded by 3 banks and ditches with a counterscarp. There was an entrance on the NE.

Whitley Castle Fort
Alston
Roman
87(NY:696487)
Just W of A689, NW of Alston. On line of Maiden Way (Roman road), by Castle Nook.
This rearward supporting fort for Hadrian's Wall

also probably controlled the lead mines of the Alston district. It was therefore massively defended by at least 7 ditches on the weakest flank. The fort's unusual diamond shape takes full advantage of terrain.

Yeavering Bell Hillfort *
Old Yeavering
Iron Age
75(NT:928293)
s of the B6351 between Kirknewton and Akeld; NW of Wooler. Steep climb.
This fort of 5.3ha, at an altitude of 360m, encloses 2 summits and the saddle between. It has a single stone rampart, 4m wide, with entrances on N, NE and s, and small annexes to E and W. The centre is full of hollows, traces of at least 130 circular huts. There was a palisade trench around the eastern summit.

——————YORKSHIRE——————
(NORTH, SOUTH AND WEST)

Acklam Wold Barrows
Acklam
Bronze Age
100(SE:796621)
Just E of Acklam, s of Norton. Both sides of road from Acklam to Birdsall.
Seventeen round barrows, thought to date to 1700–1400 BC, were dug in the 19th century, but many were later destroyed by ploughing. Each contained cremations or up to 6 crouched burials, including children. Grave goods included beakers, jet and amber buttons and a fine dagger of white flint, 18.5cm long, in one skeleton's hand.

Aldborough Town
Aldborough
Roman
99(SE:406664)
E of B6265 between Aldborough and

Boroughbridge; just SE of Boroughbridge at crossing of river Ure.
Isurium Brigantum was the regional capital of the Brigantes, a *civitas* built in the early 2nd century AD by and for native Britons, though probably with the help of Roman military architects. Not much fortification was needed by this time; the town was small (24ha) with a rectangular grid of streets. It may have covered the site of an earlier fort, and had a gate in the centre of each wall at cardinal points. It also contained a civilian amphitheatre (possibly at Studforth Hill) and baths. The houses were wooden, on stone foundations. Much rebuilding and reorganization of defences took place in the 4th century, and occupation lasted until the 5th century AD.

Most of the town lies under the modern village, but part of the sandstone town wall and its artillery turrets survives on the sw side behind the museum, as do fragments of the n gate. A large number of interesting mosaics survive: 2 in small huts in the museum grounds and others in the Leeds City Museum.

Almondbury Hillfort *
Huddersfield
Late Bronze/Iron Ages
110(SE:153141)
On Castle Hill, just se of the city, e of the A616, overlooking the Holme valley.

A small (1.1ha) fortified settlement was built here at the sw end of the hill, with a single earthen bank and an inturned entrance to the ne. An exterior ditch and counterscarp bank were added in the 7th century bc and, later, a timber-laced rampart between vertical stone faces. By 600 bc the fort enclosed 2.2ha, and 50 years later the ramparts were again increased in size and extensive annexes were added near the main entrance; an outer series of banks and ditches enclosed fort and annexes together with many acres of pasture. The fort was destroyed by fire and may have been abandoned by 500 bc, though some scholars believe the site was still in use in the 1st century bc. Much of it has been obliterated by the medieval castle. Finds in Tolson Memorial Museum, Huddersfield.

Brough-by-Bainbridge Fort
Bainbridge
Roman
98(SD:937902)
On hill e of river Bain, s of confluence with Ure, just off A684. Small museum at Cravenholme Farm. On Roman road of Craven's Way, n from Lancaster.

The fort of *Virosidum*, occupied from the 1st to the 4th centuries AD, suffered a number of tribal assaults, and was rebuilt and expanded several times. The earliest structure – an earthen rampart enclosing timber buildings – was reinforced with stone after AD 160. Later, extra barracks were added for an auxiliary unit.

Carl Wark Hillfort
e of Hathersage, sw of Sheffield
Iron Age?
110(SK:260815)
On a nature trail high on Hathersage Moor, n of the A625.

This rectangular enclosure of 0.9ha is on a promontory of millstone grit protected by steep slopes on 3 sides and by a fortification of stone backed by turf to the w. A wall 3m in height survives here. The fort had an inturned gateway in the sw corner, 1.5m wide, and a simpler entrance on the e. Dating is uncertain: probably late Iron Age with some possible Roman and even post-Roman use.

Castle Dykes Henge
Aysgarth
New Stone Age
98(SD:982873)
On spur above Wensleydale and Bishopdale. Tracks from just sw of Aysgarth.

This slightly oval henge monument has a bank, 60m in diameter, with an internal ditch. The original entrance faced e (other breaks in the bank are probably modern) and the monument is thought to date to the late 3rd or early 2nd millennium bc.

Castleton Rigg
Settlement
Westerdale, se of Guisborough
Late Bronze/Iron Ages
94(NZ:682041)
nw of road from Castleton to Westerdale. s of Castleton by road down to Danby High Moor and Rosedale Head.

A narrow spur cut by two earthworks – one at the above map reference, the other at NZ:684048 – these used to be stone-faced, and the more southerly supported a continuous wall; a few big stones survive on

Roman mosaic pavement from Aldborough Roman Town

its crest. Between the 2 barriers were a series of fields, barrows and circular huts dating to *c.* 1000–500 BC. Another series of barrows, fields and systems can be seen nearby at Crown End (NZ:668076).

Cawthorn Camps *Roman*
Cropton, N of Pickering **94(SE:784900)**
N of road from Cropton to Newton-on-Rawcliffe. Leave the A170 (Thirsk to Pickering) at Wrelton, and follow minor road N to Cawthorn.

A unique set of 4 camps, on the edge of the Tabular Hills, these are best seen in winter when bracken is low. One pair cuts into and is later than the other. All were thought to be 'practice camps': in each pair, the troops lived in one and constructed the other. They date to the early second century AD. Two were never permanently occupied, but the more substantial pair may in fact have been permanent forts since, passing

Right: ***Cawthorn Camps****, North Yorkshire (after I. Longworth)*
Below: ***Carl Wark Hillfort****. Iron Age*

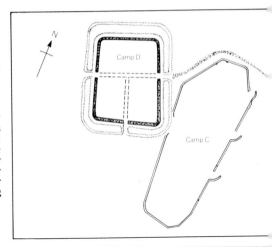

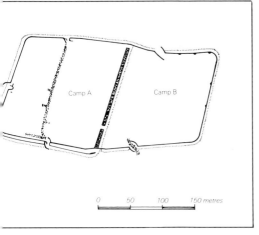

through the site and continuing to the N, there is a fine stretch of Roman road, Wade's Causeway, running for 2km over Wheeldale Moor.

Danby Rigg Promontory
Fort
Bronze/Iron Ages

2km s of Danby, SE of Guisborough **94(NZ:710065)**
Between Danby Dale and Little Fryup Beck. Track from North End Farm and Crossley House Farm.

This impressive site on a steep spur has a 'necropolis' of hundreds of small stone cairns with a stone circle in their midst. This ring cairn has a worn rubble bank, 12m in diameter, and only one of its 4 tall stones survives (1.5m high). The cairn contained some cremations. The 'cemetery area' is bounded by a wall crossing the spur; to the s is another stone circle (18m across) and some small cairns, and then a big set of earthworks, the 'Double Dike' (3 banks, 2 ditches). The area has a number of upright stones; there is a possible settlement with fields on the moor (NZ:718064) and others in the dales round the ridge.

No burials have been found in the small cairns, which have also been interpreted as clearance mounds or industrial waste.

Danby Rigg Promontory Fort, North Yorkshire, showing the position of the cairns (after F. Elgee)

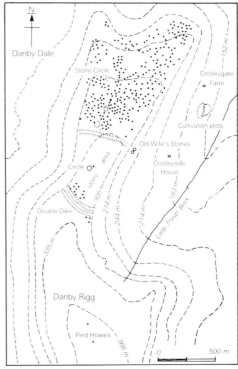

Devil's Arrows Standing
Stones *
Bronze Age

Just w of Boroughbridge **99(SE:391666)**
From Boroughbridge, take lane w to Roecliffe; stones are on either side. Visible from the A1.

This monument, part of the Thornborough/Hutton Moor religious complex (*qv*), consists of 3 huge

*One of the **Devil's Arrows Standing Stones***

stones, each naturally weathered into a fluted shape at the top. they stand in a fairly straight line on a N/S axis, at a spot leading down to the best ford over the Ure. The largest is 6.8m high and the holes they stand in are 2m deep; they are of millstone grit, quarried at a source over 10km away at Knaresborough. There used to be 4 or 5 stones in a line; one was pulled down in a search for treasure, and dragged away to form a footbridge over a stream. Until the 18th century, the fair of St Barnabas was held near the stones on Midsummer's Day. The site's name derives from a legend of the devil trying to destroy an early Christian settlement at Aldborough by firing arrows from Howe Hill – his aim was poor.

Duggleby Howe Round Barrow ✱ *New Stone Age*
Duggleby   **101(SE:881669)**
Just SE of village by B1253 to Sledmere.
   One of the largest barrows in N Britain, it contains about 5000 tons of chalk, and still stands 38m in diameter and 6m high. A large central pit-grave and a shallow double-grave beside it contained the bodies of 10 old men, youths and children together with objects such as bone pins, arrowheads and a fine flint knife. The mound itself, which, though round, dates to the late New Stone Age, contained 50 cremations of the Beaker period (2500 - 2000 BC) accompanied by bone pins and transverse arrowheads. Finds in Mortimer Archaeological Museum, Hull.

Folkton Round Barrow

Folkton Wold   *Bronze Age*   **101(TA:059777)**
W of Hunmanby, SW of Filey, SSE of Flixton.

This small, isolated round barrow comprises 2 concentric ditches round a central burial area, with a mound of chalk layers interspersed with earth, flint and stones. Excavated in the 1860s, it contained a male and female burial with a bell beaker; they were reburied in prehistoric times without their skulls, and covered with a cairn of flints. The ditches also enclosed the burials of 4 more adults and a child. Between the ditches was the grave of a 5-year-old containing 3 squat drums of solid chalk from the seacliffs. These objects, now in the British Museum (copies in Mortimer Archaeological and Transport Museum, Hull), are 10-12cm in diameter and engraved with geometric designs and stylized faces. Their function is unknown (toys? goddess figures?) but they are thought to date to *c.* 1700-1400 BC. There are many tumuli and earthworks in this area.

Goldsborough Signal Station

Goldsborough   *Roman*   **94(NZ:835152)**
NW of Whitby. A few hundred metres from the cliffs; E of track from Goldsborough to Kettleness.

In the 4th century AD, the Romans built a chain of signal towers on headlands from the Tyne to Scarborough (p. 210) and Flamborough Head as a defence against raiders. This is the best-preserved example; it has an outer wall, over a metre thick at the base, with rounded corners strengthened by circular bastions, and it enclosed an area about 32m square. A gate in the S wall led into an unpaved courtyard round the central signal tower; this building, of wood on a stone foundation, about 14m square, had 2 or 3 storeys and was up to 30m high. The whole was surrounded by a berm and ditch, and the courtyard contained a well. Only a large mound, but no stonework, is visible at present. Excavations revealed that the tower's occupants had a varied diet of meat, fish, fowl and molluscs. Early in the 5th century, the tower – like others along the coast – was attacked and burned to the ground. Skeletons of two defenders and a dog were found.

The function of these towers was to keep watch on suspicious/hostile shipping, and to signal to one another or summon cavalry from inland stations. Despite an estimated range of 20km, their use must have been limited to very clear weather.

Grassington Settlement and Field System

Grassington   *Iron Age/Roman*   **98(SD:995655 to SE:004656)**
On moors N of village.

The settlement comprises a large group of stone hut-circles on Lea Green; they cover 0.8ha, and are associated with 110ha of rectangular 'Celtic' fields; the latter are a network of stone and turf banks, up to 1m high, enclosing oblong fields up to 120m long and 22m wide, with much variation between narrow and nearly square shapes. There are other hut-enclosures scattered among them.

Hanging Grimston Long and Round Barrows

Thixendale   *New Stone/Bronze Ages*   **100(SE:810608)**
By Stone Sleights, on both sides of (Roman) road running SE from Leavening.

Located on a narrow, steep-sided plateau (SE:808608), the long barrow was excavated in 1868, and dated recently to *c.* 3540 BC; it covered a collapsed and burned mortuary house containing abundant charcoal, a human leg-bone and 4 heaps of young pig jaws representing at least 20 animals. Their tusk-points had been broken off. The barrow is now only 1m high; originally it was some 24m long, 15m wide, with side ditches 8m wide, 1.8m deep. The E end had a wooden façade.

The round barrows, which date to the Bronze Age (1700-1400 BC), contained burials, some in oak coffins. There were originally 11 such round barrows in an arc round the long barrow, but most are now flattened. One (SE:806613) contained 11 burials in a limestone circle. This group of monuments yielded beakers, collared urns, jet buttons, etc. The finds are in Mortimer Archaeological and Transport Museum, Hull. There are many other tumuli to the E of Leaving, towards Wharram Percy.

High Bride Stones

Stone-circles

Grosmont, SW of Whitby   *Bronze Age*   **94(NZ:850046)**
On Sleights Moor; road and track ESE from Grosmont to A169 passes between Bride Stones and Flat Howes.

These stones have traditionally been interpreted as the remains of 2 circles, with only 3 stones surviving in each, and the tallest being 2m high. Other single standing stones exist in the area. It has recently been suggested that the 'circles' are, in fact, the sparse remains of stone *rows*, stretching some 137m across the moor. The monument is thought to date to the Bronze Age (2000-1400 BC), like the Flat Howe barrow (NZ:855046), which has a ring of stones.

Hutton Moor Henges

Hutton Conyers,   *Bronze Age?*   **99(SE:353735,**
Cana, Nunwick   **361718 & 323748)**
In angle between A61 and A1, N and S of road from Sharow to the A1.

The 3 henges form part of the group of religious monuments in the Ripon area between the rivers Ure and Swale. Like those at Thornborough (*qv*), they comprise circular areas surrounded by a bank and ditch, but they are poorly preserved and heavily ploughed. They are thought to date to the early Bronze Age (2000-1500 BC). Hutton Moor has both internal and external ditches, entries on N and S, and a diameter of 170m. Nearby, to the S, is the Cana henge, of similar size and construction. Between these 2 are a few barrows. The smaller Nunwick henge has no external ditch.

Ilkley Moor Rock-carvings and Monuments *

Ilkley   *Bronze Age*   **104(SE:118476)**
Tracks lead S and up into the moor from Ilkley.

The N and W edges of the moor have a series of stone monuments and of grouped engravings on flat rock outcrops, thought to date to the Bronze Age. Many of the engraved cup-and-ring marks need good light to be seen clearly. Some fragments of the engraved Panorama Stone are enclosed by railings near St Margaret's Church, Ilkley (SE:115473). On Woodhouse Crag, by the reservoir, is the Swastika Stone (SE:096470), which may be Iron Age; while a steep, short climb from the cattle grid between Ilkley and the Cow & Calf Hotel leads to the 'Hanging

*Overleaf: **Ilkley Moor***

Above: **Ilkley Moor Hanging Stones**

Opposite: **Ilkley Moor**. *The curvilinear form of this 'swastika stone' suggests that unlike the other carvings on the moor it may date from the Celtic Iron Age*

Below: **Ilkley Moor**, *West Yorkshire, rock carvings and other monuments (after B. M. Marsden)*

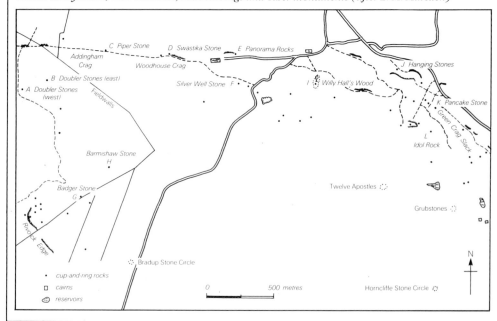

Stones' group (SE:128467). There are at least 8 stone circles on the moor. The 'Twelve Apostles' circle (SE:127451) is 16m in diameter, but most of its stones have fallen or disappeared. Forty-six close-set stones survive of the circle near Horncliffe House (SE:134435) and 20 of the Grubstones Circle (SE:136447).

Ilkley Roman Fort *Roman*
Ilkley **104(SE:116478)**
Covered by the church and the Manor House Museum, near the bridge over the river Wharfe.

Olicana, only 1.4ha in extent, was one of the small Pennine auxiliary forts built for more mobile, less heavily armed troops; it was rectangular, with an earth rampart and wooden internal buildings. Part of the w wall, 21m long and 1m high, survives behind the museum.

Ingleborough Hillfort *Iron Age*
NE of Ingleton, NW of Settle **98(SD:742746)**
From B6255 near Storrs Cave, track via Crina Bottom, and stiff climb.

One of the very few hillforts of the N Pennines, this summit plateau is, at 716m, one of the highest in Britain. It was 6ha in extent, and defended by a huge wall of millstone grit, 4m thick, which is now collapsed in most places. Some parts of the wall were faced internally with large upright slabs. The main entrance was on the SW, and stone hut-circles can still be seen inside the fort, which is dated to 300 BC–AD 100. Being a windswept and bleak site, it is unlikely to have been permanently occupied.

Loose Howe Round Barrow * *Bronze Age*
NW of Rosedale Abbey **94(NZ:703008)**
N of road from Rosedale Head/White Cross to Rosedale Abbey.

This barrow, located at an altitude of 430m on the moors, is 2m high and 18m in diameter. Excavation showed that it contained a water-logged oak-trunk coffin. The (disintegrated) body had been laid on a bed of rushes and straw; a piece of shoe survived, as did a bronze knife by the hip, and offerings of hazel branches/nuts, the latter indicating an autumn burial. With the coffin was a dugout canoe, 3m long and 0.5m wide at the prow, although the nearest navigable water is 5km away. This burial is thought to date to *c.* 1700 BC. A secondary grave comprised a cremation in a collared urn together with a stone battle-axe, a bronze dagger and a miniature food vessel; this assemblage dates to *c.* 1400 BC.

Malton Fort *Roman*
Malton **100(SE:791717)**
In angle formed by Old Malton Road (A169 to Pickering) and the railway line to the NE of Malton. On a public open-space near the gas works and fire station.

Founded by Agricola in *c.* AD 79, the fort of *Derventio* had turf ramparts until, in *c.* AD 100, it was strengthened with a stone rampart behind 2 deep ditches. It was damaged in the northern rising of AD 196 but, after reconstruction, became a storage centre in the 3rd century for the corn from the Wolds villas. It was damaged again during raids by Franks and Saxons in the 4th century. Little is now visible except for portions of the ramparts on the NE and SE sides. Finds are housed in the museum in the old town hall, Malton.

Scambridge Long Barrow and Dykes * *New Stone/Iron Ages*
Allerston **101(SE:892861 to 914866)**
NE of Pickering. Track N from A170, 1.5km E of Allerston.

The long barrow is 50m long, 16m wide. At its E end, 3m high, there was a trench containing the scattered remains of 14 people, some completely burned *in situ*. The barrow was made of limestone boulders enclosed in a drystone wall, and dates to *c.* 3500–2500 BC. To W is Givendale Dyke, leading N to Oxmoor Dykes; to E are the Scam Dykes and other earthworks and tumuli.

Scarborough Signal Station *Roman*
Scarborough **101(TA:052892)**
On Castle Cliff, accessible only through Castle.

The site, chosen for its defensive qualities, was first occupied in the early Iron Age, *c.* 550 BC: about 30 pits have been found, presumably for grain storage. On the same spot, in the late 4th century AD, the Romans built a signal station, one of the series of such towers on the NE coast (*see* Goldsborough, p. 205). It comprised a square tower in a courtyard protected by a stone wall with bastions at each corner, and an external ditch. It was probably destroyed in the early 5th century.

Nothing is now visible of the Iron Age settlement. The E side of the signal station has gone over the cliff; the outline of the rest has been marked in concrete on the turf, and the ditch is visible to the S and W. Some medieval chapels obscure part of the site.

Stanwick Fortifications * *Romano-British*
NW of Stanwick St John, **92(NZ:180115)**
SE of Barnard Castle
Halfway between the A66 and A67, E and W of the B6274, SE of Caldwell.

First built in *c.* AD 47, the site consisted of a fortified enclosure of 7ha on the S side of the stream. Before AD 60, another 53ha were added to the N, including a stretch of the stream, and a stone-faced rampart was built, 12m wide, 3m high, with an external ditch that was 12m wide and 4m deep. Finally, in a massive project, another 243ha were added to the S in *c.* AD 72, resulting in earthworks, almost 10km in length, that were the biggest in Britain: no doubt to protect expanses of pasture, since cattle remains dominate in the site's animal bones. The fort was thought by Sir Mortimer Wheeler to have been the stronghold of the anti-Roman Venutius, chief of the Brigantes and husband of the pro-Roman Cartimandua (*see* p. 46). His final phase of construction was not yet completed when the Roman 9th Legion attacked and overran the fort. An iron sword in a wooden scabbard was found in a water-logged part of the ditch, and a skull, cut off at the 4th vertebra, had sword-cuts visible on the eye-socket and forehead.

Most of the site is low lying, hidden by trees and undulations; it is best seen from 'The Tofts', the earliest part of the site, just s of Stanwick church. Part of the ditch, N of the Stanwick-to-Forcett road, is preserved for public viewing. There is a small museum on the site, and other finds are in the Yorkshire Museum, York, and the British Museum.

Staple Howe Farmstead *Iron Age*
E of Scampston **101(SE:898749)**
S of the A64. NE of Malton. Track from near Knapton Grange.

A farmstead on a flat-topped chalk hillock over-looking the Vale of Pickering, this site comprised an oval wooden palisade enclosing an oval hut, 9m long, which had stone walls and contained a clay oven and hearth. Later, this was replaced by 2 round timber huts and a big 5-post rectangular granary. These huts also contained ovens, hearths and a loom. Masses of animal bones were found (cattle, sheep, pig) with abundant pottery, and carbonized grains of club wheat have been radiocarbon-dated to 450 BC. The positions of the huts and granary are clearly marked.

Thornborough Henges * *New Stone Age?*
NE of West Tanfield,   **99(SE:285795 to 289788)**
at Thornborough
On either side of small road running NE from West Tanfield to Thornborough and the B6267.
Part of the concentration of monuments between the Swale and Ure (*see* Hutton Moor, p. 205), these 3 henges stand in line, almost a kilometre apart, run-ning NW/SE and surrounded by 28 round barrows. The henges are almost circular, about 275m across, with 2 entrances (on NW and SE) and surrounded by a bank (originally 3m high) with internal and external ditches, about 20m wide and 3m deep. The bank was originally covered with white gypsum, from deposits down the river Ure. The henges are threatened by gravel-working; the northern one is protected by trees, and, therefore, the best preserved. The most accessible is the central henge, which overlies an earlier *cursus* monument or 'ceremonial avenue', running NE/SW for over a kilometre.

The *cursus* had flanking ditches, 45m apart, with a bank on the inside of each; it is only clearly visible from the air, but can be seen in section in the disused gravel pit to the SW of the central henge, near the rail-way line. The *cursus* is probably of the New Stone Age, but the henges may date to the early Bronze Age (2000 – 1500 BC).

Victoria Cave Cave-dwelling *   *Old Stone Age*
Longcliffe   **98(SD:838650)**
NE of Settle. Road and track climbing NE from Longcliffe towards Malham.
This cave, at an approximate altitude of 400m in the limestone cliff of Kings Scar, has 3 chambers and an entrance facing the SW. It was occupied by hyenas in the later Ice Age, and their bones are associated with those of hippopotamus, woolly rhino and ele-phant. Later layers contain bear, fox and red deer, denoting an improvement in climate. At the cave-mouth were found worked rods of reindeer antler, and another, decorated with engraved wavy lines, was found inside. These implements are thought to date to c. 10,000 BC. A broad harpoon of red deer ant-ler, with barbs on either side, suggests occupation at the very end of the Ice Age (c. 8000 BC). Coins of the 2nd and 4th centuries AD have also been found, together with pottery, bronze brooches, spindle whorls and bone combs.

450m to the N, the small Jubilee Cave (SD:838656) contained material of the New Stone, Bronze and Iron ages, as well as of the Roman period. Finds from Victoria Cave are in Tot Lord's Pig Yard Museum in Settle and the British Museum.

Wincobank Fort   *Iron Age?*
In the NE suburbs of Sheffield   **110(SK:378910)**
East of Firth Park and Wincobank, between the B6086 and B6082.
An oval hillfort of 1ha, it had a rampart, a ditch (up to 2m deep) and counterscarp bank. The ditch and counterscarp have gone on the N side. The rampart, now only 1m high, consisted of rubble and timber-work faced with stone. The timber caught fire at some point and some of the rubble became a vitrified mass. An out-turned entry existed on the NE.
The site is undated. Finds in Sheffield City Museum.

York Colonia and Fort *   *Roman*
York   **105(SE:600520)**
Standing on a natural causeway across the marshy Ouse valley, linking the E and W halves of the county, York (*Eburacum*) was of great importance to the Romans – especially as the river was navigable up to this point, so that sea-ships could sail up from the Humber to the camp walls and deliver supplies directly. Troops were already permanently stationed here by AD 71. The rectangular fort, built to house the 9th Legion (approximately 6000 men) enclosed some 20ha. Fortifications were made more perma-nent between AD 79 and 85, when the earlier clay rampart was faced with timber, and were rebuilt in c. AD 105. Later the 9th Legion was replaced by the 6th, which was stationed at York until the 4th century. The emperor Septimius Severus died at York in AD 211. In the early 4th century the fort gained 6 internal towers and 2 massive angle towers with polygonal fronts.

Most of the remains visible today date to this last phase. Two of the fort's main streets are followed by Stonegate and Petergate. Apart from the collections in the Yorkshire Museum and Castle Museum, there are a number of structures to be seen. The Multi-angular Tower, the western angle tower of the fort, is in the Yorkshire Museum gardens; it is almost 6m high, with medieval additions at the top, and next to it is a 13m stretch of the fort's wall, 4m high.

Behind the Merchant Taylors' Hall – and best seen from the city wall – is the East Corner Tower, which was a rectangular internal tower; its remains are 2.7m high. In front of it, and stretching almost to Monk Bar, is part of the fortress wall (with the medie-val city wall above). Another portion of wall survives near the theatre, in the St Leonard's Place gardens.

Few internal structures are visible. A portion of bath-house can be seen (with the landlord's permis-sion) in the cellars of the Mail Coach Inn (St Samp-son's Square). A vaulted sewer, 46m long, survives at the junction of Swinegate and Church St; it was found in 1972, is up to 1.5m high, and is entered through a manhole (visits possible by prior arrange-ment with the Yorkshire Museum).

Finally, the recent project of strengthening the Minster's foundations led to a number of discoveries including column bases and a fine example of painted plaster; these are on view in the Minster's Undercroft. A broken column stands opposite the Minster, and there is a column base under the Trea-surer's House.

HADRIAN'S WALL

The frontier work known to most of us as Hadrian's Wall, or simply as the Roman Wall, is in very truth, even in its ruin, still the finest of any on the bounds of the Roman Empire. Designed with precision to span the shortest line in England between sea and sea – that between the Tyne and the Solway – it offers a marvellous combination of historical interest with beauty of setting.

There are two good reasons for treating this unique monument as a whole rather than as a number of separate sites. One is that it was built to a coherent plan, while the changes brought about by the experiences of war present a general picture of the military history of the Romans in north Britain. The other reason, even more important for this guide, is that the length of Hadrian's Wall provides an ideal object for a holiday pilgrimage of several days. To enjoy to the full its magnificent central stretch through the wild Pennine country, this part of the pilgrimage should certainly be made on foot.

Yet another advantage in treating the Wall as a whole is that its history will inevitably also include that of the second frontier fortified by the Romans, though held intermittently and for a much shorter time. That is the Scottish Antonine Wall across the even narrower isthmus between the Forth and Clyde. Since so little of it survives, it does not merit special attention, yet it has its own fascination for anyone interested in the struggle between Rome and the British freedom fighters.

The first Roman whose name is writ large in the history of both walls is Julius Agricola. He probably arrived in Britain as governor in the summer of AD 78, at a time when the conquest of lowland England was complete, while most of the warlike tribes of the west and north maintained their fierce independence. Agricola, whose biography was to be written by his son-in-law Tacitus, was a great fighting general, a brilliant strategist with a keen eye for the lie of the land. He more than any other individual succeeded in breaking resistance in the north of England and Scotland and might well have brought the whole of Britain into the empire had his conquests been followed up.

His method of advance was to hold conquered areas in a net of military roads and strategically sited forts. Between AD 79 and 84, he completed the conquest (though not the pacification) of the powerful Brigantes whose territory comprised all the north of England, then swept on through the Scottish Lowlands up to the edge of the Highlands where his forts, including the legionary stronghold of Inchtuthil (p. 248), commanded the passes.

His onslaught forced the wild Caledonian tribes to unite and to face him in pitched battle. This was the famous battle of Mons Graupius fought late in AD 84 somewhere on the approaches to Inverness. Holding his precious legionaries in reserve and engaging only auxiliary troops, he routed a force of some 30,000 tribesmen.

All the Lowlands were now secure and Highland resistance broken for a generation. But the total conquest that would so greatly have changed our history (and made Hadrian's Wall unnecessary) was not to be. Agricola was called back to Rome and soon the failure to go forward was to lead to retreat.

Agricola had built two main roads for his advance into Scotland, one leading west of the Pennines to Carlisle and then up Annandale, and an eastern road – known to us as Dere Street – running from York to Corbridge, over the Cheviots and on to Inveresk. Both roads were well fortified and linked by cross routes. It was in this way that the lines of the two frontiers were to be determined.

Agricola had at once appreciated the military possibilities of the two isthmuses. In AD 79, at the end of his first campaign, he had reached the Tyne – Solway line, corresponding roughly to the northern limits of Brigantian territory. Strong forts were built at Corbridge (p. 217) and Carlisle, at the points where the eastern and western roads to the north were to cross the isthmus. A road was built between them, extending well down the Solway estuary. It was this cross road, to be known as the Stanegate, that was to play an important part in plans for Hadrian's Wall.

By the next year, Agricola had reached the Forth – Clyde isthmus and here, too, he established a fortified frontier base from which to advance. Much as the Tyne – Solway line had ethnic significance as the northern limit of the Brigantes, this isthmus corresponded with the northern limit of the lowland tribesmen who could be recognized as Britons. Beyond it the Caledonian peoples were described by Tacitus as being quite different: with their reddish hair and big limbs, he likened them to the Germans.

Agricola's defensive system held for some time after his recall, although attacks by Dacians on the Danube frontier led indirectly to the withdrawal of the legion from Inchtuthil, a reduction in manpower that ended all possibility of further conquest and, before long, caused a withdrawal from Agricola's northern forts to provide men to hold the Forth-Clyde frontier.

During Trajan's reign, which began in AD 98, there was a military disaster of some kind in Britain and the decision was taken for a further ordered withdrawal, this time to the southern isthmus, to the line of the Stanegate where Carlisle and Corbridge were reinforced by further forts and fortlets. So by AD 117, when Trajan died in the midst of his Asian conquests, the retreat from Scotland was over and the approximate line of his successor's great work already chosen.

The accession of Hadrian was a turning point in the destiny of the Roman empire: expansionism was to be given up in favour of consolidation behind secure frontiers. To this sensible purpose, the new emperor devoted his reign.

His most northerly frontier was ripe for such treatment, for war had broken out in Britain once more-probably a combined uprising of the Brigantes and their Lowland Scottish neighbours. It was firmly put down, and by AD 122, when Hadrian came in person to his troublesome province, it was obvious that a strong military barrier should and could be built. In Germany, he had been satisfied with a massive wooden palisade to secure his boundary, but here in Britain he laid plans for 'one of the most remarkable constructions of any emperor at any time'. Having decreed the building of a stone wall so great in conception that it was to bring glory to his name nearly 2000 years later, Hadrian departed, leaving the execution to the governor, Platorius Nepos, a most able man who was also his friend.

The original intention was to maintain the existing seven forts along the Stanegate, well to the rear of the new wall. While the Stanegate took the low route provided by the valleys of the Tyne, Irthing and Eden, an ideal high route for the Wall was formed by their northern crests. This was at its best in the magnificent central section where the spread of volcanic rock known as the Whin Sill falls in craggy precipices commanding the northern approaches in a way that delights tourists as much as it must have reassured generations of Roman soldiers on patrol.

The specification was for a wall with well-masoned facings and a fill of stones and mortar, 10 Roman feet (3m) wide and 15 feet (4.5m) high with a rampart walk and parapet. At every Roman mile was a fortlet with a gate tower through the Wall, and barracks and kitchen for a small garrison. Between these milecastles, two turrets were built into the Wall with steps up to the rampart walk and (it is assumed) a lookout post on a flat roof. This design provided an observation and perhaps signalling point every third of a Roman mile along the entire length, from Newcastle (*Pons Aelius*) to the Solway coast at Bowness. A formidable ditch was to be cut in front of the Wall except where nature provided a precipice.

Inevitably in a vast undertaking of this kind, there were changes of plan in the light of experience. Since these were all in the direction of greater strength and effectiveness, it seems that the Britons gave more trouble than had been expected. It may well be that the intention of cutting off the Brigantes from their northern friends itself caused rage of a kind known to us from Berlin.

The building of Hadrian's Wall, demanding high engineering skill, was entrusted to contingents from the three legions then in Britain. Starting from Newcastle, they worked in sections of about five miles, one party laying Wall foundations and raising milecastles and turrets, while another built the wall itself. Wall building, which was to consume over a million cubic metres of quarried stone, proved to be by far the more laborious task, so that the other party soon forged ahead. It was when they had reached the Irthing while the ten-foot Wall was only up as far as the North Tyne crossing (at present-day Chollerford) that important changes were decided upon.

It was probably persistent attacks from the north that determined the top brass to give up the old Stanegate forts and, in their stead, build a rather larger number right on the Wall with gate towers opening northward, an arrangement that would enable troops to be deployed far more quickly to meet any attack.

The second major change, presumably to balance the fort building by a compensating reduction in labour and materials, was to reduce the width of the Wall from ten to eight feet. Along the central section where the broad foundations had been laid, the footings can be seen running two feet behind the narrower wall-as clear evidence of a change of plan as any archaeologist could wish. This is supported by the remains of turrets and milecastles taken down to make way for the forts. At much the same time, the eastern flank was secured by running the narrow wall another four miles to abut on the Tyne estuary at Wallsend.

A third drastic change was made as the cohorts advanced their work west of the river

Irthing. Here the wall and the milecastles were built not of stone but of turf and timber, a variation that some attribute to a lack of limestone for mortar, others to a need to speed up a grandiose construction which had fallen badly behind schedule. The turf wall was 20 feet (6m) wide at the base and probably 12 feet (4m) high plus a palisade; the turrets were stone-built as before. Soon, however, the stone wall was to be extended to a little beyond Birdoswald, and later was to replace the turf one along its entire length to Bowness.

When the position of the wall forts had been fixed, the last important addition, the Vallum, was built to the south of them. This consisted of a formidable ditch flanked on each side by turf-faced banks some six feet (2m) high, making a wide open strip-overlooked by watch towers – in principle, much like the Iron Curtain frontiers in parts of Eastern Europe. Unauthorized persons of any kind would have great difficulty in crossing the Vallum: all traffic, civilian or military, would be obliged to use the official crossing places. These were marked by openings in banks corresponding with a stone-sided and gated causeway across the Vallum ditch. One served each fort and milecastle, and also gave access to the military road running along the south side of the Wall.

Although the Wall was built to face north, the strength of the Vallum suggests that there were still freedom fighters among the Brigantes, and that dividing them from their allies to the north was one of Hadrian's main objectives. Certainly his Wall was never meant to be defended against concerted attack like the walls of a city or castle. Essentially it was a patrolled barrier from which continuous watch could be kept and through which both cavalry and infantry could be rushed to drive off or round up enemy bands. Whenever serious fighting did break out, we have to envisage grim scenes such as those carved on Trajan's Column in Rome to commemorate the latter's victories against the Dacians, also a warlike and rebellious people: villages burning; inhabitants fleeing; herded captives; women and children led away; Roman soldiers returning from battle carrying severed heads.

By AD 128, by far the greater part of the frontier works was completed. The garrison numbered some 9500 men, all auxiliary troops recruited from many subject peoples of the empire. Cohorts of foot soldiers or wings (*alae*) of mounted men, 500 or 1000 strong, were stationed in each of the forts,

the cavalry on either flank and the infantry along the centre. The greatest danger was in the west, where the country was difficult and the population hostile. To meet this threat, a cavalry *ala* of 1000 men was held at Stanwix, near Carlisle, its prefect being the commanding officer of all forces on the Wall. Here, from command HQ, a signalling system along the road enabled him to communicate with the legionary legate at York in minutes.

Any attempt to picture the frontier would be incomplete if it left out the settlements of civilians that grew up near the forts, usually to the south of the Vallum. In contrast with the military buildings, their little houses, temples, workshops, taverns and shops would have had a crowded and unplanned appearance. As for the inhabitants, though most were probably Britons, they must surely have included a polyglot sprinkling of camp followers from the homelands of the troops.

These words about the early history and construction of Hadrian's Wall may serve to give visitors an idea of this supreme monument to Roman military power and the heroic persistence with which they applied it even in these faraway misty lands. By using the excellent site guides, zealous visitors can detect much of the archaeological evidence from which the story has been pieced together by diggers and scholars.

The Wall was, of course, to have an important place in British history until the final collapse of the Roman empire, but as the work of later centuries is hard to distinguish on the ground, they can be recalled only in outline. Until the middle of the second century AD, the most significant events centred on changes in imperial policy as to whether the frontier should be held on the Tyne – Solway or the Forth – Clyde line.

It now seems astonishing that no sooner was Hadrian dead (AD 138) than his successor, Antoninus Pius, determined upon a reoccupation of the Scottish Lowlands. Before lichen had time to soften the great work of Hadrian's legionaries, Antoninus campaigned against the still troublesome Lowland tribes, then raised a stout turf wall with close-set forts across the isthmus from west of Carriden to Old Kilpatrick. When this, the Antonine Wall (p. 243), was finished, probably by AD 143, Hadrian's frontier was thrown open – the milecastle gates removed and the Vallum ditch and banks slighted. Most of the forts seemed to have been maintained by only handfuls of men, but the garrisons were largely redeployed in the north.

Within ten years, the Brigantes had risen

again and, with Hadrian's Wall open, were able to renew their league with the Lowland tribes. So serious was the turmoil and the loss of life, even among the legionaries, that replacements for all three legions had to be brought from Germany, while the Antonine Wall was evacuated. Not for long, however. Rome reacted with such vigour that, by about AD 158, both walls had been restored and both were remanned together. At the same time, many forts from the Pennines to the Antonine Wall were rebuilt, among them Corbridge, Hardknott Castle and Birrens.

After two decades of troubled peace while the two walls were held, untamed Caledonians from north of the Antonine Wall broke through it and succeeded in killing a general at the head of his troops. Once again Rome had to send harsh punitive expeditions and the Lowlands were brought under control. This accomplished, the frontier was withdrawn to Hadrian's Wall, where it was to remain.

All might now have gone well in north Britain had not the British-based usurper Clodius Albinus denuded it of most of its soldiers, causing all the old troubles to boil up once again. Hadrian's Wall was so badly damaged that the restoration work under the emperor Septimius Severus was extensive enough to lead some early historians to believe that he had been the original builder. By the time the ailing emperor himself was in Britain, with his empress and their sons Caracalla and Geta, to win a great victory over the Caledonian insurgents, the Wall was in good order once more.

The emperor died in York in AD 211 (a unique distinction for that city) and it was left to his son, Caracalla, a character not generally admired, at last to pacify the north. By this time the Brigantes had already settled down and Caracalla made treaties with the tribes in Scotland, including the Caledonians, that allowed them some autonomy, though under military control. Hadrian's Wall became the base for this control, its garrisons supported by outposts to the north of it. Forts such as Birrens, and High Rochester (p. 196) and Risingham (p. 198) on Dere Street being restored or rebuilt.

During this time of relative tranquility, the civilian settlements outside the Wall forts – traders, craftsmen, veterans and camp followers of all sorts – grew in size and security of tenure. Some were even allowed to edge northward beyond the old line of the Vallum. As the numbers of civilians grew, more young men could be recruited to the auxiliary forces, while Roman citizenship became more widespread. The old hard divisions – civil and military, native and Roman – were becoming blurred. True, the peace was again disturbed in AD 296 when the Caledonians, now to be called Picts, attacked and damaged the Wall, but Rome was still resilient: the Picts were punished and the frontier restored.

During the following century, the chief danger to the province no longer came from the north but from the sea-raiders (p. 58). In the decade after AD 360, when the empire was reeling before barbarian onslaughts, those against Britain mounted to a climax. This came in AD 367, the year of the 'Barbarian Conspiracy', when the improbable happened: the various peoples among the sea-raiders and other barbarians set aside their enmities and united against the unhappy province. This unexpected conspiracy was dreadfully successful: leading figures of government were killed or captured, the army demoralized, and Hadrian's Wall, hitherto impregnable when fully garrisoned, was now overrun. The countryside was at the mercy of robber bands and looting soldiers.

It is remarkable that Rome still had the ability and determination to defend its northern frontier, but after a time of agony it did so. The Roman general Count Theodosius reached Britain with reinforcements and cleansed it of marauders, and Hadrian's Wall received its fourth and last restoration. The building work was inferior to that of the old legionaries; some gates were simply walled up, while the outpost forts were abandoned – there were to be no more Roman soldiers north of the Wall. At the same time, it seems that the civil settlements were deserted, the inhabitants moving into the forts until they resembled fortified villages. Headquarters buildings and granaries became dwellings, and the discovery of their lost trinkets suggests that women were to be found in barrack rooms.

Until recently, it was thought that all troops had been withdrawn from the Wall by the last quarter of the fourth century, but archaeology has shown otherwise. Although the garrisons of the forts were much reduced and probably were little more than a local militia, they seem to have held out until the end of the century. So Hadrian's Wall saw the last of its defenders only a decade before the fatal year of AD 410, when Rome fell before the Goths and the Emperor Honorius formally released the province from his collapsing empire, bidding the Britons look after themselves.

EAST-TO-WEST ITINERARY
—————OF HADRIAN'S WALL—————

The Wall and its Vallum have been suffi-ciently described, but the forts perhaps need further description. The legionaries built their forts to a standard plan, though in dif-ferent sizes according to the garrisons needed. On the Wall there were two sizes: about 1.2 hectares for 500 infantry and about 2 hectares for 1000 infantry or 500 cavalry. The walls were of good masonry, 1.5 metres thick, with a massive double gate in each side and internal towers. The ground plan was shaped like a playing card – a rectangle with rounded corners. In normal infantry forts, the north wall is flush with the Wall, a central gate tower with double gates serving as the sally port; while in those designed for cavalry, the fort projects beyond the Wall far enough to accommodate sally ports also in the east and west sides, three gates being needed to allow mounted men to debouch in good order.

As for internal buildings, rows of barracks (or barracks and stables) stood at either end, while across the centre were the comman-der's house and granaries, with the head-quarters building between them. All were stone-built and the headquarters was a place of some dignity with a colonnaded forecourt, a large hall with tribunal and the regimental shrine and strong-room beyond it. This cen-tral block might also include a hospital, while outside the fort were baths that could serve the men as a clubhouse.

Before setting out on the itinerary, one curious historical development linking Roman with much later military history needs to be explained. After the crushing of the 1745 rebellion, General Wade built a much-needed road across the Pennines from Newcastle to Carlisle. On the eastern side he took advantage of Hadrian's frontier, in parts using the actual base of the Wall for the hard-core of his highway. Thus for much of the way between Heddon-on-the-Wall and Sew-ingshields, where it veers to the south-west, Wade's road, now the B6318, runs between the Wall ditch and the Vallum.

—————— THE PRINCIPAL SITES —————

Hadrian's Wall was built by men of the 2nd, 6th and 20th Legions working from east to west, so the itiner-ary will follow in this direction.

Wallsend (*Segedunum*)   88(NZ:305661)
The Wall was extended to this point on the Tyne estuary when it had already been built westward as far as Chesters. It was carried right down to the river, where there was a quay. The fort has been built over but its outline is marked by white stones in the sur-face of the streets.

Newcastle (*Pons Aelius*)   88(NZ:250640)
This was the starting point for the building of the Wall. There was a small fort on the site of the present castle and a bridge, probably wooden, over the Tyne. Aelius was the family name of Hadrian and so it seems that Hadrian's Bridge (*pons*) marked the beginning of Hadrian's Wall. The Vallum is first known at Arthur's Hill, a kilometre or two w of the town centre.

Benwell (*Condercum*)   88(NZ:217646)
This was a cavalry fort manned by Asturians from N Spain. It is now covered by houses and a reservoir, but had some special features, including an aqueduct and a forge where local coal was burned. Looking odd among modern housing are 2 structures outside the fort. One, in Broombridge Ave, is the little Temple of Atenociticus, a local deity unknown elsewhere. The head of his statue, which stood in the apse, can be seen in the University Museum of Antiquities, New-castle, as can the altars that flanked it. The second, at the foot of Denhill Park Ave, is a stone-built causeway across the Vallum ditch giving access to the fort (p. 00). It is well worth seeing, since of all such crossings, this is the only one to survive.

Denton   88(NZ:198655)
Here, at the bottom of Benwell Hill, the first piece of the 'broad wall' visible above ground lies to the left of the road. 180m further on is a well-preserved turret set within the wall.

Heddon-on-the-Wall   88(NZ:137669)
A small section of the Wall is again visible to the left of the road near the junction of the B6528 and B6318. On Great Hill, still E of the village, the Vallum is in excellent condition with the ditch cut through solid rock.

Rudchester (*Vindovala*)   88(NZ:112675)
This was once a cavalry fort, but although its out-line can just be traced on the ground, there is nothing else to be seen except a rock-cut tank in the orchard of the farm.

Corbridge. On the site of an Agricolan fort, Corbridge (Corstopitum) grew into a military supply base for the army. Many buildings survive from the campaign of the Emperor Severus, including this granary

Halton *(Onnum)*   87(NZ:996685)

Before reaching the site of this fort, there is a good section of the northern Wall ditch to be seen near Wallhouses. *Onnum* itself was another cavalry fort astride the Wall but, as at *Vindovala*, nothing survives above ground. Passing visitors may like to know that, in the 4th century, an extension was added to the fort, giving it an L plan, a rare infringement of the usual strict military standardization. It is well worth pausing 800m w of Halton where Dere Street (now the A68) passed through the Wall by a gateway known as the Portgate. Excavation discovered its foundations just sw of the present roundabout – which, a rare concession, was resited to allow the work to be completed.

Corbridge *(Corstopitum)* *   87(NY:982648)

From this roundabout, visitors should leave the B6318 to go some 4.8km s down Dere Street to the unique and very interesting site of *Corstopitum*. Its buildings cover a flat hilltop immediately w of Corbridge village and sloping southward to the River Tyne. The hill commands a fine view over Corbridge and the Tyne Valley – the first of many that will reward travellers as they move westward.

Corstopitum can be said to be both extensive and deep, for it spreads over some 16ha, while below the surviving buildings, dated to the late 2nd to 3rd century, are hidden a series of forts down to that built by Agricola at this vital junction of his two roads, Dere Street and the Stanegate.

One of the attractions of the place is that it is so much like every military base and depot in all times, including the present. It served as an arsenal, a store for grain and other supplies and, in particular, had workshop space for units maintaining the buildings, tools and equipment of the Wall garrison. It was also an important depot for supplying the campaigns of the Emperor Severus in Scotland (p. 215), but it inevitably developed less directly martial interests as it became a settlement for trade, relaxation and retirement.

The principal buildings to be seen today represent its many functions. In the N is a very large courtyard building with rooms all round – probably a storehouse, though one that was never completed. The rooms along the s side were converted into shops. To the w of the storehouse runs an aqueduct that probably discharged into a tank through an ornamental spout, such as that of the famous Corbridge Lion, from another part of *Corstopitum* (now in the site museum). w of that again are 2 granaries, among the best of their kind in Roman Britain.

To the s, a street divided these buildings from 2 walled compounds for the legionary units, that to the E enclosing their officers' houses, barracks, headquarter buildings, stores and clubhouses (or Naafis), that to the w workshops, where much evidence for armaments manufacture was found. Facing the street on either side of the compounds are rectangular buildings thought to be temples. The site museum houses religious sculptures as well as legionary inscriptions.

Portgate to Chesters

Returning to the Wall by Dere Street, there is plenty to see before reaching the Chesters fort. Climbing the hill immediately to the w, well-preserved stretches of the Vallum and Wall ditch run on either side of the road and continue along the hilltop. On the left at the beginning of the descent to the North Tyne is Fallowfield, site of Roman quarries where one soldier cut an inscription which translates as 'Flavius Carantinus's Rock'. His self-assertion has brought him immortality for his inscription appears in many learned works, while the stone itself is now on view in Chesters Museum. Going steeply downhill, about 230m beyond Planetrees farm, a chunk of wall stands in a field to the left, but the best remains are at Brunton, where the road leaves the line of the Wall to reach Chollerford bridge. In the garden at Brunton, the Wall stands 2.6m high and holds one of the best preserved of all the turrets.

The last monument on this stretch is only 180m E of Chesters: it is the abutment of the bridge across the North Tyne built on the line of the Wall to enable patrols and other traffic to cross freely. It can best be reached by a footpath from Chollerford bridge. The Wall runs down to a square tower on a massive stone platform from which the bridge sprang. The tower presumably gave access to the bridgeway, but its lower storey housed a millwheel turned by a neatly constructed mill race. The river has shifted a little to the W so that the opposing abutment has been carried away – although its foundations can be seen in the river bed when the water is low. So, too, can the bases of 2 of the 3 piers with cut-waters pointing upstream. The third is hidden below the E bank. Piers of an earlier bridge have been found in the masonry of the abutment and one of the midstream piers.

Chesters *(Cilurnum)** 87(NY:912701)

The approach to this well-known fort is from lodge gates about 1km w of Chollerford bridge along the B6318. Here, in the wooded valley, there is something pleasantly rural about this ruined fort, in contrast with the stark and sternly military atmosphere of its chief rival, Housesteads. Fences to separate visitors from farm animals add to the informality (and inconvenience) of the place. Most of the buildings to be seen today were already excavated by John Clayton in the mid-19th century. His collection of antiquities from the Wall is in the museum at the lodge entrance.

This is a large (2.3ha) fort astride the Wall, originally garrisoned by cavalry. The way in is through the N gate, where the sockets for hinges can be seen in the E portal. Keeping straight on, the visitor passes between blocks of barracks – though only those to the E have been partly uncovered – into the headquarters building. Here it is worth lingering, for there is nowhere else in Britain where the look and life of a regimental HQ of Roman days can be more clearly imagined. The courtyard was colonnaded, as the column bases show, and furnished with a well. A wall with 5 openings, no doubt once arched, divides it from a spacious hall with a tribunal from which the CO would have heard disciplinary cases or harangued his men. Beyond it are 5 rooms, the central one being the regimental shrine from which steps lead down to a vaulted strong-room where soldiers' pay and other treasures were kept – a few coins were found between the paving stones. When Clayton first uncovered the strong-room, an iron-studded oak door still closed the entrance.

This is the showpiece among the internal buildings of *Cilurnum*, though the big house next door to it shows that in the cold north the commandant had the comfort of central heating (by hypocaust) and his own private baths.

It is well worth walking round the walls, particularly noticing the E and W gates abutting on the N face of the Wall, and the well-preserved towers and gate

on the S end of the fort. In a guard-room in the S gate, one of those finds was made which, like Flavius's name-cutting, suddenly brings one in touch with an individual. It is a bronze plate (now in the site museum) conferring Roman citizenship on an auxiliary soldier at the end of his 25 years of service.

If visitors walk down towards the river, they will come upon what is probably the best-known, because most photogenic, building at Chesters. This is the large regimental bath-house. Immediately inside the entrance is the spacious changing-room with latrines on one side and a line of round-topped niches on the other which, at a guess, may have held the bathers' clothes. From there, having stripped and perhaps relieved themselves, they had a choice of hot dry-rooms of the sauna type or of steam-rooms. Off the main hot-room to the SW there are 2 alcoves that held hot plunge baths.

Chesters to Carrawburgh

On this stretch, the Wall is sometimes visible on the right, most conspicuously at Black Carts farm where there are the remains of a turret. 1km further and visitors are at the top of Limestone Corner (NY:876716) with a marvellous prospect before them. The eastern half of Hadrian's Wall, where one can trace it only in bits and pieces, is behind and, westward, Wall and Vallum run straight ahead for mile after mile through untamed country, much of it bare but nobly furnished with tree clumps and glimpses of water. Away to the N, moorlands run free to the Scottish border.

The misnamed Limestone Corner is itself of great interest, for here is the first encounter with the Whin Sill (p. 213); cutting through its tough dolerite was a problem for the Roman engineers. The Vallum ditch was truly cut, but with the Wall ditch, the natural fall of the land was almost protection enough and the engineers did not complete their work. Blocks of stone lie along the edge, and one large chunk was left in the middle of the ditch. The wedge holes cut in it show how it would have been split up before being lifted with block and tackle.

Carrawburgh *(Brocolitia)* * 87(NY:858712)

This is the first of the infantry forts of the central section (p. 213). As its long axis runs N/S, it is its short northern wall and gate that are flush with the Wall. It stands up conspicuously as a platform of the standard playing-card shape, but there are no internal buildings to be seen. The bath-house was outside the w gate.

Carrawburgh (Brocolitia). *Roman fort of Hadrian's Wall*

Chesterholm (Vindolanda). *Roman fort of Hadrian's Wall*

The great interest of Carrawburgh (pronounced *-bruff*) centres on the civilian settlement that was built on the low-lying marshy area to the sw of the fort. Here 2 religious buildings have been uncovered, for (as has been seen at Benwell) while the imperial cult had its shrine inside each fort, a variety of cults were practised in the settlements. The first is a 3rd-century temple of Mithras, always a popular cult with the Roman army (p. 51), which was excavated

in 1949 and proved to be in an exceptionally good state of preservation. It is a long, narrow building that would have been low and dark to represent the cave of the bull-slaying myth. Having passed through an annexe and screen, the worshippers entered the sanctuary where they would have reclined on the raised side-benches, flanked by sculptures of Mithras's two companions symbolizing, respectively, light and life, darkness and death. Of the 3 altars dedicated by prefects of the Batavian cohort stationed at *Brocolitia*, one showed the god as charioteer of the sun with rays round his head that could be illuminated by

Housesteads *(Vercovicium)* 87(NY:789687)

Advancing w from Carrawburgh, there are several small camps to the s of the Wall, and some way before Sewingshields the road diverges to the left while the Wall continues along the edge of the Whin Sill, rising in noble ridges with Broomlee and Greenlee loughs gleaming below.

After King's Crag and Busy Gap, the Wall approaches Housesteads fort at an oblique angle from the NE. This is the most visited of all the forts, partly because it is set among the finest stretches of the Wall itself, and partly because it can be seen and understood in its entirety. Indeed there is a perfect view of the fort from the carpark, looking like a model of itself in the completeness of its defences and many interior buildings. In comparison with the romantic feel of Chesters, this might be called a classic site.

It lies with its long axis E/W along the crest of the Whin Sill with the Vallum running straight through the hollow to the s. The buildings are such as we have now come to expect, but are exceptional in having all been excavated and planned at the end of the last century. Some are now overgrown, but the most interesting are well maintained. The headquarters building is very much like that at Chesters, but the commandant's house on its s side is far more complete, built on a civilian plan with many rooms round a central courtyard. The granaries to the N of it had a ventilated floor raised on stone pillars; the building to the w was a hospital.

The 3rd-century garrison, the 1st Cohort of Tungrians (a tribe of the Tongres region in Belgium) was 1000 strong, and 10 barracks were needed to house its men. These, as usual, are long, narrow blocks occupying both ends of the fort. A feature that always rouses interest is the latrine in the SE corner. A sewer runs round it – which was flushed with water from one of several tanks, probably filled from adjacent roofs. There would have been multiple wooden seats over the sewer.

The foundations of the walls with their internal towers and 4 double gates are particularly worth seeing for their completeness. There used to be a story that the legionaries built the N gate according to rule, although the precipitous Whin Sill rendered it useless. This is nonsense: a ramp that led up to the gate was removed when the gate was excavated. It is inside this N wall that the base of a turret and the foundations of the 3m wall belonging to Hadrian's original plan are exposed to view (p. 213).

The civilian settlement at Housesteads was large since it was the central frontier market. The outlines of 'strip-houses', once shops, taverns and the like, are visible outside the s gate, and there were cult buildings including a mithraeum. Sculptures and inscriptions, which were numerous in the settlement, are now in the Chesters Museum and the University Museum of Antiquities, Newcastle. The site museum outside the SE corner contains, as well as a full plan and model of the fort, a strange sculpture of 3 hooded deities.

a concealed lamp. These sculptures can be seen in a restoration of the temple in the University Museum of Antiquities at Newcastle.

The second building, excavated as long ago as 1876, is a shrine enclosing the spring of the goddess or water nymph, Coventina, which stood on the fence line between the mithraeum and the road. Unfortunately little is now visible, but it yielded a fascinating assortment of votive offerings, including small altars, sculptures and over 13,000 coins. The coins show that offerings were still being made to the nymph late in the 4th century.

Chesterholm *(Vindolanda)* ✻ (NY:770664)

About 1.5 km w from Housesteads, a minor road runs s, heading for Birkstow and the A69 at Bardon Mill. On a spur on the far side of it are the fort and settlement of Chesterholm. Close by the burn, a tall, columnar milestone still stands in its original place beside the Stanegate. (The only other milestone *in situ* is at Temple Sowerby in Cumbria, p. 191.) The

Hadrian's Wall *near Cawfields*

earliest fort on the site may date back to Agricola (p. 212), but the one visible today, with 2 gates, some lengths of wall and excavated headquarters building, dates from c.AD 300 with later reconstructions.

Since Chesterholm was taken over by the Vindolanda trust, it has been generally known by its Roman name of *Vindolanda* and its greatest interest centres on the excavations and reconstructions undertaken by the trust on the w side of the fort. One can walk from the w gate down the main street of the civilian settlement between 2 lines of 'strip-houses', long, narrow buildings with their narrow frontage on the street. Most of these would have been shops and taverns, but 2 may conceivably have been married quarters, while the last, and largest, building on the right is almost certainly a *mansio*, an official post-house for the Stanegate. These were set up to accommodate messengers and officials travelling on government business. There they changed horses for their light carriages, had a meal and a bath, rested or stayed overnight. The fort baths adjoin the 'strip-houses' to the N, while away to the s of them lie the trust's replicas of the different forms of the Wall and its installations. One can see the 'broad wall' with a turret, the 'turf wall' and one of its milecastle gates and the Wall ditch. Though already looking slightly dilapidated, these replicas do make it easier to visualize Hadrian's Wall when it was alive with military activity over 1800 years ago.

Finally, the museum in Chesterholm House to the SE of the fort is full of the most fascinating finds from the settlement and the early forts – everything from jewellery to a bath sandal, and from writing tablets to a letter about a soldier's socks and underpants. The trust has made *Vindolanda* a place not to be missed. Further to the w along Stanegate, it is possible, but difficult, to trace the earthworks of many camps, some used by the wall-builders, but others built as military exercises.

Housesteads to Great Chesters

The 10km between these 2 forts can be judged the finest, most exhilarating, of the entire frontier. The escarpment of the Whin Sill rises to rough crags with steep falls between them; the Wall, rising and falling with it, adds movement and a bold emphasis to the scene. It is country to stir even the most sedentary to take to their legs, and those whose walking must be car-based can use carparks at Housesteads, Steelrigg and Cawfields.

There are several installations to be noticed along this part of the Wall – which itself is in good shape, the s face having been restored. Not far to the w of Housesteads, there is a milecastle standing high enough for the spring of the N gate arch to be in place. Here, as in other milecastles, the gateway has been narrowed for security, in this instance in the time of Severus (p. 215). On the E side of the fortlet are barrack foundations, and there was a timber store on the w. Another milecastle can be seen by Castle Nick (NY:760676) – reached by a small road off the B6318 to Steelrigg carpark.

The Wall now climbs to its highest point (375m) at Winshields Crag, and the Solway Firth comes into view. Descending to the Cawfields milecastle, the Vallum is visible running in straight stretches along the valley to the s, and it is often possible to distinguish the many breaches made in it when the Antonine Wall was in commission (p. 214).

Great Chesters (*Aesica*) 87(NY:704667)

This is a small (1.2ha) infantry fort with its long E/W axis on the line of the Wall. It was excavated as long ago as 1897 and something of the headquarters building, the commandant's house and the barracks can be identified, but the whole fort is sadly neglected. The w gate has a special interest for archaeologists, since it shows successive narrowings of the gateway and a final complete blocking up. The bath-house to the SE of the fort was supplied by a long, winding aqueduct from the Caw Burn.

Carvoran (*Magna* or *Banna*) 86(NY:665657)

Some 2.5km beyond Great Chesters, after a switchback course over the Nine Nicks of Thirwall, the Wall leads the walker to Carvoran, one of the Stanegate forts lying s of the Vallum. It can also be reached by a minor road and footpath from the B6318. *Magna* seems to have been a late addition, built towards the end of Hadrian's reign. There is little to be seen of the fort beyond its NW angle-tower, but it stirs the imagination to know that it was garrisoned by a cohort of Hamian archers from Syria. The chief attraction is now the private museum in converted farm buildings at Carvoran House. The displays illustrate the life and times of the Roman soldier in Britain and, more particularly, of course, his life on Hadrian's frontier.

Carvoran to Willowford 86(NZ:622665)

From Carvoran the Wall goes downhill to Greenhead (where it is crossed by the B6318) and so on to Gilsland, which can show a fine piece of it in the vicarage garden. On the w bank of the Poltross Burn there is a milecastle of some interest. On the E side of the gate through the Wall (one of those where a partial blockage survives) are steps that once led up to the rampart walk. It was by making a projection from this flight that it proved possible to estimate the height of the Wall at 15 Roman feet (4.5m). Much of the interior of the fortlet is occupied by 2 barrack blocks.

Crossing the little road from Gilsland to Denton, there is a fine stretch of the Wall, still as much as 14 courses high and armed with 2 turrets, running down to the river Irthing. This, of course, is the beginning of the 'Narrow Wall', and the foundations intended for the 'Broad Wall' (p. 213) can clearly be seen projecting like a wide step along its s foot.

The ruin of Willowford Bridge (NY:622665) over the Irthing is, deservedly, one of the well-known features of Hadrian's Wall. It is quite striking to look at, and for those who like to work out historical puzzles, it presents clues for what appear to be 3 reconstructions. As at the Chesters bridge (p. 218), with which Willowford has much in common, the river has shifted quite a long way w, leaving the E abutment on dry land while burying or destroying the western piers and abutment. The Wall originally ended in a turret, with an abutment to the N, giving access to a bridge carrying the Wall on stout arches. The turret was then dismantled and a larger tower built against the Wall a little to the E, while the abutment was enlarged and extended with narrow, paved channels probably, as at Chesters, carrying millwheels. Later it seems that the abutment was again enlarged and the piers lengthened, possibly to carry a wider bridge. The easternmost of the 3 piers survives.

Beyond the river, the Wall, with a milecastle, can be seen on the top of Harrow's Scar - by road, it can only be reached by way of Gilsland and the minor road off the B6318 to Lanercost, which soon leads on past Birdoswald.

Birdoswald *(Camboglanna)* *   86(NY:615663)

This fort was first intended for cavalry and was built astride the 'turf wall', which was levelled to make way for it. In fact, it came to be manned by an infantry cohort, and the stone replacement to the 'turf wall' was given a slightly more northerly course to join with the N wall of *Camboglanna* on the standard infantry plan. This divergence, slight though it was, has left a unique section of the 'turf wall' exposed. It parts from the stone Wall near Harrow's Crag on its line towards the S side of the E gate of the fort where it is just visible crossing the adjacent field. W of the fort, it runs on to rejoin the Wall at Wallbowers. (Enthusiasts should follow the Lanercost road for about 2km, and turn right at Appletree, by a barn that was formerly a cottage. Here, after only about 70m, they will find, on the left, a section through the 'turf wall' showing the characteristic bands of dark and light soil left by piled turves.)

While the interest of specialists tends to be focused on the 'turf wall' and certain peculiarities of the Vallum at this point, the fort of Birdoswald repays inspection, particularly of its walls, gates and towers. Those who walk round them will be further rewarded by a lovely view of the Irthing from the SW corner. If the interior were to be excavated, Camboglanna would certainly rival Housesteads and Chesters.

Birdoswald to Carlisle

It would be a very great advantage to visitors if the Birdoswald fort were to be dug and conserved as it deserves, for then their pilgrimage could end on a strong note. It must be admitted that, W of this point, although there are noteworthy details on the one hand and the interest of the grand strategy of the Wall on the other, Hadrian's Wall loses its spectacular appeal. Those who are not hooked on the idea of following it to the very end might well turn aside here to see Lanercost Priory (largely built of stone from the Wall) and the marvellous Anglo-Saxon cross shaft at Bewcastle.

Those true to the frontier can find the first point of interest in the milecastle at Wallbowers, about 3km W of Birdoswald, where the 'turf wall', rejoining the stone Wall, is visible crossing the fields as it approaches the milecastle. All the way from here to Bowness, the builders raised the stone Wall on the line of the turf one, incorporating its stone-built turrets (p. 214) in their own work.

A little way W of Wallbowers along the Lanercost road, there is a lodge on the left with a path to the Roman quarries of Coombe Crag (NY:591650) where, among other inscriptions, 3 soldiers carved their names: Securus, Justus and Maternus. Further along the road again, before it reaches Banks village, is Pike Hill, an eminence with wide views in all directions, chosen by the Romans as the site for a tower that was most probably a part of a long-distance signalling system. Just to the E of it is Banks East Turret (NY:575647), a fine example of a 'turf wall' turret still standing 14 courses high. A fair piece of the Wall adjoins it.

This turret is of further interest in that the first Hadrianic extension of the stone Wall ended here (p. 214), the 'turf wall' being allowed to stand, probably until late in the 2nd century when the stone replacement was continued to Bowness.

Immediately to the W of Banks village and N of Lanercost there is a milecastle (NY:562646) and a stretch of Wall standing 3m in height - though refaced in the 19th century. This is the last piece of the Wall itself that can be readily seen, and it must be said that associated sites are not much to look at.

About 11km W of Birdoswald, there was a fort above the Cambeck in the grounds of Castlesteads House, but there is nothing to be seen of it, and nothing is worthy of comment until, after another 13km, the church of Stanwix marks the south-west quarter of the once-great fort of *Petriana*. To accommodate its 1000-strong wing of cavalry, it covered over 3.6ha and some notable sculptures have been taken from it - yet today it is represented by no more than a modest hump in the churchyard.

From there, the Wall ran straight on across the flats to cross the river Eden to the N of Carlisle.

Carlisle *(Luguvalium)* and on to Bowness   85(NY:399561)

Carlisle, as has already been mentioned (p. 212), was one of Agricola's key strong points, standing on the junction of the Stanegate with the western route to Scotland. When the fort of *Luguvalium*, which seems to have been centred on the present marketplace, was supplanted by Stanwix, the fort developed into a town. Later still this settlement was walled - and it is thought probable that the medieval city walls are, in part, built on Roman foundations. Excavations already in progress should clear the many obscurities of the early history of Carlisle. Roman remains from this end of the frontier are exhibited in the Carlisle Museum and Art Gallery in Tullie House in Castle St.

After skirting Carlisle to the N the Wall headed WNW for the Solway Firth. There was a fort at Burgh (Bruff) by Sands (the church stands in its southern part), and from there the Wall crossed Burgh Marsh to another small fort at Drumburgh. Beyond this point, there is a last view of the Vallum running N of the lane from Glasson to Old Carlisle. So, marching along the Solway coast, Hadrian's great Wall reached its terminus at Bowness, where the last fort *(Maia)* was built parallel with the shore while the Wall itself was carried down into the waters of the Firth.

Bowness (85 - NY:225628) guards the lowest fordable point on the Solway, but for a long way further S, the coast was exposed to attack by boat from Scotland. With their unfailing thoroughness, the military built a coastal road with forts at Beckfoot, Maryport, Burrow Walls and Moresby, and between them fortlets and towers comparable to the milecastles and turrets of the Wall. Until recently, it was believed that there was no continuous barrier here, but now excavation is proving that, in some stretches at least, the forts and other strong points were enclosed between ditches - taking the place of the Wall ditch and Vallum. There may also have been a stockade.

So it can be said that in defence against the enemy expected from both land and sea, the

Hadrian's Wall *near Gilsland*

legionaries raised a strongly fortified frontier of some 115 kilometres and on a scale so grand that even the poor ruins that survive fill all who see them with wonder. Perhaps here on the Cumbrian coast there is so little to be seen that the peregrination is ending with a whimper. However, travellers will certainly come away with their most compelling memories of the dramatic Pennine miles and will be able to say with Camden, who knew the Wall four centuries ago, 'Verily I have seene the tract of it over the high pitches and steepe descents of hills, wonderfully rising and falling...'

225

SCOTLAND

Scotland, so much the greatest and loftiest part of our highland zone, has scenery wonderfully diversified by the variousness of its rocks and the faulting and upheavals that have raised and broken them, yet it can be quite simply divided into three principal areas. There are the Southern Uplands, the Central Lowlands and the Highlands & Islands. The divisions between them run diagonally from south-west to north-east, following the main geological faulting – as shown, for example, in the Great Glen.

The Uplands, stretching from sea to sea, are at their highest in the extreme south-west, with some fine, wild scenery primarily due to large, granite masses rising to hills of over 610 metres. There is also plenty of fertile soil, and this is a region quite rich in prehistoric monuments of all periods, particularly in chambered tombs. To the east of Nithsdale, almost to the coast, the Upland hills are rounded, partly covered with grass and partly with bog and heather. Even where broken by the fertile Tweed valley, there are isolated hills of volcanic rock. The monuments of these eastern Uplands, in what is now called Borders, are dominated by great numbers of hillforts, similar to those of Northumberland, most of them small but some of much greater size and importance.

The southern boundary of the Central Lowlands is not well defined but stretches roughly from Lothian down to the Water of Girvan, south of Ayr. The northern boundary, in contrast, is mightily bounded by the scarp of the Highlands, a geological faultline following the north side of Strathmore down to the Clyde estuary. While predominantly low-lying and fertile, it is broken by hills such as the Pentlands, Ochils and Sidlaws. In all of this region, early prehistoric remains are few and far between, but there is a scatter of good hillforts, especially in Strathmore, and Roman forts from Agricola's campaigns and the Antonine Wall.

With the Highlands & Islands, the region is too vast and varied to have any coherence. The huge central mass of the Grampians and the north-west Highlands is virtually barren of antiquity except for a few sites in the major valleys such as Strathspey. As a glance at the Ordnance Survey map of ancient Britain shows, the distribution of ancient monuments of all periods is largely coastal, though there is an area rich in circles and forts extending inland round the Dee and the Don north-west of Aberdeen. Monuments cluster thickly round the Moray Firth, and it is from here all up the coast to the rolling plains of

Caithness that chambered tombs, lacking around Aberdeen, again become numerous.

The sharpest contrast is, of course, between the relatively unbroken isleless east coasts and the deep sea inlets, peninsulas and (reputed) 737 islands of the west and north – a drowned coastline like that of the Norwegian fiords. Here the great numbers of chambered tombs in Strathclyde (including Arran), and those on so many of the western and northern isles, give a powerful impression of these megalith builders as mariners, following the seaways fearlessly in search of likely landfalls where there was pasture and cultivable soil – maintaining the seaways, too, for communications that may have covered both trade and ceremony.

It is also along these same coasts that, towards the end of prehistoric times, communities and families were building so many small forts and duns – and evolving the unique architecture of the brochs.

There are no traces of the Old Stone Age hunters in Scotland. It was only well after the retreat of the ice, probably not before about 6000 BC, that Middle Stone Age hunters, fishing folk and food gatherers arrived in small numbers. Later in the period, groups seem to have settled to live as strandloopers along the coasts, accumulating huge middens of shells mingled with the bones of fish, birds and small animals. Such middens, together with tools, have been found in Macarthur's Cave and other rock shelters in and near Oban, and also on the Argyll coast, but are best seen on the south shore of the Firth of Forth at Inveravon, just east of Grangemouth. Though generally subsisting on such small fare, these east coast dwellers seem sometimes to have been able to feast on stranded whales.

It is with the New Stone Age and the arrival of the first farming peoples by sea and by land that Scottish prehistory leaps from poverty to an almost bewildering abundance. This transformation began probably fairly late in the fourth millennium BC, when builders of long barrows spread from the north of England into the south and east of Scotland at much the same time as builders of megalithic tombs settled the coasts and islands from Wigtown to the Shetlands – a truly remarkable passage in our prehistory. The simple chamberless long barrows (or cairns) are thinly scattered across the Southern Uplands, very sparse in the Central Lowlands, then again scattered in eastern Tayside and Grampian, all areas where there are virtually no chambered tombs. They were also raised north of the Moray Firth, but here many, though by no means all, contain stone chambers.

These long barrows with their presumed English origin are of interest as representing the burial rites of the New Stone Age peoples over a considerable part of Scotland, but they are not visually attractive, and from this point of view, it is a relief to turn to the wonderful range of megalithic chambered tombs of the west and north. The types and distributions have been described earlier (pp. 22-27) so that here it is only necessary to particularize a little more closely.

The group of small passage graves in Dumfries & Galloway, usually with round cairns, have been named by archaeologists after a modest example, the White Cairn of Bargrennan to the north-west of Newton Stuart. Several more examples are in this area of what was west Kircudbrightshire.

In this region, there is an overlap between small passage graves and examples of the far more striking chambered tombs to be seen in such numbers round the Firth of Clyde, especially concentrated on Arran, Bute and the Kintyre peninsula.

The parallel-sided chambers, most often with long trapezoidal mounds (cairns) and often opening on to crescent-shaped forecourts, can very properly be called gallery graves. Present archaeological opinion, however, favours the view that they were developed locally from simple, rectangular, dolmen-like chambers that later were elongated and divided into sections as the builders became wealthier and more ambitious. However this may prove to be, the two tombs of Cairnholy (p. 235), in a fine position above Wigtown Bay, are specimens of the simpler form of chamber, although with a forecourt, while Carn Ban (p. 268), high up in South Arran, is a well-preserved example of the fully evolved gallery grave, with a five-metre chamber divided into three sections. Crarae (p. 269) is a very similar tomb within the famous grounds of Crarae Lodge.

Tombs of this Clyde variety can be discovered up the Strathclyde coast (formerly Argyll) as far as the Firth of Lorne. Further north, chambered tombs of any kind are almost lacking until, entering Highland, Skye is on the fringe of the 300 or more northern passage graves. These all qualify for the name in having a narrower passage leading into a chamber, but otherwise display such a range of design in both chambers and cairns, some most bizarre, that one can imagine adventurous groups, having reached the limits of

land, settling down to invent every conceivable elaboration for their sacred tombs, giving rein to inventiveness and fantasy. These passage graves are few in Skye, plentiful in the Outer Hebrides, outstandingly so in North and South Uist; there are some near both coasts of what was Ross & Cromarty and they swarm in Sutherland and Caithness. Settlers in the Orkneys raised many tombs, including some of the most extraordinary, although those who braved the ocean for the Shetlands were less ambitious but still inventive builders.

The greater part of the chambered tombs of Skye and the Outer Hebrides follow more or less closely the typical passage grave plan; in the smaller tombs, the chamber is often roofed with a single large capstone. The forecourts may be v-shaped rather than crescent-shaped - as in the excavated Rubh' an Dùnain in Skye (p. 256). Good and relatively massive examples in North Uist are Barpa Langass (p. 273) and Marrogh (p. 279). Clettraval (p. 276), in the same island, with its long, originally wedge-shaped cairn, shows architectural influence from the Clyde tomb builders.

On the mainland of the Highland region, in Sutherland and Caithness, where construction was affected by the use of the local smooth flagstone, tomb designers began to make use of upright slabs projecting edgeways into passage and chamber to support drystone walling, sometimes in effect dividing the chamber into two or three sections - as well seen at Skelpick (p. 256) and Kinbrace (p. 255), both in Sutherland. Skelpick is set in one of the immense double-horned long cairns of the area, also splendidly represented by the Yarrows and Cnoc Freiceadain tombs in Caithness (p. 253). It is thought that the idea of raising long barrows, which were sometimes additions to existing tombs, may have been taken over from the builders of simple long barrows of the east and south (p. 21). That round and long cairns might be built by the same communities appears in the well-known 'Grey Cairns' of Camster (p. 252), one of which is a colossal double-horned cairn, the other a large round one. Before turning to the northern isles, a salute should be given to yet another Caithness monument - Ham (p. 255) - as the northernmost chambered tomb on the mainland of Britain.

The Orkneys are so overwhelmingly endowed with fine prehistoric monuments - and with bird life, too - that a month of the long days of early summer could happily be devoted to them. It is impossible here to do more than pick out a few of the most extraordinary of the chambered tombs – leaving the rest to be pursued using the Gazetteer. One general observation worth making is that, while a large number of these extraordinary tombs are the product of the local inventiveness already referred to, there is a group, dominated by Maes Howe, that must surely have been created by an incursion, perhaps led by some great family, who arrived with their supreme tradition of megalithic funerary architecture already at its height.

Perhaps the most remarkable works of local talent are the 'stalled' tombs of Orkney, which must certainly have come from an imaginative enhancement of the passage graves divided by projecting slabs common on the adjoining mainland. The islanders multiplied these paired slabs to produce a very long, narrow, rectangular chamber divided into compartments – of which Mid Howe on Rousay island (p. 260) is the greatest, over 23 metres long and with a dozen compartments. (Although the entrance way through the long mounds of these strange tombs was diminutive, they are still classified as passage graves.) A very odd variant of the stalled cairn is to be found in Huntersquoy (Eday, p. 257) and Taversoas Tuack (Rousay, p. 265), both of them double-deckers with one chamber built on the roof of a sunken, lower chamber.

Another unique creation of the ancient Orcadians is the Dwarfie Stane (p. 257) on Hoy. Here a passage and two side cells have been hewn in a roughly rectangular block of natural sandstone. The entrance is provided with a large slab to close it.

So much for native inventiveness. There remains Maes Howe and a small group of tombs related to it. Enough has already been said earlier (p. 27) about this cruciform passage grave in its huge round barrow, its foreign counterparts and even its legend of buried treasure, to convince us that the power that built it came immediately from overseas. That there are links here with the new Grange tombs in Ireland appears to be confirmed by the zigzags, circles and chevrons carved on the derivative Holm of Papa tomb off Papa Westray (p. 257).

This is the place to mention the truly marvellous village of Skara Brae, for it is now thought almost certain that its inhabitants were the builders of Maes Howe. The villagers, who bred cattle and sheep, furnished their snug thick-walled houses with dressers, beds, cupboards and small water tanks all constructed of flagstones. It can be assumed that other prehistoric houses now reduced to forlorn hut-circles may have been equally well supplied with wooden furnishings.

Few travellers are likely to fly or sail to the Shetlands for the sake of antiquity – although to see the noble, tranquil scene that holds the world's finest broch – Mousa – might almost be lure enough. Anyone who flies there for whatever main purpose should cover the kilometre from the airport to the seashore at Jarlshof, an extraordinary accumulation of dwelling places beginning with a few houses perhaps as old as Skara Brae and ending with a broch and wheelhouse. Among the chambered tombs, there are a number of the distinctive Shetland 'heeled cairns' with shallow concave façades. Two good specimens, the first on Mainland island, are Punds Water (p. 267) and, the best of all, Vementry on the island of that name (p. 267).

Returning to the mainland, it is only necessary to recall the compact group of passage graves ringed about with standing stones near Inverness, since they are sufficiently described on pages 33–6 and represented in the Gazetteer by Balnuaran of Clava (p. 250).

Chambered tombs must be the greatest interest of Scottish prehistory and so take pride of place in any account of it. For the later New Stone Age, Scotland possesses at least a dozen henges, generally following the eastern side of the country just as they do in England. One of the most important, because full excavation has made it a part of the long history of the site, is Cairnpapple (p. 240), west of Edinburgh. The other most visitable henges are in the north: Broomend of Crichie (p. 239) in Grampian (Aberdeenshire), and Muir of Ord (p. 256) in Highland (Ross & Cromarty), both having two entrances. But the finest by far are the two famous circle henges of Orkney: the Ring of Brodgar and Stenness. The bank and ditch at Stenness are much eroded and only four stones of the circle survive – but these are about five metres high. The Ring of Brodgar is beautifully situated between lakes and is far more complete. No bank is visible, but the ditch is wide and deep and 27 stones are standing out of a ring that once numbered 60.

Free-standing stone circles, generally assumed to belong to the Bronze Age, are to be seen throughout Scotland except in the main mountain massifs of Highland and Grampian and along the Highland coast.

Many are on remote moors and hillsides, sometimes among stone rows, menhirs and cairns, but there is not the same separation between circles and chambered tombs as exists in the south, and the circles much more often contain burials within the central area.

It will be best to make a brief survey, region by region, selecting a few of the most important or attractive, but remembering that many more find places in the Gazetteer.

Circles are quite frequent across the Southern Uplands but are somewhat concentrated to the west in Dumfries & Galloway. Here the outstanding example is the Twelve Apostles, just outside Dumfries. This is the fifth largest ring in Britain – but it never had more than 12 stones. Moving up the west coast, there are many circles on Arran, with a remarkable large group on Machrie Moor (p. 270), where there are also cairns and chambered tombs. Several of these enclosed graves of the full Bronze Age. Further north on the coast of Strathclyde (Argyll), Temple Wood (p. 273) is a perfect ring close by the Nether Largie standing stones and a line of five round cairns unique in Scotland. This is in the Kilmartin valley, with its many monuments evidently a sacred area. Mull has a circle with a very tall menhir outside it, attractively set on a patch of good land on the mountainous south coast.

In the Outer Hebrides there are striking megalithic circles, some of them, in fact, oval in plan, along the southern coasts of North Uist, including one near the chambered tomb of Barpa Langass (p. 273). On Lewis, circles cluster round the shores of Loch Roag, but all are dwarfed in extent and interest by the famous Callanish circle, avenue and rows (fully described on p. 274). This extraordinary monument – 'the Stonehenge of the North' – has attracted elaborate astronomical interpretations by Dr Alexander Thom and others.

In Sutherland and Caithness, such free-standing circles as there are tend to be small – though a few in Caithness are larger, while those of Learable Hill (p. 256) are worth seeing for their association with stone rows and cairns.

In the north-east, the circles surrounding the passage graves of the Clava group near Inverness (p. 250) have to be mentioned though they cannot qualify as free-standing. The greatest interest lies further east where clustered in the foothills of the Grampians in former Aberdeenshire are recumbent stone circles with graded uprights rising to flank one large recumbent block. No fewer than 74 of these circles have been identified.

In central Scotland, where these monuments are not common, there is the fine and fully excavated circle of Croftmoraig (p. 246), where the stone ring had been preceded by a horseshoe of wooden posts.

There are cup-and-ring carvings at Croftmoraig, and these are sometimes found on Scottish megaliths and cists as well as on natural rocks. They are common in the south-west, for instance in Arran (Stronach Wood), and in Strathclyde (Argyll) where examples are Achnabreck (p. 268) and Carn Ban (p. 268).

There is no doubt that, while some stone circles were being put up before the end of the New Stone Age, most of the free-standing variety date from the Bronze Age of the second millennium BC. The Beaker Folk reached Scotland in considerable numbers, particularly its eastern part, and, as in England, took an interest in circles and henges as sacred places and sometimes left traces in chambered tombs. Although perhaps the evidence is shaky, it seems that neither they nor their full Bronze Age successors, who interred their dead in cremation urns, were as fond as their English contemporaries of raising barrows (cairns) over the graves. There were, however, many exceptions: at Cairnpapple, there was a Beaker burial in the cairn and cinerary urns added when it was enlarged, and there is said to have been a beaker in the fine fat round cairn of Memsie. There are some notable examples in Strathclyde (Argyll), such as Dunchraigaig (p. 270) securely dated to the Bronze Age, Kintraw (p. 270) and, above all, the five Nether Largie cairns already mentioned. In Lothian, Penshiel Hill (p. 244) has two equally good neighbours, south and east of Gifford. Greenhill Barrow (p. 238) in Fife yielded Bronze Age finds, including an elaborate jet necklace, while among the Orkney Knowes of Trotty, one contained gold discs and amber.

As in the south, hillforts began to be built towards the end of the Bronze Age, from the eighth century BC, and were common from the beginning of the Iron Age. Again as in England, the earlier builders were usually content with a single wall or earthen rampart, often laced or framed with timbers. It was when these caught fire that 'vitrification' took place (p. 38). The overall distribution shows a marked contrast between the regions east and south of the Highland massif, where there are numbers of fair-sized, true hillforts, and west and north of the massif where forts large enough to have contained village communities are relatively rare. Instead, the coasts and islands are lined with more or less strongly defended homesteads, including the characteristic duns. This small scale must have been largely dictated by the very limited amount of good soil available, and one has to imagine family groups each cultivating its section of the narrow coastal strip or valley bottom.

Right across the Southern Uplands, hillforts abound, except in the more rugged hills west of Nithsdale. Near the centre, Burnswark, with its Roman camps, dominates Annandale, while forts congregate most thickly between the Tweed and Forth. Here is Eildon Hill North (p. 232), the largest hillfort in Scotland, crowning an ancient volcano above Melrose, and at one time the *oppidum* of the tribe of the Selgovae. With nearly 300 round huts still visible from the last stage of its history, Eildon Hill ranks as a town. It seems to have been abandoned after AD 80, when the Romans reached the area and built their now vanished fortress of Newstead at the foot of the hill. This part of Borders (Roxburghshire) has many substantial hillforts, including Hownam Rings (p. 232) where excavation revealed a history of five centuries, and Woden Law (p. 233), a multivallate fort with Roman siege works below.

The Central Lowlands, so poor in surviving prehistoric monuments, now come into their own with a number of good hillforts, the best on the eastern side. In the south-east, between Edinburgh and Dunbar on a hill rising boldly from the East Lothian plain, is Traprain Law, *oppidum* of the Votadini, very nearly as large as Eildon Hill and the only other hillfort settlement that can be called a town. In this area, Arthur's Seat (p. 240) in Edinburgh is probably the best known of Iron Age fortifications, but it makes no great show today. Tayside and Grampian can mount the best display of important and highly visitable hillforts in all Scotland. In a small area (in Angus) west of Montrose is Finavon, an excellent example of a timber-laced, vitrified fort, while those neighbours, the Brown and the White Caterthun hillforts, make a striking pair and the White is credited with 'the most imposing ruined wall in Britain'. Inland, near Balbeggie and within sight of Birnam Wood, Dunsinane must be mentioned if only for the sake of that name – but the fort itself is worth seeing.

Of a number of hillforts round the Moray Firth, Craig Phadrig is conspicuous at the east end of the Beauly Firth, and its two ramparts, dated to 370–180 BC, are both heavily vitrified. North of Inverness, sizeable forts become rarer–only Garrywhin, one of the few in Caithness, deserves special mention for the stone slabs that back its single rampart at the entrances.

Here in the far north, the interest in Iron Age defence works shifts to brochs, those family strongholds that were devised by the Pictish people and were in use during the centuries on either side of the beginning of our era. Of the five or six hundred that have been identified, only about a dozen are outside the northern mainland and the western and northern Isles. There is a little group in the Tay–Tweed region and a very few in the south-west (Wigtownshire), one of them the Ardwell broch (p. 234) on a rocky spit projecting into the sea, a typical enough site even so far from the main broch country. Two of the best-preserved mainland towers are Dun Telve and Dun Troddan (p. 254) which, in Invernesshire, are still very much on the southern fringes of the territory. On the extreme east coast of Caithness, the remotely situated Ousdale broch has many interesting features well preserved and invites the more adventurous visitor. In the Western Isles, Boreraig is one of several good, upstanding brochs in Skye, while for anyone who can reach Lewis, Dun Carloway (p. 277) is strongly recommended–it towers up among the ruins of later dwellings.

These are all notable monuments, but for most people who have any awareness of these strange strongholds fringing Scottish shores, the broch *par excellence* is Shetland's Mousa in its simple perfection. Mousa stands well over 12 metres high, and no one knows whether many other brochs were equally tall, or whether this was built (surely by professionals) to be the pride of some supreme Pictish chief of the Isles.

By the time Agricola began his brilliant campaign for the conquest of Scotland, brochs were not only still inhabited but new ones were almost certainly still being built. Tidings of the Roman victories probably reached their owners, for news always travelled far more quickly than most people today like to think. They perhaps even saw Agricola's fleet sail by–but their lives were not to be affected.

An outline of the history of the Romans in Scotland is given in the section on Hadrian's Wall. This includes some account of the Antonine Wall of the Forth–Clyde isthmus and its changing fate as the Roman frontier shifted to and fro, while the scanty remains of this Wall find a place in the Gazetteer. Now it is only necessary to mention the most important and visible of the other military works the legions left behind them.

For the most part, they are forts related to the east and west roads that Agricola first built during the years of his command. In the south-west, commanding Annandale, there is the large and strongly defended fort of Birrens (p. 234). First established by Agricola, it was used also in Antonine times. Just to the north is Burnswark hillfort with the Roman siege works that are believed to have been built as a military exercise. This road went on to Crawford, then met the crossroad from Newstead to the west of Lyne fort.

The eastern road, known as Dere Street, can be very clearly seen and followed from Woden Law (p. 233) to the series of Roman camps at Pennymuir (p. 233), south-east of Jedburgh, the best of their kind in Scotland. It went on to the big fort at Newstead (which had a signal station on Eildon Hill, p. 232), then to the fort and supply base on the Firth of Forth that can still be seen at Cramond (p. 243).

North of the Forth–Clyde isthmus, Agricola planted a strong advance fort at Ardoch, which later became an outpost of the Antonine Wall. From here, after his victory of Mons Graupius, Agricola was able to push up into Angus, establishing forts at the Highland passes and his great fortress at Inchtuthill (p. 248), only held for a few years after AD 83, and now recognized as having provided us with a perfect plan of a great fortress.

SOUTH AND EAST SCOTLAND

BORDERS

Addinston Hillfort
Iron Age?
Addinston 73(NT:523536)
N of Lauder. 1.6km E of Carfraemill. Minor road NE to Addinston from A697.

An impressive and well-preserved oval enclosure, 80 by 50m, with a pair of massive ramparts and external ditches. In the NW sector, the ramparts are still up to 5m high. A few grass-covered stone hut-circles can be made out inside. The site is undated.

Cademuir Hill Hillforts
Iron Age?
Peebles 73(NT:230375/225371)
3.2km SW of Peebles. S of A72 and of by-roads from Kings Muir and Kirkton Manor. SE of Kirkton Manor, SW of Kings Muir.

The first fort (NT:230375), at the top of the SW part of Cademuir Hill, has superb views along the valleys of the Tweed and Manor Water. A ruined stone wall with entrances on the NE and SW encloses up to 40 foundations of timber-framed houses. It seems to have been a minor *oppidum* and was probably abandoned after the Roman arrival in AD 80.

The other, smaller fort is built of stone on a lesser summit of the same ridge. Like Dreva Craig (*qv*), its outer defences have a *chevaux de frise*, a series of upright boulders to the E. The enclosure is irregular, and the massive drystone wall is still substantial.

Coldingham Loch Hillfort
and Settlement
Iron Age?
Coldingham 67(NT:899688)
2.8km N of Coldingham, 1.6km W of St Abb's Head. Take B6438 NE to Coldingham from A1, then farm road from Northfield.

This D-shaped fort, located on a knoll near the cliff-top, has an arc formed by 2 ramparts with a median ditch, and an entry on the S. After the fort

fell into disuse, it housed a settlement featuring a number of stone hut-circles (probably after the 2nd century AD). Four other small settlements are located in the area.

Dreva Craig Hillfort *
Iron Age?
Broughton 72(NT:126354)
1.6km SE of Broughton, and E of the A701. Take minor road SE from Broughton to B712. Just by river Tweed.

An unexcavated fort in a superb setting with tremendous views along the valley, and controlling the Biggar Gap and hence communication between the Upper Tweed and Clyde, it has 2 massive walls of rubble enclosing an oval area that contains a later settlement (stone hut-circles). Other clusters of hut foundations occur around the fort, especially to the NW. The most important feature is an imposing *chevaux de frise* defence, as at Cademuir (*qv*), i.e. rows of upright stones placed at a vulnerable point to break up enemy charges. About 100 stones survive on the SW side of the fort, with many more fallen or broken. They cover an area 30 by 21m, and stand up to 0.8m high. There may have been another set along the ridge to the NE, later incorporated into a secondary settlement.

Drumelzier Barrow
New Stone/Bronze Ages
Broughton 72(NT:124327)
3.2km S of Broughton. Just S of gamekeeper's cottage at Ford. By-road S from B712 near its junction with A701.

The first structure here was a kerbed cairn, 9m in diameter, covering a cremation pit. Later it was restructured round a central cist containing a beaker and some flint tools. Finally, at least 6 more cists were inserted into the cairn as well as a decorated stone slab. Half of the cairn has collapsed thanks to erosion.

Earn's Heugh Forts and
Settlements
Coldingham

Iron Age?
67(NT:892691)

On summit of Tun Law Hill near the sea, 3.2km NNW of Coldingham (qv).

The two enclosures in this spectacular site have lost part of their earthworks over the precipice. That in the SE was the first, with a single rampart, an external ditch and an entry on the W. The NW enclosure was larger, and partly covered it. It has 2 ramparts with a median ditch, and an entry on the W. Finally, a settlement was placed inside a single rampart, entirely within the NW fort, probably around AD 150–400; there are several stone hut-circles.

Edin's Hall Fort, Broch
and Settlement *
Preston

Iron Age/Romano-British
67(NT:772604)

3.6km NW of Preston. Farm road N from junction of B6355 and B6365 (W of Preston). Signposted.

These sites, on the NE side of Cockburn Law, are named after the giant Etin, who is supposed to have lived in the broch. The oval hillfort, probably Iron Age, is on a slope with very few natural defences, and therefore had double ramparts with external ditches, and an entrance on the W. Some time later, in its eastern half, a massive drystone broch was built, the only one in this region. Its walls are 5m thick and still up to 1.5m high; there are 3 sets of rooms in the wall, guard-rooms flanking the entrance passage, and door-checks. Traces survive of outer defence works, and the broch may date to the 40-year interval (after AD 100) between the 2 Roman occupations of the area. Finally, a settlement was placed in the western half of the disused hillfort, probably in the late 2nd century AD, and obliterated the NW defences. Lengths of walling and stone hut-circles can be seen.

Eildon Hill North Hillfort
and Signal Station *
Melrose

Iron Age/Roman
73(NT:555328)

1.6km S of Melrose. Reached from N by signposted 'Eildon Walk' from B6359 s to Lilliesleaf, then steep climb. From S, take by-road W from A6091.

This 16ha hillfort is, with Traprain's Law (p.244) the biggest in Scotland. There is a legend that King Arthur and his knights are in an enchanted sleep beneath it, and that the hill is so full of gold that sheeps' teeth turn yellow after feeding there! It is thought to have been the *oppidum* of the Selgovae tribe, but was abandoned after the Romans arrived in AD 79.

The fort grew in 3 phases on the flat summit, a position of great natural strength, and by the end, there were 2 concentric heavy ramparts. Inside, there are almost 3000 flat platforms for wooden huts: a population of 2000–3000 has been estimated. Only a tiny fraction has been excavated.

After AD 79, the only occupation was at the western end, where the Romans placed a small, wooden signal station: all that remains is a 10m diameter shallow ditch. They also built a great fort and supply base at Newstead, at the NW foot of the hill (NT:571344) but no surface traces of it survive. Finds in the National Museum of Antiquities, Edinburgh.

Green Knowe Settlement
Peebles

Bronze/Iron Age
73(NT:212433)

4.8km NW of Peebles. By-road linking A72 and A703. In Harehope Farm.

This typical unenclosed platform settlement, which faces 2 others at the NW foot of White Meldon Hill, has 9 platforms. The 4th from the N end was excavated and found to have a circle of postholes, 8m across; crude sherds lay on the floor. Recent work has produced radiocarbon dates of the late 2nd millennium BC. A cairn, 100m to the N, contained a number of Beaker burials and cremations, with 30 perforated bone buttons and 110 jet disc-beads.

Haerfaulds Fort and
Settlement
Cambridge

Iron Age?/Romano-British
73(NT:574501)

In Lauderdale, NE of Lauder. Follow A697 to Cambridge, then by-road to NE; after 1km, turn NW on farm road to Blythe; beyond farm, walk across moor to W.

The impressive remains of the fort's 3m thick, timber-laced rubble wall stand on open moorland, by a steep drop down to a stream, and enclose an oval area. A number of later stone hut-circles are visible inside. The fort is undated, but the settlement is probably Romano-British.

Hownam Law and Hownam
Rings Hillforts
Morebattle

Late Bronze/Iron Age?
74 & 80(NT:796220 & 790194)

E of Jedburgh, SE of Morebattle. Hownam Rings (NT:790194) is just E of Hownam.

Hownam Law is a large (8.5ha) fort with a single, massive wall enclosing over 150 shallow platforms for timber-framed houses. A later, small, embanked structure is located in the NE corner, and the entrance is on the SW.

Hownam Rings, at the N end of a long hilltop, is protected by steep slopes on nearly all sides. Excavation revealed a long and complex sequence of occupations and reconstructions, starting with a 0.6ha settlement within a single palisade, followed by a thick drystone wall, and finally a set of 4 ramparts with external ditches. This multivallate system was probably built to meet the 1st Roman advance. The outer 2 ramparts are only visible on the W, while the inner 2 are still over 1m high. After the defences were abandoned, an open settlement was established inside in Roman times (traces of hut-circles).

There are standing stones nearby (NT:792193): 16 low stones running E/W, called the Eleven Shearers, supposedly local folk turned into stone for working in the fields on the Sabbath.

The Mutiny Stones
Long Barrow
Longformacus

New Stone Age
67(NT:623590)

7.2km WNW of Longformacus, SE of Gifford. S of the B6355. Farm track and walk.

This long cairn, apparently unchambered, still stands to an impressive 3m high despite much stone-robbing. It is 85m long and 23m wide at the broad NE end. The monument, aligned E/W, is also called the Mittenfull of Stones: the Devil was carrying stones in his mitten to build a dam across the Tweed, but the mitten burst and spilled the stones on the moor.

Northshield Rings Hillfort
Eddleston

Iron Age?
73(NT:257494)

N of Peebles, 2.4km NNE of Eddleston, E of the A703. On ridge E of Eddleston Water and S of Portmore Loch.

A well-preserved but undated fort of 2 structural phases, it dominates the valley. An inner rampart/

ditch has 3 entrances; 2 outer banks and ditches are concentric with each other though not with the innermost.

Pennymuir Forts (Camps)   *Roman*
Jedburgh   **80(NT:755140)**
SE of Jedburgh, just NW of Woden Law (qv) and N of Chew Green (qv). W of minor road NW from Tow Ford. Dere Street (from the Tees to the Forth) goes through the centre. N of Pennymuir Farm.

These 3 temporary camps, 2 of which are well-preserved, housed the Roman troops who held training exercises on Woden Law. They are marked out by rectangles of ramparts with external ditches. The largest camp (18ha), probably the earliest, could house 2 legions of 5000 men in tents. Its massive rampart is still impressive in places (up to 1.2m high, 4.6m thick, with a ditch of similar dimensions). Five large gates are visible. A 2nd camp occupied its SE corner and used its defences on 2 sides. The 3rd camp, less visible, is to the NE.

Rubers Law Hillfort   *Iron Age & later*
Hawick   **80(NT:580155)**
10km E of Hawick, in angle between A698 (to N) and A6088 (to S). By-road S from Denholm or N from Bonchester Bridge, then moorland walk.

This fort, in a spectacular setting, has at least 2 structural phases: the earlier is an enclosure of 2.8ha with a rampart far below the summit. The later wall, which includes some reused Roman stones (probably from a signal station) only encloses the summit itself. A hoard of Roman bronze vessels found on the SE side of the mountain is now in Hawick Museum.

Tamshiel Rig Walled
Settlement and Fields   *Iron Age & later*
Hawick   **80(NT:643062)**
16km SE of Hawick. Between A6088 (to N) and B6357 (to W). Tracks S from A6088.

A stone-built farmstead associated with a D-shaped 13ha field system. The first settlement, an Iron Age bivallate enclosure, was replaced by a walled settlement with a number of stone hut-circles.

Whiteside Hill Hillfort *   *Iron Age*
Romannobridge   **72(NT:168461)**
2.4km SE of Romannobridge. E of B7059 from Romannobridge S to A72. Take by-road just N of Newlands Church.

A well-preserved, conspicuous hillfort with tremendous views along the valley of the Lyne Water, it underwent several phases of construction. An initial enclosure with a single rampart and ditch was extended by 2 more concentric ramparts and ditches. Later, the fort was greatly reduced in size, and there are traces of hut-platforms inside.

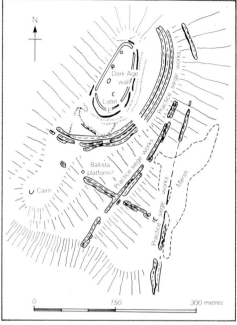

Woden Law Hillfort and Siege Works, Borders *(after Royal Commission on Historical Monuments [Scotland])*

Woden Law Hillfort and
Siege Works *   *Iron Age/Roman*
Nether Hindhope   **80(NT:768125)**
14km SE of Jedburgh. By-road S from Hownam, then by green road (Dere Street) up from Tow Ford southward over Kale Water. Steep climb. Just N of Chew Green (qv).

This well-preserved multivallate fort is located strategically by the pass through which Dere Street runs, the best route through the N Cheviots. It underwent 3 phases of construction: an oval enclosure with a single stone wall was expanded by 2 outer ramparts and median ditch; both of these were systematically destroyed soon after construction. Finally, an oval enclosure with a rubble wall and 4 round huts was built inside during post-Roman times.

The fort is especially noteworthy as the site of training exercises by Roman troops at Pennymuir (*qv*). On 3 sides of the fort, well away from the ramparts, is a well-preserved complex of Roman siege works: banks, ditches and artillery platforms. When they were built, the hillfort was no longer occupied.

——— CENTRAL ———

Castlehill Wood Dun   *Iron Age/Romano-British*
SW of Cambusbarron   **57(NS:750909)**
4.8km SW of Stirling on NE face of Touch Hills. S of the A811 and near by-road from Stirling SW to B818.

An oval dun with a thick drystone wall and an entrance with door-checks on the E. Traces of a stair exist inside, to the N of the entrance, and 2 narrow wall-chambers seem to have been used as kilns for

corn-drying. Excavation in 1955 produced finds of the 1st or 2nd century AD.

Glenlochay Rock Carvings   *Bronze Age*
NW of Killin   **51(NN:532358)**
Take A827 N from Killin, and branch left up Glen Lochay. Carvings between road and river.

A long, glaciated lump of schist is decorated with

cup-and-ring marks for nearly 20m: one of the best collections in the country. Other examples occur nearby.

Stockie Muir (Aucheneck) Chambered Long Barrow
New Stone Age
NW of Glasgow   **64(NS:479814)**
8km WNW of Strathblane. 8km SE of Loch Lomond.
NW of Burncrooks Reservoir. 3km walk W from
A809.

A conspicuous mound of stones, originally 18m long and up to 9m wide: the shape is now rather indistinct. Two big boulders stick out near the E end, and the remains of a large chamber are visible just to the w, with one lintel stone still in place.

Tor Wood Broch
Iron Age
Torwood   **65(NS:833849)**
NE of Denny, 3.2km NW of Larbert, just W of A9.
Woodland path from by-road W from Torwood and
A9. Site of Roman road runs NW/SE here.

One of the best preserved of the few South Scottish brochs, it stands at the edge of a steep ridge, with a superb view to the N. Most of its outer face is obscured by debris, but the inner is clearer. The massive wall, 6m thick, is pierced in the E by a lintelled entrance passage with door-checks and a bar-hole. The courtyard, 10m across, has a number of cupboards, a stair-lobby and a scarcement in the inner wallface. Finds are in the National Museum of Antiquities, Edinburgh, and in Falkirk Burgh Museum.

DUMFRIES & GALLOWAY

Airswood Moss (King Schaw's Grave) Cist in Barrow
Bronze Age
NW of Langholm   **79(NY:259933)**
5.6km NW of Bentpath. Cist stands in dry patch of
Airswood Moss, part of Bank Head Hill. W of B709
in moorland.

The cairn was originally 16m in diameter: after 150 cartloads of stones were removed in 1828 to build a dyke, a large cist was discovered in the centre. This now stands exposed, aligned NE/SW. One of its sides is a single big slab; one end slab and the massive cover are still in place.

Ardwell Broch *
Iron Age?
Ardwell   **82(NX:066446)**
On rocky spit on Ardwell Point, 6.4km SW of
Sandhead. Take by-road SW from A716.

A typical broch located on a knoll close to the sea. The wall is 4m thick, the courtyard 9m across, and the entrance passage faces the sea. Extra defence is provided by a wall and ditch that cut the neck of the promontory. Unexcavated.

Barsalloch Point Fort
Iron Age
Port William   **82(NX:347413)**
On cliff edge, 2.4km SSE of Port William, and just E
of A747. Steep walk from road. Signposted.

A small (0.1ha) promontory fort, it comprises a D-shaped enclosure formed by the cliff-edge and an arc consisting of 2 ramparts with a deep, wide median ditch. The entrance was on the NE. A mesolithic hearth with geometric microliths was found near here and radiocarbon-dated to 4050 BC.

Birrens Fort
Roman
Middlebie   **85(NY:219752)**
In Annandale. 1.6km S of Middlebie, W of by-road
going NW from B722 near Eaglesfield, or from B725
SE from Middlebie.

The Roman fort of *Blatobulgium*, one of the biggest and most important in SW Scotland, was an outpost for Hadrian's Wall after the Antonine Wall was abandoned. It stands at the confluence of Mein Water and Middlebie Burn and on the main Roman route from Carlisle to W Scotland. Burnswark *(qv)* is 4km to the NW. Originally a turf-rampart camp in the 1st century AD, it grew in the 2nd century to have 6 concentric banks and ditches, now only fully preserved on the N side. Excavations found stone buildings inside, but these are not visible at present.

Broomhillbank Hill Hillfort
Iron Age?
9.6km N of Lockerbie   **78(NY:131911)**
E of A74 and old Roman road. Approach from A74
by farm road and hill climb.

An oval fort with a fine situation on a summit, and with tremendous views all around. It has a double rampart with wide median ditch and 2 entrances.

Burnswark Fort, Siege
Works and Fortlet *   *Iron Age/Roman*
Ecclefechan   **85(NY:185785)**
5.6km SE of Lockerbie, E of A74. By-road leaving
B725 to NE of Ecclefechan leads to hill. Roman road
nearby runs NW/SE. 4km NW of Birrens (qv).

The 7ha hillfort, in its very dominant position, grew from a small, oval enclosure to the irregular shape seen today. The original defences – banks with a double palisade – were soon transformed into an earth-and-rubble bank with stone-facing. There were timber houses inside the fort. Recent excavations have provided radiocarbon dates of 525 and 500 BC. Today, the most impressive ramparts are those at the N, the easiest approach to the fort.

As at Woden's Law (p. 233), the deserted hillfort was later (2nd century AD) used for training exercises by the Romans – probably those stationed at Birrens *(qv)*. They made 2 practice siege camps below the hill, to the NW and SE (the former being too far away to be effective in a real siege) and the hillfort was bombarded with live ammunition to simulate battle conditions: excavations in the hillfort produced 67 lead sling-bolts and sandstone *ballista*-balls, all fired from below.

The southern camp is very well preserved and most impressive, with its rectangle of ramparts with gates. In front of its northern gates, facing the hill, are 3 massive artillery platforms. In the NE corner of the camp is an earlier, small fortlet of the 2nd century AD.

Cairnholy I and II Chambered   *New Stone/*
Long Barrows *   *Early Bronze Ages*
SE of Creetown, SW of
Gatehouse of Fleet, near coast   **83(NX:518541)**
By-road N from A75, then farm road 3km W of
Auchenlarie.

Two Clyde cairns in a fine setting by Wigtown Bay. The first is the more impressive; having lost its covering cairn, its ruined bipartite chamber can be seen, and the 6 tall stones of the horned forecourt stand

Cairnholy I Chambered Long Barrow. *New*
Stone Age/Early Bronze Age

Opposite: ***Cairnholy II Chambered Long Barrow***. *The second of two chambered long cairns with megalithic chamber and portal stones*

out clearly. The trapezoidal cairn was originally over 50m long and 15m wide. Excavation showed that 5 fires had been lit in front of the tomb's entrance during the period of use. Inside the tomb were cremated human remains, together with pottery and flint arrowheads showing affinities with Ulster. Some pitchstone fragments came from Arran. After a last use in the 3rd millennium BC, the tomb was blocked up. Finally, a Bronze Age burial was inserted into the chamber, with a cup-and-ring-marked stone beside it.

The smaller cairn, 150m to the N, is less impressive and has no forecourt façade, though it does have a NW portal stone some 3m high. Its bipartite chamber of large slabs is still visible. Its dating is similar: like its companion, it was blocked at the end of its use.

Finds are in the National Museum of Antiquities, Edinburgh. The site's name may be derived from *Carn Ulaidh* ('treasure cairn').

Cardoness House Rock Carvings
Gatehouse of Fleet *Bronze Age* 83(NX:565535)
4.8km SW of Gatehouse of Fleet, along the A75. Near the coast.

Three fine slabs, collected locally and decorated with cup-and-ring marks, are kept in the garden of Cardoness House.

Cardoness House rock carvings. A good specimen of inscribed stone with cup-and-ring marks and other related symbols

Castle Haven Galleried Dun
W of Borgue *Iron Age* 83(NX:594483)
Take A755 W from Kirkcudbright, then B727 SW to Borgue. Coast road W from village to a point 200m E of Corseyard 'tower' where dun can be seen on the foreshore.

This drystone ruin, covered in ivy, is D-shaped, with a wall along a low cliff-edge to the W as the straight section. It has been considerably restored. The hollow wall contains 3 stretches of gallery, with 6 doors leading into the interior. The main door, with checks, is on the N; and the inner wallface has traces of stairs to the wallhead. A narrow door through the S wall leads to the beach via steps in a natural rock-cleft. Excavation of the dun produced some typical Iron Age artifacts.

Cauldside Burn Stone Circle, Barrows, Rock Carvings *

Anwoth   *Bronze Age*   **83(NX:529571)**

Between Gatehouse of Fleet (to SE) and Creetown (to NW). 4.8km WNW of Anwoth church, by Cauldside Burn, on lower slopes of Cairnharrow Hill. Not far from Glenquicken (qv).

The great cairn, 20m in diameter and 3m high, is the best preserved in the group, and stands by a heather-covered swamp; its cist is visible at the top. Just to the S is a circle of 10 thin slabs: there may originally have been 20. Two stones can be seen 120m to the NE (the taller has fallen), which may be the remains of another circle, and lead to a ring cairn, now overgrown, with a cist sunk in the ground inside it. About 360m N of the burn, on the hillside, is a remarkable spiral, 60cm across, carved on a block of whinstone. There are also cup-and-ring marks.

Drumtroddan Rock Carvings

2.4km ENE of Port William   *Bronze Age*   **83(NX:362444)**

Just NE of junction of A714 and B7021. Due S, near the coast, are a stone circle (NX:361420), standing stones (NX:362415) and other cup/ring marks on the shore (NX:366406).

A fine set of carvings, fenced off in a field on Drumtroddan farm, they are located on several stretches of rockface. There are cups, some with concentric rings and occasional radial grooves and connecting channels. There are 2 others nearby at Big Balcraig and Clachan. About 360m S are 2 upright 3m stones, with one fallen between them.

Glenquicken Stone Circle
Bronze Age
4km E of Creetown **83(NX:509582)**
Approach by minor road and 'Old Military Road'.
By Englishman's Burn.
Said to be the most perfect centre-stone circle in the British Isles, it comprises a ring of 28 unimpressive close-set boulders, 16m across. However, the centre stone, about 1m from true centre, is a pillar of granite nearly 2m high, 1m thick and about 4 tons in weight. The circle's interior is strewn with cobbles. There was a 2nd circle in a field to the NW (now destroyed) and there is a circle of 9 boulders with a centre stone about 2km to the SSE (NX:517560). *See also* Cauldside Burn.

Mullach Hillfort
Iron Age
NW of Dalswinton **78(NX:929870)**
11km NW of Dumfries along A76; E of the A76. At crossing over river Nith, take farm road to NE and climb hill to SW.
A hillfort with a superb location and extensive views over Nithsdale, it comprises an oval enclosure with 2 concentric rubble walls unusually far apart: the space between was perhaps a stock-enclosure. The walls have become a vitrified mass in several places owing to the burning of the internal timber framework. Unexcavated. Just over 1km to the S was the great Dalswinton Roman fort (of which nothing is left), probably the HQ for all of SW Scotland.

Torhousekie Stone Circle ✱
Bronze Age
Wigtown **83(NX:382565)**
Close to the S of the road from Wigtown to Kirkowan.
This is an exceptionally well-preserved circle of 19 granite boulders. It is very slightly flattened in plan, with the stones increasing in size towards the SE. At the centre are 3 further boulders, 2 large ones with a smaller block between them. Diameter about 18m.

Trusty's Hill Hillfort
Iron Age?
Just E of Anwoth, just W of Gatehouse
of Fleet **83(NX:589561)**
Turn off A75 to Anwoth, footpath from village.
This small fort has an inner defence comprising a rectangular layout of vitrified wall. There are outer defences of banks and ditches lower down the slopes. Unexcavated. The entrance on the E lies between 2 rock outcrops, the southernmost of which bears carvings of 3 Pictish symbols: a 'monster', a double disc with Z-rod, and a circle with 'horns' and a stylized face. These probably postdate the fort's abandonment, and are attributable to *c.* AD 700.

Twelve Apostles Stone Circle
Bronze Age
SE of Holywood, NW of Dumfries **84(NX:947794)**
S side of B729, just W of its junction with A76, just N of New Bridge.
Also known as Holywood, this ranks as the 5th largest ring in Britain. It is an ellipse, 87 by 74m, and 11 of its original 12 stones survive, though only 5 are upright; the tallest is 1.8m high. A great number of axes have been found in the vicinity, including some from Great Langdale (*see* Pike of Stickle, p. 191). Another circle of 9 big stones, 1km away, by the Nith, has now disappeared.

Tynron Doon Hillfort
Iron Age?
SW of Penpont **78(NX:820939)**
W of A702, 5km W of junction with A76. By-road to W, and hill climb.
A spectacular fort on a steep hill, it has an oval enclosure with a ruined stone wall, and outer defences of 3 great ramparts and ditches; the outer ramparts are still impressively high (up to 6m) in places.

FIFE

Clatchard Craig Hillfort
Iron Age
Just SE of Newburgh **59(NO:244178)**
Immediately S of A913 and just S of railway, above Tay estuary.
A large, well-defended fort which controlled a pass through the Ochils, it has been partly quarried away. It underwent at least 3 structural phases, but traces of the last (constructed in the early Middle Ages) are almost completely destroyed.
As at Hownam Rings (p. 232) it grew at some point to a multivallate complex, with up to 5 ramparts round the summit.

Collessie Barrow
Early Bronze Age
Collessie, SE of Newburgh **59(NO:288131)**
Just N of A91, 185m SE of Collessie Church. Standing stone at NO:293133.
This cairn was once huge – 35m in diameter and 4m high – and still stands 25m across. In 1876 a gang of labourers removed 1000 cartloads of stones in 8 days, and exposed the internal structure. There was a ring of sandstone blocks inside, with its interior filled with clay on which fires had been lit. The floor was covered in charcoal and burned bones. A cist in the centre contained a crouched burial and 2 beakers. Elsewhere in the cairn a later burial yielded a riveted bronze dagger with gold mounting. Finds in National Museum of Antiquities, Edinburgh.

Greenhill Barrow
Bronze Age
2.4km SW of Balmerino **59(NO:345228)**
On S side of Firth of Tay. Take by-road NW from A914.
A round kerbed cairn, 15m across and 1.5m high, it had an upright slab buried at its centre, and a cist beside it. The barrow also contained a number of other minor cists and pits that yielded cremated bones, pottery vessels, and 72 jet necklace-beads.

Lundin Links Standing Stones
Bronze Age
Lundin Links **59(NO:404026)**
NE of Leven, NW of Earlsferry. Just N of A915 on Forth estuary, at Largo Bay. On W edge of Lundin Links.
Three thin standing stones, ringed by iron railings on a golf course, may be a setting rather than part of a destroyed circle. Two are 5m high and taper towards the top; the 3rd is shorter. From here one can see the Bass Rock, 25km away to the SE, and it has been suggested that the stones were used for observations on minimum moonrise and moonset. Bones from a complex kerb-cairn near here have been radiocarbon-dated to 390 BC.

Norman's Law Hillfort and Settlement*/Iron Age
NE of Newburgh **59(NO:305203)**
w of Luthrie NNW of Cupar. Take farm road N from A913.

A large hillfort in a fine situation, with magnificent views over the Firth of Tay, it encloses the whole hill-

top with a stone wall, and has a big annexe on the SW side. The summit itself is also enclosed by a massive stone wall that may represent the final construction phase. A number of stone hut-circles inside and on the ruined ramparts indicate a later switch to open settlement.

GRAMPIAN

Barmkin of Echt Hillfort*
Iron Age?
NW of Echt **38(NJ:726071)**
Due w of Aberdeen and s of the A944. Take B977 SW from Dunecht, then farmtrack/moorland path to w.

This large hillfort has – like Brown Caterthun (p. 00) – an unusual number of ramparts and entrances. The innermost defence is a circular enclosure, 112m across, with a ruined stone wall. Outside is a 2nd wall, with entrances in line with the innermost. Beyond this stand another 3 concentric ramparts enclosing a total area of 150m diameter. There are 5 entrances through them, lined by flanking walls, but 3 of them face unbroken inner walls. Several phases of fortification are represented.

Barra Hill Hillfort
Iron Age
SW of Oldmeldrum, NNW of
Aberdeen **38(NJ:803257)**
s of junction of A920 and B9170. Take B9170 SW from Oldmeldrum, then farm road to E. There are standing stones just to the s (NJ:801249).

A fort with some similarities to Barmkin of Echt (see above), it has an inner stone wall with a single entrance on the E; outside this stand a pair of ramparts and ditches with 3 entrances, 2 of which have flanking walls. The inner wall is thought to be later than the rest. A big boulder on the site is a glacial erratic.

Broomend of Crichie Henge
New Stone Age
1.6km s of Inverurie, immediately s of
Port Elphinstone **38(NJ:779197)**
Just E of A96, between road and river Don. Standing stone to s at NJ:784179, also just E of A96.

A great circle-henge with opposing entries on N and s in its outer bank, its total diameter is over 35m. Inside stood a ring of 6 stones, of which only 2 remain: a 3rd was added in the 19th century (AD) and bears carvings of Pictish symbols. Excavation revealed an unusual sunken cist grave in the circle's centre, with a skeleton. Several cremations and Bronze Age artifacts were also found inside the circle, and indicate a primary date of c. 1700 BC.

There used to be a splayed avenue of standing stones in a double row over 18m wide, running for 400m from a sandbank to the s (near some cists with Beaker period burials) to the circle-henge and on to a larger stone circle, 50m N of the henge. This larger circle comprised 3 concentric rings, but it has completely disappeared, as has the avenue except for one stone 175m s of the henge.

It has been suggested that this important megalithic complex may have had some astronomical significance. Owing to the sandy soil, it has been estimated that the henge could have been built by 20 people in less than 2 weeks.

Dunnideer Hillfort
Iron Age?
1.6km w of Insch **37(NJ:613281)**
SE of Huntly, NW of Inverurie, N of B9002. There are standing stones s of the B9002 (NJ:618274).

This hillfort, highly conspicuous since there is no higher point between here and the sea, was robbed of stone for the ruined medieval tower that now crowns the summit. The inner rectangular enclosure has a heavily vitrified wall, and traces of a well at the w end. There are 2 outer ramparts lower down the hill, which seem to be incomplete, being marked by trenches at some points.

Little Conval Hillfort
Iron Age
3.2km w of Dufftown, on s side of
Spey valley **28(NJ:295393)**
s of junction of A95 and A941. Take B9009 SW from Dufftown, and then moorland paths.

Fortification was never finished round this 550m-altitude eminence. There were to be 4 lines of defence, but for the most part they are laid out only by marker trench, with some completed stretches of massive wall to be seen here and there.

Loanhead of Daviot Recumbent Stone Circle*
New Stone/Bronze Ages
6.4km WNW of Oldmeldrum **38(NJ:747289)**
Take A920 to NW from Oldmeldrum, and then w on by-road. Or take B9001 NW from Inverurie and then E on by-road. Signposted.

An important ritual ensemble of the 3rd and 2nd millennia BC. Conspicuous from a considerable distance, the circle is typical of its class in that it has a huge recumbent stone (now fractured by the cold) between 2 tall uprights, and the other uprights diminish in height the further away from the recumbent stone they are. The stone next to the eastern flanker has a line of 5 cupmarks on its inner face. The circle is over 20m across; at its centre was a small rectangular timber structure, later replaced by a ring cairn of small boulders. Fragments of skulls, including over 50 from small children, were found in the centre, together with a layer of burning.

Five standing stones have very small cairns around them containing cists and cremated bones. An adjacent cremation cemetery was enclosed by 2 lines of stones and ditches. At its centre was a cremated body.

It has been suggested that the megalithic monument may have had some astronomical significance.

Mither Tap o' Bennachie Hillfort
Iron Age
3.6km SSE of Oyne **38(NJ:683224)**
sw of junction of A96 and B9002. Take by-roads/footpaths to s.

This high and holy granite tor, the 'Mother of the Top', is crowned by a fort with tremendous views. It is hard to make out the plan, since ruined walls stand amid great masses of boulders and blocks. The huge outer wall runs round the base of the tor, over 30m below the summit. Several stretches can still be identified. There are traces of (probably later) stone hut-circles between the defences and above the upper wall.

Loanhead of Daviot Recumbent Stone Circle. New Stone Age/Bronze Age

Raedykes Fort (Temporary Camp) *Roman*
NW of Stonehaven **38 & 45(NO:841902)**
N of A957 and W of B979. Approach on by-road.
There are 4 ring cairns at NO:833906.

A curiously shaped camp, it follows the terrain and covers 38ha. Gorse and bracken have obscured much of it, but one can still see that, in order to compensate for the easier approaches (the slopes being less steep here), the N and E ramparts were built especially high.

Tap o' Noth Hillfort *Iron Age*
2.4km NW of Rhynie **37(NJ:485293)**
S of Huntly. Take A941 NW from Rhynie, and then farm road/footpath.

The 2nd highest fort in Scotland, it is visible from the sea to the E, and has superb views. It is overgrown, but one can still see a massive (6m thick) inner wall, heavily vitrified in places, and traces of a well at the S end. An outer wall can be seen further downhill to the N and E.

——— LOTHIAN ———

Arthur's Seat Hillfort *Iron Age*
Edinburgh **66(NT:275728)**
Includes the peak of Arthur's Seat and Crow Hill, occupying much of Holyrood Park.

A major hillfort which was once as large and important as Traprain Law (*qv*) and Eildon Hill (p. 232), it is now reduced to the ruins of its massive stone walls at the E, the easiest approach. Thanks to ploughing, there are no signs of dwellings inside the fort. The site was probably one of the major strongholds of the Votadini tribe.

Black Castle Hillfort *Iron Age*
4.8km SE of Gifford **67(NT:580662)**
Take B6355 SE from Gifford; fort is just S of the road. Green Castle Fort is just beyond at NT:582657.

A medium-sized fort, 110m in diameter, its outer defences were never finished. An inner enclosure surrounded by a stone rampart contains 2 stone hut-circles that may be a later addition. There is a ditch between the inner and outer ramparts, and entrances on W and S.

Cairnpapple Henge
and Barrow * *New Stone/Bronze Ages*
2.4km ESE of Torphichen, 3km N of
Bathgate **65(NS:987717)**
By-roads E from B792, or N from the A89.
Signposted. Small museum. Entrance fee. Leaflet available, and custodian's hut has explanatory model.

Standing on a basalt hill W of Edinburgh, from which one can see from coast to coast (Bass Rock and the Arran mountains) on a clear day, this is one of the most important sites in early prehistoric Scotland. It had a complex history: the earliest phase was a series of 7 pits that, like the Aubrey Holes at Stonehenge (p. 108), were filled with cremations. Fragments of axes from Great Langdale (*see* Pike of Stickle, p. 191) and Craig Lwyd (p. 300) were found on the New Stone Age land surface.

In the 2nd phase (Early Bronze Age), a circle-henge was constructed: i.e., a bank and rock-cut ditch, with wide entrances on N and S, and containing an egg-shaped setting of 24 standing stones up to 1.5m high. Near the centre was a cove of 3 massive

Above: **Cairnpapple Barrow.** *A most complicated site of the New Stone Age and Bronze Age. These stones marked one of the Beaker burials*

Below: **Cairnpapple Henge and Barrow,** *Lothian (after E. W. MacKie)*

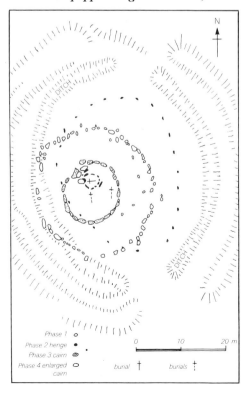

Phase 1 ○
Phase 2 henge ●
Phase 3 cairn ⊗
Phase 4 enlarged ○
cairn

burial † burials ‡

0   10   20 m

stones, facing wsw– rather like those at Arbor Low (p. 169), Avebury (p. 97) and Stanton Drew (p. 115). Also inside the henge were 2 crouched burials with beakers. None of the standing stones now survives.

In the 3rd phase, a huge cairn, over 13m in diameter, was built in the western half of the henge, using material from the bank and the circle. It stood over one of the beaker graves and also covered a cist burial. The cairn was then enlarged to 30m across, with a kerb of boulders around it, and 2 cremations were placed in it. Finally, to the E of the henge, 4 full-length rock-cut graves were made, probably in the Iron Age.

A concrete cover now shows the outline of the cairn: one can descend an iron ladder into the interior and see the grave settings.

Castle Law Hillfort
and Souterrain
Iron Age/Romano-British
sw of Woodhouselee   **66(NT:229639)**
s of Edinburgh, N of Penicuik. Just NW of the A702. Approach by farm road.

This is a typical multivallate fort, where a palisade trench was replaced by a single timber-reinforced rampart; and 2 ramparts and ditches were added outside. There were entrances on the s, w and E. In the eastern part of the ditch, between the outer ramparts, there is a well-preserved souterrain, probably built just after the Roman occupation. It is long and high, and a large bee-hive chamber opens off it.

The Chesters Hillfort
Iron Age?
Drem   **66(NT:507782)**
N of Haddington, sw of North Berwick. s of railway and B1377, near junction with B1345. By-road SSE to site.

241

Despite the robbing of stonework, this small multivallate fort is still impressive. It was vulnerable, since it is overlooked by a steep scarp. There are 2 massive ramparts with external ditches, and traces of 6 more ramparts further out. Entrances were on the ESE and possibly the w. Unexcavated.

Cramond Fort and Supply Base   *Roman*
Cramond   **65 & 66(NT:190768)**
On NW edge of Edinburgh, on the shore of Firth of Forth. Turn N at roundabout on A90 along Whitehouse Rd. Fort close to Cramond church.

A supply depot for servicing the Antonine Wall by sea, it was built c. AD 142, 18km E of the Wall's end. The Wall itself ran from Carriden to Old Kilpatrick on the Firth of Forth, half the length of Hadrian's Wall. Built in about 139 as a base for campaigns further N, it was abandoned by 163. Cramond later played an important part in Severus's campaign in the 3rd century. The visible parts of the fort are next to the church, and a model of the fort is on show in Huntly House Museum. Half a kilometre to the w, on the shore, is 'Eagle Rock' (or Hunter's Craig, NT:184774); a large niche in its seaward side contains a very worn sculpture, once interpreted as an eagle, but now thought to be a figure of Mercury.

East Cairn Hill Barrow   *Bronze Age*
West Linton   **65(NT:122596)**
On summit of NW edge of Pentland Hills. NNW of West Linton, SE of Harperrig Reservoir and the A70, NW of the A702. By-road and old Drove Road from West Linton or SE from A70 just beyond Harperrig Reservoir.

A large cairn in a superb position with very extensive views in all directions.

Harelaw Hillfort   *Iron Age?*
4.8km SE of Gifford   **66(NT:546631)**
Northern spur of Lammermuir Hills. Take by-roads and moorland walk s from Gifford and the B6355. Not far from Kidlaw Hillfort (qv). Settlements to NE/E.

A large fort on a rocky summit with fine views, it comprises a massive timber-laced stone wall, with traces of outworks. The latter are particularly clear in the SW, the only vulnerable approach, where 2 ramparts with external ditches cut off all access except for a narrow pathway to the fort's entry on the w.

Kidlaw Hillfort   *Iron Age?*
Gifford   **66(NT:512642)**
4.4km SW of Gifford. Just E of Kidlaw Farm. Approach as for Harelaw (qv).

A fine round fort, 110m across, it has been reconstructed to a great extent, and comprises 3 ramparts with external ditches, and entrances on the w and E. There are traces of later homesteads inside.

Newbridge Barrow   *Bronze Age*
Newbridge   **65(NT:123726)**
3.5km W of Edinburgh city limits, SW of Edinburgh airport. Immediately SW of the point where the A89 crosses the M8/9. Enclosed by wall.

A large and impressive earthen mound, it was opened in 1830, and a fine riveted bronze dagger was found. Three standing stones close by, up to 2m high, may be all that remains of a circle. A 4th, further E, may be an outlier.

Traprain Law Hillfort. Iron Age. (Cambridge University, Crown Copyright)

North Berwick Law Hillfort *   *Iron Age*
Just SE of North Berwick   **66(NT:555843)**
0.8km S of North Berwick on precipitous hill, E of
B1347.

This fort has a fine position above precipitous
slopes, but its surviving remains are sparse since
much of the drystone walling has collapsed downhill. Stretches of up to 3 concentric walls can be seen,
and the lowest enclosure has numerous and well-
preserved stone hut-circles and platforms.

Penshiel Hill Round Barrow   *Bronze Age?*
Penshiel Hill (in Lammermuir
Hills)   **67(NT:637635)**
11km ESE of Gifford. High up on NE side of Penshiel
Hill. Moorland walk S from the B6355, W of
Whiteadder Reservoir.

A large cairn, it has a broad, flat top and a wide surrounding ditch. Beyond this is a low bank, and thus
the monument closely resembles a bell barrow.

Traprain Law Hillfort *
(Oppidum)   *Iron Age*
3.2km SW of East Linton.   **67(NT:581747)**
By-roads S from A1 between East Linton and
Haddington. Standing stone at NT:578742, and
another at NT:581769 (immediately N of the A1).

Despite its unimpressive and inaccessible
remains, this is thought to be one of the most important sites in the late prehistory of northern Britain.
The hill, shaped like a 'harpooned whale', was first
fortified in the 8th century BC with a small (4ha)
enclosure. This then grew, in 4ha stages, to a final
enormous 16ha in the 1st century AD, when it was the
largest in Scotland, together with Eildon Hill (p.
232). It was the *oppidum* of the Votadini tribe, controlling a large area and many lesser forts, and contained stone huts and craft specialists. Unlike Eildon
Hill, it was not deserted during the period of Roman
occupation, which indicates some treaty at work. It
was later reconstructed twice, in the face of destructive raids by Picts during the 2nd and 3rd centuries.
Finally, in the 4th century, the fort's size was reduced
by a quarter, and a massive stone wall, 3.6m thick, was
built round the hill: it is the remains of this wall that
are most striking today. In 1919 a huge haul of high-
quality Roman silver plate, perhaps loot from pirate
raids, was found hidden on the W slope of the hill, and
is now in the National Museum of Antiquities, Edinburgh.

——— TAYSIDE ———

Abernethy (Castle Law)
Hillfort   *Iron Age*
Abernethy   **58(NO:183154)**
Just SW of Abernethy and Newburgh, SE of Perth.
4.8km ESE of Bridge of Earn. Take by-road S towards
Strathmiglo: it leaves A913 halfway between
Abernethy (to E) and junction with A912 (to W)
and goes round the foot of the fort's ridge.

A small hillfort dominating the confluence of the
Earn and Tay, it has 2 massive stone ramparts. The
outer face of the inner rampart has 2 rows of rectangular beam-sockets, both longitudinal and transverse.
There is a rock-cut well inside the fort. Finds from

Traprain Law Hillfort. Iron Age

19th–century excavations suggest a date of the 2nd/ 3rd century BC, and are now in the National Museum of Antiquities, Edinburgh.

Airlich Stone Circle
Bronze Age
Trochry **52(NN:959386)**
SE of Aberfeldy, SW of Dunkeld. Immediately S of the A822 and the river Braan. Moorland walk.

A small stone circle, with no stone over 1m in height, it is nevertheless quite striking. A circle of 9 stones stands on a low bank, and inside is another circle of 8 smaller stones.

Ardoch Fort and Camps*
Roman
Braco **57 & 58(NN:839099)**
Close to E side of A822. 1.8km N of junction with A9. NE of Dunblane, SSW of Crieff. Roman road headed NE from fort and passed fortlet at NN:861129.

A forward defence for the Antonine Wall, this is a well-preserved and impressive site despite its lack of visible stonework. The fort was a permanent legionary base, and, like the Wall, its wide ramparts had a stone base with turf above. The rectangle contained the usual military buildings of wood and stone; outside was a series of 5 parallel ditches, and the E and N entries are still visible as causeways across them. A final turf rampart encloses the whole system.

To the N and NE there are traces of 6 larger, temporary camps whose outlines overlap each other and the fort. Chronology probably ranges from the 1st to the 3rd centuries AD.

Braes of Taymouth Rock Carvings
Bronze Age
Kenmore **52(NN:793447)**
Scattered cup-and-ring markings in Upper Strathtay. Boulders E of Tombuie Cottage (NN:789448).

This boulder-strewn hillside displays some fine engravings. There are others throughout the region of Upper Strathtay between Logierait and Fearnan.

Brown Caterthun Hillfort
Iron Age?
Bridgend **44(NO:555668)**
NW of Brechin. Take by-road NW from Brechin via Little Brechin. It passes between this fort (to NE) and, to the SW, White Caterthun (qv). Signposted. Parking space. 720m footpath to site.

Situated only 1.2km NE of White Caterthun, this fort is much smaller, a little lower and less impressive overall. Nevertheless, it has a complex defence system: 6 concentric ramparts with a bizarre system of entrances. The inner, massive stone rampart has one entrance (on N), the next 3 have 9 each, and the last 2 have 8 each. Unexcavated.

Clach Na Tiom Pan*
Chambered Long Barrow
New Stone Age
11km SW of Amulree, SSW of Aberfeldy **52(NN:830330)**
In Wester Glen Almond. Take A822 S from Amulree, then W on private road along N bank of river at Newton Bridge.

Impressive remains of a Clyde cairn of wedge shape. The chamber is close to the wide E end; it was divided by 2 septal slabs and had a portal. A little to the W was a 2nd chamber with septal slabs, and a 3rd even further W. A 4th has now disappeared. Immediately to the S (NN:831328) is a small, late stone circle.

Clach Na Tiom Pan

Croftmoraig Stone Circle and Rock Carvings
New Stone Age
3.2km NE of Kenmore **52(NN:797472)**
Just S of A827 to Aberfeldy. Near S bank of river Tay.

An imposing and well-preserved stone circle. The original New Stone Age structure was altered in the early Bronze Age. It started as a horseshoe of 14

wooden posts, which was then replaced by an oval of standing stones – the present inner ring – with 3 more in an arc to the SE; one of the NE stones has cupmarks. At this point the site became a henge, with a bank round it, and a cupmarked stone just to the SW. Finally, the outer stone circle was added on the bank, using the arc already present, and 2 further outliers were placed on the E as an entrance. There have been suggestions of alignments on the midsummer sunrise.

Dundurn Hillfort *Iron Age?*
6.5km w of Comrie **51 & 52(NN:707233)**
Just s of the A85 and river Earn. On rocky knoll near E end of Loch Earn.

Situated just w of Kindrochet *(qv)*, this fort comprises a complex of ruined walls, courtyards and compounds all over the hill. It is thought to have also been a Pictish stronghold, and was besieged in AD 683.

Above: ***Croftmoraig Stone Circle***. *First raised in the New Stone Age, Croftmoraig was altered in the early Bronze Age*

Right: ***Clach Na Tiom Pan Chambered Long Barrow***. *An outlying example of the kind of chambered long cairn common on the south-west coast*

Dunsinane Hillfort
Balbeggie, s of Coupar Angus

Iron Age?

53(NO:214316)

Take B953 NE from the A94 and from Balbeggie; by-road N to Collace. Fort is to E of the by-road.

A conspicuous fort with fine views, it comprises a massive inner rampart that may have been timber-laced (i.e., traces of vitrification) and 3 smaller external ramparts. A small souterrain found inside the fort no longer survives.

Finavon Hillfort
Aberlemno

Iron Age

54(NO:506556)

6.4km NE of Forfar, s of the A94 and river South Esk. Just W of Aberlemno and the B9134. Take farm road towards Finavon Castle: it skirts the fort. Close to Turin Hill hillfort (qv).

The first vitrified hillfort to have been dated, this site has produced radiocarbon-dates of 590, 410 and 320 BC. The great rectangle-formed by the ruined, vitrified stone wall that still stands over 2m high in places-contained a rock-cut cistern or well on the E (still open), and another on the W. Traces of wooden huts and hearths were found by excavators.

Inchtuthill Hillfort, Fort and Camps
Caputh

Iron Age/Roman

53(NO:115393)

3km E of Caputh. Take A984 to NE, and turn S on farm road at Spittalfield. Major Roman fortress nearby at NO:125397.

The hillfort is located near the end of a promontory, and was defended by a palisade trench and ditch across this neck of land. After the Romans abandoned the area, its size was more than doubled, and 5 ramparts and ditches were built across the promontory, using much Roman stone.

Apart from one or 2 marching camps, the fort of *Pennata Castra* was the northernmost site in the Roman empire: a massive fort, it was briefly occupied by the 20th Legion (6000 men), and had a typical layout. It was intended to be the centre for Agricola's campaigns into Scotland, and construction was begun in AD 83, but Agricola was recalled within 4 years, and the fort was completely dismantled, so as to leave nothing of use to hostile forces. Timber was taken down, nails removed, glass and pottery smashed; even the hospital drain was jammed with gravel. Excavation revealed that a million unused iron nails, weighing 12 tons, had been hidden in a workshop pit, being too heavy to take s. Today, the fort is part of a golf course, and visible structures are limited to the hollow of the ditch on the E, and a massive rampart on the s. A small stone bath-house stood outside, to the SE.

Kindrochet Chambered
Long Barrow *New Stone Age*
Comrie **52(NN:723230)**
4.8km W of Comrie along A85, and just E of Dundurn fort (qv). Just S of road and river Earn, on flats. Approach by farm road.

This great mass of stones, a Clyde cairn, is on an E/W axis, and was surrounded by a kerb. One can still see its internal features: 3 cists, laid out in a row along the E/W axis. The best preserved is the segmented central cist, which was found to contain a leaf-shaped arrowhead.

Machuim Stone Circle *Bronze Age*
Fearnan **51(NN:682401)**
5.4km SW of Fearnan, NE of Killin, immediately NW of the A827. Near shore of Loch Tay.

This graded oval of 6 massive stones, 6m in diameter, stands on a mound 13m across.

Monzie Stone Circle *Bronze Age*
Crieff **52(NN:882242)**
3.2km NE of Crieff. On lowest slopes of Milquhanzie Hill, just W of A822. By-road and farmtrack to NW from Gilmerton. There is a standing stone at NN:879242.

This small monument, set in a wide, flat field, is really a kerb cairn, less than 5m across. The 10 kerb boulders are graded for size, with the tallest placed opposite a cupmarked specimen on an E/W axis. A fierce fire had burned in the centre, and by the nor-

thern kerb was a small cist containing the cremated remains of an adult and an infant. A large outlier boulder, 3m sw of the cairn, is profusely decorated with 46 cup-and-ring marks. It was connected to the kerb by a crude causeway, resembling the situation at Balnuaran of Clava (p.250).

Roromore Dun *Iron Age or later*
Fortingall **51(NN:626468)**
11km w of Fortingall, NE of Killin. S of Glen Lyon. By-road and farm road to right bank of Allt a' Chobhair (waterfall at NN:625467).

A very well-preserved dun with a massive wall and an entrance in the N. The wall was robbed for stone to make the (now ruined) rectangular structure inside the dun, but survives as a great grassy mound with numerous boulders in it.

Strathgroy Barrow *Bronze Age*
2.4km E of Blair Atholl **43(NN:897649)**
N of A9, farm road to Strathgroy and steep hill climb.

A substantial round cairn, 40m across, with traces of a peristalith (surrounding kerb). A cist, possibly a secondary feature, can be seen at the top.

Turin Hill Hillfort and Duns *Iron Age*
Aberlemno **54(NO:514535)**
5.6km NE of Forfar, just SE of Finavon (qv). Take

B9134 NE from Forfar to Aberlemno, or the B9113 ENE from Forfar; the fort is S of former, N of latter. Approach by farm roads.

The fort stands on a long ridge with superb views. It had at least 2 phases of construction, the earlier of which comprised an oval enclosure with 2 ramparts. Later, a much smaller enclosure was made inside, with a single, possibly timber-laced stone wall. After the fort fell into disuse, a round dun was constructed, in part, on the northern section of the later wall; its entrance is on the SW. A 2nd dun was built 130m to the W, and a 3rd 130m to the E.

White Caterthun Hillfort * *Iron Age*
Bridgend **44(NO:548661)**
Approach as for Brown Caterthun (qv).
Signposted. 360m path to the site.

Much bigger, a little higher and more impressive than its companion. Two really massive concentric stone walls comprise the inner defences and enclose an oval area; the innermost is said to be the most imposing ruined wall in Britain, with rubble spread to over 12m in width. It is said to have been built by witches as a fairy stronghold, and the stones were carried in an apron; one day the apron-strings broke, and the stones fell out.

The outer defences, 2 banks with a median ditch, enclose 0.7ha in all. There is rock-cut cistern or well inside the fort, at the W end.

NORTH AND WEST SCOTLAND AND
THE WESTERN ISLES

HIGHLAND

Achany Chambered Barrow *New Stone Age*
Achany **16(NC:571019)**
8km S of Lairg. Immediately E of B864 and W of river Shin, railway and A836. Right bank of Grudie Burn, by B864 bridge. Settlements and field systems and a stone circle to E/SE, on E side of A836.

This cairn was originally 18m across; much of its covering has gone, and its rectangular chamber, divided into 2 halves, is now exposed. The mound's entrance is still marked on the NE by a kerb and an arc of boulders.

Achavanich Standing Stones * *Bronze Age*
Achavanich **11(ND:188418)**
1km SE of Achavanich. E of A895, and immediately E of by-road running SE from Achavanich to Lybster. Near S edge of Loch Stemster, and to S of Hill of Rangag (qv). Chambered cairn just to SE (ND:189417).

A horseshoe-shaped setting of stones, open to the SE. There may originally have been up to 60 stones, but a score have been removed. The surviving ones are tall, thick flagstone slabs, set at right angles to the perimeter, with their broad faces towards each other. By the northernmost stone is an early Bronze Age cist of 4 slabs.

Achu Chambered Barrow *New Stone Age*
Spinningdale **21(NH:671911)**
1.2km NNW of Spinningdale and A9. Take by-road NW from Spinningdale towards Bonar Bridge, then moorland walk. Other cairns to W and SSE.

This short, horned cairn, 15m long, has a passage leading in from an entrance in the façade on the ESE to a polygonal chamber; the latter is made of big stone slabs and drystone walling, with a corbelled roof 2m high.

Badnabay Chambered Barrow *New Stone Age*
Scourie **9(NC:219468)**
Immediately next to A894, 6.4km NE of Scourie, 1.6km W of Laxford Bridge.

The only remains of this mound, originally 12m across, are the stones of the polygonal chamber, which still stand to 1m in height.

Balnuaran of Clava Chambered Barrows (Ring Cairns) * *New Stone/Bronze Ages*
10km E of Inverness **27(NH:756443)**
Take B9006 E from Inverness, and by-road to SE just before junction with B851. On the right bank of river Nairn, just E of Culloden battlefield. Signposted.

An impressive necropolis of 3 large cairns, each sur-rounded by a graded kerb and a graded stone circle.

Achavanich Standing Stones*. Standing stones set in a truncated oval. Some 40 of the flagstone slabs survive: probably set up in the early Bronze Age*

Balnuaran of Clava Chambered Barrows. New Stone Age/Bronze Age

All 3 now have their central chambers open to the sky. The 1st (sw) cairn and the 3rd (ne) have passages that align exactly, and possibly point to the midwinter sunset. The central ring cairn is non-aligned, and has no passage.

Some stones at cardinal positions in these monuments bear cupmarks. It is thought that the mounds are Neolithic and the stone circles Bronze Age. A similar monument at Raigmore, near Inverness, has been radiocarbon-dated to c. 3000 BC.

Just w of the central ring cairn is a small kerb cairn that contained an inhumation; one of the kerb stones has cupmarks.

Ben Freiceadain Hillfort   *Iron Age?*
Summit of Ben Freiceadain   **11(ND:059558)**
13km SE of A836 and Reay. Take by-road ESE from A836 to Shebster, and S to Loch Shurrery. Then moorland walk eastward. Alternatively, take B870 from Thurso and then by-road SW between Loch Calder and Loch Olginey to Dorrery; then moorland walk.

The most northerly large hillfort on the British mainland, it has vast views over Caithness, Orkney and the Sutherland Hills. It has a single, massive wall, and an entrance (WNW) lined with upright slabs. A ruined chambered cairn stands on the summit. Numerous chambered cairns and standing stones occur in the area round the fort.

Ben Griam Beg Hillfort   *Iron Age?*
10km NW of Kinbrace (*qv*)   **10(NC:830412)**
W of A897. Take B871 WNW from Kinbrace, and tracks towards hillfort: long walk and very steep climb. Or go W from A897, but marshy.

The highest hillfort in Scotland (590m), it has a stone wall, 2m thick, with an entry on the N. Further down, on the S side, there are traces of walled enclosures.

Boreraig Broch   *Iron Age*
Boreraig, Isle of Skye   **23(NG:195532)**
8km NW of Dunvegan. Take A863 to SE, then B884 to WNW. After Colbost, continue on by-road N along shore of Loch Dunvegan. Broch is between by-road and shore, to E of road.

A typical and well-preserved broch, with walls up to 3m high externally, and an entrance on the W; traces of a gallery and a scarcement can be seen. The broch stands in a rectangular enclosure.

Caisteal Grugaig Broch   *Iron Age*
Letterfearn   **33(NG:866251)**
On headland between Loch Alsh (to W) and Loch Duich (to SE). By-road NW from A87 at Shiel Bridge, or ferry S from Ardelve on A87 W of Dornie.

A very well-preserved example with a wall up to 4m high and with cells and galleries visible within the wall both at ground – and at 1st-floor level, together with part of a staircase. The entrance (NE) has doorchecks and a bar-hole. One odd feature is that the floor slopes steeply down towards the entrance, but the scarcement ledge is horizontal.

**Camster Chambered Long
and Round Barrows ***   *New Stone Age*
Camster   **11(ND:260442)**
10km S of Watten and A882, on W side of by-road from there S towards Lybster. Brochs and standing stones occur just to N. A couple of km N of Camster and just W of Loch of Camster. Signposted.

The two 'Grey Cairns of Camster' were well restored in 1966. The stalled round cairn, about 100m W of the road, is 18m across and 3.6m high. An entrance in the E leads through a narrow, lintelled passage that is well lit by a modern skylight, but so low that one has to proceed on hands and knees. After a dark antechamber, one reaches the well-lit burial chamber, a round corbelled structure, 3m high. Excavators in

Camster Chambered Round Barrow. Of the two Grey Cairns, this is the round one, covering a passage grave where legless skeletons were found

1865 found charcoal, ashes and potsherds in the chamber, and 2 legless skeletons propped up in the passage, which had subsequently been blocked.

The long cairn, 200m N, is one of the largest in the country: 60m long and up to 20m wide. It is double-horned, with external steps, and contains 2 burial chambers that were originally in 2 separate round cairns before being covered by the long one. That nearest the (NE) façade divided, polygonal was a high, corbelled structure. The other, halfway along the cairn's length, is tripartite. Both open on to the SE, and their passages had to be extended when the long cairn was built.

Cinn Trolla Broch
Kintradwell   *Iron Age*
        17(NC:929081)
4.8km NE of Brora. Take A9 to NNE. Broch is just between road and railway, near coast.

This broch, 10m in diameter, has a wall up to 5m in height, containing chambers and a stair-lobby. The large entrance passage has 2 door-checks and a 'guard-chamber'. In the SE part of the courtyard is a well with steps leading into it.

Cnoc Freiceadain and Na Tri Shean
Chambered Long Barrows *
Shebster   *New Stone Age*
        11(ND:013653)
7km E of Reay, WSW of Thurso. Take by-roads SE from A836. Cairns are on Hill of Shebster, just W of road N from Shebster to Achreamie. Just S of Upper Dounreay stone rows (qv).

The 2 long cairns, on the northern summit of Shebster Hill, stand at right angles to each other, and 120m apart. The 1st is 67m long, and has horns at the narrow NE end. It may have contained chambers made of slabs. Its companion, to the S, has extensive views over Orkney and Caithness. It is a huge cairn, 75m in length, with horns at both ends, and probably also contains chambers.

Corrimony Chambered Barrow * *New Stone Age*
Corrimony   **26(NH:383304)**
At head of Glen Urquhart, 13km W of Drumnadrochit, SW of A831. By-road W to Corrimony; cairn is immediately to N of road, on right bank of river Enrick. Signposted.

This well-preserved monument, similar to those of Balnuaran of Clava (qv) comprises a kerbed cairn, 15m across, surrounded by a circle of 11 stones, 21m across. A low passage leads to a central, round corbelled chamber, now open to the sky. The large capstone, now on top of the mound, has cupmarks on it.

Craig Phadrig Hillfort *
Inverness   *Iron Age*
        26(NH:640453)
2.4km W of city centre and A9. Take A82 to SW and then by-road N, or A862 to W; then tracks S and uphill. Signposted.

Although located on a hilltop, this fort is in the middle of a forest, and its layout is not easy to distinguish. A rectangular area is enclosed by 2 turf-covered ramparts, of which the inner still stands 4m high externally. Excavations found little inside, but radiocarbon-dated the ramparts to 370 and 180 BC. The site was also occupied in Pictish times: its gates flew open for St Columba, and it became the first Christian foundation in the Highlands.

Culbokie Dun
Culbokie   *Iron Age or later*
        26(NH:603587)
8km NE of Conon Bridge, on SE side of Cromarty Firth. NNW of Inverness. Take B9161 NE from A9 at Duncanston: the dun is to the E of it, just S of Culbokie.

This site, also known as Carn Mor, is a good example of the several duns in the area: an inner ring-wall, over 2m thick, encloses an area 17m across. A double circle of ramparts, with median ditch, surrounds it. All entrances are on the WSW.

253

Corrimony Chambered Barrow, *showing the central corbelled chamber. New Stone Age*

Duchary Rock Hillfort
Brora   *Iron Age?*   **17(NC:850050)**
5km w of Brora. Near s extremity of Loch Brora.
Take by-roads n from A9, via Doll, and peat track.
Carrol Broch stands just to the ne, nearer the loch
(NC:855053).

A site in a superb setting with tremendous views
and very strong natural defences, it still has fine
traces of a massive wall on the nw, with an entrance
passage. Steep slopes or cliffs gave protection on all
other sides. Unexcavated.

Dun Deardail Hillfort
Glen Nevis   *Iron Age*   **41(NN:126702)**
5km se of Fort William, above and to w of by-road s
up Glen Nevis. Approach from bottom of Glen (stiff
climb) or from Blarmachfoldach, to w.

A vitrified fort, also known as Glen Nevis Fort, it
has a massive, ruined wall with an entry on the nw,
and a later wall across the enclosure. There are traces
of outer defences on slopes to the w and s.

Dùn Grugaig Dun *
Elgol, Isle of Skye   *Iron Age*   **32(NG:535124)**
On Strathaird peninsula, sw of Broadford. Take
A881 sw to Elgol, then hill road 2.5km to extreme se
coast of peninsula.

This small, sub-rectangular dun is very strong,
being located on a narrow promontory with sheer
sides. A short wall, over 4m thick, with an upper gallery, cuts off the neck of the promontory; its entrance
has a door-check and bar-holes. There are some
remains of a thinner wall round the enclosed area.

Dun Lagaidh Fort and Broch
Blarnalearoch   *Iron Age*   **20(NH:143914)**
n of Blarnalearoch, 2.8km sse of Ullapool across
Loch Broom (on s side of loch). Approach by boat,
or track following w side of loch, nw from A835.

A small fort on an isolated ridge beside the loch, it
has strong natural defences and a strategic position
at the loch's narrowest point. It comprised an area of
78 by 27m, enclosed by a massive timber-framed
wall, with another one at the easiest approach, to the
e. A narrow gate stood on the s, near the cliff edge.
Vitrification of both walls occurred when the fort
was burned, an event dated by radiocarbon to 490–
460 bc. Later, a massive drystone dun was built at the
e end: it has an entrance with two door-checks and a
'guard-cell'.

Dun Telve and Dun Troddan
Brochs *   *Iron Age*
Glenelg   **33(NG:829173 & 834173)**
3km se of Glenelg (se of ferry to Skye). By-road e up
Gleann Beag from Eilanreach. Brochs are on either
side of road, on edges. Chambered cairn further
along road at NG:845167.

After Mousa (p. 266) on Shetland, these are the
best-preserved brochs in Scotland, a class of building
that is Scotland's great achievement in the art of drystone masonry. They stand less than 0.5km apart, and
are still 10 and 7.6m high respectively. Dun Telve has
a central court almost 10m across, and a wall 4m
thick at its base, with passages, stairs and chambers
within its thickness. Two scarcements and upper
galleries are visible. Dun Troddan is similar, though
smaller. Excavation in 1920 revealed a ring of 10 postholes in its courtyard.

Dundornaigail (Dùn
Dornadilla) Broch *
Allt na Caillich   *Iron Age*   **9(NC:457450)**
14km nw of Altnaharra (A836). In Strath More, s of
Loch Hope. Take by-road nw from Altnaharra to Allt
na Caillich: broch is on w edge of road, by river. Or
go s on same by-road (along e shore of Loch Hope)
from Hope (on A838) at n end of Loch Hope.

Probably a late example of this type of monument, it still stands to a height of 6.7m in places, and is over 14m across. Modern buttresses hold up the outer face. A massive triangular lintel stone is still in place over the entrance. In its height, proportions and overall size, this monument is very similar to Dun Carloway (p. 277) on Lewis.

Garrywhin Hillfort, Horned Barrow and Stone Rows
New Stone/ Bronze/Iron Ages
Ulbster **12(ND:313413 fort)**
11km ssw of Wick, near coast. Take A9 ssw from Wick; by-road to w at Thrumster. Sites are just w of Loch Watenan. The Yarrows sites (qv) are just to N.

The fort, surrounded by marshy land except on the N, has a single massive stone wall, with impressive entrances, especially on the N.

The chambered cairn, also known as the Cairn of Get, is 500m w of the loch (ND:313411); a passage leads from the sw to a rectangular antechamber and a circular chamber, which contained flint arrowheads, potsherds, inhumations and cremations. It was originally in a small round cairn, which was later converted into a long structure with horns at either end.

NNE of the cairn stands a small round barrow from which 6 rows of small, upright stone slabs radiate down the slope at intervals of about 2.5m. In 1871, there was an average of 8 stones per row, but some have since disappeared. The barrow contained a cist with an inhumation.

Ham Chambered Barrow
New Stone Age
Ham **12(ND:238738)**
By the coast. Take by-roads NW from A836, halfway between Dunnet (to w) and Mey (to E). NE of St John's Loch.

The northernmost chambered cairn in mainland Britain, it is a grass-covered mound, 19m across and 2m high, with a passage leading to a chamber with a corbelled roof.

Hill o' Many Stones
Bronze Age?
Mid Clyth **11(ND:295384)**
sw of Wick, NE of Lybster. Take A9 NE from Lybster towards Wick; farm road to NW. Stone rows are beside it, to sw. Signposted.

In boggy moorland, 600m from the main road, about 200 small stones stand on the s slope of a low hill. The stones, less than 1m high and a few centimetres wide, are set out in 22 parallel rows. There is an average of 8 stones in each row, and they may be designed to lead the eye up the slope to a cairn on the top. A fallen standing stone is 46m to the w, on the ridge, and may have played a role in lunar observation. Some scholars believe that the rows have an astronomical function, as a grid for plotting maximum moonrise in summer and winter.

Hill of Rangag Standing Stone
Bronze Age?
Rangag, just N of Achavanich *(qv)* **12(ND:176448)**
Conspicuous, on E edge of A895, 1km N of Latheran.

A massive rectangular stone, 3m high. There is another marked at ND:184451, 800m to the ENE.

Hill of Rangag Standing Stone. Bronze Age

Keiss Broch
Iron Age & later
Keiss **12(ND:353611)**
12km N of Wick. Just N of Keiss harbour, SE of A9.

A largely reconstructed example: its wall is up to 4m thick, with an entrance on the SE, and modern buttresses outside. There are secondary enclosures both inside and outside, and another broch a few hundred metres to the NW.

Kinbrace Chambered Barrow
New Stone Age
Kinbrace **17(NC:876283)**
3.6km SSE of Kinbrace, E of A897, just SE of its crossing of Kinbrace Burn.

This disturbed mass of fallen boulders still has traces of a horned forecourt at the N end; its chamber was tripartite, with a corbelled roof over the central section. The entrance passage led in from the E. More settlement and field systems, and cairns/chambered cairns are located between here and Kinbrace, E of the A897, and there are more w of Kinbrace and N of the B871.

Laggan Hillfort
Iron Age
Laggan **35(NN:582930)**
On nose of ridge separating Strathspey (to N) from Strath Mashie (to s). Approach from sw along ridge by taking woodland paths from A86.

A fort with strong natural defences, its only easy approach was from the sw, along the promontory ridge. The enclosing wall, still up to 3m high, follows the contours of the crag.

Learable Hill Stone Rows and Circles
Bronze Age
Kildonan Lodge **17(NC:892235)**
In Strath of Kildonan (or Strath Ullie), 14km NW of Helmsdale. W of A897 and the river, 2km N of Kildonan Lodge. Moorland walk of 1km after crossing river. 6km from Kinbrace (qv).

This collection of standing stones, rows, circles and cairns starts 600m NW of Learable farmhouse, and is near one of the few passes between the E and N coasts. The parallel and splayed stone rows, for which an astronomical purpose has been suggested, point eastwards. An isolated standing stone, 35m s of the main rows, is marked with an incised cross; 30m to the SE is another fan-shaped arrangement of stone rows, with abundant cairns all over the hillside, while 120m to the W is a stone circle with 5 upright stones still in place. Another badly damaged circle exists in this group of monuments.

Muir of Ord Henge
New Stone Age
Muir of Ord **26(NH:527497)**
0.4km SW of Muir of Ord, on golf course, just w of A862 and railway. Standing stone to s at Windhill (NH:532484).

This henge has 2 opposing entrances; the external bank is 34m in diameter, while the ditch, interrupted by 2 causeways, is over 1m deep in places, and filled in elsewhere.

Ousdale Broch *
Iron Age
Ousdale **17(ND:071188)**
Between Helmsdale (to SW) and Dunbeath (to NE). 6km SW of Berriedale. On right bank of Ousdale Burn, between A9 and sea.

This broch, partly reconstructed after excavation in 1891, is remote and well preserved; its lintelled entrance is on the SW, and has 2 door-checks and a 'guard-cell'. A scarcement ledge can be seen. A massive wall defends the broch on 3 sides, while a sheer slope down to the burn gives protection on the others.

Rubh' an Dùnain Chambered Barrow and Broch *
New Stone/Iron Ages
Glenbrittle House, Isle of Skye **32(NG:393164)**
Near tip of remote headland on SW coast. From A863 near Drynoch, take B8009 w to Merkadale; then by-road s to Glenbrittle House, and moorland coastal walk of 5.5km by Loch Brittle.

This round cairn, still over 3m high and 20m across, is a passage grave with the entrance in a crescent-shaped forecourt on the E. The lintelled passage leads to a bipartite antechamber and a polygonal chamber, originally corbelled. It contained human remains, Neolithic pottery and a beaker representing later use. Finds in the National Museum of Antiquities, Edinburgh.

500m to the SE (NG:395159) is a semi-broch, or

galleried promontory dun, on a small headland – now even smaller thanks to erosion of the cliffs. A massive, curved wall, still up to 2.6m high, with an entrance with door-checks, cuts off the promontory. It is made of large squared stone blocks; an inner scarcement can be seen, and some galleries in the wall. A cave nearby (NG:399162) yielded Beaker pottery and traces of later ironworking.

St John's Point Promontory Fort
Iron Age
Mey **12(ND:310751)**
3.2km NE of Mey, N of the A836. Take by-road N from A836, then footpath to point.

The northernmost promontory fort on the British mainland, it comprises a defence cutting off the headland from cliff to cliff. A ditch has a slight external mound and an inner stone rampart, 3m high. The entrance is near the w end.

Skelpick Long Barrow *
New Stone Age
Bettyhill **10(NC:723567)**
In Strathnaver, 4.8km s of Bettyhill. Take A836 s, then by-road s to Skelpick just before crossing river. Barrow is 1km beyond Skelpick Bridge, E of the burn.

This large cairn, almost 60m long, has horns at both ends. A passage leads in from the N façade to 2 lintelled polygonal chambers: some of the capstones are huge (3m long). There are more cairns further N (NC:715590) and SW of Skelpick (NC:718550).

Upper Dounreay Stone Rows
Bronze Age
Dounreay **12(ND:012659)**
By-road SE from A836 to Upper Dounreay. Walk to N end of Shebster Hill. Just N of Cnoc Freiceadain (qv). Chambered cairns to NW and SSE.

About 100 stone slabs comprise the remains of 13 rows aligned WNW/ESE. It is thought there may originally have been 20 in each row, and some of the rows may lead the eye to a 'cist' of 4 slabs just above them.

Yarrows Chambered Long *
Barrow and Standing Stones
New Stone Age
Loch of Yarrows **12(ND:304432;**
316432 standing stones;
313441 rows)
10km SSW of Wick. Take by-roads WSW from Thrumster and A9 to the loch; then moorland walk. Not far from Garrywhin (qv).

The cairn may originally have been a smaller, round mound, which was later covered by a double-horned kerbed long barrow. A 2nd long cairn, 270m away, was destroyed in the last century. The survivor is large, and has a short passage from the E façade to a tripartite chamber.

On the crest of a ridge are 2 fine standing stones, 2.5 and 2m high, while there are stone rows in the vicinity, and the broch of Yarrows by the loch (ND:308435).

ORKNEYS

Blackhammer Chambered Long Barrow
New Stone Age
Brinyan, Rousay **6(HY:414276)**
3.4km w of Brinyan pier, just N of the B9064. Knowe of Yarso (qv) is 1km NW; Taversoas (qv) is 1.2km E.

This rectangular cairn, 22m by 8m, has an entrance in the middle of the long s side: its passage leads to a rectangular central chamber, divided into 7 compartments (14 stalls) by 6 pairs of projecting stone slabs. The monument is now covered by concrete, with skylights set in. Excavations found fragments of 2 human skeletons, plus sheep, oxen, red deer and birds such as gannet, cormorant and goose.

Burrian Broch*
Iron Age & later
Point of Burrian, North Ronaldsay   **5(HY:763514)**
1.8km SE of South Bay pier. On cliff near S extremity of island.
The broch's wall, 4m thick, encloses a courtyard 7.5m across, and still stands to more than 2m in height. The entrance is on the SE, and a scarcement and mural chamber are visible. Later buttressing exists outside. The building was subsequently transformed into a wheelhouse, and later occupied in Pictish times. The promontory has supplementary defences in the form of 4 ramparts and ditches. Finds in the National Museum of Antiquities, Edinburgh.

Calf of Eday Chambered Barrow
New Stone Age
Calf of Eday   **5(HY:579387)**
90m from SW shore of island.
There are 2 small mounds here, both cruciform passage graves. This one overlooks a small house of Shetland type, and comprises a mass of stones with an entrance passage on the E, leading to a chamber with 3 pairs of dividing stones, making 4 compartments (8 stalls).
The island also has Iron Age houses, a house of Skara Brae type and 2 souterrains.

Cuween Hill Chambered Barrow
New Stone Age
Finstown, Mainland   **6(HY:364128)**
1.2km SE of Finstown and the A965, NW of Kirkwall. Farm road from Finstown or from Grimbister.
A restored round cairn of the Maes Howe subgroup, it overlooks the Bay of Firth. Almost 17m across, it has a low, narrow passage that leads to a rectangular corbelled central chamber with 4 side cells; one of the latter has an annexe. Excavation found 8 inhumations, as well as the skulls of 5 people and those of 24 dogs.

The Dwarfie Stane Rock-cut Tomb*
New Stone Age?
Quoys, Hoy   **7(HY:243005)**
NNE of Rackwick, S of Bay Quoys. Just SE of by-road from Rackwick to Bay of Quoys.
This monument is perhaps the only rock-cut chambered tomb in Britain and, indeed, is unique in northern Europe. Located on a steep moorland hillside, it comprises a huge rectangular block of red sandstone, 8.5m long, 4.5m wide and 2m high. The vertical W side has a rectangular entrance to a low, narrow passage, 3m long; its closing slab lies outside. At the end of the passage, on either side, is a small 'cell', each separated from the passage by a 30cm kerb of uncut rock. The cell on the right has a 'pillow' of uncut rock at its inner end, and tradition has it that the site was the home of a diminutive 'giant' (troll?) and his wife.

Gurness Broch
Iron Age & later
Georth, Mainland   **6(HY:383268)**
On coastal headland (Aiker Ness) NE of Georth. By-roads NE from A966. Site museum. Leaflet available.
The only survivor of the 11 brochs formerly in this area, it used to be further from the sea: subsequent erosion has removed some of the earthworks and

buildings. Apart from its ground-floor gallery, the broch has typical features such as an entrance passage with door-checks; guard-cells; a scarcement; and an upper gallery and stairway presumably reached by ladder. The interior is full of secondary structures built of sandstone slabs.
It was protected by strong and complex outer defences: there are a number of enclosures and, beyond them, 3 great stone-lined, rock-cut ditches, each in front of a rampart; the innermost rampart has external projecting bastions, a feature unique to Iron Age Britain. A great causeway crossed the ditches in line with the broch's entrance. Excavation inside the rampart wall found the remains of a kitchen midden, containing 5 bronze rings still on the fingers of 2 severed hands.
In a later stage, a 'courtyard house' like those at Jarlshof (p. 266) was built over the ruined enclosures; and finally, to the NE, a typical Viking longhouse was constructed.

Holland House Standing Stone
Bronze Age?
South Bay, North Ronaldsay   **5(HY:753529)**
0.4km N of South Bay pier.
Also known as the Stan Stone, this great slab of flagstone is 4m high, up to 1m wide and only 10cm thick at the base. A small oval hole, possibly natural, pierces it at a height of 2m. Records indicate that, in 1794, local people gathered here to dance and sing in the moonlight at New Year.

Holm of Papa Chambered Barrow*
New Stone Age
Papa Westray   **5(HY:509518)**
On E coast of Holm of Papa, to E of Papa Westray.
This huge long cairn, 35m long and 16m wide, occupies almost 5 per cent of the island's length, and could never have been built by the population of this tiny island alone. Situated at the highest point, it has an entrance on the SE, which leads into the long side of a central dry-walled burial chamber; the passage is now closed, and the visitor enters down ladders via manhole covers in the modern concrete roof. The chamber is tripartite, and it is unique among Orkney cairns in that 10 small, low doors lead from the sides – and 2 more from the end – to 14 small, corbelled side chambers, 2 of which are double. The chamber walls display some rare examples of Scottish megalithic art: zigzags, circles and chevrons.
The island also has some early Neolithic houses, and a small stalled chambered cairn.

Huntersquoy Chambered Barrow*
New Stone Age
Eday   **5(HY:562377)**
NE end of island, W of B9063. 6km N of Bay of Backaland pier; other chambered cairns to N (HT:560382, 564388).
This small (10m diameter) cairn is both storeyed and stalled, like that of Taversoas (qv). The lower chamber was reached by a passage from the E, the upper from the W. The latter's floor was a clay layer above the lower chamber's lintels. The roof of the upper chamber has gone; both storeys were divided into stalls.

Isbister Chambered Long Barrow
New Stone Age
Isbister Farm, South Ronaldsay   **7(ND:469844)**
Near E cliffs of island, 363m ESE of farm. Go S on A961 to its end, then E on B9041 towards Isbister.

257

This turf-covered, rectangular mound contains a tripartite stalled chamber with 3 side cells; it is especially remarkable for the human remains found in it: the leg bones were in one chamber, the arms, vertebrae and pelvic bones in another, and the skulls (all male) arranged in pairs in the corners and at the cell-openings. They were accompanied by stone tools, axes, etc., and bones of sheep, oxen, eagle and crow.

Knowe of Yarso Chambered
Long Barrow *New Stone Age*
Brinyan, Rousay **6(HY:404281)**
3.2km w of Brinyan pier, just n of B9064. nw of Blackhammer (qv) and Taversoas (qv) barrows.

A rectangular cairn, edged with drystone walling, its entrance leads from the e to a burial chamber over 7m long, divided by 3 pairs of slabs into 4 compartments. Excavation found human bones heaped in the corners, comprising at least 29 individuals: 17 were represented only by skulls, 15 of which were arranged in a line, facing the wall, opposite the entrance passage. There were also the bones of sheep and 30 red deer, and a dog; Beaker pottery, arrowheads and scrapers were also found. Fires had been lit in a number of places in the chamber. Red deer bones have produced a radiocarbon date of 2275 BC.

Maes Howe Chambered Barrow* *New Stone Age*
Finstown, Mainland **6(HY:317127)**
ne of Stromness, sw of Finstown, and just n of A965. Nearby to sw are the Stones of Stenness (qv) and, to the nw, the Ring of Brodgar (qv). Leaflet available. Admission fee. Interior often humid.

This passage grave, one of the wonders of the prehistoric world, and one of the best examples of prehistoric architecture in Europe, is the finest megalithic tomb in the British Isles, rivalled only by New Grange, near Dublin. The circular, grassy mound, 35m across and over 7m high, is built on an artificially levelled platform, and comprises alternating layers of earth, peat and stone. It is surrounded by a ditch, 15m away; this was cut down 1.8m to bedrock, and is 13m wide. Peat from its base recently gave radiocarbon dates of 2020 and 2185 BC.

The passage into the mound is on the sw, facing the midwinter sunset. 2m inside is a doorway, whose perfectly cut closing-slab stands just beyond it in a recess in the wall; when this door was closed, it would have left a 45cm gap between its top and the lintel – and, in a situation similar to the 'window' at New Grange, it has been found that the rays of the sun would have entered here, but only at midwinter sunset.

Up to this point, the passage is built of normal masonry. Beyond, it is constructed with huge stone slabs: in fact, for the last 5.6m, the walls and ceiling are made with 3 single blocks, 1.3m wide, 18cm thick, and weighing 3 tons each.

The passage leads into a tall chamber, 4.6m square, which was originally over 4m high, with a superb corbelled roof. The walls still stand to about 4m, with modern restoration above. In each corner, there is a projecting square monolith to help support the roof. Three of the walls have a square hole, about 1m

Maes Howe Chambered Barrow, shown in plan and section (after A. Gibb)

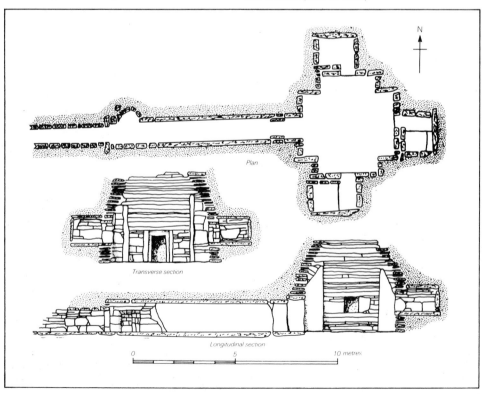

Plan

Transverse section

Longitudinal section

0   5   10 metres

Above: **Maes Howe Chambered Barrow**. *The grassy mound, 35m across, that covers the finest passage grave in Britain*

Below: **Maes Howe Chambered Barrow**. *The fine masonry of local flagstone. Details of the main chamber with opening to a side cell*

above the floor, which open out into small chambers, thus making a cruciform passage grave; these may have been burial recesses. The original blocking stones lie in front of them.

Whatever the identity of those buried here, it is likely that they were accompanied by wealth. Twenty-four runic inscriptions in the chamber were made in the 12th century AD by Vikings who broke into the tomb; 4 of these refer to treasure being removed. There are also pictorial carvings (dragon, walrus, serpent knot). Excavators in 1861 found only a fragment of a human skull, and some horse bones and teeth.

The building stone for Maes Howe was brought from a considerable distance, and the huge labour which it represents is eloquent testimony to the power of its occupant(s) or the motivation of the builders. The workmanship is consummate: huge slabs were accurately levelled, dressed and plumbed; and although the monument contains no mortar, it is still impossible to insert a knife blade between some slabs.

**Mid Howe Chambered
Long Barrow and Broch*** *New Stone/Iron Ages*
Rousay **6(HY:372307 & 371308)**
By w coast, near cliffs of Scabra Head. w of by-road joining B9064 (at Westness) to Wasbister. Another chambered cairn and broch on coast a little to s (HY:373297).

This impressive monument is the largest-known stalled cairn: it is 32.6 by 14.5m, and is built of flagstones and edged with drywalling in a herringbone pattern. It is now under a huge protective shed, so that visitors can see it from above and walk round it. An entrance in the s leads to an enormous burial

chamber, over 23m long, which is divided by tall upright slabs (up to 2m high) into 12 compartments/24 stalls. Most of the stalls on the E side have a stone bench or platform. Unburned skeletons were laid on or under these, comprising 25 people (including 6 adolescents and 2 children); only 6 had skulls, and their teeth were worn and infected. Very little cultural material was found, but there were many bones of oxen, sheep, voles and birds, and abundant limpet shells.

Close by is a good example of a broch, one of an original 3. Located on a spur between 2 creeks, it was protected by water on 3 sides at high tide. On the 4th side, 2 ditches cut through the narrow promontory, with a massive wall in between. The broch itself is similar to Gurness (*qv*) in that it is by the shore and has a ground gallery surrounded by massive outworks. In addition, both sites contain and stand amid

a complex of later structures.

The broch's wall is 4.5m thick and still stands 4m high. Its well-preserved entrance is on the W, and has some lintels still in place, door-checks, bar-holes, gaps for spear-thrusting and 2 guard-cells. A scarcement ledge is visible and, below it, a door to a mural stair and other rooms and a gallery. The courtyard contains later structures of huge flagstones. Rock-cut steps lead down from the broch to a 'harbour'. Finds in the National Museum of Antiquities, Edinburgh.

Quanterness Chambered
Barrow
New Stone Age
Mainland   **6(HY:418129)**
Immediately s of A965, between Kirkwall (to SE) and Finstown (to W). Just NE of Wideford Hill (qv). Not yet open to public, but interior resembles Quoyness (qv).

This great tomb of Maes Howe type was excavated in the 1970s, and produced a wealth of information. It is 24m in diameter, and built of local flagstones. A passage leads from the E to the main chamber in the centre, 3.5m high, with a fine corbelled roof. Six rectangular side-chambers open on to it. The main chamber's floor was covered in a thick pile of burned and smashed bones, earth, stones and charcoal. Only one of the side-chambers was excavated, and, together with the central area, the tally was 157 humans, almost all under the age of 30, suggesting a figure of 400 for the tomb as a whole. There were also bones of sheep, oxen, red deer, dog, birds and fish, but not much cultural material: 34 pots, 3 polished stone knives. The human bones have produced a number of radiocarbon dates from 2640 to 1920 BC, and the monument has been interpreted as a family tomb used for 500–1000 years. It has been estimated that 7000 man-hours were required to build it. In its forecourt stood a well-preserved round house, which has been radiocarbon-dated to the 1st millennium BC.

Quoyness Chambered Barrow
New Stone Age
Els Ness, Sanday   **5(HY:676378)**
On E edge of Els Ness. 3.2km SE of Roadside. Tracks s from B9069.

Another member of the Maes Howe group, this ovoid cairn resembles Quanterness *(qv)* in that it has 6 side-chambers opening off the main chamber. The latter rises to a height of 4m, with a sophisticated corbelled roof; the 6 side-cells are irregular and low. Human bones have produced radiocarbon dates of 2240 and 2315 BC.

Ring of Brodgar Circle
Henge *
New Stone Age
Loch of Stenness, Mainland   **6(HY:294134)**
On neck of land between Loch of Stenness (to SW) and Loch of Harray (to NE). Just on SW side of B9055 (reached via A965 from Stromness or Finstown). Just NW of Stenness (qv) and Maeshowe (qv). Signposted.

The finest and biggest stone circle in Scotland, it is also one of the most complete and beautiful in Britain. Moreover, with Stenness, it is the most northerly circle-henge in the British Isles. This is a Class 2 henge monument, with 2 opposing

Ring of Brodgar Circle Henge. New Stone Age

entrances (NW/SE) through the bank and ditch. The latter was rock-cut, up to 3m deep, 9m wide and 142m in diameter; the bank is internal. It has been estimated that the henge would have taken at least 80,000 man-hours to build: i.e., 3 months' work for 100 labourers.

There were originally 60 stones, in a circle of 113m diameter; 27 of them survive, with remains of 13 more, and the tallest is 4.6m high. They are of the local red sandstone, which splits easily and naturally. Four stones bear later carvings (runes, a cross, an anvil, etc.). The site may once have been linked to Stenness by a line of stones, to form a complex like Avebury (*qv*).

It has been claimed that Brodgar is a lunar observatory, using 3 natural foresights such as the W cliff of Hoy to the SW, but many of the orientations relate to surrounding cairns rather than the stone circle. There is an outlier, the Comet Stone, 150m to the SE.

Skara Brae Village
Settlement *   *New Stone Age*
Bay of Skaill, Mainland   **6(HY:231188)**
10km N of Stromness. Just SW of B9056, which is reached via A967. Footpath round edge of bay. Admission fee. Guidebook available.

This 'British Pompeii', one of the most famous prehistoric settlements in Europe, was preserved by being buried by sand in a storm – the occupants clearly left in a hurry. In 1850 another storm revealed the ruins of the best-preserved Neolithic village in Europe. There are 9 huts built of large, flat blocks of stone; they are thought to have had roofs of organic material, and one is now covered with a glass roof. The huts are small, squarish constructions, from 4 to 6m across, with walls over 1m thick. They were linked by covered stone alleyways. Low doorways led to a narrow passage in the hut wall, with bar-holes; inside were well-built central hearths. Presumably owing to a scarcity of timber on the island, the furniture was also made of stone: there are upright 'dressers' for storage, and, on either side of the hearths, stone 'beds'.

Right: **Skara Brae Village Settlement**. *Interior of a house with hearth, box bed, dresser and water tank all of stone*

Below: **Skara Brae**, *Orkney (after E. W. MacKie)*

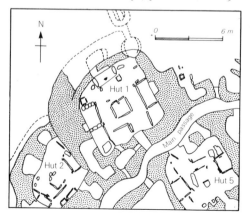

Recesses in the walls served as cupboards, and privies are known (e.g., Hut 5 has a mural cell with a drain leading from it), a feature unmatched in that period except in Minoan Crete. Clay-lined tanks in some hut floors are thought to have been used for soaking limpets for bait. It is possible that the site originally overlooked a freshwater lagoon, rather than the seashore. The whole settlement was surrounded and almost buried by its rubbish dump of ash, bone, shells, dung and sand, which protected it against the elements.

Excavation found pottery; cooking vessels containing animal bones; basins of stone and whale-bone, some containing colouring materials; stone tools; beads and pendants; an ox shoulder-blade shovel; and abundant remains of sheep, cattle, fish and shellfish. Recent excavations have also found grains of barley. They have also shown 2 earlier phases of occupation: the foundations of 4 earlier huts, and a hut with midden material beneath

those; but the construction and finds are the same in all layers. The site has produced 5 radiocarbon dates from 2480 to 2370 BC. It is estimated that this was a village of 7 or 8 families – 30 or 40 people – who would have been responsible for such monuments as Maes Howe. Some finds are on show at the site, but most are in the National Museum of Antiquities, Edinburgh.

A storm in 1976 uncovered the remains of another building some 25m w of the main site.

Stenness Circle Henge* *New Stone Age*
Stenness, Mainland **6(HY:301125)**
By s tip of Loch of Harray. 6.4km ENE of Stromness; just N of junction of the B9055 and A965. To NW is the Ring of Brodgar (qv) and to NE is Maes Howe (qv). Signposted.

Like the Ring of Brodgar, this monument was originally a henge, but it was of an earlier phase, with a single entrance on the NW. The plain here

had been cultivated, but was covered by weeds and grass when the henge was built. The ditch, not a perfect circle, was dug to 2m depth: 1200 tons of sandstone had to be quarried, a task involving 100 people for 3 months. On the W it contained decayed wild plant remains, mixed with twigs and bones of sheep, oxen and dogs or wolves. The ditch is now half-filled, and the outer bank, 61m in diameter, is greatly weathered.

The circle was made of tall, unshaped slabs of local flagstones. Perhaps even quarried from the ditch, they are only 30cm thick and up to 5m high. They were originally 12 in number, forming a circle 31m in diameter, but only 4 survive.

The 'dolmen' inside the circle is a mistaken 1906 reconstruction, and should be ignored. It is now known that the centre of the circle had a rectangular setting of stones, rather like the hearths at Skara Brae (*qv*), made of horizontal slabs. A post stood off-centre in this, and outside were the

Stenness Circle Henge. *New Stone Age*

remains of a timber structure and pairs of standing stones. The timber structure, which overlay the site of a 'cove' of 3 stones, gave a radiocarbon date of 1730 BC, while animal bone in the ditch has been dated to 2356 BC; the circle has also been dated to 2238 BC. Small pits inside the circle, filled with earth mixed with barley, nuts, seeds and fruit-stones, have been radiocarbon-dated to AD 519.

The huge 'Watch Stone', 5.6m high, stands 170m to the NNW, at the narrowest point of the land, and

may have formed part of a line linking Stenness to the Ring of Brodgar. A 2nd outlier, the Barnhouse Stone, is 700m to the SE. Another slab, the Stone of Odin, stood to the N of Stenness. Destroyed in 1814, it had a head-sized perforation halfway up its 2m height; courting couples made vows while holding hands through it, and it was linked to legends of fertility and cures. In the 18th century, Stenness was known as the Temple of the Moon, Brodgar as that of the Sun. People met here on New Year's Day to dance and feast.

Finds are in the National Museum of Antiquities, Edinburgh.

Taversoas Tuack (Taversoe Tuick) Chambered Barrow *
New Stone Age
Brinyan, Rousay
6(HY:426276)
1km w of Brinyan pier, immediately N of B9064. To w/NW are Knowe of Yarso (qv) and Blackhammer (qv) cairns.

Like Huntersquoy (*qv*), this is a double-decker tomb. Originally a round cairn, 9m across, it is in a spectacular setting with extensive views. A passage from the s leads to the subterranean rectangular lower chamber, divided into 4 by upright slabs. Excavation yielded human bones, potsherds and a granite macehead here. The passage and this chamber are roofed with stone lintels, and this ceiling forms the floor of the upper chamber, at ground level. Most of this chamber has gone, but it was entered from the N, and it opened off on either side of the passage, which continued beyond it for over a metre. Excavation found cremated bone here. A trapdoor now leads to the lower chamber from the upper.

The line of the lower chamber's entrance continued to the s as a shallow trench, and 6m away was a small, oval subterranean chamber cut into the rock. The sides of this were lined with drystone masonry, and its flat roof, only 1m above the floor, was found to be of stone lintels; Neolithic pottery was discovered here, and it is thought to be a miniature tomb.

Unstan (Onston) Chambered Barrow
New Stone Age
Stromness, Mainland
6(HY:282118)
3.2km NE of Stromness, just N of A965 on little peninsula in Loch of Stenness. Standing stones to w (s of A965) at HY:272117.

This well-preserved, slightly oval cairn, 13m across, is similar to Knowe of Yarso (*qv*), and seems to have been built in 2 concentric rings of stonework. It is now covered by a concrete dome, but its interior is intact. A 4m passage leads to a chamber at one end, which is unusual for having one side-cell. The chamber is divided by upright flagstones into 5 compartments (10 stalls) and stands almost 2m high. Its roofing construction is unclear. The side-cell contained 2 crouched burials, while the chamber had human bones in each compartment as well as animal bones, burned bones and charcoal, flint arrowheads, and fragments of at least 22 pottery vessels including many characteristic Unstan bowls (round-based vessels

Above: ***Unstan Chambered Barrow****, interior.*
New Stone Age

Below: ***Unstan Chambered Barrow****, exterior.*
New Stone Age

decorated with incised geometric designs). Some potsherds had impressions of barley grains.

Wideford Hill Chambered Barrow *New Stone Age*
Kirkwall, Mainland **6(HY:409121)**
3.2km wnw of Kirkwall, on s side of A965, on slopes of Wideford Hill. Near Quanterness (qv). Signposted.

This round passage grave, perched on a hill, is of Maes Howe type; it was twice enlarged, and comprises 3 concentric rings of stonework, each of which has a vertical outer face. It is almost 13m in diameter. A narrow, low (0.6m) passage leads from the w to a central corbelled chamber, over 31m long and 2.5m high. There are 3 side-chambers. It had been ransacked before exploration in 1849, and no human remains were found.

SHETLAND

Burra Ness Broch* *Iron Age*
Gutcher, Yell **1(HU:556957)**
2.6km s of Gutcher, on ne tip of headland. Farm track s from the A968 and Gutcher to North Sandwick, then moorland.

An impressive broch with a wall 4.5m thick, and a scarcement 4m above the floor. Its outworks have been destroyed by ploughing, and it is known that, in the 18th century AD, the broch stood in a cornfield that reached to the shore.

Clickhimin Fort, Broch and Settlement* *Iron Age & later*
Lerwick, Mainland **4(HU:465408 broch)**
On sw outskirts of Lerwick, just n of A970, on s edge of Loch of Clickhimin. Guidebook available.

A complex site with fortification from several periods, its earliest occupation took the form of a late Bronze Age farmhouse (like those at Jarlshof, qv), with 2 sleeping areas round a central hearth. Its remains can be seen to the nw of the broch; part of a paved outhouse stands just to the n. In the early Iron Age, a 3-storey blockhouse was built (the lower part survives) with a massive, drystone wall around it, and a landing stage in front of the entrance on the se. The blockhouse, which resembles that of Ness of Burgi (qv), had a central passage with door-checks and bar-holes; a large hut and cattle byres stood behind it.

Later, the loch's exit to the sea was blocked, and its transformation to a freshwater loch caused flooding of the site. A breakwater was built, and an incomplete inner ring wall, but this idea seems to have been dropped in favour of building a strong, stone broch, 20m across and up to 15m high, which still stands over 5m high. Its entrance on the w had a fortified door.

Finally, more peaceful times seem to have arrived, the defences were partly demolished, and a large wheelhouse was built inside the broch, like the smaller ones at Jarlshof. This was probably occupied from the 2nd to the 9th centuries AD.

Finds in the National Museum of Antiquities, Edinburgh.

Jarlshof Village Settlement, *New Stone/Iron*
Broch and Other Dwellings* *Ages & later*
Sumburgh Head, Mainland **4(HU:397096)**
On coast of Sumburgh Head, 0.8km s of Sumburgh Airport, and just s of the A970. Signposted. Admission fee, small museum; guidebook available.

Like Skara Brae (p. 262), this site was preserved by windblown sand (that only gradually covered it, in this case) and uncovered by violent storms in the last

century. Half of it has been eroded away by the sea. The earliest remains, dating to the early 2nd millennium BC, are houses of Skara Brae type, and can be seen on the landward side of the museum: a few portions of an oval hut, which yielded bones of sheep and oxen, and abundant shellfish.

The late Bronze Age settlement was more substantial: 6 dwellings are known, very similar to Stanydale (qv), with a large chamber at the back facing on to a central courtyard area. They were associated with enclosures and field systems defined by drystone dykes; excavators found bones of sheep, cattle, pigs, fish, seals and wildfowl, shellfish and evidence of corn-growing. Quernstones are still in place. One house was the workshop of a bronze smith, with over 200 fragments of clay moulds (for socketed axes, swords, pins, etc.) round a casting pit.

In the early Iron Age, round stone huts were built with souterrains nearby. Later, a broch – now much eroded by the sea – was built, together with a number of large oval houses. In the 2nd/3rd century AD, fine wheelhouses were constructed – they are still well preserved – and Vikings built farmsteads here in the 9th century. The site's long-term popularity may be due to the safe harbour provided by West Voe, to the E, and by the good, well-watered land in this area.

The name Jarlshof comes from Walter Scott's novel *The Pirate*, in which a 16th-century house here was called this.

Finds are in the National Museum of Antiquities, Edinburgh.

Mousa Broch* *Iron Age*
Mousa, off Sandwick, Mainland **4(HU:457237)**
On w coast of Mousa, e of Sandwick. 18km s of Lerwick. Take A970 s, by-road to Sandwick, and boats. Guidebook available.

One of the major archaeological monuments of Europe, this masterpiece is by far the best – in preservation, height and plan – of the 500 brochs known. All of its features are bigger and better conceived than those of its fellows. It still stands 13.3m high; its overall diameter is 15.25m and that of its courtyard 5.5m. The first 3.8m of its height is solid, thus providing a very stable base. A passage leads in from the w (the seaward side) and has door-checks and a bar-hole. The centre of the courtyard has a hearth. Six openings in the wall lead to 3 recesses and 3 large rooms inside the walls, each of which has 3 or 4 wall cupboards. There are 2 scarcements for upper floors, above which the walls are hollow. There is a total of 6 superimposed circular galleries, and a narrow stair leads through them to the top – access to the staircase was by ladder only.

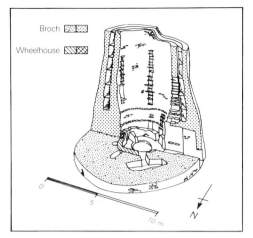

Broch ▨▨
Wheelhouse ▧▨

Mousa Broch, Sandwick, Shetland, showing the plan and elevation (after E. W. MacKie)

It is known from the *Orkneyinga* saga that the broch was still impregnable in the 12th century AD. The remains of a secondary wheelhouse can be seen inside.

Nesbister Hill Walled Cairn   *Bronze Age*
Nesbister Hill, Mainland   **4(HU:403454)**
On summit of hill, 8km NW of Lerwick, near Whiteness. SW of the A971.
This cairn has a superb location with extensive views. Although the best preserved of the round, stone-built cairns of Shetland, it is somewhat dilapidated. A small cist of 4 big slabs is visible at the centre.

Ness of Burgi Fort＊   *Iron Age?*
Near Sumburgh Head, Mainland   **4(HU:388084)**
On narrow peninsula, W of Sumburgh Head. 2.4km S of Sumburgh Airport, off A970. Not far from Jarlshof (qv).
This rocky promontory was cut by 2 deep ditches, with a massive wall (still almost 2m high) between them. A remarkable, rectangular drystone blockhouse – one of only 3 known (*see* Clickhimin) – with massive walls stood just inside these defences. The entrance passage through the centre has doorchecks, a bar-hole and some lintels still in place. It cut the building in 2, each half having an internal chamber; the eastern is entered from the passage, the western from the exterior. A 3rd chamber at the S end has mostly gone over the cliff. Excavation produced very few finds.

Punds Water Chambered Barrow   *New Stone Age*
Mangaster, Mainland   **3(HU:325713)**
Just W of A970, 4km SW of Sullom and 11km NNW of Voe. Near S edge of Punds Water.
A large, well-preserved cairn, conspicuous in barren moorland amid rock outcrops and lochs, it is a heel-shaped structure of white quartzite boulders. The corners somewhat resemble horns like those at Yarrows (p. 256). A passage from the centre of the

15m façade leads to a trefoil-shaped central chamber that, though now roofless, is in good condition, with walls standing to 1.4m in height.

Ronas Hill Chambered Barrow   *New Stone Age*
Ronas Hill, Mainland   **3(HU:305835)**
Near summit of hill dominating Ronas Voe. 8km NNE of Hillswick, W of A970. Steep climb.
Located on the highest peak in Shetland at 487m, this cairn is much mutilated, but still stands over 2m high. A short passage leads from one of the long sides to a single chamber.

The Rounds of Tivla Ring Cairns   *Bronze Age*
Haroldswick, Unst   **1(HP:615107)**
Between Haroldswick (to NE) and Baltasound (to SSE), in moorland W of A968.
Among the cairns of Crussa Field (HP:615109), these 3 stand out because their mounds are surrounded by low, concentric retaining circles of stones.

Stanydale 'Temple'   *New Stone Age*
Bridge of Walls, Mainland   **3(HU:285503)**
2.4km ESE of Bridge of Walls, 2km N of Gruting. By-roads SSE from A971. Signposted. Cairns to N at HU:285513.
This enigmatic heel-shaped building is made of rough stone blocks, with an entrance in the shallow crescent-shaped façade. The wall is up to 4m thick, enclosing an oval chamber; the inner wall opposite the entrance has 6 shallow recesses. The beaten-earth floor has 2 large post-holes, lined with stone, which contained carbonized spruce – probably obtained as driftwood floating in from America. The posts may have held a roof of organic material, but it is also possible that the building was open to the sky.
There are similarities in plan and construction to some houses and tombs of the period, but its size and internal fittings set it apart. Its function is unknown, though there are suggestions of a role as a palace or temple or other public building. Finds of pottery show that it was in use for a long time – possibly even until the Iron Age. Large quantities of barley have been found.
It stands within a group of 5 houses, with 4 more close by; one small, oval house with a thick wall contained a hearth, a bench, wall cupboards and a small inner room. There are also several standing stones nearby, forming a rough arc to the S; and other settlements and field systems exist in the area (HU:281483 and 277484).

Vementry Chambered Barrow＊   *New Stone Age*
Vementry, off Mainland   **3(HU:296609)**
Small island S of Muckle Roe, 11km WSW of Voe. From the B9071 at Aith, take by-road along W side of Aith Voe to nearest point, where boat is needed to cross 200m sound. Another chambered barrow to NW (HU:289612).
This magnificent circular, stone-faced cairn, 8m across, stands on a heel-shaped platform of big stone blocks with a façade 11m across. The passage still has lintels in place at its inner end; it leads to a trefoil-shaped chamber. The monument, on the summit of the highest hill on the island of Vementry, is one of the best-preserved chambered cairns in Shetland.

──────────── STRATHCLYDE ────────────

Achnabreck Rock Carvings *Bronze Age*
Lochgilphead **55(NR:856906)**
3km NNW of Lochgilphead. Take A816 to NW, farm
road NE to Achnabreck, then forestry track for
400m beyond farm. Signposted. Standing stones to
S (NR:856899) and N (NR:847929), and cup/ring
marks to NW at Cairnbaan (NR:839911).

Britain's largest site with rock carvings (including
135 cup/ring marks) is located in a pine plantation,
with extensive sea views, and comprises 3 large areas
of schist outcrops. A fence encloses some 1800
square metres. It lives up to its Gaelic name 'Rock of
the Host' in displaying a tremendous range of forms
and techniques, with fine carvings next to crude.
Almost all are fairly shallow, so it is useful to bring
water to make them stand out. There are many cups
of different sizes, and some have up to 7 rings (one
such cup is a metre in diameter). Most have a radial
groove. There are also double, triple and horned spirals. The outlines of some figures were deformed to
avoid irregularities and crevices in the rock surface.

Arbory Hill Hillfort* *Iron Age?*
Abington **72(NS:945238)**
Clydesdale, NW of Moffat. 1.6km ENE of Abington, by-
road E from A74 and cross river. Steep climb. Just N
of Crawford fort and settlement (qv).

A fine, well-preserved fort on a promontory overlooking the Clyde and its Roman road. A stone-walled
enclosure, with entrances on the E and SW, is surrounded by 2 ramparts, over 2m high, with external
ditches. The ramparts each have 5 entrances. The
interior has traces of timber-framed houses, and a
rectangular stone foundation.

Ardifuir Dun *Iron Age*
Kilmartin **55(NR:789969)**
Turn W of A816 to Poltalloch, then on by coastal
road past Duntrune fort and castle to the dun. Very
near coast.

This well-preserved structure's location on a flat
valley bottom left it vulnerable to attack from a high
crag to the W. The circular wall, still 3m high,
enclosed a courtyard 20m across. The broad, paved
entrance passage has door-checks and a guard-cell. A
scarcement can be traced, and there is a mural stair
and a gallery.

Auchagallon Stone Circle
with Barrow *Bronze Age*
Auchagallon, Arran **69(NR:893346)**
On W coast, opposite Brodick. N of junction of B880
and A841, and just by junction of A841 and by-
road E to the B880. Just N of Machrie Moor
monuments (qv). Standing stone to N
(NR:891364).

A circular cairn in an impressive location, surrounded by a circle of 15 kerbstones. The total
diameter is over 14m.

Ballymeanoch Standing Stones *Bronze Age*
Kilmartin **55(NR:834965)**
2.5km S of Kilmartin. Visible just W of A816, and
just S of turning W to Poltalloch. Near Ardifuir (qv),
Dunchraigaig (qv) and Nether Largie (qv). There
are many other monuments in this area.

There are 3 groups of stones here: a row of 4, running N/S, of which the tallest is over 4m in height; a pair
to the W; and a fallen perforated stone to the NW that
has cupmarks, as do 2 of the 1st group. The carvings
are very weathered, and only visible in slanting sunlight. The perforated outlier is said to have been used
for sealing bargains and betrothals. The setting of
stones is comparable to nearby Nether Largie.

100m SW of the stones is a denuded henge monument: i.e., a weathered bank and ditch with 2
entrances; inside was a probably secondary circular
cairn, 21m across, which housed 2 cists, one of which
contained beaker fragments.

Benderloch Forts and *Iron Age/*
Duns *Romano-British*
Port Selma, Benderloch **49(NM:903382)**
On Benderloch peninsula, NE of Oban. W of A828 at
Port Selma on ridge at head of Ardmucknish Bay.
Standing stones to S (NM:904380) and NE
(NM:907388), and other cairns in the area.

The earliest structure on this rocky ridge was a
timber-laced wall around the summit. It was
replaced by a small rectangular fort, now vitrified,
and by a round dun, also probably vitrified.

Bodsberry Hill Hillfort *Iron Age*
Crawford **78(NS:963169)**
Clydesdale. 4km S of Crawford on A74,
immediately E of A74. Roman road at foot of hill
follows valley road to SE to Roman camp at
NS:995159, and on to Roman fortlet at NT:031139.

This fort is in a superb, scenic setting, dominating
the valley and the approaches to the Dalveen Pass.
The enclosure has a massive stone-faced rampart,
with 4 entries, and contains traces of a few timber-
framed houses and a well. There are extra defences
on the NW and SE, but elsewhere the steep slopes provided adequate protection.

Carn Ban Chambered Barrow *New Stone Age*
Arran **69(NR:991262)**
W of Whiting Bay, 5km SW of Monamore Bridge.
From A841, take by-road W (at Monamore Bridge),
footpath and moorland walk to S. Not far N of
Kilmory Water.

This well-preserved Clyde cairn is a long mass of
stones with a crescent forecourt and façade at the E
end. A tripartite chamber has a corbelled roof over
2m high.

Clachaig Chambered Barrow *New Stone Age*
Kilmory, Arran **69(NR:950214)**
Near S coast, just S of A841 and W of Kilmory.
Stands in farmland on old raised beach.

An oval Clyde cairn, it has a chamber, divided by a
septal slab. Excavation found the remains of 12 adults
and 2 children, with pottery, a flint knife and a long
stone axe. A secondary, small cist contained a food
vessel. There are other cairns in the area.

Cow Castle Hillfort and
Settlement *Iron Age*
Coulter **72(NT:042331)**
Clydesdale, S of Biggar. Take A702 SW from Biggar,
and take by-road to SE at Coulter. Just to NE, in

Arbory Hill Hillfort from the air. Iron Age (?) (Cambridge University Collection, Crown Copyright)

Borders region, are White Hill fort and settlement (NT:055338) and Mitchelhill Rings fort and settlement (NT:063342).

A large D-shaped settlement was placed at the SW end of a ridge, and was protected by a single rampart with external ditch. A smaller D-shaped structure was built on the same spot in a later phase. Both contain traces of timber-framed houses. There are other stretches of rampart and ditch in the vicinity, and another settlement at the other end of the ridge.

Crarae Chambered Long Barrow *
New Stone Age
Crarae   **55(NR:987974)**
4.8km SW of Furnace, just W of A83, in Crarae Forest Garden. N shore of Loch Fyne.

A long Clyde cairn, it had a paved forecourt area and a drystone façade, and a chamber made of large slabs. Two enormous caches of seafood remains were found in it – at least 5000 seashells comprising 15 different species, including periwinkles. They had all been eaten.

269

Crawford Fort and Settlement
Iron Age
Crawford **72(NS:952219 fort; 945216 settlement)**
1.6km NW of Crawford, s of Arbory Hill fort (qv).
Take by-roads to N from A74 at Crawford and cross
river Clyde. Roman road follows E bank of Clyde
here, and goes N from Crawford. .

The oval fort has remains of a stone rampart, with an external ditch on the sw, with traces of another rampart on its outer lip. The settlement, on an isolated knoll, has a single rampart with 4 entrances, and contains clear traces of 8 timber-framed houses.

Dumbarton Rock Fort
Iron Age
Dumbarton **64(NS:400745)**
Steep rocky knolls on s outskirts of Dumbarton,
overlooking Firth of Clyde.

An impressive site, in a striking location on an isolated volcanic plug. No prehistoric remains are known, but it is highly probable that it was occupied at this time by the Dumnonii. It was certainly a fortress in the early Middle Ages, and the rock is now covered by later defences and structures. The name is thought to mean 'Dun of the Britons' and the site thus to be the capital of the old British kingdom of Strathclyde.

Dunchraigaig Barrow with
Long Cist
Bronze Age
Lochgilphead/Kilmartin **55(NR:833968)**
9.5km NW of Lochgilphead, s of Kilmartin. In wood
just W of A816. Just NW of Ballymeanoch stones
(qv). Signposted.

This cairn was originally over 30m across and still stands 2m high. Three stone cists were found in it, containing inhumations and cremations, pottery vessels, a stone axe and a flint knife. The cist on the s is built of boulders and covered by a huge capstone over 4m long. Just N of here, w of the road, are the cup/ring markings of Baluachraig (NR:831970); very well preserved, they are protected by a railing.

Dun Skeig Hillfort and Dun
Iron Age
Clachan **62(NR:757572 to 757574)**
Near shore at mouth of West Loch Tarbert. 16km SW
of Tarbert on A83. Farm road N from Clachan and
hill climb.

The oval hillfort has a superb location on an isolated steep hill, with extensive views. It had a single stone wall, only visible here and there. At its s end was constructed a big, oval dun, which also had a thick timber-framed wall, now heavily vitrified. At its N end was built a small drystone dun, still well-preserved. Its entrance, on the E, has door-checks and a bar-hole.

Kildonan Dun
Iron Age
Saddell **68(NR:779278)**
10.4km NE of Campbeltown, 4km s of Saddell
Abbey. Just E of the B842.

A reasonably well-preserved galleried dun on top of a rocky knoll, its massive walls enclose a D-shaped area. The main entrance on the w is wide, like that of Ardifuir (*qv*), and has door-checks and a bar-hole. Opposite the entrance is a small cell, and, to the N, there is a double mural stair.

Kildoon Hillfort
Iron Age
Maybole **76(NS:299075)**
2.4km s of Maybole. Take by-road s from Maybole
or w from B7023 just N of Crosshill.

This fort, on a basalt ridge, had a single timber-laced rampart, now vitrified; the western approach

has 2 extra ramparts with external rock-cut ditches. A later monument on the ridge has obliterated part of the defences.

Kintraw Cairns and Standing
Stones
Bronze Age
Kintraw **55(NM:830050)**
A little less than halfway from Lochgilphead N to
Oban. Just E of A816 at NE end of Loch Craignish.

In this fine location, with splendid views, there are 3 small cairns and one large kerbed cairn; the latter, 14.6m across, and over 2m high, had a bipartite cist in its NW sector containing cremated bones and carbonized wood; a posthole was also found inside the cairn. The mound had been covered in brilliant white quartz. Close by, to the sw, is a leaning stone nearly 4m high, which probably belongs to a small kerb cairn. There have been forceful claims that this site was an observatory of the midwinter solstice: e.g., with a siting from the large kerb cairn's summit across the top of the leaning stone to the midwinter sunset. Some scholars believe that there is an artificial sighting platform – an almost level rubble pavement behind 2 adjacent boulders that form a notch – cut into the steep hillside NE of the cairns; others, however, are equally certain that this feature is completely natural, perhaps made by extreme frost in glacial times.

Machrie Moor Stone Circles
and Standing Stones *
Bronze Age
Tormore, Arran **69(NR:910324)**
Between A841 (to W) and B880 (to E), just s of
Machrie Water and the Auchagallon monuments
(qv). Footpath E from A841 near bridge over
Machrie Water.

This complex of monuments comprises 6 stone rings, one of which (NR:921325) was discovered under the peat (formed since the Bronze Age) as recently as 1978; it has 10 low sandstone pillars, with a posthole between each pair. Of the other 5 circles, 3 are of granite lumps, and 2 of sandstone columns. Diameters range from 6 to 18m, and the group seems to have accumulated rather than been set out with an overall design. The most interesting is the double circle known as 'Fingal's Cauldron Seat' (NR:908323): an inner ring of 8 granite boulders, 11.5m across, surrounded by an egg-shaped setting of 15 granite stones. From its centre (where there is a ruined cist), one can see all the other circles and standing stones in the vicinity. One stone in the outer circle is perforated: Fingal the giant is said to have tied his dog Bran to this while heating his cauldron on the inner ring. Several other circles had cists at their centre, some of which contained food vessels.

Nether Largie Barrows *
New Stone/Bronze Ages
Kilmartin **55(NR:828979)**
N of Lochgilphead on A816. Barrows lie within 1km
s from Kilmartin on w side of A816. Not far from
Dunchraigaig (qv) and Temple Wood (qv). All
signposted.

The Kilmartin valley is filled with prehistoric sites – cairns, circles, standing stones and engraved rocks – being a key route centre for sw Scotland. It is unique in Scotland in having a line of 5 cairns, the earliest dating to the New Stone Age, the others to the early Bronze Age; thus the line may span 2000 years of use.

The northernmost *Glebe* cairn (NR:833989) is a huge mass of pebbles, 33.5m across and 4m high,

Right: *Nether Largie South Cairn*. One in the line of round cairns in the Kilmartin region. This South Cairn has a segmented chamber with huge capstones

Centre: *Nether Largie North Cairn*, interior. Another of the round cairns in the Kilmartin region. This North Cairn has a cist with cup marks and bronze axe carvings visible on the capstone

Below: *Ri Cruin Cairn*. This cairn is one of the unique line of round cairns in the Kilmartin region. There are 3 cists, one with carvings of the Bronze Age. (Part of the Nether Largie Barrows)

Dunchraigaig Barrow with Long Cist. *This Bronze Age cairn was originally 30m across and still stands 2m high*

Temple Wood Stone Circle. An unusual monument: the stone circle encloses a slab burial cist

housing 2 stone cists that contained food vessels; the cists are no longer visible. *Nether Largie North* (NR:831985) is 21m across and still stands to a height of almost 3m. A modern trapdoor gives access to a large central cist, which has numerous cupmarks and carvings of axe-heads on the underside of its capstone, and others on an end slab.

200m further s stands *Nether Largie Centre* (NR:831984), an originally kerbed cairn, 32m across, whose 2 empty stone cists are now uncovered, with possible cup and axe carvings. 450m further is *Nether Largie South* (NR:828979)–the Neolithic cairn–which housed a burial chamber of large stones, divided into 4 compartments, containing cremated burials and pottery. The edge of the cairn had 2 later, intrusive stone cists of the Beaker period.

Finally, in a wood 850m ssw stands *Ri Cruin* (NR:826971), 20m across, which houses 3 stone cists, the southernmost of which displays axe-head carvings; another possible depiction of a boat or halberd has now gone, but a cast can be seen in the National Museum of Antiquities, Edinburgh.

Quothquan Law Hillfort   *Iron Age*
Just ENE of Thankerton   **72(NS:988385)**
5.4km w of Biggar. Take by-roads to Thankerton and beyond, from A72 sw of Biggar, or e from A73 beyond its junction with A72.

A very conspicuous hillfort situated in a bend of the Clyde, it began with a single rampart, and was later extended to include the western face: this annexe contains traces of a number of timber-framed houses.

Temple Wood Stone Circles
and Standing Stones   *Bronze Age*
Kilmartin   **55(NR:827978)**
Directions as for Nether Largie: about 180m sw of Nether Largie South. Signposted. Near Ballymeanoch (qv).

Thirteen stones in a copse are the remains of an original 20 that stood in a circle 12m across. They were set within a weathered bank, and at the centre was a stone burial cist. One of the circle stones has pecked spiral carvings at its base. A slightly smaller circle was found recently in this wood.

Nearby, 300m to the s, is the 'x'-shaped setting of the 5 'Nether Largie standing stones' (NR:831985). The central stone has a number of cupmarks. It is thought that this setting may have had an astronomical function, perhaps in conjunction with the circle and a notch in the western mountains, to form a lunar observatory.

A couple of small burial cairns have recently been excavated in and near the main circle.

WESTERN ISLES

Barpa Langass Chambered
Barrow*   *New Stone Age*
Langass, North Uist   **18(NF:837657)**
8.4km ssw of Lochmaddy. Just s of A867, on slopes of Ben Langass. 1km NE of turning to Langass. Stone circle just beyond Langass at NF:842651.

A conspicuous and well-preserved round passage grave, 24m across and over 4m high, it has a peristalith of small flat slabs. An entrance in the forecourt on the E side leads to a fine polygonal chamber, built of 7 huge, upright slabs, with drystone above, and a roof of 3 large lintels, 2m above the floor. Finds (National Museum of Antiquities, Edinburgh) included potsherds and a flint arrowhead of Beaker type.

**Beinn a' Charra Standing
Stone** *Bronze Age*
Stoneybridge, South Uist **22(NF:771321)**
*12km NW of Lochboisdale. On w slopes of Beinn a'
Charra. Just E of A865 and N of East Loch Ollay.*
    This stone is 4m in height, 1.5m wide and 0.6m
thick.

**Callanish Chambered Barrow
and Standing Stones*** *New Stone/Bronze Ages*
Breasclete, Lewis **8(NB:213330)**
*20km w of Stornoway, 3km s of Breasclete, on
promontory just w of the A858. Other burial
chambers, standing stones and stone circles along
A858 in this region. Signposted. Leaflet available.*
    This complex site, the 'Stonehenge of the North', is
2nd in importance only to that site, and it is equally
enigmatic. It comprises a unique setting of megaliths, on a promontory into Loch Roag. The principal
feature is a flattened circle of 13 tall slabs of the easily
split Lewis gneiss; the ring is 13m across, and one
stone, 4.6m high, stands near its centre. This slab,
and 2 of those in the circle's eastern arc, are on the
perimeter of a now roofless chambered round cairn
of the New Stone Age; squashed between the stones,
it is the smallest such cairn in Britain (7m in diameter) and has a bipartite chamber. There is another
low cairn just to the NE of the 1st, and another of the
circle's megaliths forms part of it. A single stone, 3m
sw of the circle, may be all that remains of an outer
ring.
    It should be noted that this impressive circle is
nevertheless quite modest: even the tall centre stone
weighs only 5 tons, and at most would have required
20 people to haul and erect it. The stones are
undressed and ungraded.
    Running NNE from the circle, there is a slightly
splayed avenue of 2 rows of tall stones, culminating
in 2 particularly tall specimens: 19 stones are still
standing in this avenue, which is 83m long and 8m
wide. Single rows of stones lead in other directions
from the circle: 4 to the w (12m), 4 to the ENE (15m)
and 6 southward (27.4m). The overall shape is therefore that of a cross; it is thought that the 3 single rows
are uncompleted avenues.
    There have been many claims of astronomical
alignments at the site: e.g., the northern avenue
points s to a possible horizon marker for the
moon's setting at its most southerly declination.
However, recent analysis of 46 possible alignments
found that 45 were unsatisfactory, while the accurate 46th could be due to chance.
    The site is visible from a considerable distance,
and forms part of a group of circles along, and very
close to, this stretch of the coast: such as Cnoc
Ceann, 1km SSE (NB:222326); Cnoc Fillibhir Bheag,
a double ring 1.3km SE (NB:226326), and 4 others
near the head of East Loch Roag, notably Garyna-
hine (NB:230303).
    Callanish is also called *Fir Bhreig* ('false men')
and *Tursachen* ('place of mourning/pilgrimage').
Until the last century, couples would go there to
make their marital vows, and there is a legend that
any marriage first consummated among the stones
would be especially happy. Another tale is that the
stones are local giants turned to stone by St Kieran
for refusing to be christened. In a time of famine, a
white cow appeared from the sea, and told women

*Callanish Standing Stones. New Stone
Age/Bronze Age*

Above: **Callanish Standing Stones** on a
promontory of East Loch Roag

Right: **Callanish Chambered Barrow and
Standing Stones**, Lewis, Outer Hebrides (after
A. Burl)

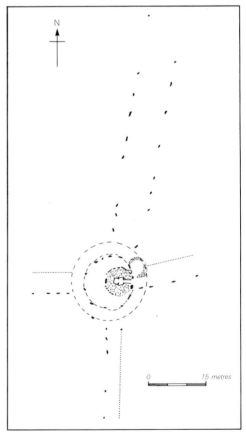

to take milk-pails to the circle, where they
received a pailful each night.

In the vicinity, 2 phases of prehistoric ard cultivation have been found, and there are some field
systems (NB:218326).

Clach an Trushal Standing
Stone
Ballantrushal, Lewis   **8(NB:376538)**
*Near NW coast, 4km NNE of Barvas. Just NW of A857 at
Ballantrushal.*

Bronze Age

This stone is one of the tallest and most striking
in Scotland. It is 6m high, almost 2m wide and
1.8m thick at the base.

Clettraval Chambered Long
Barrow and Dun/Farm *
Hosta, North Uist   **18(NF:749714)**
*17km W of Lochmaddy, E of A865 near Tigharry and
Hosta. Footpaths; just below S summit of the
Clettraval ridge.*

*New Stone/
Iron Ages*

The wedge-shaped cairn, 29m long, stands out
on open moorland. It has a fine, well-built peristalith, and a straight façade of tall slabs. The chamber's floor is gneiss bedrock; now roofless, it is
divided into 5 compartments by septal slabs. It
contained quantities of Neolithic and Beaker pottery. There is a standing stone to the W of the
cairn.

The site also has an Iron Age farm: a free-standing stone wheelhouse with 8 radial stone piers,
and a surrounding farmyard enclosure comprising
work areas and subsidiary structures, most notably
a large rectangular byre to the SW. A circular dun
was built at the W end of the cairn.

Dun Carloway Broch. *The entrance passage of the broch. The galleries between the double wall show clearly behind*

Dun Bharpa Chambered Barrow

Castlebay, Barra   **31(NF:672019)**

New Stone Age

3.6km N of Castlebay, 1.6km NE of Borve. By-road E from A888 and footpath. Another chambered cairn to SE (NF:677012).

A large round cairn, it has remains of a peristalith of tall slabs. The passage is on the E, and a huge covering slab is exposed near the top of the mound, 4m up.

Dun Carloway Broch*

Carloway, Lewis   **8(NB:190412)**

Iron Age

3km SW of Carloway, and just W of the A858, between road and sea.

One of the best-preserved brochs, it stands on a rocky knoll, and in size and proportions bears a strong resemblance to Dundornagail (p. 254). Still up to 9m in height, it has a double wall, with a series of galleries linked by an intramural staircase. The main door, at the NW, has a guard-room in the

wall, and 4 doors in the courtyard give on to other rooms and the staircase. This area is supposed to be the site of battles between giants and Finns.

Kilpheder Aisled
Round-house
Iron Age or later
Kilpheder, South Uist **31(NF:734203)**
6km w of Lochboisdale. Take A865 nw to Daliburgh, then B888 to s, and by-road w to Kilpheder.

A ruined wheelhouse, resembling that of Clet-traval *(qv)*, it has a strong circular wall with an internal series of radial drystone pillars. The round area in the centre has a hearth.

Marrogh Chambered Barrow
New Stone Age
Marrogh Hill, North Uist **18(NF:833696)**
10km w of Lochmaddy, on knoll near foot of Marrogh, a steep hill on remote moorland occupying centre of ring of A865 and A867.

A round cairn, 24m across and over 4m high, it has a funnel-shaped forecourt on the e, from which a passage – with some lintels still in place – leads to a round chamber built of massive stones. Its 2 huge capstones have been displaced. An outlier stone stands 100m to the sw.

Uneval Chambered Barrow
New Stone Age
Clachan, North Uist **18(NF:801669)**
3km nnw of Clachan (at junction of A865 and A867). On shoulder of hill of Uneval, 1km w of Loch Huna. Near coast.

Located on a prominent hill surrounded by lochs, this very large, square, chambered tomb has remains of a peristalith and façade, and a short passage leads to a polygonal chamber that contained abundant Neolithic pottery and a beaker. A bipartite early Iron Age house was later built into the ne corner of the cairn; it is thought to contain a corn-drying area. Finds are in the National Museum of Antiquities, Edinburgh.

A 3m high standing stone (NF:800669) near the cairn's edge is very conspicuous from a wide area around, and is thought to constitute a plausible lunar observatory.

***Dun Carloway Broch**. The broch stands to a height of some 9 m with later buildings below it*

WALES

Looked at in simplest terms, Wales forms the central block of the rocky highland zone of Britain, its dominant promontories of Dyfed, Caernarfon and Anglesey following in sequence from that of Cornwall to the south and those of Cumbria and Galloway to the north.

Geologically, it can be divided between an 'old Wales' of the north and centre and a 'young Wales' of the south and east. While Anglesey is largely composed of the most ancient rocks, laid down long before life was stirring on earth, the main mass of 'old Wales' consists of the Cambrian mountains, centred on Snowdonia where old rocks are armoured by great masses of volcanic lava. It extends into north Dyfed, where again there are lava flows. The resulting igneous rocks produced material for polished stone axe factories in both areas; the most active, exporting its products far and wide, mostly freely to Wessex, was that of Craig Lwyd (p. 300) behind Penmaenmawr on the Caernarfon coast. Central and west Wales south of the lovely hills of Merioneth (south of Harlech) is a raised plateau largely covered by rolling moorland, and this, together with the main Cambrian range, has virtually no antiquities dating from before the Bronze Age.

'Young Wales' of the east and south is built largely of the Old Red Sandstone (often neither red nor sandstone), rising to the romantic country of the Brecon Beacons and the Black Mountains – and including the wide extent of the Coal Measures, never attractive to settlement by prehistoric man. Along the south coast of Glamorgan, and again in the extreme north-east in Clwyd, there are limestone cliffs and hills, with caves offering shelter to the Old Stone Age hunters.

Because of these caves, Wales is relatively rich in remains of this time, although humans do not seem to have penetrated the country much before the last glaciation of the Ice Age. By far the best-known cave dwelling, that of the Goat's (Paviland) Cave (p. 293) on the coast of Gower, was probably occupied considerably before the radiocarbon date of 17,000 – 16,000 BC for the young man buried there. Less well known, but perhaps even more important, are the caves in the limestone of northern Clywd. Ffynnon Beuno (p. 288) and Cae Gwyn near St Asaph were occupied at much the same time as the Goat's Cave, but Pontnewydd cave just to the north, near Rhyl, has yielded much earlier implements and also teeth and fragments of jaw of several individuals of Neanderthal type.

The cave dwellings of both the north and south are well worth visiting, but by far the greatest attraction Wales can offer to visitors in search of the prehistoric past lies in her megalithic tombs, many of them set in places so beautiful, wild or remote as greatly to enhance their archaeological interest. As already hinted in the opening paragraph, the bold promontories of Dyfed, Caernarfon and the just detached island of Anglesey offered promising landfalls for would-be settlers of the New Stone Age following the seaways from the south into the Irish Sea. It is there that most of their finest tombs can be found, although others, perhaps more easily accessible, are dotted all along the coastal plain of South Glamorgan. Their distribution is overwhelmingly coastal, the little farming communities they represent having never attempted to push into the moors and mountains of the interior. There is a puzzling absence of settlement, and therefore of monuments, from south of the hills of Merioneth along the whole smooth sweep of Cardigan Bay to the Teifi.

The one inland group of tombs is on the north-west slopes of the Black Mountains of Brecon. These are all chambered long barrows and they are so very like those of the Cotswolds that, for once, there can be no doubt that the settlements on either side of the Severn estuary were closely related. Anyone in the mood for antiquity could spend a happy week among these delectable valleys searching out the dozen or more tombs, some of them, such as Tŷ-isaf (p. 303) and Pipton (p. 303), extraordinarily complicated in plan. There are also a few chambered long barrows on the Glamorgan coast, notably Tinkinswood (p. 293) and Parc Le Breos (p. 293), and an odd, unexpected example in the Conwy valley, Capel Garmon (p. 299).

The host of megalithic tombs on the west coasts show a rich variety of forms, some with long mounds, some with round. Among the commonest are the dolmens, often with tall portal stones and gigantic capstones that seem best to fulfil the term *megalithic*. Most significant are the rare passage graves in their round cairns, of which the famous examples are Bryncelli Ddu (p. 282) and Barclodiad y Gawres (p. 282), both in Anglesey. The strange, magico-religious designs carved on their stones are close enough to the far more magnificent display to be seen on passage graves in Ireland and Brittany to prove beyond question that the builders belonged to a seaborne movement bringing colonists to the coasts of the Irish Sea.

As the Gazetteer makes plain, Anglesey has several other conspicuous megalithic tombs as well as later monuments. There is no better place to combine a seaside holiday with painless archaeology.

At the dawn of the Bronze Age, groups of Beaker Folk penetrated most regions of Wales, a few perhaps coming directly from the Continent, but more from England, spreading westward by way of the Severn, Wye and other river valleys and so settling the hitherto unpopulated central massif. There, in the dry climate of that time, they could pasture their flocks and herds. Their further interest in metal-prospecting led to direct contacts with Ireland. Moreover, they were almost certainly involved in the extraordinary venture of transporting the famous 'bluestones' from the Preseli mountains of Dyfed by sea and land to Stonehenge (p. 108).

As for field monuments associated with the Beaker peoples, a number of their typical contracted burials in cists and pits under round barrows (usually cairns) have been uncovered, and there is evidence that the Beaker Folk were concerned in raising some of the earlier stone circles.

There are, in fact, quite large numbers of round barrows to be seen on Welsh moors and mountains and along the south coast, but they are seldom impressive enough in size or number to find a place in the Gazetteer. While the earliest contain Beaker graves, here as elsewhere they were raised all through the middle Bronze Age, usually over cremation urn burials. The same can be said of stone circles, some 50 of which survive in the principality, mostly small and insignificant. On some remote moorlands such as the Mynydd Epynt, they are accompanied by menhirs, stone rows or even small avenues in a style reminiscent of the South-west.

One small group, including the Meini-Gwyr embanked circle (p. 291), can be found at the south-west foot of the Preseli mountains. The best known, however, is the Druid's Circle on Penmaenmawr, just west of Craig Lwyd stone-axe factory.

By the sixth century BC, it seems that some iron tools were in use, together with late bronze tools, and it may have been about this time or soon after that groups of iron-using Celtic peoples began to arrive and build hillforts. The second influx probably followed in the second century BC. Wales swarms with fortified settlements of all sizes, from the smallest walled single dwelling to the largest of over 50 hectares. Very many of the smallest, of less than half a hectare, are known or suspected of being post-Roman, but even

ignoring these, there are not far short of 600 that have been accepted as probably of Iron Age origin, though many remained in use in Roman times. Most of them are stone-built, either with large blocks or massive drystone walling, but along the Marches and in Glamorgan, some are of bank-and-ditch construction.

Dating is difficult for there have been few scientific excavations, and in this mountain land, digging may fail to find any datable material. As a general but by no means universal rule, just as in England, the older forts are those with single ramparts; multiple defences are later. Many of all periods show the foundations of round houses. The earliest tribesmen seem to have pushed in along the Marches, and also to have settled in Glamorgan and north and south Dyfed.

The Breiddin (p. 302) on a crag above the Severn is a relatively early Iron Age fort (succeeding late Bronze Age defences) and so, too, are Ffridd Faldwyn (p. 303), Pen Dinas (p. 291) and Carn Goch (p. 288). Frequently, of course, forts that had been established early with a single rampart later saw them multiplied. Dating remains vague but here 'later' may mean after about 150 BC. The expansion of the Belgic tribes hardly affected Wales and there appears to be no sign of their presence in any hillforts.

The Gazetteer lists a selection of the most conspicuous and rewarding hill and promontory forts from all over the principality. In addition to those already mentioned, a few others may be named for the special attractions. There are the promontory forts of the Dyfed cliffs in the south-west. Flimston Castle (p. 290) with dramatic cliff formations is the easternmost of three within the national park; St David's Head (p. 292) contains round huts and has outer cattle enclosures; Bosherton and Wooltack perhaps also deserve to be noted here. Visitors will find the most rewarding group of hillforts on the line of hills along the Caernarfon peninsula. Starting in the west, there is Carn Fadrun, conspicuous on its sugar loaf hill, then Garn Boduan, poor in defences but with good examples of round houses within. Furthest to the east of the three is the splendid Tre'r Ceiri on a summit some 450 metres high, perhaps the finest of all the stone-built forts of Britain. It has everything: gateway, posterns, rampart walks, 150 houses (rectangular as well as round)–and a superb view.

It will be realized that, owing to the long resistance of the mountain tribes, particularly of the Silures and Ordovices (p. 44) against the Romans, most Welsh forts were held for decades after their English counterparts had fallen; indeed, some were hastily repaired to meet the Roman threat. Little is known of their history at this time, but it has been suggested that Lanmelin in Gwent might have been the capital of the Silures, later moved down to Caerwent.

The general introduction has given some account of the Roman conquest of Wales (pp. 44-46) and of how it was controlled from Chester and Caerleon by a network of roads and garrison forts. How brilliantly this system was devised can be seen by a glance at any Roman map; many of the forts can still be seen. In the north, controlled by two roads from Chester, there is the fort of Caerhun in the Conwy valley, and the larger one for 1000 auxiliaries at Caernarfon (*Segontium*). A minor road centre linked with both these forts is Tomen-y-Mur (p. 301), strongly recommended for a visit. Here the ruins include a fort, amphitheatre, bath-house and parade grounds, set in a remote spot with superb mountain scenery, a place that better than any other suggests how alien troops must have felt, exposed as they were to the violence and dark spiritual forces of the barbarians surrounding them.

Central Wales, served by the main road originally pushed west from Wroxeter, has little to show, though something can be seen

of the fort of Caer Gai (p. 298), and there are two others on the north-south road that linked Tomen-y-Mur (p. 301) and Brithdir.

The southern sector is by far the best endowed, with Caerwent (p. 295), the cantonal capital of the Silures, and the legionary fortress of Caerleon (p. 295) with most to show. Glamorgan has not only the forts of Gelligaer (p. 293) and Coelbren Gaer (p. 293), but also a number of villas, including Llantwit Major. Then there is Cardiff, where the foundations of a fort built against Irish sea-raiders were rebuilt by the Marquess of Bute. There, too, and not far away, are all the treasures of the National Museum of Wales. While a southern road linked up with the central system at Carmarthen, further north Brecon Gaer (p. 301) was a large fort and road centre-first garrisoned by Spanish auxiliaries. From here one road ran on past the Y Pigwn camps (p. 303) by the unique Roman gold mines of Dolaucothi and on to join the north-south highway just below Llanio fort.

In picturing this iron network of Roman rule, it should be remembered that many of their old strongholds were reoccupied by the native Celts. It should also be remembered that far more wonderful than the survival of stony ruins is the survival of the Celtic language which, while changing on the tongues of passing generations, is still spoken today.

ANGLESEY
(part of Gwynedd)

Barclodiad y Gawres Chambered Barrow*
Llangwyfan
New Stone Age
114(SH:328708)
Between Rhosneigr (to NW) and Aberffraw (to SE).
Signposted. Leaflet available. Usually locked: key from 22 The Square, Caernarfon. Torch useful.

This round cairn, beautifully situated on a clifftop overlooking the bay, was used as a stone quarry in the 18th century; the original mound of stones (the name means the 'Giantess's Apronful') has gone, and been replaced by a concrete dome that covers the passage grave. Related to the Irish cruciform tombs of the Boyne valley and dating to c. 2500 BC, it has a 6m passage at the N leading to a polygonal chamber with 3 side-chambers. Excavation revealed the remains of 2 cremated youths mixed with sheep bones, and a hearth with remains of reptiles, fish, shellfish and small mammals. The monument is especially important for its engraved stones (3 in the passage, 2 in the chambers) whose chevrons, spirals, circles and lozenges are another link with the Irish tombs.

Bryncelli Ddu Chambered Barrow*
Llanddaniel Fab
New Stone Age
114(SH:508702)
Just SE of Llanddaniel Fab, and W of A4080, S of A5.
In fields close to farm. Signposted. Leaflet available.

The 'hill in the dark grove' is one of the most interesting passage graves in the country. It used to be thought that the site began as a circle-henge in c. 2000 BC; its ditch's diameter was 32m, and the circle had 14 stones. The subsequent destruction of this monument was thought to indicate conflict-the stones had been deliberately toppled or broken-and only 2 of them survive, on opposite sides of the cairn. A mound was then erected, 26m across, with a double kerb of stones round its edge. A roofed passage, over 7m long, leads from the NE to a polygonal chamber of 6 upright stones, one of which has a spiral carving. In the chamber is a tall, smooth, free-standing pillar. The passage has a doorway and a low bench; beyond the chamber, at the mound's centre, is a pit that contained wood and a human ear-bone, and close by is a cast of the carved

Above: ***Barclodiad Y Gawres Chambered Barrow***. *A romantic view of the round barrow covering the megalithic passage grave. Uprights in the chamber are carved with spirals, zigzags and other symbols*

Below: ***Barclodiad Y Gawres***. *The entrance to the New Stone Age chambered barrow*

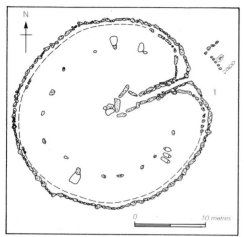

Above: **Bryncelli Ddu**, *chambered tomb, Anglesey (after Hemp)*

Right: **Bryncelli Ddu Chambered Barrow.** *The chamber of this passage grave with its ritual pillar. New Stone Age*

stone found here and now on display in the National Museum of Wales, Cardiff. The tomb itself contained human bones, flint tools, shells, etc. In front of the entrance was a forecourt and, nearby, a small ox buried in an enclosure. The mound has been kept small in order to show the central pit and the two henge-stones.

It has been suggested recently, however, that, rather than starting as a circle-henge (there was never any trace of a bank), this is simply an early 2-period structure: i.e., a first passage grave was built in a mound, surrounded by a kerb of stones and a ditch; later its passage and mound were enlarged, and a new kerb of stones was erected in the ditch, part of which was obliterated by the enlargement.

Bryn-yr-Hen Bobl Chambered Barrow*
NE of Llanidan   *New Stone Age*
114(SH:519690)
Just E of A4080, above Menai Strait. Just SE of Bryncelli Ddu (qv) and S of Plas Newydd (qv).

The 'hill of the old people' is 135m across and over 5m high. On its E side is the entrance to a small burial chamber, and there may have been a 2nd on the SW side. The entrance has a large horned forecourt. An urn containing a cremation was found at the S end. The tomb itself contained at least 20 people. The southern horn of the forecourt has a long revetted terrace attached to it.

Caer Gybi Fortlet
Holyhead   *Roman*
114(SH:247826)
On cliff at edge of Holyhead town harbour. The church of St Gybi stands within the fortlet.

This fortified landing base was built on the edge of the harbour in c. AD 300, and was presumably for warships. No doubt the Romans guarded against pirates and policed the area from this small fort that still has walls over 4m high on the outside. Three of the corners had circular towers, though only that

on the NW is still completely of Roman work, and the 4th side of the fort was open to the harbour.

Caer-y-Twr Hillfort
Holyhead   *Iron Age?*
114(SH:218830)
W of Holyhead, enclosing summit of Holyhead Mountain.

This hillfort in a superb setting on a rocky summit had no need of defences on the sheer S side; elsewhere its 7ha were enclosed by a massive drystone wall, with an entrance on the NE. Unexcavated.

Din Lligwy Walled Settlement*
SE of Penrhos Lligwy   *Romano-British*
114(SH:496862)
E of A5108. Short distance beyond Lligwy chambered barrow (qv), by woodland path. Signposted.

A strong limestone wall encloses an area of 0.2ha containing 2 round and 7 oblong huts, some of whose walls still stand to a height of almost 2m. An entrance is visible on the NE. Six hearths in 2 of the rectangular huts indicate that iron-smelting took place there. The site is thought to date to the 4th century AD.

Din Sylwy Hillfort (Bwrdd Arthur)
Llanddona   *Romano-British*
114(SH:586815)
NE of Llandonna, NW of Llangoed. Overlooking the sea E of Red Wharf Bay.

The 'fort of the Sylwy tribe' (or 'Arthur's Table') comprises an oval area of 7ha enclosed by a thick drystone wall of great limestone blocks, and further separated by a berm–though no ditch–from the steep slopes all around. There were entrances on the S and W. The site was occupied by the Ordovices in the Roman period.

Lligwy Chambered Barrow
SE of Amlwch   *New Stone Age*
114(SH:501861)
Near Penrhos Lligwy. From Llanallgo, lane past Lygwy farm. Signposted. Near Din Lligwy (qv).

Above: **Din Lligwy Walled Settlement**. *One of two well-built round huts in this walled Romano-British enclosure*

Below: **Lligwy**. *The vast capstone of this New Stone Age chambered barrow rests on only 3 of the uprights*

Most of this apparently stunted monument is underground. The chamber is actually 2m high, set into a natural fissure. There are 8 upright stones, but the huge limestone capstone – one of the biggest in Britain – rests on only 3 of them. It is 5.5 by 4.5m, 1m thick and probably weighs 25 tons. There is no trace of a mound. The tomb seems to have been entered from the E, and housed at least 30 people of all ages, together with abundant animal bones and limpet and mussel shells. The pottery implies that the monument was in use until the early Bronze Age.

285

Above: ***Plas Newydd Chambered Long Barrow***. *New Stone Age*

Below: ***Trefignath Chambered Long Barrow***. *Long cairn with early dolmen-like burial chamber in foreground and later chamber with tall portal stones beyond. New Stone Age*

Pant-y-Saer Chambered Long
Barrow *New Stone Age*
Llanfait-Mathafarn-Eithaf **114(SH:509824)**
*Lane from Red Wharf; just s of B5108 and w of
A5025, on high ground above Tynygongl. 3km s of
Lligwy (qv).*

A pit was battered out of bedrock here, and a rectangular chamber of stones was set up in it that eventually housed over 50 bodies, including 9 unborn
infants. Some of the skulls were missing. A huge capstone, 4m square, formed the roof, and an oval cairn
enclosed the site, with a drystone horned forecourt
at the w end.

Plas Newydd Chambered
Barrow* *New Stone Age*
NE of Llanidan **114(SH:519697)**
*E of A4080, above Menai Strait. In Marquess of
Anglesey's park in front of Plas Newydd house. SE of
Bryncelli Ddu (qv) and N of Bryn-yr-Hen Bobl
(qv).*

A massive burial chamber with no trace of a
mound, it has a huge capstone over 1m thick; the
entrance was on the SW where there is a small antechamber.

Trefignath Chambered Long
Barrow *New Stone Age*
s of Holyhead **114(SH:259805)**
*s of A5. Overlooking aluminium reduction plant.
Signposted. Standing stone to NW (SH:254809) at
Ty-mawr.*

This monument was thought to be a single gallery

grave, almost 14m long, divided up by cross-slabs
into 4 chambers; however, recent excavations
revealed that the situation is more complex. This is a
multi-period site, with its earliest phase dating to
3100 BC. Originally, a simple rectangular tomb was
built on the w under a small round mound; a larger
chamber with low portals was then built to the E,
housed in a long, wedge-shaped cairn with a deeply
recessed drystone forecourt like that of Capel Garmon (p. 299) and other Severn–Cotswold tombs.
This mound enclosed the 1st structure too. Finally, a
3rd chamber was built into the forecourt, with its
own drystone forecourt on the E. The mound was
extended eastward to surround it, and edged in drystone. Human bones and pottery were found inside,
and the tomb was probably used throughout the 3rd
millennium BC. The easternmost chamber has survived well; the others have collapsed.

Ty-Mawr Settlement
Romano-British
Holyhead **114(SH:212820)**
*On sw slopes of Holyhead Mountain below Caer-y-
Twr (qv). Another group of huts below on the bay
of Porth Dafarch.*

Locally called *Cytiau Gwyddelod* ('huts of the
Irishmen'), the site comprises a score of circular
huts, up to 10m across, in 2 groups (14 and 6); many
are clearly visible, with low stone walls, some
hearths still in place, and even slabs marking the
position of beds. One hut contained copper slag.
There were originally about 50 huts spread over 8ha.
Other finds include querns, mortars, spindlewhorls,
pottery and coins – probably of the 3rd/4th centuries
AD.

Trefignath Chambered Long Barrow. New Stone Age

CLWYD

Brenig Archaeological Trail* *Middle Stone/Bronze Ages*
Mynydd Hiraethog **116(SH:985576)**
In Fechan valley, E of Brenig reservoir. Nature reserve with carpark. Welsh Water Authority. Map and pamphlet available.

Over 50 sites were uncovered by excavations in this valley in the 1970s, and some have been restored and can be visited along 2 trails. The shorter trail (under 1 hour) leads from the carpark to a summer campsite of the Middle Stone Age, dated to 5700 BC and now marked by a stone; there follows the Bronze Age barrow of *Boncyn Arian* ('money hillock') comprising a central grave dating to 1600 BC, and later cremations inserted into the mound. Finally, to the S, is a ring cairn dated to *c.* 1680 BC, to which 3 urn cremations were also added later.

If the weather is fine, the 2-hour trail is worth a visit. 1km S of the carpark is a Bronze Age living-site with a restored platform cairn on it; to the E of a medieval farm *(Hen Ddinbych)* is another Bronze Age cairn with a stone kerb, built over a prehistoric hut, and to the W of the farm is another kerbed cairn.

Foel Fenlli Hillfort *Iron Age*
Llanbedr-Dyffryn-Clwyd **116(SJ:163601)**
On W edge of Clwydian range. N of A494 between Ruthin and Mold.

Located at an altitude of over 500m, this ovoid fort of 10ha has double or treble ramparts on all sides, and an inturned entrance on the W. There is a spring by the centre of the fort, and a couple of dozen hut-platforms lie unexcavated and often obscured by heather in the SW sector. There is a legend that the site was the home of the tyrant King Benlii in AD 450 – for opposing St Germanus, he and his fort were consumed by fire from heaven. This is probably a site of more than one period (from pre-Roman into Roman times).

Ffynnon Beuno Cave-dwellings *Old Stone Age*
S of Tremeirchion **116(SJ:085725)**
E of B5429. SE of St Asaph, on the W edge of the Clwydian range, S of the A55.

Both of the adjacent small caves here were occupied by humans during the Ice Age. They face S in a side valley, overlooking a stream. The upper cave, *Cae Gwyn*, contained bones of lion, bear, rhinoceros and deer, as well as stone tools. The lower, *Ffynnon Beuno*, which was used as a cattle shelter in the recent past, contained bones of hyenas, giant Irish deer, reindeer, horse and woolly rhino, as well as

stone tools such as scrapers, burins (a type dated to 32,000–29,000 BC in France) and a unifacial leaf point, all buried under layers of stalagmite.

Gop-y-Goleuni Barrow* *New Stone Age?*
Trelawnyd **116(SJ:086802)**
SE of Prestatyn, just N of A5151. Offa's Dyke just to E at SJ:105790.

After Silbury Hill (p. 104), this is the largest barrow in Britain and, like Silbury, its function is unknown: a shaft sunk in 1886 (which caused the indentation on the summit) encountered only a few bones of horse and ox. Located at an altitude of 250m, with a fine view from its summit, it covers an area of 100 by 68m, and is still 12m high. It was built of limestone blocks. This hill used to be called *Bryn y Saethau* ('hill of the arrows') because of the many flint arrowheads found there; it was traditionally associated with a battle, and there was an unlikely 19th-century story that the mound was the grave of Boudicca.

Moel y Gaer Hillfort *Iron Age?*
NE of Denbigh, just N of Bodfari **116(SJ:095708)**
Between B5429 (to W) and A541 (to SE), on small hill above river Wheeler. Just S of Ffynnon Beuno (qv).

A D-shaped fort, it had the natural defence of a steep slope on the E, and a rampart, ditch and counterscarp on the W, with a 2nd line of defence lower down. The entrance is on the NE.

Moel y Gaer Hillfort *Iron Age?*
NE of Ruthin **116(SJ:149618)**
N of A494.

This 4ha fort had double ramparts all around, and a 3rd added at the level area to the NE. There are 2 inturned entrances on W and NE.

Pen-y-cordynn-mawr Hillfort *Iron Age?*
S of Llanddulas **116(SH:914765)**
Between Colwyn Bay and Abergele, S of A55. On massive limestone outcrop E of river Dulas.

This 12ha fort, which may originally have covered 17ha, is one of the biggest and strongest in the region. It had the natural defence of steep slopes except to the N where the plateau has 2 ramparts with stone revetments, but no ditches. Beyond, to the N, is another rampart enclosing an annexe of 6ha. The fort had 3 entrances, one of which had guard-chambers, and contains a number of round hut sites. From a small gate on the E, a steep path led down to a spring.

DYFED

Beddyrafanc Chambered Long Barrow *New Stone Age*
SW of Eglwyswrw **145(SN:113346)**
Just SE of B4329, near Brynberian. Just SE of Pentre Ifan (qv).

The 'grave of the water monster' is 18m long, over 10m wide and 0.6m high. At the centre is an

unusually long (11m) and narrow (1–2m) chamber, with short rows of stones along each side.

Carn Goch Hillfort* *Iron Age*
NE of Llandeilo **159/160(SN:691243)**
On scarp S of the river Towy (Tywi). Approach by lanes climbing from road from Llandeilo to Llangadog via Glan-Towy or Bethlehem.

Above: ***Ty-Mawr Settlement***. *One of the score of round houses occupied by native Celts in Roman times. Some were equipped with querns and mortars*

Below: ***Gop-y-Goleuni Barrow***. *New Stone Age*

This 10.5ha hillfort comprises a rectangular enclosure, with massive drystone walls, 20m thick, over the ends of the ridge, and less imposing ramparts along its sides. The main entrance is on the NE, with 2 minor gates in the side ramparts. The fort contains a (probably contemporary) round-hut site and 2 (probably later) rectangular examples. A long barrow stands to the N of the fort.

Cerrig-y-Gof Chambered
Round Barrow
New Stone Age
w of Newport
145(SN:037389)
s of Newport Bay by A487.

The 'smith's stone' barrow, 11m across, has the remains of 5 rectangular chambers around its edge: 4 of their capstones survive, one of them *in situ*. Excavation in the last century revealed bones, charcoal and pottery.

Dolaucothi Gold Mines
and Aqueduct*
Roman
Pumpsaint
146(SN:665404)
NW of Llandovery. Approach by lanes turning E off A482 just s of Pumpsaint and river Cothi. Pamphlet from Cothi Arms.

The only Roman gold mine known in Britain had workings on such a scale that they must attest to either government activity or a company of great efficiency. Certainly, expensive equipment and the most advanced Roman mining techniques are in evidence. The workings (now jumbled with medieval and modern traces) extended for a mile, quarrying veins of auriferous pyrites in 3 main areas along the SE slope of the Cothi valley. Scattered mining dumps can be seen, including 2 large open dumps where pyrites was worked opencast to a depth of 10m. Some of the underground galleries, about 2m square, can still be seen; these were cut very systematically.

A wooden panning cradle was found, and part of a wooden water wheel (now in the National Museum of Wales, Cardiff). Water was brought by 3 rock-cut aqueducts from the river; the longest was 11km, and could deliver 13.5 million litres per day for washing the ore. There were pithead baths for the miners. Expert goldsmiths seem to have lived here and worked the gold *in situ*; a hoard of jewellery of the late 2nd/early 3rd century AD was found.

Traces of a Roman fort exist at Pumpsaint.

Flimston Castle Promontory
Fort
Iron Age
Castlemartin
158(SR:930946)
sw of Pembroke; s of B4319. Entry restricted by Castlemartin firing range.

Westernmost of the 3 adjacent clifftop forts within the national park and surrounded by dramatic cliff formations, Flimston Castle, to the E of the carpark, is located on a limestone promontory housing the 'Devil's Cauldron', a collapsed cavern. The peninsula is defended by a pair of banks and ditches, with another defence 20m beyond. A single wide entrance goes through the centre.

Just to the E is Crocksydam Camp (SR:936943) where another peninsula is cut by a single stone bank: it has the remains of a hut. Further E is Buckspool Down Camp (SR:954934) with 3 banks and 2 possible round huts.

Foel Trigarn (Moel Drygarn)
Hillfort and Barrows
Iron/Bronze Ages
s of Whitechurch, w of Crymmych **145(SN:158336)**
Fort crowns hill towards E end of the Preseli mountains. SE of Eglwyswrw, w of A478.

The site's name ('hill of the three cairns') is derived from the 3 great Bronze Age mounds on the summit here, said to be the burial places of 3 kings:

Cerrig-y-Gof Chambered Long Barrow. New Stone Age

Pentre Ifan Chambered Long Barrow. New Stone Age

Mon, Maelen and Madog. Aerial photography has shown that a large collection of hut-platforms pre-dated the hillfort; the latter covers a hectare, contains the cairns and has a wall of earth and stone on the w. To the e, it is protected by the steep slope. There are other semicircular enclosures to the w and n, and a number of entrances. Excavations in the last century produced potsherds and beads from the Iron Age and Roman period.

Gors-Fawr Stone Circle *Bronze Age*
Mynachlog-ddu **145(SN:134294)**
On lower s slopes of Preseli by lane running ssw from Mynachlog-ddu towards Llangolman. w of A478, sw of Foel Trigarn (qv). Signposted. Marshy in wet weather.

On an expanse of peaty moorland (the name means 'great wasteland'), one finds a perfect circle of small igneous boulders, 22m across. There are 16 surviving stones, graded in size to the ssw, but none over 1m in height. Two taller stones stand as outliers, 134m to the NNE and 13.7m apart. There are unconvincing suggestions that these are aligned on the midsummer sunrise. A number of ruined chambered tombs and some earthworks can be seen in the area.

Long House (Carreg Samson)
Chambered Tomb* *New Stone Age*
WNW of Mathry **157(SM:846336)**
Near coast by turning to Trevine. N of A487. Signposted.

This tomb, 'Samson's stone', is an impressive monument in a splendid position overlooking the bay. There is no sign of a covering mound. The polygonal chamber comprises 7 uprights, but the huge capstone (4.5 by 2.7m) rests on only 3 of them. The monument was used as a sheep-shelter in the early part of this century.

Meini-Gwyr Embanked Stone
Circle *Bronze Age*
N of Llandissilio E **145(SN:142267)**
w of A478 opposite road from Llanglydwen. Not far s of Gors Fawr (qv); other cairns, circles and standing stones in the area (e.g. SN:145270).

The only example of an embanked circle in Wales is now inconspicuous in a field on a ridge. Probably built in the early 2nd millennium BC, it comprised a ring of 17 stones, 18m across, on a circular bank 36m in diameter and 1m high, and a narrow stone-built entrance on the w; there was no ditch.

Only 2 stones now remain. Excavation revealed a Bronze Age hearth and a few potsherds in the centre.

Pen Dinas Hillfort* *Iron Age*
Aberystwyth **135(SN:584804)**
On ridge between rivers Rheidol and Ystwyth. w of A487 as it approaches town from the s.

This fort enclosing 2 peaks was originally 2 separate sites. The northern summit was enclosed by a box rampart and ditch; then the southern was surrounded by a stronger stone-faced bank of rubble, and a deep ditch; it had entrances on N and s. After a period of abandonment or destruction, the 2 forts were joined together by a revetted wall across the saddle, with an entrance to the enlarged enclosure on the e. A number of round hut foundations can be seen inside. The site's history probably spans the last 300 years BC.

Pentre Ifan Chambered
Long Barrow* *New Stone Age*
Newport **145(SN:099370)**
Just NW of Beddyrafanc (qv), s of Nevern and A487 on slopes of the Preseli mountains. Well-signposted. Leaflet available.

This portal dolmen is the best-known prehistoric monument in Wales, comprising a huge capstone, 5m long, elegantly balanced 2.5m above the ground on pointed uprights. It is thought to weigh 17 tons. Two of the 3 supporting uprights form portal stones.

There are traces of a small circular cairn that was later doubled in length to about 40m, and a horned projection with a large crescent-shaped forecourt was added.

St David's Head Promontory
Fort and Settlement *Iron Age?*
NW of St David's **157(SM:723279)**
Approach by B4583 and tracks.

A high and massive drystone wall runs 100m N/S and defends the rocky headland. Further E stand 2 banks of rubble with possible ditches between. Near the entrance gap are the remains of half-a-dozen adjacent stonewalled huts. Dating is vague – finds included pottery, spindlewhorls, whetstones and decorated shale pendants.

GLAMORGAN
(West, Mid and South)

The Bulwark Hillfort *Iron Age*
SW of Cheriton **159(SS:443927)**
Gower peninsula, on E end of Llanmadoc Hill.

The westernmost multiple enclosure hillfort is oval in shape, defended by a bank and ditch – with a wide entrance on the E – and a 2nd enclosure beyond. Further defences cross the ridge to E and W, and there are steep slopes to the N.

Cardiff Castle Fort. Built against Irish sea rovers in about AD 300. A 19th-century restoration

Cardiff Castle Fort
(Reconstructed) *Roman*
Cardiff **171(ST:181766)**
Entry from Castle St. Cardiff Corporation.

Much of the circuit of the medieval castle's walls follows the ramparts of the Roman fort. The reconstruction of part of this fort's walls and N gate – carried out at the turn of this century on the basis of excavated remains – gives a good idea of how well-defended these late shore forts must have been. The semi-octagonal projecting bastions suggest a date at the end of the 3rd century AD.

Cat Hole Cave-dwelling
Old Stone Age
w of Ilston **159(SS:538900)**
Near centre of Gower peninsula in wooded valley E
of road between A4118 and B4271.
This cave, 15m above the floor of a steep-sided,
wooded valley, is 18m deep; it was occupied in the
Old Stone Age – *c.* 10,000 BC – probably constituting a
base camp from which to exploit the higher areas of
Gower. Bones of reindeer, red deer, brown bear and
other species have been found, and flint tools including burins, scrapers and awls; an eyed bone needle
was also discovered. The cave was occupied again in
the Middle Stone Age, used for burial in the Bronze
Age, and occupied again in medieval times.

Coelbren Gaer Fort
Roman
Coelbren, NE of Neath **160(SN:859108)**
Beside short road from A4109 at Dyffryn Cellwen N
to Coelbren.
A well-preserved Roman road runs along the ridge
from Neath to Coelbren, and passes 2 fortlets or signal stations (SN:828066, 812040). The best stretch of
road, between ditches 6m apart, is at SN:873114. The
Coelbren fort is an example of a small base, of the 1st
century AD, for 500 cavalry or 1000 infantry. It was
probably abandoned *c.* AD 140. One can see the outline of the ramparts and 3 of the gates, as well as of
roads leading out of them. The fort covered 2ha, with
a 1.4ha annexe added on the E. Internal buildings
were of timber, and the defences of wood, turf and
clay. Finds in Swansea Museum.

Gelligaer Forts *
Roman
NE outskirts of Gelligaer **171(ST:134971)**
N of B4254. N of Caerphilly.
A square, stone auxiliary fort of 1.4ha, housing 500
men, it stands just SE of its 1st-century earth/timber
predecessor of 2.2ha. It had the standard layout of
2nd/3rd century forts: 4 stone walls backed by earth
ramparts, and towers at corners as well as spaced
along the sides. There were 4 gates, each with 2 portals and a guard-room at either side. A typical HQ
stood in the centre, with 6 barracks that in, as well
as a commandant's house, granaries and a bath-house
in an annexe on the SE. A ditch ran in front of 2 of the
gates, and there must have been wooden bridges
here. The site seems to have been in use until the 4th
century. The defences are visible today as earthen
mounds. Finds in the National Museum of Wales,
Cardiff.

Goat's Cave Cave-dwelling
(Paviland Cave) *Old Stone Age*
Paviland **159(SS:437858)**
In cliffs of Gower peninsula SE of Worms Head.
Reached from sands at low tide; hard to get to, and
you can be trapped by incoming tides.
This deep cleft in the rocks is one of the most
important sites for early British prehistory, as well as
for the history of British archaeology. It was here that
Dean Buckland, excavating in 1823, encountered
bones of Ice Age fauna (hyena, cave bear, woolly rhinoceros, mammoth, aurochs, reindeer and horse),
together with a headless human skeleton in a deposit
coloured red with iron oxide. Since it was impossible
at that time to envisage an association of humans
with extinct fauna, he decided that the beasts had
been drowned in the biblical Flood, whereas the
burial was a later intrusion of a Romano-British lady –
the famous 'Red Lady of Paviland'.

We now know that the skeleton is, in fact, that of a
young man, and it has been dated by radiocarbon to
c. 16,510 BC. He was in a shallow grave beside the skull
of a mammoth, and was accompanied by an ivory
armlet, a necklace of pierced teeth and shells, and a
handful of periwinkles. The cave also yielded hundreds of stone implements from an occupation dated
to *c.* 26,650 BC. At that time, it was separated from the
sea by a plain, and, facing s, would have afforded
excellent views to Exmoor, Lundy and over the Bristol Channel area. Even at the time of maximum glacial advance, ice never covered the Gower: it stopped
at Swansea Bay and Cardiff. The cave is next to a
ravine giving access to the Gower plateau, and was
probably a base camp – in fact, it is one of the principal sites of this period in Britain. It was later used in
the Middle and New Stone Ages, and in Roman times.

Maen Ceti (Arthur's Stone)
Chambered Tomb *
New Stone Age
SW of Llanrhidian, Gower
peninsula **159(SS:49105)**
Just NE of Reynoldston on Cefn Bryn.
An unusual megalithic tomb, it comprises a
bisected chamber, built of 10 uprights, 4 of which
support a huge glacial boulder as a capstone; originally weighing above 30 tons (though part is now broken off), it is over 2m thick and 4m long. There is no
trace of a mound, but some think that the chamber
stood at the centre of a ring cairn, 23m in diameter.
The name is derived from a legend that Arthur, out
walking near Llanelli, found a stone in his shoe and
threw it towards the Gower peninsula. Unexcavated.

Parc Le Breos Cwm Chambered
Long Barrow *
New Stone Age
Penmaen, Gower peninsula **159(SS:537898)**
N of Oxwich Bay, and A4118. Near Cat Hole (qv).
A transepted gallery tomb of Severn – Cotswold
type, it is a wedge-shaped cairn built of thin slabs of
drystone, and has a horned forecourt on the s end,
leading to a long gallery with 2 pairs of chambers on
either side. A couple of dozen people were found,
together with potsherds, and the tomb clearly was in
use for a long period. The capstones have disappeared.

St Lythans (Maes y Felin)
Chambered Long Barrow
New Stone Age
SW of St Lythans and Cardiff **171(ST:101723)**
S of road 1.2km SW of St Lythans village. Signposted.
Leaflet available. Close to Tinkinswood (qv).
Also known as *Gwâl-y-Filiart* ('the greyhound
bitch's kennel'), the tomb stands in fine countryside.
It comprises 3 great mudstone uprights supporting a
huge capstone. Only slight traces remain of the
mound that was probably 27m long; the rectangular
chamber stood at its E end. Some human remains and
coarse potsherds are recorded. On Midsummer's Eve
the capstone is said to whirl round 3 times and the
stones all go to bathe in the river. The field was
thought to be cursed, and it was said that the stones
would grant wishes whispered to them on Hal-
lowe'en.

Tinkinswood Chambered Barrow *
New Stone Age
w of Cardiff **171(ST:092733)**
Just S of A48. Signposted. Leaflet available. Close to
St Lythans (qv).
A well-restored, wedge-shaped Severn – Cotswold

Above: ***St Lythans Chambered Long Barrow***. *New Stone Age*

Below: ***Tinkinswood Chambered Barrow***. *New Stone Age*

mound, 40m long and edged in drystone walling, it has a burial chamber of 5 large slabs at one end under a 50-ton capstone, the biggest in Britain: it would have required at least 200 people to move it. The chamber contained at least 50 people, including 8 children, together with flint tools, pottery and the bones of sheep, pigs and cattle. Behind the chamber is an enigmatic stone-lined pit in the mound. Fragments of beakers imply that the tomb was in use until *c.* 2000 BC. The stones are said to be women turned to stone for dancing on Sunday; and there is a legend that if you sleep here on nights preceding May Day, St John's Day or Midwinter's Day, you will either die, go insane or become a poet!

GWENT

Caerleon Legionary Fort*   *Roman*
On sw edge of Caerleon   **171(ST:339906)**
NE of Newport. By the B4326. Guidebook available.

Isca Silurum, for 300 years the home of the 2nd Augustan Legion, was with Chester (p. 169) and York (p. 211) one of the permanent legionary fortresses of Britain. Housing 5000 or 6000 men, it covered 21ha and had a standard layout. The original (*c.* AD 75) earthen ramparts were strengthened with a stone revetment in the 2nd century AD, when the interior buildings were also built in masonry. The best-exposed area of foundations is in Prysg Field (at the junction of the sw and nw walls) where one can see a number of round army ovens and the square cook-houses that replaced them. There are also the remains of 4 (out of a total 64) barrack blocks, divided into 12 pairs of small rooms, each pair for 6 legionaries, with larger rooms at the nw end for the centurion. Each block held a *centuria* of 80 men.

Other features found at Caerleon include granaries; cemeteries outside the fort; and a massive quay beside the river Usk – ships of 1.6m draught could come alongside at high tide. By the Bull Inn, recent excavations have uncovered a fine legionary bathhouse with hypocaust rooms: this is now housed in a protective building.

The most impressive feature is the great amphitheatre, built *c.* AD 80, which could have held 6000 people. The only completely excavated example in Britain, it was hollowed out of the hillside, with high earthworks all around, interrupted by 8 entrances. The theatre was used not only for entertainment but also for drilling, military displays and gladiatorial combats.

The fort was still in use in *c.* AD 345 when the final rebuilding took place. There is a legend that Arthur was crowned here. There is a small museum by the church, and other finds are in the National Museum of Wales, Cardiff.

Caerwent Town*   *Roman*
Caerwent   **171(ST:469905)**
On A48 some 8km wsw of Chepstow. The present village is built on the site. Guidebook available.

The tribal capital *Venta Silurum* ('market town of the Silures') was founded *c.* AD 75 when the tribe had been subdued and had submitted to Roman administration. Its walls – originally an earth rampart with ditch, replaced by stone in the late 2nd or early 3rd century – enclosed 18ha, with buildings in a regular grid of 20 insulae, with a forum, basilica, baths, temples and a small amphitheatre. The 4 walls may have been 8m high: the best-preserved and highest (5m) stretches remain on the w and s. Further defence was provided by 2 external ditches.

Apart from the walls, the principal visible remains are the foundations of some Roman houses and shops to the w of the forum, at Pound Lane; and a small octagonal Romano-Celtic temple outside the E wall, by a caravan site. The houses at Caerwent were

Caerleon Legionary Fort. This amphitheatre for the 2nd Legion would have held 6000 men on wooden benches. Built in AD 80 it was used for parades and exercises as well as entertainments

Above: **Caerwent**. *Excavation of the Roman town of* Venta Silurum

Right: *Plan of* **Caerwent** (Venta Silurum)*, showing both Roman and modern foundations*

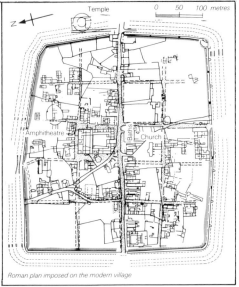

Roman plan imposed on the modern village

small and simple, modestly equipped: mosaics and hypocaust were rare, bath-houses even rarer. The town was occupied until the 4th century.

Many finds are in Newport Museum and the National Museum of Wales, Cardiff, but some fragments can be seen in Caerwent church.

Harold's Stones Standing Stones   *Bronze Age?*
Trelleck   **162(SO:499052)**
s of Monmouth. Just w of B4293.

A trio of tall, pointed stones stand, leaning at different angles, in a 12m alignment in a field at Trelleck ('village of stones'). The central stone has been shaped, and has 2 large cupmarks on its s face. The stones are an enigma, and perhaps form part of a once larger monument. They are said to be immovable, and to have been thrown from Trelleck Beacon (1.3km e) by Jack O'Kent and the Devil, in a throwing competition. The stones' name derives from a tale that they commemorate a battle won by King Harold. In Trelleck church, there is a fine carving of them on a 17th-century sundial.

GWYNEDD

Bachwen Chambered Tomb   *New Stone Age*
Clynnogfawr   **115(SH:407495)**
Near the sea, w of the A499 at Clynnogfawr. Approached by a track s from Bachwen.

Now surrounded by railings, this probable portal dolmen has 4 uprights supporting a large 3-sided capstone. There are over 100 small cupmarks on the top of this slab, with 8 more on its e side. Two grooves each link 3 cups.

Caer Euni Hillfort and
Ring Cairn   *Iron/Bronze Ages*
Llandderfel   **125(SJ:000413 hillfort)**
On a high ridge above A494, sw of its junction with A5.

The fort comprises a long, narrow oval enclosure with a stone rampart, a ditch, and a counterscarp. Some of the stonework is fused on the w side. There are entrances on the s and ne, and traces of about

Harold's Stones Standing Stones*. Bronze Age*

25 hut-circles, An obsolete crossbank in the interior marks the boundary of an earlier fort. A fine kerb circle and ring cairn can be seen nearby (SJ:993410).

Caer Gai Fort *Roman*
NW of Llanuwchllyn **125(SH:877314)**
Just NW of A494. Near s end of Lake Bala (Llyn Tegid).

Superbly located on a spur in a valley, this fort of 1.7ha has been levelled inside, but its SW and SE sides are impressive from the outside. It was occupied from *c.* AD 75 until *c.* 130, but its timber buildings were never recast in stone.

Caerhun Fort *Roman*
Caerhun **115(SH:776704)**
s of Conwy. Overlooking the Conwy valley between B5106 (to w) and A470 (to E).

The fort of *Canovium* was a bridgehead in hostile territory; it was built in the late 1st century AD, and the timber replaced by stone in *c.* 150. The fort was destroyed 50 years later, and occupied only sporadically afterwards until the 4th century. The churchyard now covers the NE section. Excavations revealed a bath-house outside to the E, a large *vicus* and a jetty and dock by the river. There was a Roman road from Caerhun to Caernarfon which can be followed over moorland for a few kilometres.

Caernarfon Fort. This fort of Segontium, established for an auxiliary regiment in about AD 78, was rebuilt in stone a century later. The approach to the regimental strongroom

Capel Garmon Chambered Long Barrow. New Stone Age

Caernarfon Fort*
Caernarfon   *Roman*   **115(SH:485625)**
On the SE outskirts of Caernarfon, by A4085.
Booklet available at site museum.

Towards the end of its occupation, *Segontium* was an advanced base for the Irish Sea fleet to protect against raiders. It was also a cavalry barracks, and guarded nearby copper deposits of considerable value. Originally an auxiliary fort, founded *c.* AD 78, it was repeatedly abandoned and rebuilt according to need. Occupation lasted until *c.* AD 383.

Nearby (SH:482624) is Hen Waliau, an enigmatic 3rd-century stonewalled enclosure that was either a storage depot for the fort, or a means of protecting the harbour from a strategic height.

Capel Garmon Chambered
Long Barrow*
SE of Llanrwst   *New Stone Age*   **116(SH:818542)**
Just E of Betws-y-Coed and just NE of A5. Signposted.
Leaflet available.

A well-preserved and carefully renovated monument, it is the best-documented Severn–Cotswold tomb in North Wales. The wedge-shaped cairn, surrounded by a revetment wall, has well-developed horns and a deep forecourt at the E end, but this is a false entrance. A passage led from the S side to a rectangular antechamber, from which a round chamber opens at either side. All is now open to the sky except the western chamber, which was used as a stable in the last century and is still covered by a huge capstone. Little was found in the site thanks to much disturbance, but bones, potsherds and flints were recovered, including beaker fragments; and pieces of white quartz were found scattered in front of the false entrance.

Carneddau Hengwm Chambered
Long Barrows*
Llanaber   *New Stone Age*   **124(SH:614205)**
Between Barmouth (to S) and Harlech (to N). Just SE of Dyffryn Ardudwy (qv). 4km NNE of Llanaber, and E of A496.

At an altitude of 261m on moorland stand 2 long barrows, side by side. The northern mound is 33m long, and has a burial chamber – possibly 2 – at the E end, and another set into the side. There is a large capstone on the W. The larger southern barrow, 57m long, is probably a multi-period monument. It has a short passage leading from the N to a small chamber in the centre; at the E end are 2 chambers, one of which is a portal dolmen with 3 tall uprights (the capstone has fallen behind them) somewhat resembling Pentre Ifan *(qv)*. On moorland nearby, to the NE, are the sparse remains of 2 stone circles, the Ffridd Newydd rings (SH:616213), now barely visible. There are other rings nearby, and many axes and flakes from Craig Lwyd *(see* Druid's Circle).

Carn Fadrun Hillfort and
Settlement
NE of Llaniestyn W of Pwllheli   *Iron Age*   **123(SH:280352)**
On summit of hill dominating the Lleyn peninsula. Lane N from Llaniestyn, then steep and strenuous climb; stout boots required.

A triangular area of 5ha, enclosed by a stone wall, was subsequently extended to over 10ha by the annexing of a rectangular area to the N. The wall still stands to a height of 2m in places, and there are entrances on N and S from which ancient trackways lead down the hill. There are some round and oblong hut-foundations inside the fort, many more on the hill slopes, a well in the annexe, and even a Bronze

Dyffryn Ardudwy Chambered Long Barrow. *New Stone Age*

Age stone cist near the early wall in the fort's centre. The site is unexcavated and undated, but it is thought that the N annexe may be late Roman.

Conwy Mountain (Mynydd y Dref) Hillfort
Conwy   *Iron Age*
    115(SH:760778)
Just w of Conwy, above and to s of A55.

This oblong fort of 3ha was protected by a steep slope to the N, and by a stone wall on other sides, enclosing about 60 hut-circles, a dense settlement. There is an entrance on the s, and a separate enclosure on the sw containing another 6 huts. Saddle querns were found in some numbers at the site.

Dinas Dinorwig Hillfort
Iron Age
Just SE of Llanddeiniolen, NE of
Caernarfon   **115(SH:549653)**
SE of B4366, w of B4547, on ridge above tributary of the Seiont. Part tree-covered.

The impressive 'fort of the Ordovices' has a fine location and comprises 1.2ha enclosed by a massive inner wall, and 2 great banks of earth and rubble. The latter are crossed obliquely by a track leading to a gateway in the stone wall. The site is thought to span the whole of the Iron Age.

Druid's Circle Stone Circle *
Bronze Age
s of Penmaenmawr, sw of Conwy and E of
Llanfairfechan.   **115(SH:722747)**
On low saddle above and s of A55. Craig Lwyd axe factory lies just to E.

The circle of 'Meini Hirion' stands on an exposed upland moor above Conwy Bay, alongside an ancient trackway – indeed, at the junction of several tracks. In this splendid setting are 30 large granite blocks

unevenly spaced on a worn elliptical bank of earth and stones, about 26m across. An entrance on the sw is marked by a gap in the bank and by 2 large portal stones. The interior was found by excavators to contain a scatter of stones over several cremations: at the centre was a tiny cist containing a food vessel and a cremated 10-year-old; another cist nearby held the same, together with a bronze knife; while a 3rd child cremation in a pit was linked to a hole lined with sandstone whetstones. It is thought by some scholars that these children were sacrifices or dedicatory offerings rather than simple burials. The monument, very conspicuous on its ridge, is thought to date to *c.* 2100 BC. One of its stones is reputed to bend over towards anyone who swears near it.

There are other monuments nearby, including the Craig Lwyd axe factory. To the E is a 5-stone ring (SH:725747) that had a dense concentration of white quartz pebbles. To the w is a ring cairn (SH:721745) dating to *c.*1780 BC, which contained the cremated remains of a young woman.

Dyffryn Ardudwy Chambered Long Barrow *
New Stone Age
Just SE of Llanenddwyn, s of
Harlech   **124(SH:589229)**
On the E side of A496 on hillside above sea. Just NW of Carneddau Hengwm (qv). Signposted. Leaflet available.

An unusual monument, it was built (according to pollen analysis) in a clearing amid thick hazel woods, and comprises 2 separate burial chambers, 8.6m apart, on a bed of white boulders. Their wedge-shaped cairn has almost disappeared. The smaller of the 2, to the w, was built 1st, in the mid-3rd millennium BC, in a small round mound. It is rectangular in shape, with 2 portal stones and a single capstone. Soon afterwards the larger chamber was constructed, and a new cairn enclosed both, with a forecourt on the E. Finds (pottery, stone pendants, etc.) are in the National Museum of Wales, Cardiff.

Garn Boduan Hillfort
Boduan
Iron Age/Roman
123(SH:311394)

Just SE of Nefyn, and N of junction between A497 and B4354. On isolated, partly tree-covered hill.

A 10ha enclosure on this rocky summit – containing some useful springs – was surrounded by a massive wall, but no ditch; it was later extended for 4ha down the western slope by an even more massive wall that still stands up to 2m high in places. There are entrances on the SE and NE, and the enclosure contains 168 hut-circles of upright slabs and laid stones. The summit also has a small fort that seems to date to the late Roman period and the early Middle Ages. The site is traditionally linked to Buan, who lived in the 7th century AD.

Hendre Waelod Chambered
Long Barrow*
SE of Conwy
New Stone Age
115(SH:793748)

SW of Colwyn Bay, above river. W of A470, near railway.

This fine portal dolmen, also known as *Allor Moloch*, has few surviving traces of its cairn. A low chamber has 2 tall portal stones, and the entrance is blocked by a thin slab that rises to the capstone, a huge block now partly resting on the ground.

Maen-y-Bardd Chambered
Long Barrow*
Caerhun
New Stone Age
115(SH:740718)

W of Roewen, SW of Conwy. Lies 300m above river Conwy. Take minor road W from B5106 to Roewen, then track.

The 'poet's stone' still has a few traces of its cairn; there is a rectangular chamber of 4 uprights and a large capstone. A burial cist in a mound stands nearby (SH:741718) and there are 2 standing stones to the W: one at SH:736716, and another, Ffon-y-Cawr (the 'giant's stick'), at SH:738717. Another pair stands at SH:742718.

Pen y Gaer Hillfort with
Chevaux-de-frise*
Llanbedr-y-Cennin
Iron Age
115(SH:750693)

S of Conwy. High above Llanbedr-y-Cennin on lane leading W from B5106.

The fort, of at least 2 periods, has 2 massive stone walls, with a 3rd on the S and N, and an entrance on the W. Its principal points of interest are the 2 areas of *chevaux-de-frise* to the W and S: these comprise densely packed groups of pointed stones erected to impede attack (*see also* Dreva Craig, p. 231, and Cademuir Hill, p. 231, in Scotland). The southern group lies between the central and outer ramparts, which implies that it predates the latter. Excavation revealed 20 huts inside and between the ramparts; one of them had been used for iron-working.

Tan-y-Muriau Chambered
Long Barrow*
NE of Aberdaron
New Stone Age
123(SH:238288)

At the end of the Lleyn peninsula near the NW end of Porth Neigwl. S of B4413.

Much of the cairn has gone, but a portal dolmen chamber remains at the NW end under a massive capstone. Further SE was a side chamber, entered from the W, and beyond here the mound is well preserved for another 27m. It is thought that the portal dolmen may have been covered by a smaller cairn that was subsequently extended.

Tomen-y-Mur Fort*
N of Trawsfynydd, S of Ffestiniog
Roman
124(SH:707387)

E of A470, by lane and gated track from Trawsfynydd.

This 1.7ha auxiliary fort, in the middle of nowhere, has magnificent views to the sea and the mountains. Built by Agricola in AD 78, it was slightly reduced in size in c. 110, when the walls were rebuilt in stone, and it was finally abandoned c.140. The site is particularly notable for its small 'amphitheatre' to the NE, the only example known at an auxiliary fort and built perhaps to compensate for the remote location. A Norman *motte*, built astride a rampart, provides a useful platform for seeing the layout of the site. Various earthworks round the fort have been interpreted as practice camps (NW), a *vicus* and bathhouse (SE), an unfinished levelled parade ground (E) and perhaps burial mounds near the amphitheatre (NE).

Tre'r Ceiri Hillfort*
Llanaelhaearn
Iron Age
123(SH:373446)

Crowns easternmost of 3 peaks of Yr Eifl. 2km W of Llanaelhaearn and A499. Steep climb.

One of the most spectacular and impressive British hillforts, the 'town of the giants', at an altitude of 450m, was a stronghold of the Ordovices. Since it follows the summit, it is a very long and narrow oval; the fine stone ditchless rampart, still up to 4m high, is largely intact and has ramps leading up to a walkway protected by a parapet. There are 2 large and 3 minor gateways; inside there are remains of about 150 stone-built huts – round (Iron Age), D-shaped, and rectangular (Roman); outside there are enclosures and terracing. Some believe that the site was a communal summer centre for pastoralists from lowland farmsteads.

POWYS

Brecon Gaer Fort*
W of Brecon
Roman
160(SO:003297)

Just N of A40 and the river Usk, by its confluence with the Afon Yscir. Pamphlet available.

This key fort of 3ha, built c. AD 80 at the junction of several important roads, was occupied by a garrison of 500 cavalry. The original earth and timber defences were replaced by stone c. 140. Military occupation lasted until c. 200, and the fort was used again c.300. It had the usual HQ, a bath-house in the barrack area, and an extensive civil settlement outside the N gate. Some of the walls still stand up to 3m in height, and the most substantial visible remains are those of the S gate, which has a guard-chamber and walls still 2m high, on either side of a double carriageway. Finds in Brecknock Museum, Brecon.

Brecon Gaer Fort. *Built* c. AD *80, this Roman fort overlooks the Usk*

The Breiddin Hillfort*   *Late Bronze/Iron Ages*
Bausley, w of Shrewsbury   **126(SJ:292144)**
Just inside Welsh border on line of Offa's Dyke.
Within triangle of A483, A458 and B4393.

A multiple enclosure in a superb location on a jagged volcanic summit overlooking the Severn, at an altitude of 365m, it has a double rampart that uses the natural contours for defence. Radiocarbon-dating has shown that the site was first fortified with a box rampart in the 9th century BC; this was destroyed by fire. Later, a massive rampart with stone revetments was built in the Iron Age. After the arrival of the Romans, the fort was abandoned, and not reoccupied until the late 2nd century AD. This occupation lasted 2 or 3 centuries. There is a stone-lined entrance on the E, with traces of Celtic fields and a small enclosure outside (SJ:298140). Inside the fort, there are a number of Iron Age hut-circles that were subsequently replaced by oblong structures.

Burfa Camp Hillfort   *Iron Age*
N of Kington   **148(SO:285610)**
Just inside Welsh border, sw of Presteigne. Wooded
hill just NW of B4362 at Knill.

A large fort of 8ha with multiple ramparts (with stone revetments) and ditches; there is an entrance on the NE and a bigger one on the NW, which has an extra line of defence forming a barbican.

Castell Collen Fort   *Roman*
Just NW of Llandrindod Wells   **147(SO:055628)**
On w bank of river Ithon, w of A483, N of A4081.

One of the best-preserved Roman forts in Wales, it was reduced in size (from 2 to 1.5ha) in the early 4th century. Still to be seen is the layout of the ramparts,

HQ, granary and bath-house. The early timber buildings of AD 78 were rebuilt in stone in the mid-2nd century.

Castell Dinas Hillfort   *Iron Age*
SE of Talgarth   **161(SO:179301)**
On spur E of A479, immediately N of Tŷ-isaf (qv).

A strong fort with massive double ramparts at its more vulnerable S side, and an entrance on the N. The site was bisected by a crossbank, and the Normans subsequently built a *motte* within the enclosure.

Cefn Carnedd Hillfort   *Iron Age*
WSW of Newtown   **136(SO:016900)**
NW of Llandinam; w of A470. Roman road goes past
to the N. Stiff climb.

Superbly located on an oval, narrow hilltop at an altitude of 277m, this strong fort of 6ha required no defences on the steep SE side, but had a triple rampart on the N side. There are entrances on NE and SW. Several phases are represented, the earliest being a small fort (1.6ha) at the SW end.

Cerrig Duon Stone Circle
and Stone Rows*   *Bronze Age*
N of Abercraf, sw of Sennybridge   **160(SN:852206)**
On w slopes of narrow valley of Upper Tawe. Easily
accessible from small road running N up valley
from A4067.

An inconspicuous, egg-shaped circle on a low hill, it is about 18m across and comprises 22 small stones, regularly spaced. It is dominated by a great block of sandstone (*Maen Mawr*, 'large stone'), 9m to the N and almost 2m high, which would have needed 40 or 50 people to move it. There are 2 tiny stones in line with it, just to the N, on the axis of the circle; it has been suggested that this arrangement marks the rising of the star Arcturus in 1950 BC, but *Maen Mawr* and its consorts are more likely to be simple directional markers. To the NE of the circle is a short tapering avenue of low stones, 46m long and 5m wide at the near end. It neither reaches the ring nor even leads towards it, but follows the easiest line of approach up the hillside from the river below. Finally, 1km to the N is another standing stone (SN:855215) set with its thin side pointing towards the circle.

Crug Hywell (Crucywel) Hillfort
Iron Age
W of Llanbedr, NW of Abergavenny **161(SO:225206)**
On Table Mountain, above small road sw to Crickhowell.

Located at 457m, near the end of a short spur, this small (0.8ha) but well-preserved fort is somewhat pear-shaped. It has a stone rampart and ditch with a counterscarp bank, and an entrance on the W side.

Dan-yr-Ogof Cave-dwelling with Dioramas
Bronze Age/Roman
NE of Abercraf **160(SN:838161)**
Just w of A4067, not far from Cerrig Duon (qv).

The main cave is visited for its spectacular stalagmitic formations, but the 'bone cave' above was occupied in Bronze Age and Roman times–finds included a bronze razor, a sword blade and a gold bead–and now houses dioramas of prehistory, featuring such things as cave-bears, sabre-toothed tigers and a family group in the Bronze Age.

Ffridd Faldwyn Hillfort *
Bronze/Iron Ages
Just NW of Montgomery **137(SO:216970)**
Approached by road to Llandyssil. sw of B4385.

This summit was occupied in the New Stone Age, but the 1st fortification was in the late Bronze Age. The first phase in this complex site was a simple palisaded enclosure, which was replaced by a box rampart. A series of twin portal gates were added; subsequently there was a fire at the site. In the early 1st century BC, the fort was extended to 4ha and the defences were strengthened with a stone revetted bank and ditch.

Gwernvale Chambered Long Barrow
New Stone Age
Crickhowell **161(SO:211192)**
Immediately s of A40. 1.6km NW of Crickhowell. Between road and river Usk. Close to Crug Hywell (qv).

Before the tomb was built, there was occupation here in the New Stone Age (querns, cereals, fruit seeds and hazel-shells have been found, dating to 3100 BC), the Middle Stone Age (dated to 4945 BC) and perhaps even the late Old Stone Age. The tomb was probably built at the end of the 4th millennium BC; it is a trapezoidal cairn, over 45m long, on an ESE/WNW axis. There is a horned forecourt at the E end, with a doubled revetment wall and a false portal. It had 3 lateral chambers–2 entered from the s, one from the N–and a 4th chamber or cist was also built in the s side. All were carefully blocked. Due to much disturbance–the A40 used to pass over the N side of the mound, and none of the capstones has survived *in situ*–skeletal material was found only in one chamber, but there was a great deal of pottery. The tomb was probably closed just after 2440 BC

Pen y Crug Hillfort
Iron Age
Fennifach **160(SO:029303)**
2km NW of Brecon on moorland hilltop on sw side of B4520. Path up from N outskirts of Brecon.

A moorland fort with triple bank-and-ditch defences (a 4th set in places) and a counterscarp bank, with an entrance on the SE. An annexe outside the entrance may be the remains of an earlier fort.

Pipton Long Barrow *
New Stone Age
SW of Pipton and Three Cocks **161(SO:160372)**
NE of Brecon on spur above river Wye. In centre of triangle formed by A479, A4079 and A438.

A wedge-shaped cairn, 30m long, it has a drystone revetment and a horned forecourt/false portal at the N end. There are 2 chambers on the w side: one is reached via a long, curved passage and an antechamber, the other having no passage. Apart from human remains, bones of cattle were found, including oxhorn cores in ritual positions in the forecourt.

Tŷ Illtud Chambered Barrow *
New Stone Age
Llanhamlach, SE of Brecon **161(SO:098264)**
On slopes to SE of Llanhamlach and E of A40. Side road E to Pennorth and Llangasty-Talyllyn.

The 'house of St Illtud' (a Welsh saint) is an oval cairn with a rectangular forecourt on the N. Near the centre of the mound is a rectangular chamber with 3 uprights and a low capstone. The uprights are decorated with faint medieval engravings–crosses, lozenges, dates–which have been attributed to shepherds.

Tŷ-isaf Chambered Long Barrow *
New Stone Age
Talgarth **161(SO:182291)**
7km SE of Talgarth and just E of A479. On side road where it crosses the Rhian Goll river.

This wedge-shaped cairn, 30m long, has a double drystone revetment with a horned forecourt and a false entrance on the N. Halfway down the mound's length, there is a chamber at either side. The western chamber contained remains of 17 people together with pottery, arrowheads and a polished stone axe; the eastern had one skeleton and remains of 6 bowls, plus 2 more skeletons in the passage. The southern end of the barrow has another rectangular chamber that housed a cremation urn of the Bronze Age. Between here and the principal chambers is the site's most unusual feature: an oval mound is incorporated into the long cairn, with a double drystone wall around it and a long entrance passage leading into a transepted chamber. Remains of several people were found here, and debate still goes on as to which of the 2 cairns was built first.

Y Pigwn Temporary Forts
Roman
SE of Llandovery **160(SN:828312)**
The forts straddle the Dyfed/Powys border, on crest of NW scarp of Black Mountain. Reached by Roman road from Llandovery or by road s from Halfway on A40.

These 2 marching camps were used early in the Roman campaigns in Wales, and probably only for a season or two. One of them partly overlies the other; the earlier is the larger (15ha). Outlines can still be seen in the ditches. A Roman road runs E from here to the cavalry fort of Brecon Gaer (qv). Near the camps are 2 inconspicuous stone rings on Trecastle mountain (SN:833311), closely adjacent to each other, but very different in size. Four stones form an alignment a little further sw.

Map 1 THE SOUTH-EAST, WESSEX, THE SOUTH-WEST

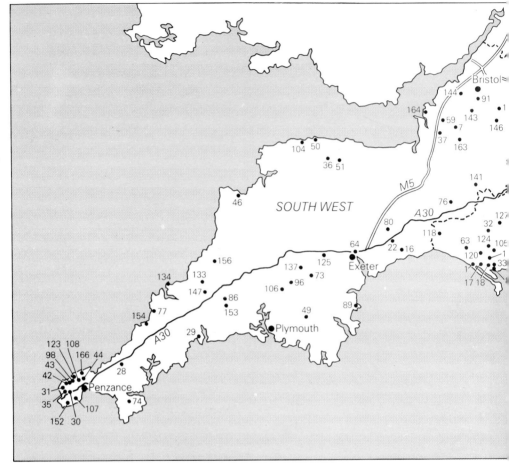

1 Abbotsbury (Iron Age? hillfort)
2 Abinger Common (Middle Stone Age pit dwelling)
3 Addington Park (New Stone Age chambered long barrow)
4 Afton Down (New Stone/Bronze Age long and round barrows)
5 Aldbourne Four Barrows (Bronze Age bell and bowl barrows)
6 Avebury Sanctuary Complex (New Stone Age henge)
7 Aveline's Hole (Old Stone Age cave dwelling)
8 Badbury Rings (Iron Age? hillfort)
9 Barbury Castle (Iron Age hillfort)
10 Bath (Roman town)
11 Battlesbury (Iron Age? hillfort)
12 Beacon Hill (Iron Age hillfort)
13 Bevis's Thumb (New Stone Age long barrow)
14 Bigbury (Iron Age hillfort)
15 Bignor (Roman villa)
16 Blackbury Castle (Iron Age hillfort)
17 Black Down (Bronze Age round barrows)
18 Blackpatch (New Stone Age flint mines)
19 Bokerley Dyke (Roman earthworks)
20 Brading (Roman villa)
21 Bratton Castle (New Stone/Iron Age? hillfort)
22 Broad Down Barrows (Bronze Age cemetery)
23 Buckland Rings (Iron Age fort)
24 Bury Hill (Iron Age hillfort)
25 Butser (Iron Age hillfort)
26 Caburn (Iron Age hillfort)
27 Caesar's Camp (Iron Age fort)
28 Carn Brea (New Stone/Iron Age hillfort)
29 Carn Euny (Iron Age village and fogou)
30 Carn Gluze (Bronze Age barrow)

31 Castle Dore (Iron Age hillfort)
32 Cerne Giant (Romano-British? hill-figure)
33 Chalbury (Iron Age hillfort)
34 Chanctonbury Ring (Iron Age and Roman hillfort and dykes)
35 Chapel Euny (Bronze Age chambered barrow)
36 Chapman Barrows and Long Stone (Bronze Age cemetery)
37 Cheddar (Old Stone Age cave dwellings)
38 The Chestnuts (New Stone Age chambered tomb)
39 Chichester (Iron Age entrenchments)
40 Chichester (Roman town)
41 Chillerton Down (Iron Age? fort)
42 Chun Castle (Iron Age hillfort)
43 Chun Quoit (New Stone Age chambered tomb)
44 Chysauster (Iron Age/Romano-British village)
45 Cissbury (New Stone/Iron Age hillfort and flint mines)
46 Clovelly Dykes (Iron Age? enclosure)
47 Coldrum (New Stone Age chambered tomb)
48 Combe Hill (New Stone Age causewayed camp)
49 Corringdon Ball (New Stone Age chambered long barrow)
50 Countisbury (Iron Age? promontory fort)
51 Cow Castle (Iron Age? hillfort)
52 Cow Down (Bronze Age round barrows)
54 Crooksbury Common (Bronze Age triple bell barrow)
55 Danebury Ring (Iron Age hillfort)
56 Devil's Dyke (Iron Age hillfort)
57 Devil's Humps (Bronze Age bell and bowl barrows)
58 Devil's Jumps (Bronze Age bell barrows)

59 Dolebury (Iron Age hillfort)
60 Dorset Cursus (New Stone Age)
61 Dover (Roman town)
62 Durrington Walls (New Stone Age henge)
63 Eggardon (Iron Age hillfort)
64 Exeter (Roman city)
65 Farley Heath (Romano-British Temple)
66 Figsbury Rings (Iron Age hillfort)
67 Firle Beacon (New Stone/Bronze Age long and round barrows)
68 Fishbourne (Roman palace)
69 Five Barrows (Bronze Age barrow cemetery)
70 Frensham Common (Bronze Age bowl barrows)
71 Fyfield and Overton Downs (Iron Age 'Celtic fields')
72 Giant's Cave (New Stone Age chambered long barrow)
73 Grimspound (Bronze Age walled settlement)
74 Halligye (Iron Age fogou)
75 Hambledon (New Stone/Iron Age hillfort and causewayed camp)
76 Ham Hill (Iron Age/Roman hillfort)
77 Harlyn Bay (Iron Age cemetery)
78 Harrow Hill (New Stone/Iron Age flint mines and fortlet)
79 Hascombe Hill (Iron Age hillfort)
80 Hembury (New Stone/Iron Age/Roman hillfort)
81 Hengistbury Head (Bronze/Iron Age promontory fort)
82 High Rocks (Middle Stone/New Stone/Iron Age hillfort and rock shelters)
83 Hod Hill (Iron Age/Roman hillfort)
84 Hollingbury (Iron Age hillfort)
85 Holtye (Roman road)
86 The Hurlers (Bronze Age stone circles)

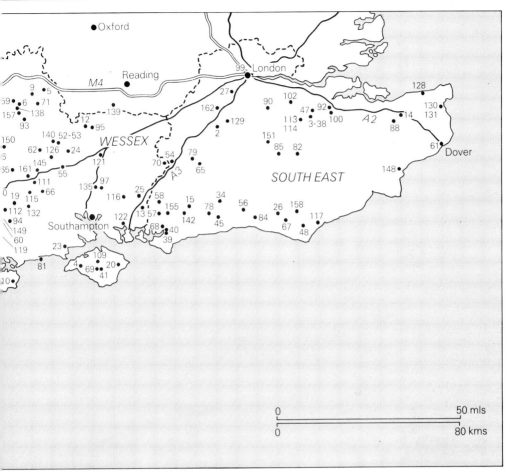

Oxford

Reading

M4

London

Dover

WESSEX

SOUTH EAST

Southampton

A2

A3

0				50 mls
0				80 kms

87 Jordan Hill (Roman temple)
88 Julliberrie's Grave (New Stone Age long barrow)
89 Kents Cavern (Old Stone Age cave-dwelling)
90 Keston Tombs (Roman cemetery)
91 Keynsham (Roman villa)
92 Kit's Coty House (New Stone Age chambered tomb)
93 Knap Hill (New Stone Age causewayed camp)
94 Knowlton Circles (New Stone Age henge)
95 Ladle Hill (Iron Age? hillfort)
96 Lakehead Hill (Bronze Age stone cists)
97 Lamborough (New Stone Age long barrow)
98 Lanyon Quoit (New Stone Age chambered long barrow)
99 Londinium (Roman city)
100 Lower Kit's Coty House (New Stone Age chambered tomb)
101 Lugbury (New Stone Age long barrow)
102 Lullingstone (Roman villa)
103 Maiden Castle (New Stone/Iron Age/Roman hillfort)
104 Martinhoe (Roman fortlet)
105 Maumbury Rings (New Stone Age/Roman henge and amphitheatre)
106 Merrivale (Bronze Age stone rows)
107 Merry Maidens (Bronze Age stone circle)
108 Mulfra Quoit (New Stone Age chambered tomb)
109 Newport (Roman villa)
110 Nine Barrows (New Stone/Bronze Age long and round barrows)
111 Normanton Down (New Stone/Bronze Age barrow cemetery)
112 Oakley Down (Bronze Age round barrows)
113 Oldbury Hill (Iron Age hillfort)

114 Oldbury Hill Rock Shelters (Old Stone Age)
115 Old Sarum (Iron Age/Roman/Medieval hillfort and castle mound)
116 Old Winchester Hill (Iron Age? fort)
117 Pevensey Castle (Roman Fort of the Saxon Shore)
118 Pilsdon Pen (Iron Age hillfort)
119 Pimperne (New Stone Age long barrow)
120 Poor Lot (Bronze Age barrows)
121 Popham Beacons (Bronze Age round barrows)
122 Portchester Castle (Roman Fort of the Saxon Shore)
123 Porthmeor (Romano-British village)
124 Poundbury (Iron Age/Roman hillfort and aqueduct)
125 Prestonbury Castle (Iron Age? hillfort)
126 Quarley Hill (Iron Age? hillfort)
127 Rawlsbury Camp (Iron Age? hillfort)
128 Reculver (Roman Fort of the Saxon Shore)
129 Reigate Heath (Bronze Age round barrows)
130 Richborough (Roman amphitheatre)
131 Richborough (Roman fortresses and monument)
132 Rockbourne (Roman villa)
133 Rough Tor (Bronze/Iron Age hut circles, hillfort, stone circle)
134 The Rumps Cliff Fort (Iron Age promontory fort)
135 St Catherine's Hill (Iron Age hillfort)
136 Scratchbury Camp (Iron Age hillfort)
137 Shovel Down (Bronze Age stone rows)
138 Silbury Hill (New Stone Age mound)
139 Silchester (Romano-British town)
140 Snail Down (Bronze Age barrow cemetery)

141 South Cadbury Castle (New Stone Age/Saxon hillfort)
142 Stane Street (Roman road)
143 Stanton Drew (New Stone Age stone circle)
144 Stokeleigh (Iron Age promontory fort)
145 Stonehenge Sanctuary (New Stone/Bronze Age henge)
146 Stoney Littleton (New Stone Age chambered long barrow)
147 Stripple Stones (New Stone Age? henge)
148 Stutfall Castle (Roman Fort of the Saxon Shore)
149 Thickthorn Down (New Stone Age long barrows)
150 Tilshead Old Ditch (New Stone Age long barrow)
151 Titsey Park (Roman villa)
152 Treen (Iron Age? promontory fort)
153 Trethevy Quoit (New Stone Age chambered tomb)
154 Trevelgue Head (Iron Age promontory fort)
155 The Trundle (New Stone/Iron Age hillfort)
156 Warbstow Bury (Iron Age? hillfort)
157 West Kennet (New Stone Age chambered long barrow)
158 Wilmington Long Man (hill-figure)
159 Windmill Hill (New Stone Age causewayed camp)
160 Winkelbury Hill (Iron Age hillfort)
161 Winterbourne Stoke (New Stone/Bronze Age barrows)
162 Wisley Common (Bronze Age bell barrow)
163 Wookey Hole (Old Stone Age/Roman cave-dwellings)
164 Worlebury Camp (Iron Age hillfort)
165 Yarnbury Castle (Iron Age fort)
166 Zennor Quoit (New Stone Age chambered tomb)

305

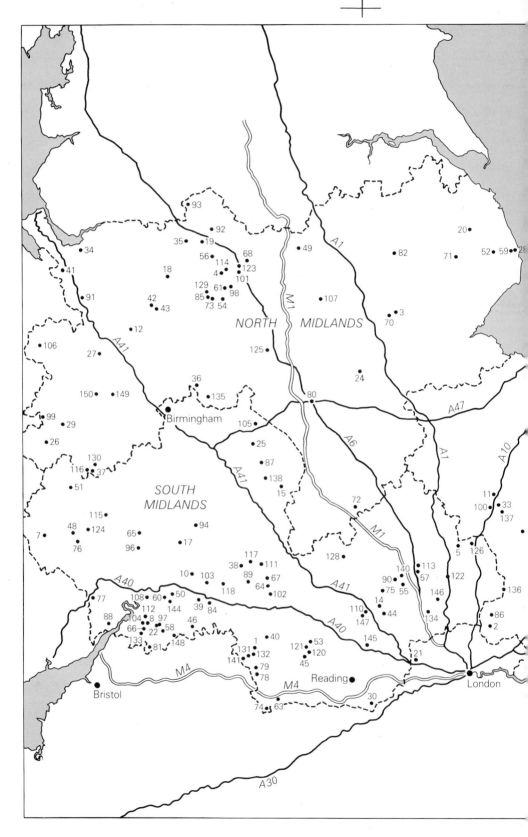

Map 2   EAST ANGLIA, THE SOUTH MIDLANDS, THE NORTH MIDLANDS

50 mls

80 kms

Norwich

ST ANGLIA

1 Alfred's Castle (Iron Age/Roman hillfort)
2 Ambresbury Banks (Iron Age? fort)
3 Ancaster (Roman town)
4 Arbor Low (New Stone/Bronze Age henge and round barrows)
5 Arbury Banks (Iron Age fort)
6 Arminghall (New Stone Age henge)
7 Arthur's Stone (New Stone Age chambered long barrow)
8 Avening (New Stone Age burial chambers)
9 Bartlow Hills (Roman barrows)
10 Belas Knap (New Stone Age chambered long barrow)
11 Belsar's Hill (Iron Age hillfort)
12 Berth Hill (Iron Age? hillfort)
13 Bircham Common (Bronze Age round barrows)
14 Boddington (Iron Age? hillfort)
15 Borough Hill (Iron Age hillfort)
16 Bradwell (Roman fort)
17 Bredon Hill and Conderton (Iron Age hillforts)
18 Bridestones (New Stone Age chambered long barrow)
19 Bull Ring (New Stone/Bronze Age henge and round barrows)
20 Bully Hills (Bronze Age round barrows)
21 Bulstrode (Iron Age? fort)
22 Bulwarks (Iron Age hillfort)
23 Burgh Castle (Roman fort of the Saxon Shore)
24 Burrough Hill (Iron Age hillfort)
25 Burrow Hill (Iron Age hillfort)
26 Bury Ditches (Iron Age? hillfort)
27 Bury Walls (Iron Age? promontory fort)
28 Butterbump (Bronze Age round barrows)
29 Caer Caradoc (Iron Age? hillfort)
30 Caesar's Camp (Iron Age fort)
31 Caister-by-Yarmouth (Roman town)
32 Caistor-by-Norwich (Roman town)
33 Car Dyke Canal (Roman dyke)
34 Castle Ditch (Iron Age fort)
35 Castle Naze (Iron Age? promontory fort)
36 Castle Ring (Iron Age? hillfort)
37 Caynham Camp (Iron Age hillfort)
38 Chastleton (Late Bronze/Iron Age fort)
39 Chedworth (Roman villa)
40 Cherbury Camp (Iron Age fort)
41 Chester (Roman town)
42 Chesterton (Roman fort)
43 Chesterton (Roman town)
44 Cholesbury (Iron Age fort)
45 Churn Farm (Bronze Age round barrow cemetery)
46 Cirencester (Roman town)
47 Colchester (Iron Age/Roman town)
48 Credenhill (Iron Age hillfort)
49 Creswell Crags (Old Stone Age cave-dwellings)
50 Crickley Hill (New Stone/Iron Age hillfort)
51 Croft Ambrey (Iron Age hillfort)
52 Deadmen's Graves (New Stone Age? long barrows)
53 Dyke Hills (Iron Age promontory fort)
54 End Low (Bronze Age round barrows)
55 Five Knolls (New Stone/Bronze Age round barrows)
56 Five Wells (New Stone Age chambered barrow)
57 Galley Hill (New Stone Age/Roman bowl barrows)
58 Gatcombe Lodge (New Stone Age chambered long barrow)
59 Giant's Hills (New Stone Age? long barrow)
60 Great Witcombe (Roman villa)
61 Green Low (Late New Stone Age chambered barrow)
62 Grimes Graves (New Stone Age flint mines)
63 Grimsbury Castle (Iron Age hillfort)
64 Grim's Ditch Running Dyke (Iron Age? earthwork)
65 Herefordshire Beacon (Iron Age hillfort)
66 Hetty Pegler's Tump (New Stone Age chambered long barrow)
67 Hoar Stone (New Stone Age chambered barrow)
68 Hob Hurst's House and Beeley Round Barrows (Bronze Age barrows)
69 Holkham Fort (Iron Age? fort)
70 Honington (Iron Age? hillfort)
71 Horncastle (Roman town)
72 Hunsbury Hill (Iron Age hillfort)
73 Ilam Tops Low (Bronze Age round barrow)
74 Inkpen Beacon (New Stone Age long barrow)
75 Ivinghoe Beacon (Late Bronze/Early Iron Age fort)
76 Kenchester (Roman town)
77 King Arthur's Cave (Old Stone Age/ Roman cave-dwelling)

78 Lambourn (New Stone Age chambered long barrow)
79 Lambourn Seven Barrows (New Stone/ Bronze Age round barrow cemetery)
80 Leicester (Roman city)
81 Leighterton (New Stone Age chambered long barrow)
82 Lincoln (Roman town)
83 Little Cressingham Bronze Age round barrows)
84 Lodge Park (New Stone Age chambered long barrow)
85 Long Low (New Stone Age round barrows)
86 Loughton (Iron Age hillfort)
87 The Lunt Fort (Roman fort)
88 Lydney (Iron Age/Roman hillfort and temple complex)
89 Lyneham (New Stone Age chambered long barrow)
90 Maiden Bower (New Stone/Iron Age fort)
91 Maiden Castle (Iron Age fort)
92 Mam Tor (Bronze/Iron Age hillfort)
93 Melandra Castle (Roman fort)
94 Meon Hill (Iron Age? hillfort)
95 Mersea Mount (Roman barrow)
96 Midsummer Hill (Iron Age hillfort)
97 Minchinhampton Common (Iron Age earthworks)
98 Minninglow (New Stone Age chambered tomb)
99 Mitchell's Fold (Bronze Age stone circle)
100 Moulton Hills (Roman round barrows)
101 Nine Stones Close (Bronze Age stone circle)
102 North Leigh (Roman villa)
103 Notgrove (New Stone Age chambered long barrow)
104 Nympsfield (New Stone Age chambered long barrow) —
105 Oldbury (Iron Age hillfort)
106 Old Oswestry (Iron Age hillfort)
107 Oxton Camp (Iron Age? hillfort)
108 Painswick Beacon (Iron Age? fort)
109 Peddars' Way (Roman road)
110 Pulpit Hill (Iron Age? hillfort)
111 Rainsborough Camp (Iron Age hillfort)
112 Randwick (New Stone Age chambered long barrow)
113 Ravensburgh Castle (Iron Age fort)
114 Ringham Low (New Stone Age chambered long barrow)
115 Risbury (Iron Age? hillfort)
116 Robin Hood's Butt (Bronze Age round barrow)
117 Rollright Stones (Bronze Age stone circle)
118 Salmonsbury (Iron Age fort)
119 Seven Hills (Bronze Age round barrows)
120 Sharpenhoe Clapper (Iron Age? hillfort)
121 Sinodun (Iron Age? hillfort)
122 Six Hills Barrows (Roman mounds)
123 Stanton Moor (New Stone Age stone circle)
124 Sutton Walls (Iron Age hillfort)
125 Swarkestone Lows (Bronze Age round barrows)
126 Therfield Heath (New Stone/Bronze Age barrow cemetery)
127 Thetford Castle (Iron Age hillfort)
128 Thornborough (Roman barrows)
129 Thor's Cave (Old Stone/Iron Age/Roman cave-dwelling)
130 Titterstone Clee (Iron Age hillfort)
131 Uffington Castle (Iron Age? hillfort)
132 Uffington White Horse (Iron Age? hill-figure)
133 Uleybury (Iron Age? hillfort)
134 *Verulamium* (Iron Age/Roman town)
135 Wall (Roman town)
136 Wallbury (Iron Age hillfort)
137 Wandlebury (Iron Age/Roman hillfort)
138 Wappenbury (Iron Age fort)
139 Warham Camp (Iron Age fort)
140 Wauluds Bank (New Stone Age enclosed settlement)
141 Wayland's Smithy (New Stone Age chambered long barrow)
142 Weasenham Plantation (Bronze Age round barrows)
143 West Rudham (New Stone Age long barrows)
144 West Tump (New Stone Age chambered long barrow)
145 West Wycombe (Iron Age? hillfort)
146 Wheathampstead Devil's Dyke (Iron Age earthwork)
147 Whiteleaf (New Stone Age barrows)
148 Windmill Tump (New Stone Age chambered long barrow)
149 The Wrekin (Iron Age hillfort)
150 Wroxeter (Roman town)

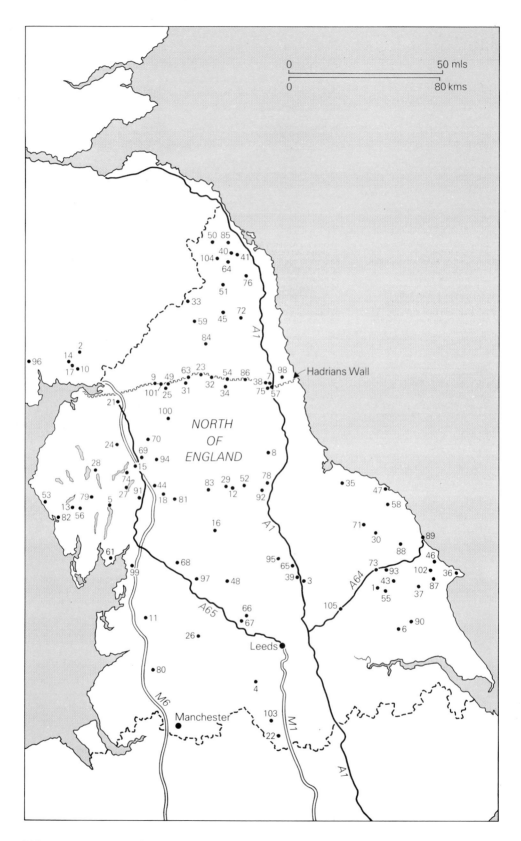

0   50 mls

0   80 kms

Hadrians Wall

NORTH OF ENGLAND

Leeds

Manchester

Map 3 THE NORTH OF ENGLAND AND HADRIAN'S WALL

1 Acklam Wold (Bronze Age round barrows)
2 Airswood Moss (Bronze Age cist in barrow)
3 Aldborough (Roman town)
4 Almondbury (Iron Age hillfort)
5 Ambleside (Roman fort)
6 Arras (Iron Age round barrow cemetery)
7 Benwell (Roman fort)
8 Binchester (Roman fort)
9 Birdoswald (Roman fort)
10 Birrens (Roman fort)
11 Bleasdale Circle (Bronze Age barrow)
12 Bowes (Roman fort)
13 Brats Hill (Bronze Age stone circles)
14 Broomhillbank Hill (Iron Age? hillfort)
15 Brougham (Roman fort)
16 Brough-by-Bainbridge (Roman fort)
17 Burnswark (Iron Age/Roman siege works and fortlet)
18 Burwens (Iron Age/Romano-British settlement)
21 Carlisle (Roman town)
22 Carl Wark (Iron Age hillfort)
23 Carrawburgh (Roman fort)
24 Carrock Fell (Iron Age? hillfort)
25 Carvoran (Roman fort)
26 Castercliff Camp (Late Bronze/Iron Age hillfort)
27 Castle Crag (Iron Age? hillfort)
28 Castlerigg (New Stone/Bronze Age stone circle)
29 Castleton Rigg (Late Bronze/Iron Age settlement)
30 Cawthorn Camps (Roman camps)
31 Chesterholm (Roman fort and settlement)
32 Chesters (Roman fort)
33 Chew Green (Roman fortlet and camps)
34 Corbridge (Roman military depot)
35 Danby Rigg (Bronze/Iron Age promontory fort)
36 Danes' Dyke (Iron Age earthwork)
37 Danes Graves (Iron Age round barrow cemetery)

38 Denton (Roman wall)
39 Devil's Arrows (Bronze Age standing stones)
40 Dod Law (Bronze Age rock carvings)
41 Dod Law Forts (Iron Age camp)
43 Duggleby Howe (New Stone Age round barrows)
44 Ewe Close (Iron Age walled settlement)
45 Five Round Barrows (Bronze Age cairns)
46 Folkton (Bronze Age round barrow)
47 Goldsborough (Roman signal station)
48 Grassington (Iron Age/Roman settlement)
49 Great Chesters (Roman fort)
50 Great Hetha (Bronze/Iron Age fort and settlement)
51 Greaves Ash (Iron Age/Roman hut-circles and enclosure)
52 Greta Bridge (Roman fort)
53 Grey Croft (Bronze Age stone circle)
54 Halton (Roman fort)
55 Hanging Grimston (New Stone/Bronze Age barrows)
56 Hardknott Castle (Roman fort)
57 Heddon-on-the-Wall (Roman wall)
58 High Bride Stones (Bronze Age stone circle)
59 High Rochester (Roman fort)
61 Holme Bank (Iron Age? walled settlement)
63 Housesteads (Roman fort)
64 Humbleton Hill (Iron Age hillfort)
65 Hutton Moor (Bronze Age? henges)
66 Ilkley (Roman fort)
67 Ilkley Moor (Bronze Age rock-carvings and monuments)
68 Ingleborough (Iron Age hillfort)
69 King Arthur's Round Table (New Stone Age henge)
70 Long Meg and Her Daughters (Bronze Age stone circles)
71 Loose Howe (Bronze Age round barrow)

72 Lordenshaws (Romano-British hillfort)
73 Malton (Roman fort)
74 Moor Divock (Bronze Age stone circles and barrows)
75 Newcastle (Roman fort)
76 Old Bewick (Iron Age hillfort)
78 Piercebridge (Roman fort)
79 Pike of Stickle (New Stone Age axe factory)
80 Pikestones (New Stone Age chambered long barrow)
81 Raiset Pike (New Stone Age long barrow)
82 Ravenglass (Roman fort)
83 Rey Cross (Roman marching camp)
84 Risingham (Roman fort)
85 Roughting Linn (Bronze Age rock carving/Iron Age promontory fort)
86 Rudchester (Roman fort)
87 Rudston (Late New Stone/Bronze Age standing stone)
88 Scambridge (New Stone/Iron Age long barrow and earthworks)
89 Scarborough (Roman signal station)
90 Scorborough (Iron Age round barrow cemetery)
91 Shap (Bronze Age stone circles)
92 Stanwick (Romano-British fortifications)
93 Staple Howe (Iron Age farmstead)
94 Temple Sowerby (Roman milestone)
95 Thornborough (New Stone Age? henges)
96 Twelve Apostles (Bronze Age stone circle)
97 Victoria Cave (Old Stone Age cave-dwelling)
98 Wallsend (Roman fort)
99 Warton Crag (Iron Age? hillfort)
100 Whitley Castle (Roman fort)
101 Willowford (Roman bridge)
102 Willy Howe (Late New Stone/Bronze Age round barrow)
103 Wincobank (Iron Age? hillfort)
104 Yeavering Bell (Iron Age hillfort)
105 York (Roman city and fort)

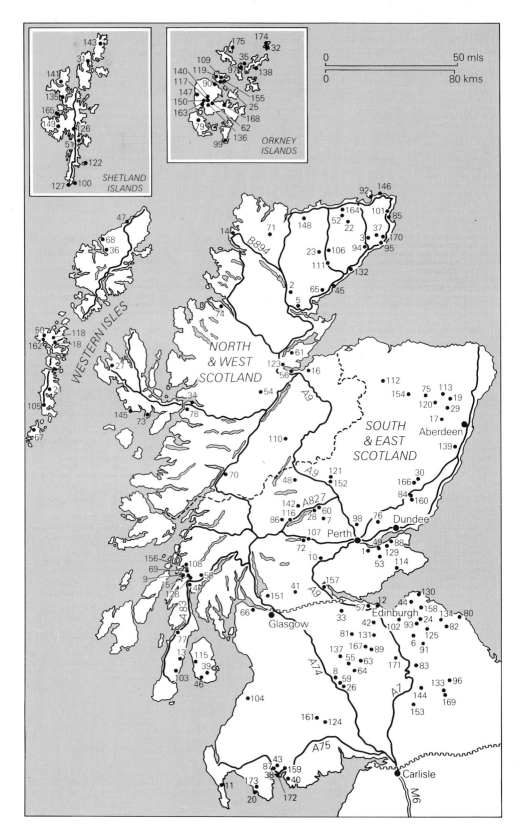

SHETLAND ISLANDS

143
31
141
135
165
149 126
51
122
127 100

ORKNEY ISLANDS

175 174
32
109 35
140 119 97 138
117 90
147 155
150 25
163 168
79 62
99 136

0   50 mls
0   80 kms

92 146
47
71 148 52 164 101 85
68 141 164 22 37 170
36 B894 23 106 3 95
94 111 132
2 65 45
5
74
50 118
162 18 NORTH 61
27 & WEST 123
105 SCOTLAND 56 16
34 54 A9 112
145 73 78 110 154 75 113
120 19
70 17 29
48 A9 121 SOUTH Aberdeen 139
152 & EAST
142 A827 SCOTLAND 30
116 60 166
86 28 7 84 160
107 98 76
72 Perth 1 49 88
10 129
53 114
156 108
69 58 41 157
9 151 A9 130
157 128 40 66 12 44 158
Glasgow 57 134 80
33 Edinburgh 82
42 102 93 24 125
81 131 6
77 137 167 89 91
13 115 55 63 171 83
103 39 8 64 133 96
46 59 144 169
26 A7 153
104
161 124
A75
87 43
38 159
173 40
11 20 172 Carlisle
M6

WESTERN ISLES

310

Map 4 SCOTLAND

1 Abernethy (Iron Age hillfort)
2 Achany (New Stone Age chambered barrow)
3 Achavanich (Bronze Age standing stones)
4 Achnabreck (Bronze Age rock carvings)
5 Achu (New Stone Age chambered barrow)
6 Addinston (Iron Age? hillfort)
7 Airlich (Bronze Age stone circle)
8 Arbory Hill (Iron Age? hillfort)
9 Ardifuir (Iron age dun)
10 Ardoch (Roman fort and camps)
11 Ardwell (Iron Age broch)
12 Arthur's Seat (Iron Age hillfort)
13 Auchagallon (Bronze Age stone circle and barrow)
14 Badnabay (New Stone Age chambered barrow)
15 Ballymeanoch (Bronze Age standing stones)
16 Balnuaran of Clava (New Stone/ Bronze Age chambered barrows)
17 Barmkin of Echt (Iron Age hillfort)
18 Barpa Langass (New Stone Age chambered barrow)
19 Barra Hill (Iron Age hillfort)
20 Barsalloch Point (Iron Age promontory fort)
21 Beinn a' Charra (Bronze Age standing stone)
22 Ben Freiceadain (Iron Age? hillfort)
23 Ben Griam Beg (Iron Age? hillfort)
24 Black Castle (Iron Age hillfort)
25 Blackhammer (New Stone Age chambered long barrow)
26 Bodsberry Hill (Iron Age hillfort)
27 Boreraig (Iron Age broch)
28 Braes of Taymouth (Bronze Age rock carvings)
29 Broomend of Crichie (New Stone Age henge)
30 Brown Caterthun (Iron Age? hillfort)
31 Burra Ness (Iron Age broch)
32 Burrian (Iron Age broch)
*171 Cademuir Hill (Iron Age? hillforts)
*172 Cairnholy (New Stone/Bronze Age chambered long barrow)
33 Cairnpapple (New Stone/Bronze Age henge)
34 Caisteal Grugaig (Iron Age broch)
35 Calf of Eday (New Stone Age chambered barrow)
36 Callanish (New Stone/Bronze Age chambered barrow and standing stones)
37 Camster (New Stone Age chambered barrows)
38 Cardoness House (Bronze Age rock carvings)
39 Carn Ban (New Stone Age chambered barrow)
40 Castle Haven (Iron Age galleried dun)
41 Castlehill Wood (Iron Age/Romano-British dun)
42 Castle Law (Iron Age/Romano-British hillfort and souterrain)
43 Caulside Burn (Bronze Age stone circle, barrows, rock carvings)
44 The Chesters (Iron Age? hillfort)
45 Cinn Trolla (Iron Age broch)
46 Clachaig (New Stone Age chambered barrow)
47 Clach an Trushal (Bronze Age standing stone)
48 Clach Na Tiom Pan (New Stone Age chambered long barrow)
49 Clatchard Craig (Iron Age hillfort)
50 Clettraval (New Stone/Iron Age chambered long barrow and dun)
51 Clickhimin (Iron Age fort, broch and settlement)
52 Cnoc Freiceadain and Na Tri Shean (New Stone Age chambered long barrows)
53 Collessie (Early Bronze Age barrow)
54 Corrimony (New Stone Age chambered barrow)
55 Cow Castle (Iron Age hillfort and settlement)
56 Craig Phadrig (Iron Age hillfort)
57 Cramond (Roman fort)

58 Crarae (New Stone Age chambered long barrow)
59 Crawford (Iron Age fort and settlement)
60 Croftmoraig (New Stone Age stone circle and rock carvings)
61 Culbokie (Iron Age dun)
62 Cuween Hill (New Stone Age chambered barrow)
63 Dreva Craig (Iron Age? hillfort)
64 Drumelzier (New Stone/Bronze Age barrow)
*173 Drumtroddan (Bronze Age rock carvings)
65 Duchary Rock (Iron Age? hillfort)
66 Dumbarton Rock (Iron Age fort)
67 Dun Bharpa (New Stone Age chambered barrow)
68 Dun Carloway (Iron Age broch)
69 Dunchraigaig (Bronze Age barrow with long cist)
70 Dun Deardail (Iron Age hillfort)
71 Dundornaigail (Iron Age broch)
72 Dundurn (Iron Age? hillfort)
73 Dùn Grugaig (Iron Age dun)
74 Dun Lagaidh (Iron Age fort and broch)
75 Dunnideer (Iron Age? hillfort)
76 Dunsinane (Iron Age? hillfort)
77 Dun Skeig (Iron Age hillfort and dun)
78 Dun Telve and Dun Troddan (Iron Age brochs)
79 The Dwarfie Stane (New Stone Age? rock-cut chambered tomb)
80 Earn's Heugh (Iron Age? forts and settlements)
81 East Cairn Hill (Bronze Age barrow)
82 Edin's Hall (Iron Age/Romano-British hillfort, broch and settlement)
83 Eildon Hill North (Iron Age/Roman hillfort and signal station)
84 Finavon (Iron Age hillfort)
85 Garrywhin (New Stone/Bronze/Iron Age hillfort)
86 Glenlochay (Bronze Age rock carvings)
87 Glenquicken (Bronze Age stone circle)
88 Greenhill (Bronze Age barrow)
89 Green Knowe (Bronze/Iron Age settlement)
90 Gurness (Iron Age broch)
91 Haerfaulds (Iron Age?/Romano-British fort and settlement)
92 Ham (New Stone Age chambered barrow)
93 Harelaw (Iron Age? hillfort)
94 Hill of Rangag (Bronze Age? standing stone)
95 Hill o' Many Stones (Bronze Age? standing stones)
*174 Holland House (Bronze Age? standing stone)
*175 Holm of Papa Westray (New Stone Age chambered barrow)
96 Hownam Law and Hownam Rings (Late Bronze/Iron Age? hillforts)
97 Huntersquoy (New Stone Age chambered barrow)
98 Inchtuthill (Iron Age/Roman hillfort, fort and camps)
99 Isbister (New Stone Age chambered long barrow)
100 Jarlshof (New Stone/Iron Age village settlement)
101 Keiss (Iron Age broch)
102 Kidlaw (Iron Age? hillfort)
103 Kildonan (Iron Age dun)
104 Kildoon (Iron Age hillfort)
105 Kilpheder (Iron Age aisled round house)
106 Kinbrace (New Stone Age chambered barrow)
107 Kindrochet (New Stone Age chambered long barrow)
108 Kintraw (Bronze Age cairns and standing stones)
109 Knowe of Yarso (New Stone Age chambered long barrow)
110 Laggan (Iron Age hillfort)
111 Learable Hill (Bronze Age stone rows and circles)
112 Little Conval (Iron Age hillfort)

113 Loanhead of Daviot (New Stone/ Bronze Age recumbent stone circle)
114 Lundin Links (Bronze Age standing stones)
115 Machrie Moor (Bronze Age stone circles and standing stones)
116 Machuim (Bronze Age stone circle)
117 Maes Howe (New Stone Age chambered barrow)
118 Marrogh (New Stone Age chambered barrow)
119 Mid Howe (New Stone/Iron Age chambered long barrow and broch)
120 Mither Tap o' Bennachie (Iron Age hillfort)
121 Monzie (Bronze Age stone circle)
122 Mousa (Iron Age broch)
123 Muir of Ord (New Stone Age henge)
124 Mullach (Iron Age hillfort)
125 The Mutiny Stones (New Stone Age long barrow)
126 Nesbister Hill (Bronze Age walled cairn)
127 Ness of Burgi (Iron Age? fort)
128 Nether Largie (New Stone/Bronze Age barrows)
129 Norman's Law (Iron Age hillfort and settlement)
130 North Berwick Law (Iron Age hillfort)
131 Northshield Rings (Iron Age? hillfort)
132 Ousdale (Iron Age broch)
133 Pennymuir Forts (Roman camps)
134 Penshiel Hill (Bronze Age? round barrow)
135 Punds Water (New Stone Age chambered barrow)
136 Quanterness (New Stone Age chambered barrow)
137 Quothquan Law (Iron Age hillfort)
138 Quoyness (New Stone Age chambered barrow)
139 Raedykes Fort (Roman camp)
140 Ring of Brodgar (New Stone Age circle henge)
141 Ronas Hill (New Stone Age chambered barrow)
142 Roromore (Iron Age dun)
143 The Rounds of Tivla Ring (Bronze Age cairns)
144 Rubers Law (Iron Age hillfort)
145 Rubh'an Dùnain (New Stone/Iron Age chambered barrow and broch)
146 St John's Point (Iron Age promontory fort)
147 Skara Brae (New Stone Age village settlement)
148 Skelpick (New Stone Age long barrow)
149 Stanydale (New Stone Age building)
150 Stenness (New Stone Age circle henge)
151 Stockie Muir (New Stone Age chambered long barrow)
152 Strathgroy (Bronze Age barrow)
153 Tamshiel Rig (Iron Age walled settlement)
154 Tap o' Noth (Iron Age hillfort)
155 Taversoas Tuack (New Stone Age chambered barrow)
156 Temple Wood (Bronze Age Stone Circles and standing stones)
157 Tor Wood (Iron Age broch)
158 Traprain Law (Iron Age hillfort)
159 Trusty's Hill (Iron Age? hillfort)
160 Turin (Iron Age hillfort and duns)
161 Tynron Doon (Iron Age hillfort)
162 Uneval (New Stone Age chambered barrow)
163 Unstan (New Stone Age chambered barrow)
164 Upper Dounreay (Bronze Age stone rows)
165 Vementry (New Stone Age chambered barrow)
166 White Caterthun (Iron Age hillfort)
167 Whiteside Hill (Iron Age hillfort)
168 Wideford Hill (New Stone Age chambered barrow)
169 Woden Law (Iron Age/Roman hillfort and siege works)
170 Yarrows (New Stone Age chambered long barrow and standing stone)
171 172 173 174 175 see above*

311

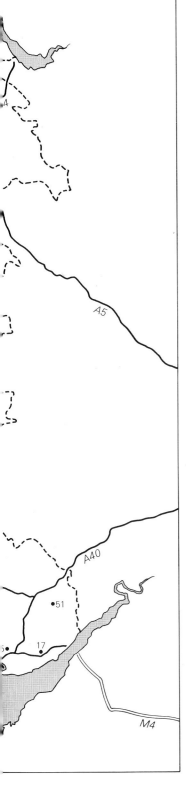

Map 5 WALES

1 Bachwen (New Stone Age chambered tomb)
2 Barclodiad y Gawres (New Stone Age chambered barrow)
3 Beddyrafanc (New Stone Age chambered long barrow)
4 Brecon Gaer (Roman fort)
5 The Breiddin (Late Bronze/Iron Age hillfort)
6 Brenig Archaeological Trail (Middle Stone/Bronze Age sites)
7 Bryncelli Ddu (New Stone Age chambered barrow)
8 Bryn-yr-Hen Bobl (New Stone Age chambered barrow)
9 The Bulwark (Iron Age hillfort)
10 Burfa Camp (Iron Age hillfort)
11 Caer Euni (Iron/Bronze Age hillfort and ring cairn)
12 Caer Gai (Roman fort)
13 Caer Gybi (Roman fortlet)
14 Caerhun (Roman fort)
15 Caerleon (Roman legionary fort)
16 Caernarfon (Roman fort)
17 Caerwent (Roman town)
18 Caer-y-Twr (Iron Age hillfort)
19 Capel Garmon (New Stone Age chambered long barrow)
20 Cardiff Castle (Roman fort)
21 Carneddau Hengwm (New Stone Age chambered long barrow)
22 Carn Fadrun (Iron Age hillfort and settlement)
23 Carn Goch (Iron Age hillfort)
24 Castell Collen (Roman fort)
25 Castell Dinas (Iron Age hillfort)
26 Cat Hole (Old Stone Age cave-dwelling)
27 Cefn Carnedd (Iron Age hillfort)
28 Cerrig Duon (Bronze Age stone circle and stone rows)
29 Cerrig-y-Gof (New Stone Age chambered round barrow)
30 Coelbren Gaer (Roman fort)
31 Conwy Mountain (Iron Age hillfort)
32 Crug Hywell (Iron Age hillfort)
33 Dan-yr-Ogof (Bronze Age/Roman cave-dwelling)
34 Dinas Dinorwig (Iron Age hillfort)
35 Din Lligwy (Romano-British walled settlement)
36 Din Sylwy (Romano-British hillfort)
37 Dolaucothi (Roman gold mines and aqueduct)
38 Druid's Circle (Bronze Age stone circle)
39 Dyffryn Ardudwy (New Stone Age chambered long barrow)
40 Ffridd Faldwyn (Bronze/Iron Age hillfort)
41 Ffynnon Beuno (Old Stone Age cave-dwellings)
42 Flimston Castle (Iron Age promontory fort)
43 Foel Fenlli (Iron Age hillfort)
44 Foel Trigarn (Iron/Bronze Age hillfort and barrows)
45 Garn Boduan (Iron Age/Roman hillfort)
46 Gelligaer (Roman forts)
47 Goat's Cave (Old Stone Age cave-dwelling)
48 Gop-y-Goleuni (New Stone Age? barrow)
49 Gors-Fawr (Bronze Age stone circle)
50 Gwernvale (New Stone Age chambered long barrow)
51 Harold's Stones (Bronze Age? standing stones)
52 Hendre Waelod (New Stone Age chambered long barrow)
53 Lligwy (New Stone Age chambered barrow)
54 Long House (New Stone Age chambered tomb)
55 Maen-y-Bardd (New Stone Age chambered long barrow)
56 Maen Ceti (New Stone Age chambered tomb)
57 Meini-Gwyr (Bronze Age embanked stone circle)
58 Moel y Gaer (Iron Age? hillfort)
59 Moel y Gaer (Iron Age? hillfort)
60 Pant-y-Saer (New Stone Age chambered long barrow)
61 Parc Le Breos Cwm (New Stone Age chambered long barrow)
62 Pen Dinas (Iron Age hillfort)
63 Pentre Ifan (New Stone Age chambered long barrow)
64 Pen-y-cordynn-mawr (Iron Age hillfort)
65 Pen y Crug (Iron Age hillfort)
66 Pen y Gaer (Iron Age hillfort)
67 Pipton (New Stone Age long barrow)
68 Plas Newydd (New Stone Age chambered barrow)
69 St David's Head (Iron Age? promontory fort and settlement)
70 St Lythans (New Stone age chambered long barrow)
71 Tan-y-Muriau (New Stone Age chambered long barrow)
72 Tinkinswood (New Stone Age chambered barrow)
73 Tomen-y-Mur (Roman fort)
74 Trefignath (New Stone Age chambered long barrow)
75 Tre'r Ceiri (Iron Age hillfort)
76 Tŷ Illtud (New Stone Age chambered long barrow)
77 Tŷ-isaf (New Stone Age chambered long barrow)
78 Tŷ Mawr (Romano-British settlement)
79 Y Pigwn (Roman temporary forts)

GLOSSARY

Agger raised causeway of Roman roads

Barrow a mound of earth and/or rubble usually covering one or more burials or cremations. The word *tumulus* is also used, while *cairn* denotes a mound of stones

Berm flat area between a bank or barrow and its ditch

Bivallate double line of bank and ditch

Broch circular building of drystone found in N. Scotland. Brochs are always open at the centre, while the wall contains chambers, stairways and upper galleries. Brochs were probably fortified homesteads

Cairn mound of stones (see *barrow*)

Capstone stone laid horizontally on the top of a *megalithic* monument

Chevaux de frise series of closely spaced stones, set upright, as a defence: they helped to break up charges by cavalry or infantry

Cist simple rectangular or square grave made from stone slabs often with a slab lid. Cists were built in the ground or above ground and were often covered by a *barrow*

Corbelling means of roofing chamber or passage, each course of stones projecting beyond the one below until the last gap is closed by a single stone or line of stones

Cove U-shaped setting of standing stones, usually in or near a stone circle.

Cursus long, narrow enclosure with a bank and external ditch at either side. Function unknown.

Dolmen simple *megalithic* structure comprising a few *orthostats* and one or more *capstones*

Dun small fortified settlement in Scotland. Duns have thick stone walls, internal rooms and galleries

Governor representative of the Roman emperor sent to govern Britain for three to five years; usually a distinguished and experienced ex-consul or successful legionary commander. The head of the army in Britain, he constituted a one-man 'supreme court' but his powers were kept in check by the *Procurator*

Henge uniquely British monument comprising a round area, 30-400m across, enclosed by a bank and a (usually internal) ditch. Class I henges have a single entrance, Class II have two opposing entries. Those that contain stone circles are called circle-henges

Hollow way trackway which has been worn deep into a hillside by heavy use

Hypocaust Roman system of central heating; the ground floor was built on a number of small pillars, enabling hot air from a furnace to circulate beneath the floor

Lynchets step-like formations on hillsides formed when colluvial material was eroded through ploughing and travelled downhill where it became piled up against field boundaries.

Megalith(ic) large stone, either a standing stone or incorporated in a monument

Menhir standing stone

Microlith(ic) very small stone tool

Midden accumulated heap of refuse, often of sea-shells mixed with bones, ash, etc.

Motte earth mound with a flat top, and surrounded by a ditch (medieval)

Multivallate Several lines of bank and ditch

Orthostats upright stones in structures such as a *dolmen*

Peristalith retaining wall or kerb of stones around a *barrow*

Potsherd fragment of a pottery vessel

Procurator official responsible only to the Roman emperor and therefore acting as a check on the power of the *Governor*. The top civil servant in Britain, the Procurator controlled legal and financial administration, taxation and censuses

Quern grain grinding stone

Revetment wall which held a mound or rampart in position

Sarsen sandstone often used in the construction of *Megalithic* monuments, in the Wiltshire region for example

Scarcement flat ledge in a wall

Souterrain underground chamber or passage, sometimes lined with drystone walls and roofed over. Used for storage and refuge

Trilithon two *orthostats* capped with a horizontal lintel. The most famous are those of Stonehenge, where mortice and tenon joints can be seen

Tumulus see *barrow*

Vicus Roman village or suburb, often developed beside a fort

Vitrification the fusing together of stones in a wall; thought to have been caused by the intense heat produced by the burning of timber-lacing in the walls

Wheelhouse drystone building in Scotland, named after its shape: partition walls, like the spokes of a wheel, run from the circular outer wall to the open space in the centre

MUSEUMS

There are many museums throughout the British Isles containing exhibits from prehistoric and Roman sites. It would be impossible to give them all in the space available and we have, therefore, listed only the most important and rewarding to visit.

Aberdeen University Anthropological Museum
Tillydrome Avenue, Aberdeen
Antiquities excavated locally, including skeletal remains of Beaker Folk (Bronze Age).

Avebury: Alexander Keiller Museum
Exhibits from excavations at Avebury and Windmill Hill.

Bath Roman Museum
Abbey Churchyard, Bath
Roman antiquities from Bath and elsewhere, including sculpture from Sul Minerva temple.

Brighton Museum and Art Gallery
Church Street, Brighton
The Hove amber cup and other exhibits from Sussex excavations.

Bristol City Museum
Queen's Road, Bristol
Exhibits from west of England, particularly from barrow excavations.

Cambridge University Museum of Archaeology and Ethnology
Downing Street, Cambridge
Artifacts from Iron Age chieftain burials and other exhibits from Cambridgeshire.

Canterbury Royal Museum
High Street, Canterbury
Roman exhibits.

Cardiff: National Museum of Wales
Cathays Park Exhibits from Welsh prehistory and subsequent Roman occupation.

Carlisle Museum and Art Gallery
Tullie House, Castle Street, Carlisle
Prehistoric and Roman exhibits.

Cheltenham Art Gallery and Museum
Clarence Street, Cheltenham
Material from Belas Knap and Cotswold excavations.

Chester: Grosvenor Museum
Grosvenor Street, Chester
Antiquities from the legionary fortress (Roman)

Cirencester: Corinium Museum
Park Street, Cirencester
Mosaics, reconstruction of a Roman dining-room and objects of everyday life in Roman Britain.

Colchester and Essex Museum
The Castle, Colchester
Impressive collection of Roman antiquities.

Devizes Museum
Long Street, Devizes
Wiltshire archaeology, including the Colt-Hoare prehistoric collection.

Dover Corporation Museum
Ladywell, Dover
Roman and Anglo-Saxon exhibits.

Dorchester: Dorset County Museum
High West Street, Dorchester
Prehistoric and Roman artifacts, including fine mosaic from Hinton St Mary and finds from Maiden Castle excavation.

Dundee City Museum and Art Gallery
Albert Square, Dundee
Local antiquities including Pictish inscribed stones.

Edinburgh: National Museum of Antiquities of Scotland
Queen Street, Edinburgh
Prehistoric and Roman artifacts, including Pictish inscribed and sculptured stones.

Exeter: Rougemont House Museum
Castle Street, Exeter
Prehistoric artifacts and Roman exhibits from Devon.

Glasgow: City of Glasgow Museums and Art Galleries
Kelvingrove, Glasgow
Prehistoric exhibits from Scottish excavations.

Gloucester City Museum and Art Gallery
Brunswick Road, Gloucester
Local antiquities, particularly the Birdlip mirror, Celtic head and Roman inscribed stones.

Hull: Mortimer Archaeological and Transport Museum
High Street, Hull
Prehistoric and Roman exhibits, including Roos-Carr images (late Bronze Age), Iron Age chariot burials and Roman mosaic pavements.

Ipswich Museum
High Street, Ipswich
Exhibits from prehistoric and Roman sites in Suffolk.

Leeds City Museum
Municipal Buildings, Leeds
Exhibits from Yorkshire excavations, including Roman mosaic pavement.

Leicester: Jewry Wall Museum
St Nicholas Circle, Leicester
Roman antiquities and mosaics.

Lincoln City and County Museum
Broadgate, Lincoln
Antiquities from local excavations, particularly the legionary fortress.

Liverpool: Merseyside County Museums
William Brown Street, Liverpool
Prehistoric artifacts from local excavations, particularly the Mayer mirror (Celtic).

London: British Museum
Great Russell Street, London WC1
Major collection of prehistoric and Romano-British artifacts.

London: British Museum (Natural History)
Cromwell Road, London SW7
Exhibits relating to prehistory of man.

London: Museum of London
Aldersgate Street, London EC1
Exhibits from London excavations, especially the Mithraic temple at Walbrook.

Maidstone Museum and Art Gallery
St Faith's Street, Maidstone
Exhibits from local excavations.

Newcastle: University Museum of Antiquities
The Quadrangle, Newcastle
Inscriptions and sculpture from Hadrian's Wall, altars from Mithraic temple at Carrawburgh.

Newport Museum and Art Gallery
John Frost Square, Newport
Roman antiquities.

Norwich Castle Museum
The Castle, Norwich
East Anglian prehistoric and Roman artifacts.

Oxford: Ashmolean Museum
Beaumont Street, Oxford
Local antiquities.

Reading Museum and Art Gallery
Blagrave Street, Reading
Prehistoric and Roman exhibits.

St Albans: Verulamium Museum
St Michael's, St Albans
Roman antiquities from the town's excavations.

Salisbury and South Wiltshire Museum
St Ann Street, Salisbury
Exhibits from local excavations.

Sheffield City Museum
Weston Park, Sheffield
Prehistoric exhibits from local excavations.

South Shields: Roman Fort and Museum
Baring Street, South Shields
Exhibits from Roman fort.

Taunton: Somerset County Museum
The Castle, Taunton
*Prehistoric and Roman exhibits, particularly Low
Ham Roman bath mosaic and artifacts from South
Cadbury.*

Winchester City Museum
Cathedral Precinct, Winchester
Prehistoric and Roman finds from Hampshire.

Yorkshire Museum
Museum Gardens, York
Roman remains.

FURTHER READING

General and regional archaeology

BORD, J. & C., *A Guide to Ancient Sites in Britain,*
Latimer, 1978.

BRANIGAN, Keith, *Prehistoric Britain: An Illustrated
Survey,* Spur Books, 1976.

CLAYTON, P., *Archaeological Sites of Britain,* Weidenfeld & Nicolson, 1976.

COLES, John, *Field Archaeology in Britain,* Methuen,
1972.

CORCORAN, John X. W. P., *The Young Field Archaeologist's Guide,* Bell, 1966.

DANIEL, Glyn (ed.), *Ancient People and Places
Series,* various authors: Central England, East
Anglia, South-east England, South-west England,
Wales, Wessex.

FOSTER, I. Ll. and DANIEL, Glyn, *Prehistoric and Early
Wales.*

FORDE-JOHNSTON, J., *Prehistoric Britain and Ireland,*
Dent, 1976.

GRINSELL, L. V., *Folklore of Prehistoric Sites in Britain,* David & Charles, 1976.

MACKIE, E. W., *Scotland, An Archaeological Guide,*
Faber & Faber, 1975.

MUIR, R., and WELFARE, H., *National Trust Guide to
Prehistoric and Roman Britain,* George Philip,
1983.

PEARCE, S. M., *The Archaeology of South-West Britain,* Collins, 1981.

PIGGOTT, Stuart, *The Prehistoric Peoples of Scotland,*
Routledge & Kegan Paul, 1962.

WAINWRIGHT, R., *A Guide to the Prehistoric Remains
in Britain* (volume 1: South and East), Con-
stable, 1978.

Prehistoric monuments

ASHBEE, Paul, *The Earthen Long Barrow in Britain,*
Dent, 1970.

– , *Bronze Age Round Barrows in Britain,* Phoenix
House, 1960.

ATKINSON, R. J. C., *Stonehenge,* Hamish Hamilton,
1956.

BURL, Aubrey, *The Stone Circles of the British Isles,*
Yale University Press, 1976.

DANIEL, Glyn, *Prehistoric Chamber Tombs of England and Wales,* Cambridge University Press,
1951.

GRINSELL, L. V., *The Ancient Burial Mounds of Britain,* Methuen, 2nd ed. 1953.

HOGG, A. H. A., *Hillforts of Britain,* Hart-Davis Mac-
Gibbon, 1975.

RENFREW, C. (ed.), *The Prehistory of Orkney,* Edinburgh University Press, 1985.

RITCHIE, G. & A., *Scotland: Archaeology and Early
History,* Thames & Hudson, 1981.

Roman Britain

BIRLEY, A., *Life in Roman Britain,* Batsford, 1981.

COLLINGWOOD, R. G. and RICHMOND, Ian, *The Archaeology of Roman Britain,* Methuen, 2nd ed. 1969.

FRERE, Sheppard, *Britannia: A History of Roman
Britain,* Routledge & Kegan Paul, 1967.

GRIMES, W. F., *The Excavation of Roman and Medi-
aeval London,* Routledge & Kegan Paul, 1968.

JOHNSON, S., *Later Roman Britain,* Routledge &
Kegan Paul, 1980.

JOHNSTON, D.E. (ed.), *Discovering Roman Britain,*
Shire, 1983.

LAING, Jennifer, *Finding Roman Britain,* David &
Charles, 1977.

LIVERSIDGE, Joan, *Britain in the Roman Empire,*
Routledge & Kegan Paul, 1968.

MARGERY, Ivan D., *Roman Roads in Britain* (2 vols),
Phoenix House, 1955.

MORRIS, John, *Londinium: London in the Roman
Empire,* Weidenfeld & Nicolson, 1982.

SCULLARD, H. H., *Roman Britain, Outpost of the
Empire,* Thames & Hudson, 1979.

WILSON, R., *Roman Forts, An Illustrated Introduction to the Garrison Posts of Roman Britain,*
Bergstrom & Boyle, 1980.

WACHER, John, *The Towns of Roman Britain,* Batsford, 1974.

Guides for prehistoric and Roman Britain

DYER, James, *Penguin Guide to Prehistoric England
and Wales,* Allen Lane, 1981.

– , *Southern England: an Archaeological Guide,*
Faber & Faber, 1973.

FEACHAM, Richard, *Guide to Prehistoric Scotland,*
Batsford, 2nd ed. 1977.

HAWKES, Jacquetta, *A Guide to Prehistoric and
Roman Monuments in England and Wales,*
Chatto & Windus, 2nd ed. 1973.

HOULDER, Christopher, *Wales: An Archaeological
Guide,* Faber & Faber, 1974.

JOHNSTON, David (ed.), *Discovering Roman Britain,*
Shire Publications, 1983.

THOMAS, Nicholas, *Guide to Prehistoric England,*
Batsford, 2nd ed. 1976.

INDEX

Numbers in italics refer to illustration captions